The practice and theory of project management

the practice and theory of project management

Creating value through change

RICHARD NEWTON

palgrave
macmillan

First published 2009 by
PALGRAVE MACMILLAN

Palgrave Macmillan in the UK is an imprint of Macmillan Publishers Limited,
registered in England, company number 785998, of Houndmills, Basingstoke,
Hampshire RG21 6XS.

Palgrave Macmillan in the US is a division of St Martin's Press LLC,
175 Fifth Avenue, New York, NY 10010.

Palgrave Macmillan is the global academic imprint of the above companies
and has companies and representatives throughout the world.

Palgrave® and Macmillan® are registered trademarks in the United States,
the United Kingdom, Europe and other countries

ISBN-13: 978–0–230–53667–8 paperback
ISBN-10: 0–230–53667–0 paperback

This book is printed on paper suitable for recycling and made from fully
managed and sustained forest sources. Logging, pulping and manufacturing
processes are expected to conform to the environmental regulations of the
country of origin.

A catalogue record for this book is available from the British Library.

Library of Congress Cataloging-in-Publication Data
Newton, Richard, 1964–
   The theory and practice of project management : creating value
   through change / Richard Newton.
      p.   cm.
   Includes index.
   ISBN 978–0–230–53667–8
   1. Project management.   I. Title.
   HD69.P75N4974 2009
   658.4'04—dc22   2008038432

10   9   8   7   6   5   4   3   2   1
18   17   16   15   14   13   12   11   10   09

Printed in China

There are a large number of people who deserve thanks for directly or indirectly helping with this book. I especially want to give my thanks to

Janet Campbell, David Caswell, Jayne Cockill, Tony Collins, Tom Connolly, Marie Dutton, James Edwards, Peter Evans, Ursula Gavin, Andrea Gaynor, Paul Gilhooley, Terry Goh, David Hirst, David Keighley, Kevin Muraski, Anna Newton, Steve Oliver, Sauming Pang, Roger Simkin and Howard Watson.

A few other people have provided great case studies but have chosen to remain anonymous. Even though they remain unidentified my thanks goes to them as well.

contents

preface

When I was given the opportunity to write this book I was excited, but also a little daunted by the challenge.

Writing a book like this is challenging because so much has already been said. There are numerous books which discuss and promote approaches to projects and change. More than this, there are quite a few *good* books on these topics. In addition, I had to consider the demanding needs of those studying for a business degree or an MBA.

I can point to the failings of many other books on implementation. Pure project management books can be turgid, strategy books can be clever without telling you how to make it happen, and change management books often repeat the same old stuff or focus on only one aspect of change. Even so, I can very quickly name a lengthy list of excellent books in each of these areas that are stimulating and helpful. For these reasons, to make this book worthwhile, I spent a long time considering what the readers' outstanding needs were, and therefore how do I make the contents original, accessible, comprehensive and most of all, useful?

Originality is difficult in subjects like strategy, project and change management, which are hardly new topics. They have been the bedrock of management journals and books for several decades. Even so, based on experience, debate and access to my clients' executives there are some new ideas in this book. But I don't claim that each aspect of the contents is unique. What I do think it has is a synthesis of ideas presented in an original way. It provides a relatively complete view of how to go from ideas to successfully implemented solutions in the complex and dynamic world of a business.

For a book to be accessible it needs to be clearly written and well-structured. I have tried to use straightforward language, only resorting to jargon where it is either the everyday speech of the business community, or when it helps by encapsulating complex concepts. Terminology is explained where I felt there was room for ambiguity. I start by defining the assumptions and principles I base my arguments upon, so there are no jumps in understanding, and it is easier to challenge the advice. Chapters and the contents are logically structured to be simple to work through. I have designed it in such a way that the chapters can be used individually if required. References are given where helpful and when credit is appropriate. I have avoided the academic style of referencing or justifying every point, as although this makes the contents more verifiable, it does not aid easy reading. Nevertheless there is a fairly extensive list of references at the end of each chapter.

To make this book comprehensive I have brought together a practical, and stimulating, synthesis of the different aspects of delivering change in businesses, which covers topics like strategy execution, project and portfolio management, benefits tracking and realization, and change management, with my views as an experienced practitioner in these fields. These topics are usually presented separately. Relatively rare is the strategist who can competently talk projects, the project manager who can comprehensively explain the strategy, or the change manager who can define the best way to plan. Yet strategy execution, change management and project management are different aspects of the same capability. (I am not claiming they are synonyms, but they are inter-related and overlapping areas of expertise.) I have tried to bring together the most useful parts from the thinking in each area that is relevant to this audience.

What of usefulness? To be useful the book has to be relevant to the specific audience it is intended for. This book's audience are existing or prospective senior managers and leaders in business organizations. I consider those studying an MBA as the primary sub-set of this category, who need not only practical advice, but the material to debate and critique that advice. I have built the contents of the book from the challenges this group will face in real life and in discussion with a range of managers and executives. This is not a project or change management primer; it is a book for those who want to manage and direct the achievement of a business's objectives through projects.

Beyond this, to me, assessing usefulness is about measuring up to four challenges:

1. *To present problems clearly*: really what are the difficulties, issues and pitfalls in executing strategy, delivering business change and reliably implementing projects? The first step to a robust solution must be a full understanding of the problem that it sets out to resolve. This understanding alone has value.
2. *To describe a workable solution to these problems*: what is a great way to go about reliably delivering improvements? Why is this a good way? What are the limits to this solution?
3. *To enable the reader to use the solution*: what does this mean to the reader and situations they may find themselves in over their careers? I do not believe in universal solutions that will deliver any project in any

organization, but there are common building blocks and experience-based lessons that can significantly increase the chance of success.

4. *To prompt further and deeper thought and discussion*: A single book cannot provide the answers to everything and I don't claim to be the sole source of wisdom. But even if you disagree with some contents, a good book should encourage debate and the development of the readers' own analysis and conclusions.

How have I set out to achieve this? The information in this book comes from two sources. First, it comes from research and analysis of the available materials on related topics. I have spent the last few years reviewing articles, journals and books and discussing them with other experienced practitioners. This is now my fifth book on project and change management. The book also draws on my own experience in successfully delivering large-scale change, and in sometimes failing to deliver needed changes. You can question whether this is an objective view. My first response is to question whether true objectivity is possible, and to ask you to consider whether what you want is objectivity – or a useful tool and a stimulus to your own thinking. I have tried to be as objective as possible, by showing the principles of my arguments; they are clear and can be debated. In the end though, it describes an approach through the lens of an experienced practitioner.

Why read my book? I have already written extensively and successfully on different parts of these topics. I have worked as a project manager and change manager responsible for delivering benefits in businesses. I have also held strategy and operational roles, acting as the sponsor of change and as the frustrated recipient of it. These varied perspectives give me an ability to reflect on being both a customer and a supplier of change. Finally, I have access to my own large network of senior managers in a number of organizations whom I have worked with on many projects. The contents are my own, but they have been enriched with the views and perspectives of others, which are documented through this book.

introduction

This book explores how projects deliver change and value in business, and how project management relates to other business management disciplines. To achieve this, the book starts by considering the perspective and needs of the general business manager, leader or executive as well as the viewpoint of the project manager.

The main audience for this book is students doing some form of management studies degree with an interest in projects, and, more broadly, in implementing strategy and change. The contents are targeted primarily at those studying for an MBA. The subject matter addresses the two separate needs of MBA students. First, the vocational need of those who want to increase their capability to work in senior management and leadership positions. Second, the academic need to understand, critique and debate the mechanisms of business.

Given the scope of the book, there is much that should be of interest to anyone in business, and it will be useful to any manager who wants to understand how to be successful in implementing projects.

This book has six related objectives:

1. To explain the key issues with regards to projects in terms of the challenge of delivering business value. Clearly understanding the problem that projects must overcome is an important step in developing the skills to deliver projects.
2. To develop a picture of the various components of a solution based on the above problem definition.
3. To encourage productive debate and thinking about the topic of projects. In business, projects are often accepted without question as the way to

deliver, rather than a way that needs to be actively thought about, discussed, and tailored to the situation.

4. To provide a perspective different from that of most project management texts, to deepen understanding from the reader's own experiences and study on project management.
5. To present potential and existing senior managers with a fuller understanding of how to achieve project success, without trying to make all managers into project or change managers.
6. To provide project and programme managers with a greater understanding of how to drive successful projects, and particularly with a more holistic view of the component parts of a full delivery competency which is broader than pure project management.

Underlying this is the aim to provide knowledge that not only encourages thinking, but is useful in practice. The remainder of this chapter introduces project management in a business context and describes the contents of the book.

Project management in context – business projects

The concept of a project and the associated discipline of project management were being increasingly formalized over the last 50 or so years. The approaches are documented into collections such as the APM Body of Knowledge (APM, 2006) or the Project Management Institute's PMBOK (PMI, 2004). These collections aim to provide a comprehensive description and framework for project management thinking. However, even their strongest advocates would not claim that they alone provide a sure guide to the successful delivery of every business project. Partially, this is due to the origins of project management in *projectized* industries as opposed to general business.

The genesis of project management as a formal discipline lies within industries such as defence and construction which by the nature of their work perform large and complex projects all the time. These are *projectized* industries, and most of their day-to-day activities revolve around a series of projects. These projectized industries have driven the development of many innovations and advances in project management, and a significant proportion of project management approaches are primarily concerned with the activity of managing projects in such an industry. But there is a different kind of organization that needs projects. This includes government departments and businesses primarily with non-project based operations, but which regularly undertake projects to implement modifications and improvements.

Most organizations carry out projects to make changes to operations or to the products and services they provide. Examples of such projects include IT systems developments, new product and service creation and introduction, performance improvement projects, costs reduction exercises and so forth. Carroll has given this type of organization the differentiating, but rather cumbersome, title of *business-as-usual organizations* (Carroll, 2006). Other writers use the simpler term *business projects*, to refer to projects in these organizations (e.g. Winter et al., 2006a). This term is used in the rest of this book.

Traditionally, the core focus of project management is the delivery of some tangible output, known in project management terms as *product*. Whether it is the construction of a bridge or the development of a new fighter plane there is a clear output that meets the specification defined at the start of the project (taking into account changes along the way). For business projects the required output is more often associated with the less tangible result of *value* rather than product, although the two are related. One of the issues facing project management today is defining a reliable approach to deliver results specified in terms of value rather than pre-defined products. In understanding how projects deliver value, questions arise as to the definition and level of flexibility of the concept of a project and whether the currently defined project management standards reflect what project managers do in practice on business projects.

This book should be of interest to someone responsible for projects in a projectized company. But it is business-as-usual organizations doing projects, often in ways that do not conform to the expectations of documented standards, to drive change and deliver value, which are the main focus of this book.

Project management and business management

Why is the subject matter of this book important, especially in the context of a readership that has the opportunity to study many other important management topics? Isn't project management a discipline that is best left to those who want to specialize in the subject? The answer is no – some understanding of project management is important for virtually every business manager. Any manager who is interested in how a business will continue to create value gains from an understanding of projects.

To explore this further, consider a very simple model of an organization's work. In this model the work of an organization can be consolidated into three main groups of activities:

o Work done in the performance of day-to-day operations
o Work done in the form of thinking and planning for the future of the organization, and the creation of a change agenda
o Implementing this thinking to achieve change – often through the mechanism of a project

Here *operations* means the everyday tasks that the organization exists to do. These include the core tasks of selecting and purchasing resources, converting those resources into products and services, selling to and serving the organization's customers and any activities that support these core tasks. It is by performing these operations that an organization achieves its goals. A business's operations are the source of the value it currently creates.

Thinking and planning for the future is essentially about identifying how an organization will continue to survive and thrive – and to do so what changes are required. This includes generating, collecting and clarifying ideas about modifications to the ways of working, structure, business model or the services and products the organization provides. The combined set of ideas is the *change agenda*. The change agenda describes how an organization can adapt to meet its future goals. The change agenda defines how a business will continue to create value, and possibly increase its value creation in future.

The change agenda may not be consolidated into one place or a coherent document; no one person or group may be able to articulate it completely; and it is constantly evolving and altering. However, one way or another, this change agenda will guide the allocation of resources to future investments. By implementing the change agenda the organization will modify its current operations or offerings to its customers in some way, converting from working in the way it works today to an alternative way.

One of the primary mechanisms for implementing the change agenda are projects. Therefore, anyone wanting to understand how future ideas convert into current operations and hence value creation should have an understanding of the mechanics, strengths and weaknesses, and methods of projects.

Expanding on this, an ability to control and achieve success from projects is an important issue for all managers because

1. *All managers have to make change*: The need to change to survive and thrive is inherent in the environment of most organizations. Businesses have to change due to competitive pressures, to take advantage of new opportunities, and to meet evolving customer and stakeholder needs. Public sector organizations are subject to the changing needs of government and the public. Ensuring an organization can and does change is core to its ongoing viability and is generally considered as a key responsibility for all managers and leaders. Unless a business changes, any value-creating capability is at risk.

2. *Projects are a key enabler of change*: The project is the management approach used to achieve a substantial proportion of the change undertaken by organizations. Investments as varied as developing IT systems, launching new products, expanding into new premises, reorganizing, outsourcing and off-shoring, and mergers as well as many performance improvement initiatives are managed as projects. A substantial proportion of business resources are invested in projects. The project is one of the key ways of moving from change ideas to improved business operations. Projects are therefore relevant to managers both because they consume significant resources and because they offer the opportunity to change future value creation.

3. *Projects have a significant failure rate*: The data on the percentage of failure varies. There are reports showing that 15% of projects fail; at the other extreme there are reports of up to 70% failure rate for change projects. This depends on the sample and the definition of success, but there is consensus that projects have not proven themselves to be a reliable mechanism for delivering change. Beyond this, even when projects result in desired change, the changes do not consistently justify the investments made. This failure rate leads to questions about how to make projects more successful, but equally to whether projects are the most appropriate management approach to deliver change. Before managers invest in projects they should have an understanding of the inherent risks in projects.

4. *Successfully achieving the desired outcome from projects cannot be fully delegated to project managers*: There are several reasons for this, including

- *Management behaviour significantly affects the likelihood of project failure*: The success or failure of projects is not just about project management competence, but is significantly affected by the behaviours and decisions of the managers and executives that projects interact with. There are approaches that the management community can use which will increase the level of project success. Conversely, ignorance of the impact of management behaviours and decision upon projects will significantly decrease the chance of project success.
- *Project management alone will not deliver successful change*: Although good project management improves the likelihood of change and project success, it does not operate in a vacuum. There is a range of other disciplines, including business analysis, portfolio management, change and benefits management, that are required. Understanding this full set of disciplines, how they interact, and who is responsible for what will support project success.
- *Projects add risk to current operations*: Although projects set out to deliver improvements in business and hence reduce longer-term business risk, they introduce operational risk and disruption to the organization's operations. Good project managers work to reduce this risk and disruption. However, risk requires the ongoing support and active involvement of business managers to overcome. Before investing in a project, managers should understand the potential negative effects of the project as well as the potential benefits.
- *Managers are accountable for project success*: The project manager is normally an agent responsible for managing a project, but is not fully accountable for its success. Projects need to be successful both to justify the investments made and to ensure the future vision of a business is achieved. The assessment of success in projects depends on the viewpoint of different stakeholders. Different people, in various roles, tend to have different views of success and different needs from projects. This means being successful, far from being objectively measured, is usually subjectively and inconsistently determined, and also has a level of complexity that is not always recognized.

Each of these points can be debated, and one of the objectives of this book is to open up such a debate. As the book progresses these statements will be explored, challenged and justified.

Project management – the business manager's perspective

There are thousands of pages, and probably tens of millions of words written on project management. My own bookshelves are crammed with everything from beginner's guides to advanced manuals. These publications include how-to-do handbooks, collections of tips and techniques, the personal reflections of experienced practitioners and academic journals.

Although project management books vary in terms of structure, there is a high degree of similarity between many of them. They appear more alike than books on management topics such as strategy, marketing or operations. Most project management texts cover very similar ground and are, perhaps obviously, concerned with managing individual projects and have been written for project managers. It is unfair to state that all project management books fit this categorization. There is a minority strand concerned with larger and multiple projects with titles including words like "programme", "portfolio" or "governance". There are also volumes by academics providing both students' textbooks and critical analysis of the subject.

Occasionally an unusual project management book appears, like Goldratt's *Critical Chain* (1997), but truly innovative books in this field are rare. This book tries to be different, even atypical, when compared to other project management texts. For a start, it is not a project management book in the normal sense of that phrase. This book will not provide the reader with all the skills to work as a project manager, although the contents will help in understanding how an organization can be more successful in delivering projects. And whilst this book will prove useful to project managers, the primary audience is not the project management community.

This book takes a different perspective from most project management texts, which are written from the viewpoint of those who *do project work*. In contrast, this book takes the perspective of those who *want projects done* or who *have projects done to them* – that is the business management community who need concepts explored, IT systems developed, new products launched, performance improved, costs reduced and changes implemented.

Many books on programme and portfolio management claim to be targeted at business managers, leaders or executives. In practice, they are usually written in the language of the project management community and address the issues of project managers. Hence, they will be read mostly by those with a professional involvement in the subject, rather than the broad business management population this book is targeted at. Even writing on the topic of project governance, which should be a subject for project sponsors and stakeholders, appears to be mostly written by project managers for project managers' consumption. The majority of project management books define how to do a project, without ever asking what managers want from projects. In contrast, this book starts by asking what do the various management stakeholders need and want from business projects, and therefore what should be done to achieve this.

To understand the importance of this difference in viewpoint consider an analogy of writing about cars and drivers. Project management books, in general, are like mechanic's guides defining how to build an engine and how to make it run. But this book is akin to a text that helps readers to go for drives, to get where they want to go, and to prepare their passengers for the trip. A mechanic's guide helps to build and fix the engine, but it will not show how to have ongoing pleasant and successful journeys. Of course, a working engine is an essential component of a car journey, and all drivers must know how to re-fuel a car. It is sensible for any driver to be able to undertake simple maintenance tasks like adding oil, changing spark plugs and lamps. It is even prudent to understand the basic structure of the car, even if it is only to have productive conversations with a mechanic about replacing break pads or the clutch. This book will help with all of the similar tasks, of course in the context of business management, but most car drivers' primary interest is to be confident they can get somewhere time after time. They do not want to be an expert in gearbox design.

The structure of this book

This book provides practical advice and an understanding of different theories of project and change management. The aim is to provide useful knowledge and to open up debate about the role of projects and how project performance can be optimized.

The chapters have been written to form a coherent framework. However, each chapter has been rendered stand-alone to enable readers to pick and choose according to need. This does mean that there is some minor repetition between chapters. There is a broad logic to the order of the chapters, but readers are encouraged to use the chapters in whatever order works best for them. Possible orders of chapters depending on a reader's learning objectives are discussed below.

Throughout the chapters two types of case studies are used. Examples of projects are given, so also are examples of how individual managers in various roles deal with projects.

The contents of the book have been derived from a practitioner's experience. Many of the ideas are sourced from the direct experience of project managers or other managers, but the references include journals and academic books as well as practitioner sources.

There is of course a cost to any book which tries to bring a synthesis from a wide range of different areas – the level of detail must be limited (unless the book is huge). This is not a weakness. It is always possible to research and learn more about the individual topics in this book, but these component topics can be better understood by being placed into a coherent framework. Many of the problems arising in projects are not due to absence of expertise in any individual area, but because of the lack of a complete and coherent understanding of the full challenge of implementing change through projects, and an understanding of how action in one area affects outcomes in another.

People with skills in all sorts of exotic project management fields can be found in many organizations – theory of constraints, earned value analysis, uncertainty management and Monte Carlo techniques – but it is a struggle to find many managers who can coherently bring together the end-to-end activities that allow an organization to go reliably from ideas to sustained change without excessive operational disruption.

The challenge of management is not to be an expert in every domain, but to have enough expertise to apply a skillset in everyday situations; to understand when it is appropriate to get help from specialists; to be able to competently manage those specialists to achieve organizational goals; and importantly to be able to analyse and critique management approaches to understand their limitations and be able to improve upon them. This book sets out to achieve this in the domain of projects.

The contents

In determining the scope of this book, some of the arbitrary or subjective boundaries that are often used when discussing project management have been avoided. The scope has been derived by analysing the work of a project manager rather than being bound by what is normally described as project management. There are chapters on topics that are not always considered as part of project management – such as requirements analysis, benefits realization and change management. Such topics, whilst arguably not project management, are essential to the successful delivery of most projects and are regularly not dealt with in any other course of study. However, a book obviously must have boundaries, and in removing one set of limitations on contents another has been applied.

To keep this book to manageable proportions I have restricted the amount of discussion on topics which are part of every manager's role (such as team management, relationship building, group dynamics, communication skills, leadership and organizational politics). It is not that these topics are not essential to project management – they are crucial. Anyone familiar with my other writings will know how much emphasis I place on the importance of skills like relationship building, communication or managing organizational politics to successful project delivery. But such skills are also essential to all management roles, and therefore may be dealt outside the context of a project management course. Anyone studying a management discipline or pursuing a management career has to learn about topics like team management, leadership and communication skills and will find many courses on them. So discussion on these topics has been limited in this book. However, it may be only on project management courses that topics like requirements analysis or benefits management are dealt with sufficiently in the context of projects, hence they have been included in the book.

The book is split into 13 chapters. The first chapter is optional, and those with a project management background or detailed knowledge may choose to skip it. However, it is recommended to at least scan it. Even very experienced project managers often only know a sub-set of the different approaches to project delivery. Table 1 describes the order and gives a flavour for the contents of each chapter.

Table 1 Contents description

	Chapter title	Overview of contents
1	Overview of project management	An introduction to project management and the associated terminology. This chapter helps those with less experience or knowledge of projects and project concepts to use the rest of the book and to put project management generally in context. It also introduces newer and alternative approaches to project management. Experienced project managers will still benefit from reading this chapter as it may cover variations of project management they are unfamiliar with.
2	Strategy, project management and the project portfolio	This chapter looks at the origins of ideas for projects, and the linkages between strategy and projects. It discusses strategy from the viewpoint of what a strategy must produce to be helpful to those responsible for projects. It also discusses how strategy can be influenced by projects and project management.
3	Selecting projects and creating the project portfolio	The challenge of reducing an enormous set of ideas to an achievable set of projects within the resource constraints of an organization. How can a project portfolio be optimized and prioritized, and what does this achieve? What happens in reality? It explains the concept and role of portfolio management.

4	Project resources and resource management	An overview of how organizations can understand their resources and capability to deliver projects. How does resource management impact the ability to deliver projects? What are the implications of different resourcing strategies (such as maximizing utilization of staff versus flexibility to respond to new needs)? What makes up the project resource pool? This chapter also introduces the Theory of Constraints.
5	Exploration and definition of requirements and designs	The basis for many projects is an understanding of detailed requirements and thereafter the design of deliverables. How important is analysis and requirements capture to project sponsors and stakeholders? What are the implications of different approaches to the outcome of the project? How should change to requirements be managed and what are the implications? How can the management community gain an understanding of what a project will deliver?
6	Planning projects	This chapter describes how to go from the position of desire for a project to a structured piece of work that is planned and has resources allocated who are actively working to complete the project. It introduces different ways of planning and discusses how planning relates to risk management.
7	Defining project success	For a project to be perceived as successful there must be a view of what success is. This chapter explores how the measures of success evolve and the perspectives of different stakeholders. The chapter also proposes how determining success measures should be approached in practice.
8	Managing the execution of projects	An overview of delivery and governance processes for in-life projects. The objective is to provide a view of how to understand, authorize, monitor and probe project progress as a project manager, sponsor or stakeholder. This chapter also looks at communication, reporting and expectation management.
9	Implementation: Delivering and sustaining change	How can projects be structured and managed to achieve the results required? What is change management, and how does it relate to project management? How change can come undone, and what needs to be in place so the results of a project are sustained after the project ends, rather than merely delivered? What are the implications for different project stakeholders? What are the effects of projects on operations and how should this be managed?
10	Achieving benefits from projects	The challenge of achieving value and measuring benefits as projects are delivered. How should the need for value shape projects, rather than just be a result of them? How does value delivery link to project progress, expectations and change? How does the delivery of different types of benefits (e.g. cost reductions, revenue increases, customer satisfaction improvements) conflict, and how should they be combined?

Table 1 Continued

	Chapter title	Overview of contents
11	Understanding and managing risk on projects	Risk management is a core part of project management; this chapter explains why. There are many sources of risk on projects. How can these be understood and what can be done about it?
12	Building a delivery capability	If project management capabilities are required how should organizations go about developing and enhancing them? What is the role of the broader organization in developing project capabilities? What resource does an organization need, and what is the role of third parties in providing access to these skills? How should project management expertise be aligned with expertise in other disciplines such as change management?
13	Context, culture and the limits to project management	This chapter introduces the implications of variations in organization and situation on approaches to projects, considering issues such as type of project, business sector and organizational culture. What environment does *change* need to be successful? What are the implications of *context* upon projects and project management? Is the idea of generic project approaches viable for business? The chapter also discusses when it is appropriate to use project approaches and project management disciplines to deliver change, but also the limits to them and when they will not deliver the results required.

The order of chapters

One of the challenges faced by the author of a book like this is determining the order of the chapters. There is no one right order or wrong order, but different orders that are appropriate to different readers. For instance, from an individual project manager's perspective the positioning of Chapter 4 may seem premature and may be considered better if placed after Chapter 6 on planning. However, from the perspective of a manager responsible across an entire organizational portfolio of projects this is a critical topic that must be understood early on. Strategy is concerned with decisions about resource allocation, and to achieve it an understanding of resource is essential.

The challenge of the ordering of chapters has been faced in three ways. First, I have ordered the chapters as I felt most appropriate given my background in projects and project management. This is somewhat different from the traditional ordering of chapters. Second, chapters are written as stand-alone units which may be read in any order as required by the individual student. To some extent the order of chapters is irrelevant, with the exception of Chapter 1; they may be used in any order desired. However, it is accepted that students may want guidance in approaching this topic. Therefore, and third, an order for using the chapters based on the needs of the specific student or group of students has been suggested. This order is represented in Diagram 1 as a "flight path" through the chapters.

Category of reader	Optional intro	Primary flight path (Primary chapters of interest)	Secondary flight path (additional chapters of interest)
❶		1 → 5 → 6 → 10 → 11 → 7 → 8 → 9	2 → 3 → 4 → Appendix
❷	1	5 → 6 → 4 → 10 → 11 → 7 → 8 → 9	2 → 3 → 12 → 13 → Appendix
❸	1	2 → 3 → 4 → 7 → 8 → 9 → 10 → 11 → 12 → 13	5 → 6 → Appendix
❹	1	2 → 3 → 4 → 7 → 8 → 9 → 10 → 11	5 → 6 → 13 → Appendix
❺	1	2 → 3 → 4 → 5 → 6 → 7 → 8 → 9 → 10 → 11 → 13	12

Diagram 1 Possible ordering of chapters by category of reader

Whilst everyone is an individual with individual learning needs, there may be five broad categories of readers for this book:

1. Those with no background in project management and studying it to learn the skills and capabilities of a project manager
2. Experienced project managers looking to expand knowledge
3. Managers looking to develop a project management capability within an organization (whilst not desiring to personally practice as a project manager)
4. Those with no intention of working as project managers, but with an understanding that it is a powerful and useful management skill that all managers should have an awareness of
5. Those looking to undertake some academic or critical analysis of project management

Every chapter has value to each category of reader, and they can be read in the order they are given in the book. However, each category of reader could take a different "flight path", utilizing different chapters in a different order. Possible "flight paths" are shown in Diagram 1.

This should be considered as general guidance only, and each reader needs to assess his or her needs individually.

Bibliography

APM (Association for Project Management). *APM Body of Knowledge*, 5th Edition, 2006.

Balogun, J. and Hope Hailey, V. *Exploring Strategic Change*. Prentice Hall, 2004.

Burnes, B. "Complexity theories and organizational change". *International Journal of Management Reviews*. Volume 7, Issue 2, 2005, pp. 73–90.

Carroll, T. *Project Delivery in Business-As-Usual Organizations*. Gower, 2006.

Cicmil, S. and Hodgson, D. "Making projects critical: An introduction". *Making Projects Critical*. Palgrave MacMillan, 2006, Chapter 1, pp. 1–25.

Cicmil, S., Williams, T., Thomas, J. and Hodgson, D. "Rethinking project management: Researching the actuality of projects". *International Journal of Project Management*. Volume 24, Issue 8, November 2006, pp. 675–86.

Crawford, L., Pollack, J. and England, D. "Uncovering the trends in project management: Journal emphases over the last 10 years". *International Journal of Project Management*. Volume 24, Issue 2, February 2006, pp. 175–84.

Goldratt, E. *Critical Chain*. The North River Press, 1997.

Hrebiniak, LG. *Making Strategy Work, Leading Effective Execution and Change.* Wharton School Publishing, 2005.

Hyvärdi, I. "Project: The just necessary structure to reach your goals". *International Journal of Project Management.* Volume 24, Issue 3, April 2006, pp. 216–25.

Kollevit, B. Karlsen, JT. and Grønhaug K. "Perspectives on project management". *International Journal of Project Management.* Volume 25, Issue 1, January 2007, pp. 3–9.

Martinsuo, M. and Lehtonen P. "Role of single-project management in achieving portfolio management efficiency". *International Journal of Project Management.* Volume 25, Issue 1, January 2007, pp. 56–65.

McKinlay, M. "A matter of perception?" *APM Yearbook 2005/06.*

PMI (Project Management Institute, Inc). *The Guide to the Project Management Body of Knowledge*, version 3, 2004.

The Standish Group. *The Chaos Report (1994).*

The Standish Group. *The Chaos Report Press Release 25 March 2006.*

Todnem By, R. "Organisational change management: A critical review". *Journal of Change Management.* Volume 5, Issue 4, December 2005, pp. 369–80.

Whittington, R. *What Is Strategy – And Does It Matter?* Thomson Business Press, 2000.

Williams, D. and Parr T. *Enterprise Programme Management, Delivering Value.* Palgrave MacMillan, 2004.

Winter, M. Andersen, ES. Elvin, R. and Levene, R. "Focusing on business projects as an area for future research: An exploratory discussion of four different perspectives". *International Journal of Project Management.* Volume 24, Issue 8, November 2006a, pp. 699–709.

Winter, M., Smith, C., Morris, P. and Cicmil, S. "Directions for future research in project management: The main findings of a UK government-funded research network". *International Journal of Project Management.* Volume 24, Issue 8, November 2006b, pp. 638–49.

1
overview
of project
management

Most people in business have had some involvement in project based activities and will be broadly familiar with the idea of projects. But a general awareness of projects is a far call from understanding the terminology and principles of project management. Anyone who wants to study or discuss project management as a discipline has first to learn the jargon and ideas of the project management community.

This chapter provides an overview of the central concepts of project management. It gives the reader an appreciation of project management and its associated terminology which will help in understanding the rest of the book. The chapter provides a flavour of the complexity of project management and gives an awareness of the management challenges projects throw up. Project management is put in context, so the reader can form an understanding of the linkages, overlaps and differences between this and other management disciplines.

The chapter acts a reference source for ongoing project management studies. Readers who have a good understanding of project management do not have to study it all, but will gain from scanning through it. The first section is aimed at the complete novice with little or no previous exposure to project management.

The chapter is a useful summary for any manager interested in project management.

A novice's guide to projects and project management

Most people have an intuitive grasp of what a project is, and have some exposure to projects in their private life. A project could be anything from decorating a room or restoring an old car to planning and going on that once-in-a-lifetime holiday.

Once we move out of the personal sphere, and into the domain of organizations, which is the context for this book, the range of endeavours that can be managed as projects is vast. Projects encompass IT developments, designing and implementing new products and services, building new facilities, and organizational change activities. A simple way to think of a project is as *something that needs to be done* and project management, a structured approach to *getting things done.*

The origins of structured approaches to *getting things done* are lost in history. Arguably, some very great ancient tasks, such as building the pyramids, must have had some form of management approach to control and coordinate thousands of people. But the traceable history of project management starts in the 20th century with large-scale engineering works initially in the defence sectors and then spilling out into civil construction. Over time project management has permeated most areas of business. Like any professional discipline that thousands of people are involved in, it has developed its own terminology – not all of it easily accessible – and a range of approaches and tools, some of which are more successful than others.

The most obvious question at this stage is what differentiates a project and project management from any other activity and any other style of *getting things done.* Surely operational management is equally about *getting things done.*

There is a range of characteristics that separate project management from other forms of management, which are discussed in detail below. At its simplest, a project is an endeavour with a known end, which once achieved finishes the project. Thus, if the project is to build a new facility, then once the facility is complete the project is over. Alternatively, if the project is to launch a new product, once the product is launched the project is complete. The same cannot be said for operational management, which will go on running the operations of a business forever or at least until the business itself is terminated.

The truth is somewhat more complex. Project management varies from other styles of management in a number of other ways, but the fact that a project has a clear end point is the most fundamental. It is worth considering two other factors about projects at this stage – their organizational scope and the source of management authority of a project manager. Most managers work within departments, functions or processes, and their authority derives from a position in the organizational hierarchy, and is typically aligned to the department, function or process they work in. Thus, the head of customer services or the finance director works within customer services or finance department respectively. Projects do not recognise such organizational boundaries. A project such as implementing a new IT system to improve the level of customer service will cut across the IT department, customer services and perhaps other functions like sales. The project manager has to be able to work cross functionally and critically, to control and manage resources such as staff cross-functionally.

Working cross-functionally is not a feature of all projects, but it is common. This leads to an issue: on what grounds or with what authority does a project manager work across departments? The head of customer services cannot normally tell finance staff what to do, and the head of finance cannot tell customer services staff what to do. Yet, this is what a project manager is required to do. A project manager's power comes from the mandate of the project and from his or her expertise as a project manager rather than being at a certain level in the organizational hierarchy.

The mandate can come from a number of sources, but typically it exists because the project is officially nominated by the organization as one it wants to do, and it has a senior manager with sufficient positional power to sponsor the project. Beyond mandate, project managers without direct power often have to rely on their ability to persuade and influence staff to work on the project.

One of the key approaches in project management is not just to get a task done, but to predict in advance how long it will take, how much it will cost and what the output will be. This task of prediction is tied up with the concept of planning. From analysis of the project's goal and decomposition of the work required into smaller tasks, a project manager will assess the work involved, determine the resources required, and then manage the project to achieve its objective against this plan. One of the most basic ways of assessing the success of a project is in completing the project within this estimation of time, cost and what it will achieve.

A final critically important feature of projects, and one that is often most uncomfortable to the novice project manager, is the fact that projects typically involve uncertainty and risk. Uncertainty exists in many ways – from whether the project outcome as understood is really what is needed or desired, whether a specific project approach will actually work, through to whether people will work at an expected level of productivity. Although a project is based on a plan, the plan is full of unknowns, ambiguities, estimates and assumptions, all of which add risk to projects. A key feature of project management is its attempt to manage and minimize risk. Activities such as clearly documenting the objectives and goals of a project, project planning and documenting requirements are all about bounding uncertainty. By sufficient analysis a project manager can limit uncertainty, and gain a perspective on the level of remaining uncertainty. This uncertainty is normally known as risk in project management terminology. Further, components of project management, in particular contingency planning, change control and most obviously risk management, are about dealing with the impact of risk and uncertainty.

As project managers' experience grows they develop a range of skills. The most obvious are formal project management skills. But project managers have to develop a broad range of management skills including technical knowledge, change management, influence and persuasion, team management, leadership, organizational politics, relationship building, negotiating and influencing and strong communication skills.

Project management as a discipline constantly evolves and a book like this represents the state at a point in time. However, the basic premises and tools of project management have been stable for some time now.

To the complete novice, project management can be a contradictory phenomenon. At one level it is intuitively obvious what a project is, but at another, like most management disciplines, it has developed its own world of obscure jargon and seemingly complex tools. The advice to the novice is to relax, as the basic concepts of project management, whilst powerful, are simple and the application of common sense is normally enough to understand them. The more complex project management approaches can be understood over time as experience and exposure to projects and project theory expand. The rest of this chapter provides a summary of the key parts and theories of project management. Much is simple, but some will require effort and consideration to fully understand.

Basic concepts

What is a project?

The starting point for an understanding of project management is to define the term *project*. For many people it is intuitively self-evident what a project is, but there is not a single universally accepted definition.

The difficulty in defining *project* is that the word is used to name a huge variety of endeavours. The range includes activities that take many years to those taking a few days, from undertakings involving thousands of people to tasks involving only one or two individuals, from technology developments to people change initiatives, and from concepts pushing the boundaries of knowledge to those using skills that have existed for hundreds of years.

There are several ways in which project management literature builds an understanding of what a project is, including

o Formal definitions
o Discussions of the characteristics of projects
o Comparison to what a project is not
o Examples of projects

Prominent project management literature contains a range of different but related formal definitions of a project. For example, a project is defined as

> *A unique, transient endeavour, undertaken to achieve a desired outcome.* (APM, 2006)

> *A temporary endeavour to create a unique product, service or result.* (PMI, 2004)

> *A complex, non-routine, one-time effort limited by time, budget, resources, and performance specifications designed to meet customer needs.* (Gray and Larson, 2006)

> *A unique set of coordinated activities, with a definite starting and finishing point, undertaken by an individual or organization to meet specific objectives within defined schedule, cost and performance parameters.* (BSI, 2000)

The significant words and phrases in such definitions give three main characteristics of projects:

1. Projects exist for a limited period of time: they are *transient, temporary* or *limited by time.*
2. Each project is different: they are *unique, one-time,* or *non-routine.*
3. Projects are carried out to reach some predefined goal: They *achieve a desired outcome* or *create a unique product, service or result* or are *designed to meet customer needs* or *to meet specific objectives.*

Whilst these three main characteristics of projects are generally accepted as being true, they do not in themselves give a complete description of projects. There are additional features that can be considered beyond this. Three important additional attributes are

4. A project is completed within some agreed constraints, normally specified in terms of cost, duration, starting and end points, and some measure of the quality of the output (as in *defined schedule, cost and performance parameters*).

5. Projects entail some level of complexity. There are many activities which exist for a limited period of time, are unique and which reach some pre-defined goal. Arguably, every time a meal is cooked it is unique, it takes a limited period of time and is done to reach a predefined goal. However, such activities are normally discounted as project because they are not significantly complex to require any special management. Complexity can be in many different dimensions, such as scale, risk, technology or the coordination of people.

6. Projects require a way of working called *progressive elaboration*. Progressive elaboration is a process by which the project definition is expanded in more detail as the project proceeds. An example of progressive elaboration is building a house. When a project is initiated to build a house perhaps the only information known is the location of the land it is to be built on. As the land is made ready, the size of the house and the number of rooms are determined. After the foundations are completed the precise layout of the rooms is defined. When the house is built more details are defined such as the colour of the walls and the nature of the fixtures and fittings. It is only necessary to define sufficient detail to be able to progress to the next stage predictably. It is important to note that in progressive elaboration the outcome of the project is not changed, but described in gradually increasing detail. Not all project managers agree that progressive elaboration is a universal characteristic of every project, but it is regarded as such by the Project Management Institute (PMI, 2004) and by writers such as Gardiner (Gardiner, 2005).

An alternative way to explore the meaning of *project* is by comparing it to what it is not, and typically this comparison is made with *operations*. *Operations* is a simplified concept in project management literature. Operations are typically specified as being continuous, repetitive and non-unique. Activities such as running a factory production line, managing a call centre or controlling the supply chain for a supermarket are operations. These activities do not have a predefined goal, and they do not stop on reaching some target. *Operations* continue performing an ongoing series of transactions that are more or less the same every time. In this way they contrast with projects' characteristics such as uniqueness, time limited-ness and predefined goals.

Another way of differentiating projects from other work is comparing them with the normal functional setup of an organization. Again the comparisons tend to be very simplistic, though they are helpful as a model. Most of the staff in organizations work within a department or division that is bounded by a functional skill-set or role. For example, there could be HR, finance, IT, sales, marketing, procurement, production and customer service departments. Most of the work of staff in business is done within their functional departments. Project managers, conversely, often work across functions as projects have to weave together people from different departments to complete their work. A business change project, as an example, may work across HR, finance, IT and operations. (This difference breaks down when project work is compared with the role of staff in a fully process-orientated organization.)

The final way of developing an understanding of a project is by listing examples of endeavours which are considered as projects. Typical examples of activities that could be considered as projects in a business are

- o Developing and implementing an IT system
- o Designing and launching a new product
- o Moving staff to a new office location
- o The integration of departments following the merger of two organizations
- o The rollout of a training course to every member of a large organization
- o Preparing a major event such as an exhibition
- o Developing a marketing campaign
- o Reducing operational costs
- o The improvement of staff capabilities or skills

Project management

The next piece of terminology to explore is *project management*. The relevant literature builds an understanding of what project management is in several ways, including

- o Formal definitions
- o Explaining what project management achieves
- o Descriptions of the components of project management

Prominent project management literature contains a range of different but related formal definitions of a project management. For example, project management is defined as

> *Project management is the process by which projects are defined, planned, monitored, controlled and delivered such that the agreed benefits are realized.* (APM, 2006)

> *Project management is the application of knowledge, skills, tools and techniques to project activities to meet project requirements.* (PMI, 2004) (Gray and Larson, 2006)

> *Project management is the planning, monitoring and control of all aspects of a project and the motivation of all those involved in it to achieve the project objectives on time and to the specified cost, quality and performance.* (BSI, 2000)

An analysis of these and similar definitions defines project management as consisting of three components:

- o A process for managing projects. This process encompasses defining, planning, monitoring and controlling projects
- o The application of knowledge, skills, tools and techniques
- o The management of the people working on the project

What project management achieves is simple to define, and almost a tautology given the definition of a project. A project has a predefined goal. Project management achieves this predefined goal (or at least strives to) – as in *the agreed benefits are realized*; or *to meet project requirements*; or *to achieve the project objectives on time and to the specified cost, quality and performance.*

There are many descriptions of the component parts of project management. There seem, almost unlike any other management discipline, to be continual attempts to define all aspects of project management exhaustively. (One of the features of project management that does not often receive much analysis is the rationale underlying these continual efforts to define what project management is in totality. It is as if the project management community, being used to trying to define projects fully, has to apply the same approach to explaining their discipline). These attempts are based on an assumption that there is a describable best way to manage a project that is widely applicable, and this best way is encapsulated in a series of definitions of *best practice*. One of the most influential explanations of best practice lies in the various bodies of knowledge or BoKs.

The best known of these are the APM's Body of Knowledge (APM, 2006) and the PMBOK (PMI, 2004). The PMBOK defines a framework for project management consisting of a generic project lifecycle and description of project organizations, and a set of 9 knowledge areas (such as project quality management), which subdivide into 44 project management processes (such as quality planning, quality assurance, quality control). The APM's BoK is somewhat broader in scope. It describes the context for project management and then defines 46 techniques organized into 6 areas (planning the strategy, executing the strategy, techniques, business and commercial, organization and governance, and people and the profession). Although someone familiar with either BoK would find much that is common when reading the other, the structures are different. For example, the 46 techniques in the APM's BoK do not neatly map onto the 44 processes in the PMBOK.

These BoKs are not the only definitions of project management. There are many methodologies which define how to manage a project. One of the most widely recognized is PRINCE 2 (The office of government commerce, 2005), which was developed for the UK Government. Knowledge of and adherence to PRINCE 2 is compulsory on many public sector projects in the United Kingdom. PRINCE 2 aims to be a generic, tailorable approach to managing projects. It does not seek to be an exhaustive definition of all skills required to manage a project, although it is a thorough methodology with many components. PRINCE 2 aims to be a working tool to be used directly in projects, whereas a BoK is more akin to a reference source (somewhat like an encyclopaedia that may occasionally be referred to). Project managers can be accredited to various levels of expertise in PRINCE 2. PRINCE 2 has been very successful in influencing the way projects are run, at least in the United Kingdom.

Beyond this, many businesses have their own approaches usually based either on a tailored form of a methodology such as PRINCE 2, on the advice of specialist consultants, or on the experiences and views of their own project management staff.

Definitions of project management describe it typically in terms of

- o *Generic lifecycle(s)*: describing the main steps that a project should go through from its initiation or start through to its close down or completion
- o *Tools and techniques*: which define the activities a project manager should do on any project (such as risk, time and scope management) whilst passing through the lifecycle of a project
- o *Additional supporting methods and advice*: information that project managers may find useful (such as information on communication skills, people management or common document templates).

One area of possible confusion is in the use of the term project management in specific and general contexts. Specifically, project management refers to the activity of managing a project, as opposed to managing a programme or a portfolio. On occasions it is necessary to refer generally to the complete set of disciplines of project management, programme management and portfolio management. They tend to be grouped under the same term as project management (with programme and portfolio management considered as sub-disciplines or extensions of project management). The difference has to be interpreted from the context.

Project manager

The central actor in a project is the *project manager*. A project manager is someone who manages projects, using the discipline of project management. It can be a term referring to both a role on a specific project, as well as a permanent job title for people who regularly work on projects.

The project manager is, as the name suggests, a management role. As such it is responsible for identifying, structuring and managing the tasks within a project rather than being personally responsible for doing all of them.

In business, typically, the project manager is not the customer of a project, but is acting as an agent of someone else who wants the project done. (See *project sponsor* and *project customers* below.)

Project manager is not a restricted title and anyone can title oneself a project manager, irrespective of skills or qualifications. There are many thousands of people who do. Sometimes the title is based on some level of accreditation in the subject, and there are a series of formal qualifications. The qualifications range from university degrees, practitioner qualifications and those awarded by professional bodies such as the APM (Association of Project Managers) or the PMI (Project Management Institute). In some organizations only those with formal qualifications are recognized as project managers, but this is not common practice in business.

There are many levels of skill, experience and competency of project managers, and this is reflected to some extent in job titles. There are titles such as junior or senior project manager, project director, programme manager, programme director and portfolio manager. As there are no universal standards, it is dangerous to draw any conclusions about an individual's competency based on his or her job title without understanding the context in which the title was given.

The components of project management

This section describes the core components of project management. Although there are many definitions of and approaches to project management they are mostly based on the same principal elements. All experienced project managers will recognise the contents of this section.

Project management is not a static discipline, and new ideas and techniques are constantly added to the subject. However, for all the debate and enhancement, most project managers mainly use the same basic set of ideas and tools. At this introductory level the principles are relatively constant.

Lifecycle

A fundamental component of project management is the *lifecycle*. Project management lifecycles are generic descriptions of the sequential stages a project goes through. Given the part of the definition of a project that it is a unique endeavour, it may seem impossible to define a common lifecycle of activities that describes what happens in all cases. This is overcome by the fact that lifecycles do not attempt to define the complete work to be done by a project team. Instead, a lifecycle provides a description and phasing of the tasks that the project manager must do to start, define, manage and complete a project. So, for example, a lifecycle may show how to define a project, but it will not contain the definition of the project, which is unique to the situation. The fact that there are different lifecycles indicates the difficulty in having a universally applicable definition.

A lifecycle provides a template to help a project manager structure work on a project. It provides a consistent way to manage projects which is therefore easier to oversee and audit. A lifecycle also provides a common vocabulary to discuss projects. When everyone in an organization understands the meaning of the names of stages of a lifecycle, such as *project initiation* or *feasibility study*, it is much easier to have constructive dialogue about projects.

Lifecycles are divided into stages, and the stages may be further divided into more detailed steps. There is usually supporting material to facilitate successful progress through the stages, such as procedures to carry out, techniques or forms to complete. Different lifecycles have different numbers of stages and are presented in various ways. There are no universal definitions of the different phases of projects, although there are widely recognized lifecycles based on methodologies such as PRINCE 2 (The office of government commerce, 2005).

A typical example of a lifecycle has the following stages:

1. *Initiation and definition*: the stage of defining the reason for the project, what is required to be delivered, and gaining agreement that the project is worth doing
2. *Planning*: the stage of detailed planning of the project which would result in a timescale, task schedule, budget and resource plan
3. *Execution and control*: the most apparent stage of a project when the project team do the work to reach the outcome desired, managed relative to the defined plan and budget
4. *Closure*: releasing resources from the project and reviewing what lessons can be learnt from the project

An alternative example of a lifecycle used for an organization that runs many projects concerned with launching new products is:

1. *Concept*: the structured definition of an idea for a product. The concept is used to gain consensus that a product is worth developing, without committing significant resources. At the end of a concept phase there should be a broad understanding of what the project will create, the likelihood of success and what it will take to achieve this success.
2. *Feasibility*: the review of a project in more detail. A feasibility study is done to gain confidence that the product can actually be created and sold.

It may include activities as varied as technical tests, market research and assessment of the impact of this project on the organization. At the end of the feasibility study it should be clear what the project will cost, how long it will take and what the outcome will be.

3. **Detailed requirements**: the collection of the full definition of the output from the project, including a product description and a definition of the services required to support the product.

4. **Solution design**: the identification and design of a solution to meet the requirements. In the case of a product, this design includes the technical specification for the product, as well as operational processes to market, sell and support the product and support its customers. In project management terminology this is the identification and design of the *deliverables* from the project.

5. **Solutions build**: the development of the new product. In other words this is the creation of the deliverables from the project.

6. **Solution implementation**: the implementation of the deliverables within an organization. This is the stage in which a business change is made, such as training sales in how to sell and customer services in how to support the product.

7. **Closure**: the handover of the product to the operational departments of a business and the release of all unused project resources. There is also a review of the business case to see if the product is meeting its expected targets.

A third example of a lifecycle is shown in Diagram 1.1 below:

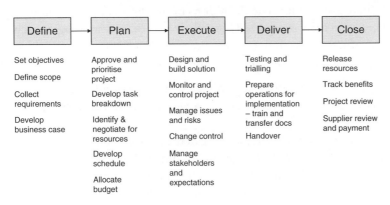

Diagram 1.1 *A project lifecycle and its component activities*

A common supporting concept in lifecycles is that of a *gate*. A gate is a decision point at the end of a stage of a lifecycle. At the gate a decision is made between three options: carry on the project to the next stage, go back and rework some of the current stage, or stop the project. So, in the previous lifecycle there could be a gate between concept and feasibility, and another between feasibility and detailed requirements. Only if the outcome from the concept and the feasibility is positive enough is the decision made to pass through the gate and move onto the next stage. Such decisions are sometimes referred to as *gate reviews*.

Lifecycles provide a structure with which a project can be quickly started. Most project managers recognise the value in them. There are many advantages to lifecycles, but there are risks as well. One risk is that unless lifecycles are applied flexibly they can constrain actions to only those that the lifecycle identifies and hence can miss out steps which are required in specific situations. In addition, for simple projects lifecycles can be inefficient by requiring a project manager to do activities which are not always required on small low-risk projects.

The choice of which lifecycle to apply is a project manager's decision. There are different approaches to manage a project. An early task of a project manager in starting a project is to choose the process to manage the project by. This choice is called the *project management strategy*. (This term should not be confused with *project strategy*, which is described in Chapter 8 and is the high-level approach for achieving a project's objectives.)

Case Study **1.1** **ONE COMPANY'S PROJECT LIFECYCLE**

Telcocom provides technology products to other businesses. Each product was bespoke for the individual customer, and a project was required as a part of every sale. This project could take several weeks or months to implement a specific solution for a customer.

The level of success in projects was variable. Some customers were very satisfied, whilst others were unhappy. The ability of senior management to track projects was poor due to limited reporting and the fact that every project was managed in a different way. In addition, constructive dialogue about projects was hampered by the lack of a single terminology to discuss projects with.

At the same time Telcocom was undergoing a cultural-change programme, aimed at moving staff away from considering the organization as a technology company to being a customer-focussed provider of business solutions. Part of this cultural change was based on staff adopting accessible everyday language rather than speaking in technology jargon.

A decision was made to develop a common project management lifecycle. The business had multiple objectives in introducing a common lifecycle which all projects would adhere to, including

- *Raising the project management success rate. The lifecycle was to be developed in conjunction with a set of methods and standards for project management.*
- *Providing an accessible and common language for the organization to use when running projects, to improve communication about projects. Partially, this was to remove some of the mystique surrounding projects, and hence everyday language was to be used. This was aligned to the objectives of the cultural-change programme.*
- *Providing a consistent way to manage projects to ease monitoring and control of projects.*
- *Combining the project lifecycle with the financial approvals process.*

The lifecycle was defined in some detail with definitions of what had to be done at every stage and how this should be done. The lifecycle consisted of seven named stages:

- *Think*
- *Define*
- *Approve*
- *Develop*
- *Implement*
- *Measure*
- *Finish*

Objectives, scope and requirements

Projects start with an idea. It could be *we need to improve sales*, or *we could have a better finance system*, or *there is an opportunity to cut costs in operations*. The idea can originate from many sources. Typical sources include business strategy (e.g. become a lower-cost competitor), compliance requirements (e.g. corporate rules, regulations or legal changes, or social pressure), the need to overcome some problem (e.g. operational issues, or not achieving some expected level of performance), or an opportunity (e.g. an idea for a new product, technology advances).

The idea that is the seed for a project can be a concept for something a business can do, such as *we can implement the new-generation software for customer relationship management*. Alternatively, the idea may be something a business needs to achieve, for example, *we must improve the way we manage our customers*.

Whatever way an idea is generated a project manager needs to know both why a project is being done and what it is expected to deliver, for example, *we must improve the way we manage our customers* (why), *which we will achieve by implementing the new-generation software for customer relationship management* (what). The former is the source of the objectives and the foundation of the business case. The latter is the basis of the requirements for the project.

One of the goals of project management is to be able to predict a timeframe and cost to complete an activity. An operational manager can make such a prediction based on his experience of previously doing the activity. As a project is a unique endeavour this cannot be done by simply reflecting on how long the last project took and how much it cost. Instead project managers strive to achieve predicting capability by seeking clarity about what a project has to achieve, and estimating how long this will take and how much it will cost by reviewing the elements of the project. A component of the early parts of most lifecycles is achieving this clarity.

The information required to plan and therefore to be able to estimate a timeframe and cost for a project is broken into four areas:

- *Objectives*: Why is the project being done? What does a project have to achieve to be regarded as a success? For example, the project will cut costs by 10%.
- *Constraints*: Are there any constraints on the project? For example, the project must be done in six months, it cannot cost more than £1m, it must meet some quality standard or it has to conform to health and safety regulations.
- *Scope*: What defines the boundaries of the project? or more prosaically, what's in or not in? For example, the project will change only customer services, the project will not impact the sales department.

o **Requirements**: What, precisely, does the project have to conform to or achieve to be regarded as complete? For example, a new customer service application will be implemented that integrates the complaint logging and billing queries systems.

Project managers start by identifying the objectives, scope and constraints on a project. In addition, they will identify the *success criteria* for a project. Success for any project includes meeting the objectives and conforming to any constraints, but may also include additional criteria such as the need to keep a key group of stakeholders happy.

The project's objectives, constraints, scope and success criteria are normally documented. This document is the central part of the project and is called *project brief* (there are other titles such as *project definition* or *scope document*). The project brief works for a project in a similar way that a strategy works for a business – it sets the direction and tone of the project.

For some projects the project brief is enough to define what the project needs to achieve. In many cases, however, it just shows the outline and boundaries. A lot more detail may be required to define what precisely needs to be achieved. This detail is defined in *requirements*.

The word *requirement* is a noun in common usage, used in multiple and indefinite ways. In project management, and particularly in IT projects, a requirement is a precise definition of need. Requirements can be very specific, such as *the IT solution must automatically calculate customer discounts and enable them to be presented whilst the customer is on the phone*. The full set of requirements will shape the deliverables or output from a project.

Requirements collection is not always necessary, but for complicated developments such as new products or IT systems it is essential. Analysis, collection and documentation of requirements is a specialist skill, called *business analysis*. On some projects the requirements collection phase can take many months, or even years, and there may be thousands of requirements. Typically, it is a phase lasting some weeks or a few months early in the project lifecycle.

Diagram 1.2 depicts the various stages in defining a project. Even though project managers seek clarity, in practice it is not possible to define objectives, scope and requirements completely and unambiguously at the start of a project. There are a number of reasons for this. There is the problem of interpretation and ambiguity inherent in language. No matter how well a project brief is written, it may be interpreted differently by various project members. Just because an objective seems clear to one person, does not mean another will not construe it differently. In addition, defining completely a full set of requirements can take a huge amount of time, and businesses are normally under pressure to complete projects quickly. Next, there is the issue of capability of project customers to know and explain what they want, and of business analysts to extract this information. Often people know

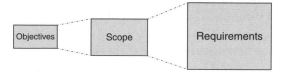

Diagram 1.2 The stages in defining a project

they need something, but cannot fully define what it is. Finally, projects can have long durations. During the life of a project, needs and requirements may change. What may have been important when a project started may become irrelevant later, and what was non-critical may become essential.

This means that there is always a degree of uncertainty and potential flux around objectives, scope and requirements. This is a source of risk for projects. If requirements continually change projects may never finish, or they may finish but deliver a no-longer desired outcome.

Project managers have various ways of dealing with this uncertainty and flux, including

- o *Progressive elaboration*: As described at the start of this chapter this is the process by which project deliverables are defined in progressively more detail as a project progresses. Project managers do not have to define all requirements to start delivering a project. They have to define enough to complete the current stage of work and to be able to estimate the length and cost of the project. As the project progresses, further details can be added.
- o *Assumptions*: Project managers make assumptions. For example, it may not be known in the development of a new product whether the product will be sold by existing sales channels, or whether new channels have to be set up. The project manager can delay the project until this is known, but often it is more productive to continue by making an assumption, such as *this product will be sold by the existing sales force*. This is a source of risk, something any manager involved in a project should understand. But it is manageable if the assumption is explicit and regularly revisited. Unfortunately, assumptions are often forgotten. Numerous projects have been completed but delivered limited benefits because they were based on assumptions that were not understood outside of the project team.
- o *Change control*: Project managers have a specific process for managing change to objectives, scope and requirements. This is called change control and is described later in this chapter.
- o *Contingency*: Project managers build contingency into their plans. Contingency is essentially a buffer of time and resources to account for various risks in a project. Depending on how risky a project is, there could be different levels of contingency.

The management and collection of requirements is discussed in more detail in Chapter 5. Handling of the risk associated with uncertainty and flux is dealt with in Chapter 11.

Plans

The most obvious manifestation of project management is the project plan. Planning is the activity that project managers are typically expected to do. A project plan is one of the main tools of a project manager.

Most people have some vision of plans based on what they think a plan looks like and what it is used for. It is important to understand that plans have many formats and several different purposes. In terms of purpose, plans aid

- o *Understanding*: Planning is a structured process; going through the process of planning develops an understanding of what a project entails in detail.

- *Prediction*: Plans provide the basis for estimating the time a project will take, the cost of a project and the resources required.
- *Allocation*: Plans provide a mechanism for a project manager to allocate the work in a project to various members of the project team.
- *Management*: Plans provide the information to assess and manage progress.
- *Communication*: Plans can be helpful to explain projects to various interested groups.

There is significant skill involved in developing a good plan. It requires experience, a structured approach, making balanced decisions, and the ability to trade off the desire for absolute understanding with the practical need to move on.

There are several steps in producing a plan, but in essence the key activities are

- Producing a list of the tasks required to complete the project
- Identifying linkages between tasks. This is used to define the order tasks must be done in
- Estimating the length of time and resources required to complete the tasks

Planning is a complicated and time-consuming activity, and there are normally many iterations of planning required. For example, the first cut of a plan may show that a task requires ten people and will take five weeks. In practice only four people may be available, or the task may need to be done in three weeks, so the project manager must revisit the plan and see whether the task can be done within these constraints.

Planning is often confused with the activity of using a software tool such as MS-Project. Planning is an intellectual activity. All a tool can do is take some of the drudgery out of determining the result from the thoughts and ideas of the project manager, and from creating a presentable plan. Planning tools are helpful, but they do not do the thinking required.

In planning, a project manager is typically balancing between three major constraints: first, the *time* the project takes; second, the *cost* of the project (or more generally the amount of resource used); and third, the *scope* of the project. These three constraints – time, cost and scope – are often called the *iron triangle* of project management.

One of the main ideas in project management is that there is a trade-off and an ongoing dynamic balance between these three dimensions of a project. A project can be done cheaper, but that usually requires reducing the scope or increasing the time. A project can be done quicker, but that often means using more resources and money, or reducing the scope. A project's scope can be increased, but that usually means the project will take longer or cost more. An objective of most projects is to optimally balance these three constraints. Traditional definitions of project success position achieving the best balance of time, cost and scope as success.

Sometimes the word *scope* is replaced with *quality*, but the principle is identical. Whether the word *scope* or *quality* is used, it refers, in this context, to what the project accomplishes or creates in terms of deliverables or outcome. (This is discussed later in this chapter.)

The starting point for a plan is the list of tasks in it. The task list is created by identifying the main blocks of work in a project. These main blocks are then repeatedly subdivided until the project manager has enough detail to be able to estimate task length, understand dependencies between tasks and estimate the resources required to do the tasks. This task breakdown is called a *work breakdown structure* or *WBS*.

The WBS is important and often goes unquestioned. There are many different ways to complete most complex tasks, so there are choices between WBSs. Depending on the way the WBS is defined, the project will be structured in quite different ways. Consider a very simple example, a project to choose a new car.

Work breakdown 1

- Define features wanted
- Review and identify cars with features wanted
- Short list in the order based on price
- Test drive top 10 cars
- Review finances
- Choose a car
- Select colour
- Order the car

Work breakdown 2

- Review finance options
- Determine budget for new car
- Select cars within the budget range
- Agree on features of the car
- Short list based on features and colour availability
- Prioritise based on reviews in press
- Test drive top 3 cars
- Choose and purchase

Both of these WBSs provide a structure to choose a new car, but they do activities in different orders and in different combinations. This will impact the time and resources required to complete the project. There are many other ways of breaking even a task as simple as this into. The different WBSs may result in quite varied approaches to buying a car. For more complex business projects the impact of selection of WBS can be much greater.

Once a WBS is defined, the plan is created by ordering tasks according to dependencies between them, estimating the length of time each task will take, and determining the resources required to do the tasks. Typically, because of resource constraints, many tasks that could theoretically be done in parallel are done sequentially.

There are many different representations of plans, which provide different information and have different strengths as ways of managing and communicating plans. Methods like *GANTT* and *PERT* are ways of conceiving and presenting plans as are the ways of managing projects.

An important concept in project management is the *critical path*. The critical path is the sequence of activities on a project plan that makes up the longest duration on a project (technically it is the series of tasks with zero slack). If any task in this sequence is delayed the project will be late, and conversely if any can be made shorter the project can be shortened. By focussing on these activities the project manager increases the chance of completing the project on time. (The term was coined as part of the *Critical Path Method* or *CPM* developed by DuPont.)

Plans are often seen as statements of fact, whereas they are just an interpretation of what needs to be done and what may happen. A plan is a living document used to understand and manage the project. It should not be considered like an architectural plan as an absolute and unchanging representation of what needs to happen.

There are many risks that can come about while planning. Assessing the risk in a plan is a skilled task. At the simplest level the risk comes from possible errors in

- o **WBS**: Have all the tasks that need to be included in the plan been included? Any missing tasks will potentially add to the cost and duration of the project and may result in the project failing. Is the WBS the most efficient and effective way to achieve the project's objective?
- o **Estimating length**: Are the times given for each task reasonable? If task length is underestimated a project is likely to be delayed. If task length is overestimated the project may end up taking longer or costing more than is necessary.
- o **Estimating resource requirements**: Are the amounts of resources required for each task reasonable? If resources are underestimated a project may not be completed. If they are overestimated it may cost more than is necessary.
- o **Dependencies**: Are all the dependencies that should exist identified, and are any dependencies identified unnecessary? Missed dependencies can cause unexpected problems. Adding unnecessary dependencies can cause delays that could have been avoided.

Refer to Chapters 6 and 11 for further consideration of these issues.

Project resources and the project team

Projects use resources. The resources required can be identified by way of the planning process. The most obvious resources a project needs are money and people. Beyond these a project may use any other kinds of resources depending on the nature of the project: for example, office space, computers and transport.

In order to carry out the identified tasks of a project, as defined in the project plan, a team of people is required. This team is generally known as the *project team*. It is this team that the project manager manages. The project manager allocates work to members of his team, and motivates and directs them in completion of the work.

Project teams vary vastly in the way that projects themselves differ: at one extreme the project manager is the project team (although usually a one-man task does not require formal project management); at the other extreme a project team can contain thousands of people with a wide variety of skill sets. A key role of the project manager in this context is to coordinate the work of different specialists.

The project manager's work usually extends beyond the people formally working on the project. One of the most important roles outside the project team is the *project sponsor*. The project sponsor is a senior manager who will support the project manager in delivering the project. The sponsor does not usually work as part of the project team, and is often only supporting the project in a part-time capacity. Project sponsors provide senior-management support to the project manager, for example, in helping to resolve major issues, providing access to the necessary resources, and making critical project decisions. Typically the project sponsor is accountable for achieving the project's defined benefits.

As well as the sponsor a project may have a wide range of stakeholders. A stakeholder can be anyone with any type of interest in the project. *Stakeholder management* is an important task for project managers supported by the project sponsor. Depending on the project, stakeholders could include the business's customers, shareholders and staff or union representatives.

Often the most important group of stakeholders of a project is the project's *customers*. There are various ways of defining the customers of a project, and this could include those people who pay for the project, those who want the project done and have the ability to shape the requirements, and those who have to use and live with the deliverables from a project. Usually these are related groups of people, but not always.

Managing the human resources required for projects and ensuring they have sufficient skills is dealt with in Chapters 4 and 12. The role of the project sponsor is explored in Chapter 8.

Managing progress and project control

Once a project manager knows the scope, objectives and requirements, and has a project plan and a project team, the execution and control phase of the project can commence. The project manager's role is to ensure that the activities required to achieve the project's objectives are completed sufficiently quickly and cost-effectively to meet the predefined timescale and budget of the project plan, and to the necessary level of quality. The essential elements to achieving this are monitoring activity, measuring progress, and identifying and taking any necessary corrective action. Arguably, the main task of any project manager is managing progress in this way.

To be able to manage progress the project manager must know what is happening. This is done by monitoring the activity of the project team. The project manager should always keep track of who is doing what, and what each task is meant to be achieving. For large projects the project manager cannot possibly monitor the activity of every individual, so this is done at a team or *workstream* level, where a workstream is a component part of a project. For example, in a project to move an office to a new location, one workstream might be locating and contracting for the new premises, whilst another might be preparing staff for the move.

Monitoring activity is not enough to control a project. The project manager must be able to use the information from monitoring to determine what progress has been made. Progress is relative both to the end objective, and to what should have been done to meet this objective. Essentially, the project manager compares what has been done versus what was expected to have been done as defined in the project plan. Without a plan measuring progress is arbitrary and subjective.

Measuring progress is not always straightforward. With an activity like booking a venue for a large event it is clear-cut whether this task has been done. Either the booking has been made or it has not. However, most tasks are more involved than this. With an activity such as collecting requirements for software development, there is often no point when the task can be categorically and absolutely be determined to be complete. Additional requirements can be added continually, requirements can always be better clarified and detailed, and assessing whether 100% of the requirements are known and documented is not simple. Making the assessment of completion is therefore often an experience-based judgement. In addition, for longer tasks it is necessary not only to understand whether they are finished, but also, whilst working on them, to understand at what stage of completion they are. In requirements capture assessing whether the task is 30 or 40% complete is a subjective estimation. Finally, project managers do not just have to judge how much of a task is done, but whether it is done to a sufficient level of quality to meet the end goals. Given the varying nature and content of projects this is a demanding challenge.

Project management provides a number of tools for assessing progress in these situations. There are special techniques, such as *Earned Value Analysis* or *EVA*, for providing assessments of project progress. Techniques such as EVA are not used universally, and often assessments of progress are based on the judgement and rules of thumb of individual project managers. Assessments of progress are there fore open to error.

So far progress has been talked about relative to the tasks on the plan. But progress is more than this. It is also about understanding what has been achieved compared to what should be achieved. Often achievement of benefits does not start until late in a project's lifecycle (for some projects it does not happen until it is complete). If a project is to cut costs in a business, no matter how much activity has been done on the project, until costs have been cut nothing has actually been delivered. Just because 10% of the tasks are completed on a plan does not mean that the project is 10% complete, or has achieved 10% of its objectives.

Having monitored activity and used this to measure progress, the project manager has to decide what action to take. Occasionally no action is required, as the project is achieving what was expected. More usually though, progress may not be according to the plan. Tasks may take shorter or longer than expected, require different resources, throw up unforeseen problems, or in doing a task it may become clear that other tasks or dependencies have been missed out from the plan. The project manager must decide how to bring work back on track with the plan, and implement this action. If this is not possible then the plan should be adapted.

In making decisions about what action to take to keep a project progressing, project managers often have to make trade-off judgments between the dimensions of the iron triangle – allocating more or less time, providing more or less resources, or increasing or decreasing the scope.

Progress and project control are discussed in more detail in Chapter 8.

Acceptance

As a project completes, it produces deliverables and the resultant outcome from them. For example, a project to launch a new product delivers the product to the sales department, and the outcome is increased revenue for the business as the product is successfully sold.

One of the later stages in most projects is some kind of acceptance of the project's outcome by the project's customers. There are various ways of achieving acceptance. For some deliverables there may be formal tests. This is typical for software development projects. For other projects accepting the deliverables is more intangible. Consider the situation of a cultural-change project to improve the organization's customer focus. Assessing this formally and accepting that the project has achieved its objective is usually subjective. It is possible to find some form of measure, but often for a change programme these are indirect. For example, it is possible to measure accurately how many staff have been to cultural events and training programmes. However, this would not constitute an actual measure of successful change.

Acceptance and testing is described more fully in Chapter 9.

Change Control

A project manager seeks, by capturing objectives, scope and requirements, and through the mechanism of a plan, to complete a project within a predefined and agreed upon budget and timescale. This is only possible if the scope and requirements stay the same. If during the life of the project objectives, scope or requirements change, then it is likely that this will impact the duration, cost or resource requirements of the project.

In practice, comprehensively and completely defining scope and requirements is impossible or at least impractical. In addition, businesses operate in dynamic markets. An idea for a new product may offer a great opportunity for increased revenues at the start of a project. Six months later, before the project is complete and when a competitor has launched a better product, the idea may not be good enough.

The answer to this problem is *change control*. Change control is a formalized project management process for managing the impact of changes in scope or requirements. (This should not be confused with change management as a discipline in its own right which typically relates to how people respond to change and managing this response – this will be explored in Chapter 9.)

A typical change-control process has the sequential steps of

1. Identifying and registering change
2. Assessing the impact
3. Seeking approval for change (usually from project sponsor and customers)
4. Accepting or rejecting change
5. Adapting the plan accordingly

It is during the second step of this process, *assessing the impact*, that a project manager determines how a change will affect the duration, resources or cost, or scope of a project.

Change control is looked at in more detail in Chapter 8.

Risk and ways to manage it

Risk is inherent in project management. As a plan is created there are many uncertainties, which means that estimates of durations and budgets may be wrong. As the project progresses events will occur that were unforeseen and which will impact the project in unexpected ways. In addition, the success or failure of the project may bring risks upon a business.

To help reduce the threat to project success from risks becoming reality, project management has the concept of *risk management*. Risk management is a formalized project management process which seeks to identify and assess risks before they occur and to take appropriate action. A typical risk management process has the steps of

1. Identifying and registering risk
2. Assessing the potential impact and likelihood of the risk
3. Determining action in response to the risk
4. Implementing action
5. Monitoring results of action

There is significant ongoing debate about risk management in the project management community. There are many processes and advanced tools to support the identification and management of risks. For all but the largest projects, the typical way risks are assessed in business relies on subjective assessment of impact and likelihood of risk. Although this is intuitively obvious and intellectually simple, it is questionable whether this truly is the best practice.

The concept of *contingency* was introduced in the section on plans. Contingency is one mechanism for dealing with risk. Contingency is essentially a buffer in the form of time and money to account for differences between what is planned and what may happen in reality. The amount of contingency should be related to the degree of risk in a project, which in turn is related to the level of familiarity of the project. A project for a telecom operator to provide circuits to a customer is a regularly repeated and well-known activity. It is therefore low-risk and needs limited contingency. At the other extreme a novel project in an unknown area using leading-edge technology is comparatively highly risky and therefore needs more contingency.

Although from a general management perspective contingency can look simply like bad planning, it is an essential component of a well-designed project plan.

Assessing contingency can be complex, but in practice project managers often use simple rules of thumb. The more unfamiliar the project the greater the percentage of contingency added.

A *contingency plan* is a plan to do some alternative or additional activities on a project contingent upon the occurrence of an identified risk. For instance, in a project to implement management information software there is a risk that the project may be delayed. The contingency plan is to develop and implement some spreadsheet-based reports in the interim. When the project manager reaches a point at which the risk of being delayed is sufficiently high this contingency plan is implemented.

Risk management is looked at in more detail in Chapter 11.

Other disciplines and tools

What has so far been described provides a very short overview of the central components of project management, and should not be considered as exhaustive. Individual components have been the subject of considerable amount of studies, and there are many sources dealing with them in detail. Activities such as planning and risk management are simple for small projects, but highly skilled and specialist disciplines in their own right for the largest of projects.

There are many peripheral processes and tools that project management methods provide. Also, most project managers tend to build up their own set of approaches learnt on the job. The components include everything from forms, document templates and procedures to specialized techniques which are applicable only to specific types of projects.

Project governance

Projects need to fit within the normal management processes and framework of controls within a business. Decisions must be made about the direction and contents of projects. Authorizations may be required to permit the use of resources on a project. The spending on projects must be aligned with the budgeting processes.

Management need to understand project progress, as well as gain an insight into project's successes and failures.

This is achieved through *project governance*. Governance is a broad concept within project management, and project managers use the term in various ways which refer typically to the interactions with senior managers and executives.

Project governance is touched on again later in this chapter and looked at in more detail in Chapter 8.

Larger and multiple projects – programmes and portfolios

Project management has been used in a huge number of situations to manage varied activities. Over the years as experience has developed, project management has been refined and enhanced. One of the areas of enhancement is managing larger and multiple projects which throw up additional challenges. This has led to the emergence of the associated disciplines of *programme* and *portfolio management*.

Large projects and combinations of projects are associated with a range of issues to resolve which traditional project management is not sufficient. For example,

- *Scale*: The largest of projects involve additional difficulties in terms of coordination and control of many different aspects, in a similar way that managing a business division of 5000 people differs from managing a team of 5 even though the basic principles of good management do not change.
- *Complexity*: There are many areas of increased complexity in larger projects: for example, the management of inter-dependencies between projects. These inter-dependencies may be related to task completion, risks or resources.
- *Resource management*: As organizations try to implement multiple projects in parallel they will hit resource constraints. This can be resolved by allowing staff to work on several projects at once, but this will tend to extend project timescales. Alternatively, organizations can prioritize between projects and limit the number underway at any one time, attempting to match project needs to the available resources. Project management does not provide tools for project selection and organization-wide resource management.
- *Risk*: Executives are often not deeply concerned with the outcome of individual projects within a large organization. The cost of an individual small project and the risk it exposes the organization to is limited. However, when many projects or an individual mega-project is considered, it consumes a significant percentage of organizational resources and may expose the business to material risk.
- *Governance and control*: Making decisions about and keeping track of an individual project is normally not complex. Doing this for a set of hundreds of projects, which is not an unusual amount for a large business, is difficult.

As the discipline of project management has evolved, these issues have become more apparent, so the concepts of *programmes* and *portfolios* have grown with the associated disciplines of *programme management* and *portfolio management*.

There are several different possible interpretations of the word *programme*. Various commentators use the terms in slightly different ways. A programme can be defined as

- *A sequential chain of related projects*: A programme is usually associated with multiple projects. Because of resource constraints, or simply to avoid trying to manage too complex an activity at any one time, projects may be broken into phases. Each phase is a complete project, but at the end of it a further project is started that builds on the previous one. For example, a new HR management system may be too complex to implement in the whole of a multi-national. So, the implementation is split into sequential phases, with each phase limited to one division or geographic area of the business.
- *A set of connected projects with a common goal*: A programme is sometimes defined by a business objective. For example, a business may embark on an endeavour to reduce its operational costs (opex) by 20%. This will require many different projects in various parts of the business. The combination of these projects is a programme. "Programme management is the way of coordinating projects that have a shared business aim" (Thiry, 2004).
- *An endeavour which leads to organization change*: Some commentators use the term programme specifically in the context of organizational-change activities. Hence a cultural-change endeavour is often called a cultural-change programme.
- *An activity that has both project and operational components*: To people outside of the world of project management the boundary between project and non-project activity can be seen as artificial. Business-change programmes often have a mixture of pure project-based activities as well as operational-management tasks. (Traditional project managers may struggle with this combination.)

There is no right or wrong answer to this debate, but it does highlight the need to ensure clarity. When talking to anyone about programmes, programme management or programme managers it is worth checking for coherence in terminology.

In addition, programmes are sometimes considered as a series of unrelated projects done in parallel using some common resources. This definition is increasingly fulfilled by the alternative word, *portfolio*. The word portfolio has been adopted from the finance-sector term *investment portfolio*. An investment portfolio has a balanced collection of financial assets whereas a project portfolio has a collection of projects.

In the context of this book the following definitions will be used:

- *Programme*: a related series of projects which contribute towards a common goal. This goal may be an organizational change. *Programme management* is an advanced extension of project management providing additional tools, techniques and approaches to delivering complicated programmes. A *programme manager* is responsible for managing a programme in a similar way that a project manager is responsible for a project. In practice there is a significant overlap between the skills of a project and a programme manager, but programme managers tend to be more senior and have broader experience.
- *Portfolio*: a diversified set of projects (and programmes) that are being delivered using a common set of resources to support the achievement of an organization's objectives. Portfolio management relates to project management, but it also has linkages to business strategy and governance.

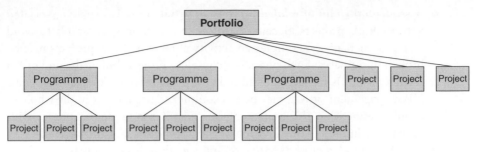

Diagram 1.3 Projects, programmes and portfolios

One way to consider portfolios, programmes and projects is in terms of a hierarchy. An organization has one or more portfolios made up of series of programmes and projects. The programmes in turn are made up of series of projects. Programmes are made up of projects, but not all projects are part of a programme. This is shown in Diagram 1.3.

Portfolios are explored more in Chapters 2 and 3.

Project Management Office

The Project Management Office (PMO) is a central function that exists in many organizations to support project managers and project management. It may alternatively be called the Project Office or the Programme Management Office.

The role varies from organization to organization. A PMO is usually created only when there are multiple projects in existence (though one may be set to support individual large programmes). This variability in role is shown by the PMI's definition of a PMO as

> *An organisational body or entity assigned various responsibilities related to centralized and coordinated management of those projects under its domain. The responsibilities of the PMO can range from providing support functions to actually being responsible for the direct management of a project. (PMI, 2004)*

Typical responsibilities include collecting and aggregating information from projects, such as weekly reports and resource requests. PMOs can be the aggregator of project information and can act as the gateway to projects for senior managers. PMOs often own project management standards within and organization and ensure compliance with them. More sophisticated PMOs analyse plans and other reports across projects to support cross-project issues, and risk and dependency management. PMOs can also take responsibility for knowledge management across the project management community in a company.

Alternative views

Throughout this chapter the lack of universal consensus on definitions of and approaches to project management has been stressed. Much of the difference of opinion is something for project management theorists to worry about. But even at this preliminary level it is helpful to gain a flavour of different perspectives, some of which will be explored later in the book.

This section provides an introduction to some of the more important alternative views of projects and project management.

Unique, transient, predefined goal?

Three fundamental characteristics of projects were identified early in this chapter. Projects are first *unique* and *non-repetitive* endeavours; second, last for *a limited amount of time*; and, third, *aim at some predefined goal*. In practice, there are endeavours considered as projects that challenge each one of these characteristics. The boundary between projects and operations is not as clear-cut as theory often suggests.

The degree of uniqueness of projects varies considerably. There are some projects that are truly unique, such as building a novel type of space rocket. Even at a high level it is not easy to define what is required to complete the project. The plan will bear limited relationship to any other plan.

Other projects have unique elements, but share similarities with previous endeavours. Consider new product development (NPD). Every new product has a degree of uniqueness, but enough products have been launched to have a detailed and standard series of steps that apply to most developments. In a sector like fast-moving consumer goods (FMCG), NPD is a repetitive activity. For many businesses most new products are closely related to previous products, and the plan to develop them will be very similar in structure to previous developments. NPD can be considered as a project, but it can also be viewed as a process.

Some types of projects follow almost exactly the same activities every time, but the context or situation will vary. For example, in performing a financial audit, the context and scale are different each time, but many of the activities and deliverables are exactly the same. Nevertheless, a project approach can help in ensuring focus on the end goal, a completed audit.

The next characteristic of projects is that they have a limited duration. Most business projects are transient, as short as a few weeks to as long as a year or two. Yet preparing for the Olympics is definitely a project, and it takes many years. A build-operate-transfer (BOT) contract, often used in the development of electricity power stations, can be considered as a project, and it may last for over a decade. Some government activities considered as projects continue even longer.

It is true that all these projects are finite in length, but so are all human activities. For limited duration to be a differentiating characteristic other activities must go on for even longer. The primary comparison for projects is with operations, often presented as continuous and relatively unchanging. In reality there are operational activities that continue for less time than many projects, especially in the business culture of constant change. With the mindset of continuous improvement, operations rarely exist unaltered for long periods of time.

Finally, traditional project management considers a defined goal not only as a characteristic of a project, but also as an essential prerequisite for success. Many projects conform to this ideal – moving office locations has a clear outcome known from the start of the project. However, there are situations where this is not true. For instance, in organizational change, beyond knowing that improvement is required, the specific goal is often not defined. It tends to become apparent as the project progresses. In some software projects rather than understanding the outcome at the start, prototypes are used to explore what the customer really wants. In both cases the goal emerges and evolves as the project progresses. Pollack (Pollack, 2007) applies the term *soft paradigm* to denote projects with such non-traditional characteristics.

The conclusion is not that traditional definitions of projects are worthless, but that they can only provide guidance. Projects exist on a spectrum relative to many criteria, and the characteristics are a useful starting point for understanding projects. Projects *typically* have unique elements, are relatively short in duration and aim at a predefined goal, but the full variety of projects cannot be understood by applying simplistic categorizations.

Iterative and incremental developments

There are many different perspectives on project lifecycles. One area where significant research and study has been done on lifecycles is in IT software development projects. The traditional approach to creating software is a *waterfall* approach. A *waterfall* is a type of lifecycle, similar to a standard project lifecycle. A typical waterfall has the sequential stages of requirements capture, analysis, design, coding and testing. In a waterfall a stage is completed in its entirety before moving onto the next stage. Thus, for example, no coding is done until design is complete.

IT projects managed as waterfalls have delivered many reliable and complex IT systems. However, they suffer from a number of problems. Four major problems are

- o *Time to deliver value*: For complex systems the time from start of the project to end may be several years. A business gains no return on its investment until the whole project is complete.
- o *Impact of change*: During the long life of a waterfall project, needs can change (it can be argued that it is inevitable). In a waterfall project if changes occur late in the lifecycle they can be disruptive. Changes can lead to re-planning and significant additional cost. Programmes have been extended by years due to changing requirements. Many waterfall project failures occur as a result of continually changing needs.
- o *Involvement of customers*: In a waterfall project the customer is involved in requirements capture phase, and then again in testing. In reality customers do not always fully understand what they want, and cannot envisage what a project will deliver. The deliverables the customer sees, for the first time at testing, may not meet expectations or needs.
- o *Ability to manage*: In a large-scale waterfall project the level of complexity can be high, and the real ability of some developers to understand and manage such complexity is questionable.

A series of alternative approaches have emerged, which are usually categorized as *iterative and incremental developments* or *IID* (Larman and Basili, 2003). There are many variants of these approaches (such as RAD or Rapid Applications Development, and more recently AGILE). These variants all differ, and in some cases extend beyond the goals of an IID lifecycle. But, the basic principles and objectives are similar across these approaches.

IIDs try to overcome the problems of waterfall methods by:

o *Delivering quick incremental improvements*: In IIDs the aim is to deliver incremental improvements in software rapidly. Rather than spending four years delivering a complete system, an iterative development develops small enhancements on a regular basis. So, a customer may see monthly or even weekly delivery of functional improvements and hence achieve business value more quickly. (Some projects time-box the maximum time between deliveries as short as one day).

o *Embracing change as inevitable*: By breaking the work into these small chunks it is far easier to integrate changing needs into software. Rather than using change control as a gate into a project, IID developers tend to embrace change as a fundamental reality and part of the process.

o *Involving customers on an ongoing basis*: In IID programmes customers are involved not simply at the start and end of the project, but remain a core part of the project team throughout its life. By using techniques such as *prototyping*, whereby customers are presented with simple examples of deliverables which are then improved on iteratively, customers are less likely to be surprised by the end point and can explore their real needs as the project progresses. (This type of emergent discovery of requirements is not the same as progressive elaboration, as detail is not only increased, but the goal can change as customers experience deliverables and learn.)

IIDs have their own problems, but they have proven to be effective in many areas. Although they have been applied primarily in software development, they provide lessons for other business projects – such as the way programmes can be phased into small chunks to give rapid business value.

There is no barrier in project management to the use of IID, but some project managers are uncomfortable with them. In many ways, business improvement approaches, such as Six-Sigma, have more in common with these iterative ways of working than with traditional projects.

AGILE development is explored in Case Study 6.2, in Chapter 6.

Critical Chain

Goldratt has applied his theory of constraints (Goldratt,1990) to projects and developed the critical-chain approach to project management (Goldratt, 1997).

Critical chain was formed by looking at some of the weaknesses of managing by critical path. Critical-path focus considers the sequence, timing and dependency between activities. Critical chain goes beyond this and considers the impact of resource constraints. Goldratt identifies issues with resource constraints impacting the completion of tasks as the key reason for project delay.

Critical chain identifies a series of problems with normal styles of project management (and use of critical path) and overcomes them. Key areas include

o *Task duration estimates*: Goldratt claims that when task length is assessed people typically estimate to give themselves an 80–90% probability of completion within the time of estimation. In critical chain, task lengths are estimated to give a 50% certainty of completion in time. Although this may mean individual tasks overrun, across a complete project the risk of overrun is smaller as any overruns will balance with other tasks completing ahead of schedule. Risk is further reduced by the use of a central buffer to call on when tasks do over-run. This alone is claimed to be able to reduce project length by 20%.

o *Student syndrome*: This is the tendency to start tasks as late as possible, meaning that the likelihood of over-running increases. It also means that when a task is completed early the benefit to the project is lost as the subsequent task does not start straightaway, but also tends to wait until as late as possible. In critical chain planning is done "back to front", working from the completion date, and each task then starting as late as possible. When started, tasks should be finished as soon as possible and the next task started as soon as its predecessors are complete.

o *Multitasking*: Critical chain sees multitasking as inefficient because of the overhead of set-up time every time someone swaps between tasks. Critical chain forbids resource multitasking and insists on dedication to a single task until completed, for all resources working on tasks on the critical chain.

o *Resource buffers*: Traditional project management techniques may add contingency buffers for time and budget. Critical chain adds resource buffers for resources on the critical chain to reduce the risk of delay and loss of resources to some other task.

One of the key aspects of critical chain is to plan the project around scarce resources, and use resource buffers to remove the risk of losing resources if tasks over-run.

Proponents of critical chain claim it is both faster and cheaper than other project management approaches such as CPM.

Beyond the iron triangle

Traditional project management handles projects in such a way as to find an optimal balance between time, cost and scope. This is something that many project managers and project management texts hold as sacrosanct. However, such an approach can be overly simplistic.

For a start, the iron triangle tends to swap the terms scope and quality as if they are synonymous. They are treated both as measures of project accomplishment. This may be true, but they are arguably quite different measurements of accomplishment. One way to consider the difference is to view scope as a measure of how much a project produces, whereas quality is a measure of how well a project produces its output.

In addition, there may be any number of other critical dimensions to a project. For example, in rapidly changing situations time is often important, but so can be flexibility in the design of deliverables. Producing a flexible deliverable that can be changed again may override needs to meet a specific timeframe or cost. In some mission-critical situations risk is a more important factor than either cost or time. The fact that a plane must be able to fly safely will override the need to develop a new plane within a limit of time or cost.

It can be argued that in these examples flexibility and risk are simply dimensions of quality. However, the problem with combining criteria like these as part of quality is that they can become lost in the detail, and they are treated as part of a single dimension to be balanced against time and cost, whereas in reality the balance has many more dimensions.

The iron triangle makes no reference to customer satisfaction. Yet, however well a project is run, and no matter what quality deliverables are produced, unless customers are satisfied the project is not likely to be considered as a success. In most other business endeavours customer and broader stakeholder satisfaction is placed at the core of decision-making and measurement of success.

Another perspective on the iron triangle is to change the way project managers view conformance to the triangle. Traditional project management tends to focus on the balance between the components of the iron triangle. Consider a project that has to be completed within £1m of budget and 6 months of time. Normally, as long as cost is below £1m and duration is less than 6 months, the project is a success. Increasingly projects are not being set objectives in terms of conforming to some criteria, but in terms of achieving as much as possible. So, the real objective is *as quickly as possible*, or *as cheaply as possible*. Hence a cost of £1m and a time of 6 months are absolute limits and not the definition of success.

The reality of projects

So far this chapter has presented information on formal definitions, agreed approaches and the supporting discussion and debate about project management. Reality often differs from the theory, and formal processes are not always followed.

To begin with, terminology is regularly used imprecisely. Job titles tend to be relevant only in the context of the organization they are given out. Often the term *project manager* is applied to anyone who manages projects, irrespective of what approach they use. One business's programme manager is another's project manager. Many project managers view programmes simply as large projects. This interpretation is not favoured by the project management theorists, but it is a common way the term is used in practice. Hence there are some programme managers who are responsible for endeavours that just happen to be relatively large compared to those of the project managers they work with.

In reality, for all the methods, rules, processes, tools and advice, many project managers are pragmatic about how they manage and successfully deliver business projects. Businesses also are pragmatic in how they use project management and appoint project managers. Although there is a trend towards greater accreditation of project managers, there are still many project managers with little or no formal training in the subject, and who have no awareness of the existence of, let alone the contents of, the various BoKs and formal methodologies. (There is little research which shows the benefits of formal methods and training.)

Arguably, project management is more than a set of predefined knowledge. There are many successful project managers who have never been formally trained in project management. Partially they have learnt the tools and techniques of project management from other skilled project managers. But it is also true that project management can be considered as a mindset or approach to work. Important parts of this mindset are a drive to seek clarity and unambiguous definition to any piece of work, and a completer–finisher mentality. Although the formal project management processes will help, it is often the drive to progress and overcome any barriers and problems that make projects more or less successful.

Traditional views of project management present it in a mechanistic way, as if by following a predefined process the desired result will occur. In practice, and increasingly in research, there are alternative views of the role of the project manager. Pollack (Pollack, 2007) points out the increasing switch to the "soft paradigm" where project management is as much about facilitating as it is about managing. Simon (Simon, 2006) uses the terms *sense maker*, *game-master*, *web weaver* and *flow-balancer* to describe the varying roles of project managers in different contexts. There is increasing consensus in academic circles that the traditional views of project management tell only a part of the story.

It has to be recognized that at times projects are messy and unpredictable. The rational reductionist view that all projects can be understood by analysing the problem they set out to solve and breaking it into perfectly determinable component parts has its limits (Jaafari, 2005). In some situations projects are as much about developing understanding as they are about creating deliverables. Core project management tasks such as definition, planning, design and execution can be less sequential stages and instead become parallel activities with ongoing feedback between them. In these situations project management ceases to be about managing a known lifecycle, and instead becomes a creative and flexible style of leadership. Specific triggers for flexibility in project management have been identified (e.g. Gallo and Gardiner, 2007).

The traditional predetermined linear approach still has value in many situations and as an ideal, but it needs enhancement, and in some contexts replacement with more intuitive solutions. This often requires project management to be more context-specific and less generic. One approach proposed to this is *complex project management* (Dombkins, 2007). Complex project management is dependent on the competencies of *complex project managers*. At the time of writing there is no consensus on complex project management. It is strongly supported by its advocates and enhanced by competency standards for complex project managers. On the other hand it has numerous critics who accuse it of being a fad without a researched evidence base (e.g. Whitty and Maylor, 2007).

The relationship between project management and other management disciplines

Project management does not operate in its own universe, and is inter-related with other management disciplines. The final section of this chapter introduces some of the most significant interactions.

Strategy

Projects and project management have a relationship with strategy, but defining this relationship can be complex. If project management is a term open to differences of opinion and interpretation, then *strategy* is even more so. Most people have an intuitive view of what strategy is, but there are many varied interpretations. For now it is enough to view strategy as the management discipline that sets the direction for an organization and decides at a high level what activities will be undertaken.

The relationship between projects and strategy is essentially in three areas:

- Project management can support the development of strategy by providing an understanding of what an organization is capable of doing.
- Project management can support strategy by developing high-level plans of implementation timeframes and costs.
- Project management provides a way to execute some strategies.

A strategy may start as unconstrained innovative thinking, but the strategy must be achievable within the constraints an organization operates under. Organizations have limited supplies of money, people and time. An understanding of what resources are available and what existing activities are already under way can be provided through portfolio management.

Project management approaches can help in developing high-level plan for strategy implementation. Although such plans usually have high margins of error in them, they can provide indicative views of how long it will take to implement a strategy.

Once a strategy has been agreed upon, it needs to be implemented. Strategies often require projects to execute them, and in some cases need projects to experiment and determine options for resolving problems. However, the execution of strategy is much more than the delivery of projects, and the project agenda is normally broader than the strategic agenda.

The relationship between strategy and project management is looked at in more detail in Chapter 2.

Operations

Projects are usually contrasted with operations, but this does not mean there is no relationship between the two. The operational departments of an organization are the primary customers for projects aimed at operational improvement, and also a source of resources to work on projects.

Projects will therefore interface with operations at several points, including

- Operational departments defining their requirements upon projects
- Projects requesting for and being allocated resources from operational teams
- Projects providing improvements to operations, whether this is enhanced infrastructure, IT systems, or business processes, or other forms of organizational change.

Although projects are often meant to benefit operations, from an operational-management perspective projects are not always welcome because they

- *Utilize valuable resources*: In an era of cost constraints, operational departments are usually under pressure to minimise headcount. Every project that needs team members to work on project activities increases the difficulty for operational management to complete their normal operational workload.

- o *Cause disruption*: By implementing change, projects often disrupt the working of operations. Even where projects are implementing improvements to operations a period of disruption and difficulty for operations to achieve their performance targets is inevitable.

Financial management and control

The financial management and control functions of a business are interested in projects for a number of reasons, including

- o Projects consume resources, and this has to be assessed, approved and managed like any other budget. This starts with developing an assessment of the costs and benefits of projects, the creation of business cases and continues through approval processes.
- o During project execution resource consumption must be monitored. This can be done in line with normal budget-tracking mechanisms (although tracking project costs and resource consumption is somewhat different from tracking an operational budget).
- o Projects provide benefits back to the business. These benefits have to be tracked and measured.
- o Project intentions have to be built into budgets and the annual planning process, with the complication that projects sometimes take longer than a year and therefore have cross-budget cycles.

In addition, like operations, the finance department may be the customer of projects and may need to provide expert resources to support projects.

Human Resources

Projects throw up some unusual HR challenges which need to be carefully managed. Examples include

- o Projects take people from their normal job role to work on project tasks. This can cause disruption to normal operational work and can give HR functions the headache of having to find temporary staff to backfill permanent staff on projects.
- o Projects require team members to work under the direction of a project manager rather than their normal line manager. This can lead to problems with motivation and control of staff. In addition, performance appraisal and rewards processes, which tend to remain in the control of line managers, can be problematic. This problem can be exacerbated by the fact that project managers are often contract or interim staff.
- o Projects have variable demands for resources. Unlike normal functions which create annual headcount budgets, projects typically do not.
- o The recruitment, management and allocation of project managers can be difficult if there is no project management function, as they often do not fit within normal functional-departmental staff profiles.

Change management

The phrase *change management* has a wide variety of interpretations. Some project management practitioners consider project management and change management as synonymous. In contrast some change management experts have written large volumes on change management without referring to projects or project management once.

Depending on the definition of *change management* its relationship with project management varies. This is context-specific and will be explored in a number of parts of this book, including Chapters 9, 12 and 13. What can be said generally is that

- Project and change management are overlapping disciplines. Both support the implementation of change in organizations.
- From a change management perspective projects can be considered as one mechanism for implementing change.
- From a project management perspective change management can be considered as a skill set that is required on some projects.

Case Study 1.2   A SHORT HISTORY OF ONE PROGRAMME

A business providing services to residential customers wanted to enhance its main product. The enhancement required a complex technical development, the building of some new infrastructure and operational changes in sales, customer services and technical support. The product was to be launched with a major marketing campaign. The programme to deliver and launch this new product was expected to take 12–18 months and cost about £100 million.

A programme manager was appointed. He brought four people together to develop the programme brief and identify the main parts of the programme. This group ran workshops and brainstorming sessions with subject matter experts from across the business to develop a better understanding of requirements and the work necessary to fulfil these requirements. This took several weeks.

Based on the information gathered the programme manager was able to produce an outline plan. The plan was sufficient to show that the proposition was viable. But there were too many assumptions and missing details to permit the accurate costing and scheduling of the programme.

A more detailed feasibility phase was started. This had a team of 20 people, aiming to produce a budgeted plan and a business case. This team worked for another three months exploring detailed needs and options to meet these needs. At the end of this stage the programme manager was able to produce a fuller plan and a business case.

The programme was ready to move into development. So far, expenditure was limited, but development would necessitate considerable spending. Given the scale of the programme, and the risks associated with it, board permission was required to continue. The board was not due to meet for another six weeks.

The six weeks passed. The time was not fully productive, but significant effort was spent collecting information and developing a board presentation.

The board met and authority was given to start the programme, but only a portion of the required budget was approved. The board members had outstanding questions, which the programme manager had to answer by the next meeting to gain full approval. However, as long as the authorized budget was not exceeded, work could commence.

It was now November, about six months since the programme manager had started work. Yet, only now was the programme commencing in the eyes of many people in the business. As the programme was continued the programme team was enlarged, and now had about 100 people on it.

The CEO continually reiterated that the programme had to be complete by October of the following year. At this stage the programme manager realized that to meet the CEO's deadline additional help was required from a specialist technology developer. The in-house team were struggling with some parts of the work, and letting them continue to do the work was too risky. A supplier was identified, and they were engaged. The contract was complex, but a fixed price for the work was agreed. The fixed price removed budgetary risk, but it created some tension. Although the supplier always acted professionally, they continually pushed to cut corners to ensure they delivered profitably.

In January the board gave complete approval for the programme. Gaining this approval had taken a significant proportion of the programme manager's time.

Unfortunately, in February, a competitor improved and lowered the prices of its product. To remain competitive with this competitor's offering meant reducing the expected sale price of the new product. As a response, the costs of the programme had to be contained, and where possible reduced.

The programme now had both a fixed timescale constraint and considerable cost pressures. As a consequence the scope of the project was constantly reviewed to see if everything was necessary. Several non-essential product features were removed.

In March, focus groups were held with small groups of customers to get their views on the proposed product. Customers were generally enthusiastic, but had some critical feedback on some areas of the product. This required changes to specifications, and parts of the product had to be redeveloped.

These changes added a month to the development, but the end date remained fixed as October. Consequently, subsequent tasks had to be done more quickly. This was achieved by doing more work in parallel, which required additional resources on contract basis. Also a number of shortcuts and compromises were taken. The time allocated for testing was shortened.

The product was launched successfully on the last day of October. The budget was marginally exceeded. The product sold very well, though there was an increase in customer complaints due to an ongoing stream of regular faults.

Following the launch, a second programme was started to provide some of the missing product features and fix some of the initial problems.

Case Study **1.3**   **WHAT IS PROJECT MANAGEMENT?**

Kevin Muraski is an experienced programme director. He has worked for several organizations involved in high technology, telecommunications and media. He is currently a programme director at BT. In this case study he answers the question – what is project management?

Kevin Muraski

I don't think this is a question you can answer absolutely. Project management is not one thing.

Let me try and answer it to some extent. I always try to look from a client's perspective, as a project manger's job is to help his or her clients achieve their goals. Project management needs to be tailored to different clients. Of course there are many common elements to every project, and it builds from a common basis, but there are unique elements depending on the situation.

Good project management is about adding value to the business; to do this it has to add value to the client, and to achieve this it must be tailored to that client's needs. In the same way that you can't universally answer the question "what is a business problem" or "what are manager's needs", you can't universally say "what is project management".

For me, project management is as much about a personal relationship with your client as it is about a specific discipline. Of course, all clients want things delivered, but the way they want them delivered changes. Let me list some examples: the client's desired level of visibility and involvement in the project differs; the level of interaction and control they want varies; the amount of detail they are capable of giving in terms of scope and requirements varies; and the client's skills and ability to directly add value to a project differ. They usually know what they want to achieve – but not how. They may or may not be of some help in delivering the project. They may want only support – or they may want the project manager to take over completely.

The project manager's role has to vary depending on the client's skill, expectations, needs and interest in getting involved in the project. In some situations the project manager's role has to expand to take account of a client's lack of skills. For example, some clients can very clearly specify what they want and can really successfully sponsor a project – some others cannot and the project manager has to help them. But there has to be a limit to this. A project manager is not there to compensate for the lack of a client's own abilities to do the job they are meant to do. For example, I often have to work with ill-defined or "fluffy" objectives, where it is not clear what is wanted. A project manager can facilitate a dialogue and can help the client in exploring what they want – and it's often worth putting in considerable effort into this. But, if at the end of the day the client does not know what they want and it cannot be extracted from them, it's not the project manager's role to define it without the client's knowledge.

In helping a client there are occasionally situations where what a client wants is not really in the interest of his business. This takes great skill to manage.

One thing to understand is that it is possible to shape what your client needs and expects from a project manager. Expectations are based on experience. If you give your clients a good experience and keep them informed at the right level, use them when you need them but otherwise leave them alone, they will start to trust you and both give you the support you need and also leave you to get on with your job.

MAIN LEARNING POINTS FROM CHAPTER 1

- Projects exist for limited periods of time, are unique and achieve a predefined goal. The predefined goal is described in terms of objectives, scope and requirements (why and what).
- Projects are typically completed within agreed constraints, usually defined in terms of time, cost and quality (how). These are arrived at through the process of project planning.
- Projects have a degree of complexity and are subject to progressive elaboration.
- Project management is a set of tools and techniques applied by a project manager for managing projects. Project management defines projects in terms of generic lifecycles. It includes approaches for scoping, planning, resourcing and controlling projects. It has a range of tools such as change control and risk management.
- Projects are one element in a hierarchy of temporary endeavours that also includes programmes and portfolios.
- There are many different views on the best way to approach projects – including approaches such as critical chain and AGILE.
- Project management links into other management disciplines including strategy, operations, financial management, HR and change management.

REVIEW QUESTIONS AND EXERCISES

1. Review a selection of project literature and produce a comprehensive list of the most important pieces of terminology. Which terms are universally accepted and which are more contentious? What is your view?
2. Case Study 1.1 shows an outline lifecycle for a project. Expand these steps by defining what you expect to happen at each stage. What supporting materials (processes, tools, document templates etc) would help in completing each stage? Can you improve on this lifecycle? How?
3. Is it possible to define a management discipline in a single body of knowledge? What are the strengths and weaknesses of doing this? Do you think a body of knowledge can truly reflect best practice?
4. Select an activity that you would like to do in your private life. Define the scope, objectives, constraints and the main requirements. What are your success criteria? Who are the main stakeholders in this activity and what are their success criteria? Define three alternative work breakdown structures for this activity. Which is the best? Why?
5. How do you see the reality of projects, as following a predetermined lifecycle or as being more flexible in approach? What are the benefits and risks of each approach? Identify several situations and explain how predictable the project management approach will be in each.
6. Considering the programme in Case Study 1.2, do you think this programme was successful? Why? What would you have done differently? How does this relate to your own experiences of large programmes?
7. Considering the Case Study 1.3, how do Kevin's views on project management contrast with the rest of the chapter? What do you think is most important?

Suggested Reading

This chapter provides enough foundation-level knowledge to read any of the further chapters in this book, so there is no requirement for further reading. However, for the individual who does, there are many good texts on project management. They vary from the minimal to the thorough and from the traditional to the radical.

The first option here is a very simple but practical text to give an opportunity for rapidly gaining a feeling for running a project. The second is a much fuller explanation of project management processes and tools. The final suggestion is a more student- or academically-orientated book:

Simple introductory text:

- *Project management step-by-step.* Richard Newton. Prentice-Hall, 2006

Fuller overview of project management:

- *Project Management: The Managerial Process.* Clifford F Gray and Erik W Larson. McGraw-Hill International, 2006

Student-orientated view of the subject:

- *Project Management – A Strategic Planning Approach,* Paul D Gardiner, Palgrave MacMillan, 2006

Bibliography

APM (Association for Project Management). *APM Body of Knowledge*, 5th Edition; 2006.

APM (Association for Project Management). *Directing Change: A Guide to Governance of Project Management,* 2004.

BSI (British Standards Institution). *Project Management – Part 1: Guide to Project Management.* BS 6079–1 (2000).

Dombkins, D. *Complex Project Management: Seminal Essays by Dr David H Dombkins.* BookSurge Publishing, October 2007.

Jaafari, A. "Project Management in the 21st Century". *Project Perspectives, Periodical of Project Management Association Finland.* Volume XXVII, 1/2005, pp. 34–41.

Gallo, M. and Gardiner, P. "Triggers for a flexible approach to project management within UK financial services". *International Journal of Project Management.* Volume 25, Issue 5, July 2007, pp. 446–57.

Gardiner, P. *Project Management. A Strategic Planning Approach.* Palgrave Macmillan, 2005.

Goldratt, E. *Critical Chain.* The North River Press, 1997.

Goldratt, E. *What Is This Thing Called Theory of Constraints and How Should It Be Implemented?* The North River Press, 1990.

Gray, C. F. and Larson, E. W. *Project Management: The Managerial Process.* McGraw-Hill International Edition, 2006.

Larman, C. and Basili V. "Iterative and Incremental Development: A Brief History". *IEEE Computer,* Volume 36, Issue 6, June 2003, pp. 47–56.

Maylor, H., Brady, T., Cooke Davis, T. and Hodgson, D. "From projectification to programification". *International Journal of Project Management.* Volume 24, Issue 8, November 2006, pp. 663–74.

Maylor, H. *"Project Management".* Third edition. FT Prentice Hall, 2005.

Morris, P., Crawford, L., Hodgsone, D., Shepherd, M. and Thomas, J. "Exploring the role of formal bodies of knowledge in defining a profession – The case of project management". *International Journal of Project Management.* Volume 24, Issue 8, November 2006, pp. 710–21.

PMI (Project Management Institute, Inc). *The Guide to the Project Management Body of Knowledge,* version 3; 2004.

Pollack, J. "The changing paradigms of project management". *International Journal of Project Management.* Volume 25, Issue 3, April 2007, pp. 266–74.

Raffoni, M. "Got a need for speed? What you can learn from rapid application development". *Harvard Management Update,* November 01, 2000.

Royce, W. "Managing the development of large software systems". *Proceedings IEEE Westcon,* August 1970, pp. 1–9.

Simon, L. "Managing creative projects: An empirical synthesis of activities". *International Journal of Project Management.* Volume 24, Issue 2, February 2006, pp. 116–26.

Whitty, S. and Maylor, H. "And then came complex project management". *21st IPMA World Congress on Project Management,* June 2007.

The Office of Government Commerce. *Managing Successful Projects with PRINCE 2.* 5th Edition. The Stationery Office Books, 2005.

Thiry, M. "Program management: A strategic decision making process". *The Wiley Guide to Managing Projects.* Wiley, 2004.

2
strategy
project management
and the project portfolio

There are few management discussion topics which do not sooner or later involve the word *strategy*. There are many different views on the meaning of, processes for and value of business strategy, but whatever perspective is taken, strategy has remained central to management theory and practice for many years. Most parts of management link to strategy, and project management is no different.

This chapter discusses strategy, project management and the selection of a portfolio of projects and programmes. It provides the reader with an understanding of the central relevance of project management to an organization.

The chapter answers two questions:

o What is the relationship between strategy and project management?
o What else, apart from strategy, influences the selection of an organization's portfolio of projects and programmes?

Introduction

The primary challenges for executives, and the goals of strategy, are deciding what a business should do and determining how it should be achieved (Manning, 2001). To the strategist, the answer lies in strategy formulation and execution. To the project manager, the solution exists in the selection of a project portfolio and its implementation through projects. At first glance the strategist's and the project manager's answers seem unrelated, but they are linked. Strategy informs, and to some extent defines, the project portfolio. However, this chapter will show that the relationship between strategy and project management is more involved than this.

There is a conundrum in understanding the relationship between projects and strategy. The relationship is often stressed in project management theories, without really being explained. Simple statements about projects being aligned to, or derived from, strategy are about as far as they often go. But the relationship is seen as important. This contrasts with strategy theories which often completely ignore projects and programmes. This can even be true for descriptions of strategy implementation or execution.

Strategy can be a contentious topic, and it is beyond the scope of this book to explain the role of strategy and describe the ways to create strategy. There is much debate as to what a strategy is, what it exists to achieve and how it can be developed (e.g. Whittington, 2000). However, there is a broad consensus amongst management theorists and practitioners that having a strategy is good for business. The companies that thrive most are those with the best and most successfully executed strategies.

Project management theories often use strategy as their starting point. Like the relationship of a building process to an architectural plan as the starting point for erecting a house, the relationship between strategy and project management is shown as logical, linear and in one direction only. However, this chapter shows that the relationship between strategy and project management is more complicated and bidirectional than most theory indicates. In addition, it explains how it is oversimplistic to assume that all projects originate in the development of strategy. Choosing what to do, and getting it done, is influenced by more than strategy.

(Simplistic definitions of strategy are not always helpful to project managers. Often, when there are problems on projects, wistful statements such as "if only we had a strategy" can be heard, though the individual making the statement may not be clear as to what a strategy is and whether one does actually exist or not. In making this sort of statement, what people often mean is "if only I had an answer to an issue that is causing me a problem right now", which even the best strategy may not provide).

There are two complementary trends that help in defining the relationship between strategy and project management:

o *From the perspective of strategy* the growing interest in strategy execution as opposed to strategy formulation, and the realisation that the best defined strategy in the world is worth nothing if it is not successfully implemented (e.g. Hrebiniak, 2005). If a strategy fails it is normally during implementation rather than during strategy creation. Whilst approaches to strategy execution often do not explicitly mention project management, and instead talk in general terms about change, they still can be helpful in understanding the relationship between projects and strategy.

o *From the perspective of project management* the understanding that the historical focus of project management on managing projects in the optimal way (doing projects right) is not enough. There also needs to be an approach to ensure that the optimal set of projects is being undertaken (doing the right projects) (e.g. APM, 2004). Strategic alignment is of increasing prominence and importance in project management–related journals (Crawford et al., 2006).

This chapter explores the overlap of strategy execution and project portfolio selection, and will present strategy and project portfolio management as different stages of one process rather than separate or unrelated activities in a business.

Chapters 2 and 3 can be used independently, but are closely related. This chapter is largely theoretical, whilst the next is more practical. Chapter 3 looks at the mechanisms for project selection and prioritization, and describes project portfolio management.

From strategy to project management

Why is the relationship between strategy and project management important? Many businesses operate as if strategy and project management are unconnected realms of management. Typically, they involve independent groups of people at different levels in the organizational hierarchy, who use unrelated concepts and capabilities and produce completely dissimilar types of output. Project activities and strategy are often uncoordinated. A strategy manager and a project manager may never meet, and if they do may use mutually incomprehensible jargon.

Going further than this, all of the following points emphasize the separation between the disciplines:

o Many strategy books, even those that are explicitly concerned with strategy execution, do not mention projects or project management.
o Parts of strategy can be implemented successfully without reference to project management.
o Projects can be delivered without being aligned to strategy.
o Strategy is not the source of all projects in an organization.

It can seem that there is a limited relationship between strategy and project management. Is there, or should there be, a closer relationship? The answer is yes. Strategy and project management, and strategy and portfolio management are closely related activities.

The relationship between strategy and project management is complicated and multi-dimensional. A perfectly valid strategy can be implemented without project management, and projects can be delivered without recourse or reference to strategy. Yet generally, good project management has a strong relationship with strategy in a number of separate ways, and the execution of most strategies will result in projects. The fact that there is often a gulf between those parts of an organization that define strategy and those that manage projects is a weakness rather than the ideal order of things. Project management is one of the most important mechanisms for delivering strategy (Longman and Mullins, 2004).

One difficulty is that strategy is not one thing developed in one way. Making generic statements about something that is inherently different from organization to organization can be problematical. At one extreme, a strategy is the end point of a deliberate activity resulting in a documented set of intentions that is widely communicated. For some organizations strategy emerges over time and whilst commonly understood, it is rarely formally discussed. At the other extreme, there are organizations in which there is only the vaguest strategy in any practical sense. Even for those organizations that have a formalized and documented strategy, its format varies considerably. For large corporations the strategy may have many layers, whilst for a small local business it may be explained in a few sentences.

To explore the relationship between strategy and project management it is helpful to have a common *strategic* vocabulary and a shared model of how it is executed. There are many different models using varied terminology. Let us look at a simple model of strategy based on an amalgam of standard theories. This model also explains how strategy generally influences the activities performed in the organization:

- An organization has a *corporate strategy*, which sets the direction for a company. Typical components of a corporate strategy include decisions about what lines of business an organization should be in, and how resources should be allocated between different lines of business.

- This corporate strategy is interpreted and converted into a series of sub-strategies. These sub-strategies are relevant to parts of the business only. For larger organizations, which are split into a set of independent business units, there will be business unit–level strategies. Business unit strategies aim to achieve competitive advantage in an industry or sector. The sub-strategies also include functional strategies such as IT, HR and marketing strategies. These are grouped together in this chapter under the title *functional and business unit strategies*.

- Each strategy is defined as a hierarchy of information. This book uses the terminology presented in the hierarchy as in Diagram 2.1. A strategy starts by defining a *mission* statement. This statement contains, in one or a few sentences, a summary of why an organization (or business unit) exists. There are many possible ways to achieve this mission, and an organization assesses these options and makes strategic choices resulting in one or more chosen *strategies*. A strategy tends to be directional rather than specific. Strategies are refined into specific *objectives*. Achievement of objectives is defined in terms of reaching a level against one or more defined *metrics*.

- The nature of such a hierarchy is that in moving down the layers the information tends to become more detailed, and often has a shorter life. An organization's one-or-two-sentence mission statement will only

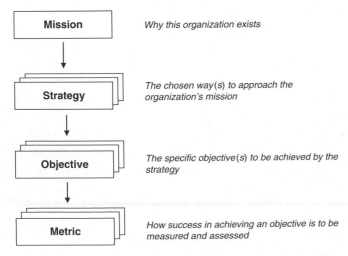

Diagram 2.1 A typical strategy hierarchy

occasionally, if ever, be modified; whereas pages of objectives and metrics will be adjusted on an annual basis.

- o Strategy has no value unless it is executed. The effective execution of strategy is achieved in two ways. First, a strategy may explicitly state that a certain action should be undertaken. For example, a strategy may define a specific investment should be made, or a particular programme undertaken. However, much of strategy implementation is not about explicit commands, and is concerned with influencing the day-to-day activities of an organization such that they are aligned to the strategy. Being aligned to the strategy means that an activity is consistent with the strategy and incrementally helps the organization reach strategic objectives and improve on the metrics. Take the situation of a strategy to compete by being a low-cost competitor. Daily decisions and activities should generally try to contain or reduce costs in the business. Any decision or project that increases costs in the business is not aligned to the strategy.

- o The day-to-day activities of the organization, including projects, tend to be aligned with the strategy. This alignment of organizational activity with strategy is not an accident, but the desired outcome. Whatever strategy is defined to be, success relates to an organization's ability to implement and manage compliance to its intended strategy (Dietrich and Lehtonen, 2005). Alignment is achieved by a combination of leadership direction and decision-making, and management influence and fiat, by controls exercised through performance measures consistent with the strategy, and by incentives that are based on achieving strategic goals.

- o Although day-to-day activities tend to be aligned with strategy there are activities which are accepted as "must do" irrespective of strategy. For example, operational problems arise which were not foreseen in strategy formulation. Even though the strategy does not explicitly state that it must be done, operational problems have to be resolved. Sometimes the resolution requires new projects. In addition, external pressures, such as changing legislation and regulation, or evolving areas of public interest create the need for activity and action in the business which may not be directly aligned to the strategy.

    One of the main challenges of management is retaining a good balance between the resources allocated to short-term problems versus ongoing achievement of the *strategy*.

- o In addition, there are some activities which should be aligned to strategy but are not. There are many reasons for this, including:
  - Lack of understanding of the strategy
  - Time lag between strategy formulation and its successful communication to the organization
  - Ambiguity or conflicts between different parts of strategy
  - In some cases, a deliberate choice of action contrary to the strategy by individual or groups of empowered managers

A key role of the leadership in the organization is to minimize or eliminate these non-aligned activities.

This model of strategy is debatable, but it can be enhanced and detailed. There will be organizations that do not conform to these assumptions. But it is a sufficient and reasonable basis to build an understanding of the relationship between strategy and project management.

Selecting the right projects

Strategy and project management are intuitively related, but often can appear independent. The strategy manager usually knows little or nothing about the practice of project management, and similarly the project manager is often not aware of the various tools and approaches to strategy formulation. The strategy manager is concerned with developing and implementing the right strategy, and the project manager typically is concerned with delivering projects in the right way.

The primary link between strategy and project management comes from the use of projects as a mechanism for the implementation of strategy. A strategy manager should seek to ensure that the projects necessary to achieve the strategic goals are initiated. Conversely, project managers should try to ensure the projects they are responsible for are aligned to strategy.

Implementing strategy is about ensuring resources in a business are allocated to achieving the strategy, rather than any other non-strategic goal. The strategy manager who ignores what projects are selected loses control of a significant part of the resource available to achieve the strategic objectives. Equally, the project manager who solely concerns himself with delivering projects in the right way can easily end up managing irrelevant activities.

The challenge for project managers is to understand how the project they are delivering relates to the organization's strategy. The question, "are we delivering the right projects" is both a strategic and a project management issue. Answering it provides the linkage between the domains of strategy and projects management. This is shown in Diagram 2.2.

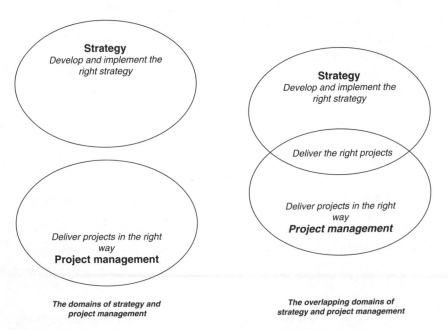

The domains of strategy and project management

The overlapping domains of strategy and project management

Diagram 2.2 The domains of strategy and project management

The *right projects* are those that contribute to the organization's mission, by generally helping to realize the chosen strategies, and specifically achieve the selected objectives and metrics.

An alternative way to interpret Diagram 2.2 is to consider the dual objectives of project managers. First, they need to deliver projects in the right way. Second, they must ensure that the project is successful. If there is a business strategy, a project cannot be considered as successful unless it is aligned to that strategy (Morris, 2005).

Strategic alignment of the portfolio

What does *deliver the right projects* mean? At the most simple level it means having the right set of projects in the organization's project portfolio. The relationship between strategy and project management is achieved by strategy populating this portfolio. Portfolio management is the realization of a business's strategy (Cooper et al., 2001).

The project portfolio is essentially a prioritized list of ideas for projects an organization wants to undertake. The corporate strategy identifies the changes an organization needs to make, and these changes are implemented as projects. (What a project portfolio consists of in practice and how it is formed is discussed in detail in Chapter 3.)

The output from strategy formulation creates the portfolio, as shown in Diagram 2.3.

In reality, the relationship is more involved than this. Strategy provides a range of outputs which either directly or indirectly informs the project portfolio (See Diagram 2.4). This includes

- o *Ideas*: the explicit statement of the right projects to undertake. These are typically derived from strategies or strategic objectives. A corporate strategy may, for example, define the need to expand to a new geographic region resulting in projects to set up operations in those regions. Alternatively, a strategy to reduce costs in a business may lead to a strategic objective of implementing greater automation in an area of the business.
- o *Direction and metric*: broader directional guidance derived from mission statements and strategy, which may also be converted into more specific

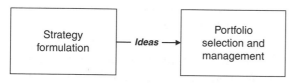

Diagram 2.3 Strategy populates the project portfolio

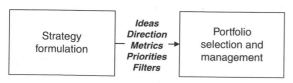

Diagram 2.4 The multiple impact of strategy on portfolio selection

metrics and performance indicators. This can be as simple as *differentiation through improved customer services.* If a business decides that it will compete on the basis of premier levels of customer service, this strategic intent informs decisions across the business. This in turn will lead to more customer service–related projects. Such strategy does not directly define the projects, but encourages the focus on improving customer service, and in time this gives birth to related projects.

o *Filters*: clarity over what a business will *not* be involved in. For example, a corporate strategy may determine that a particular line of business is to be disbanded, or is to be treated as a *cash cow*. Profits will be taken, but investment will be limited. Such guidance provides a clear filter for portfolio selection, and any project proposals relating to this line of business are rejected. Moreover, although classical theory shows a flow from strategy to projects, in reality project ideas will be conceived all the time in a business irrespective of the strategy. The ideas can then be compared to the strategy – and either accepted or filtered out as non-compliant.

o *Priorities*: guidance as to the relative importance of different activities in a business. The more strategically important a project is, the higher priority it should be given (Chapter 3 shows it is more complex than this, but this is the fundamental principle). Most businesses have to keep a tight management control on the costs of operation, the volume of sales and the price of goods and services sold. However, the specific balance between costs, sales volumes and prices will vary dependent on strategy. A strategy may determine that the most important goal for a business is to grow its customer base. In such a growth phase, a business will be more focussed on volumes than costs and margins. Projects focussed on cost reduction will be prioritized lower than ones focussed on growing the customer base such as launching new products or enhancing sales capabilities.

Strategy and the lifecycle of projects

Strategy has an impact beyond the selection of projects and can influence the entire lifecycle of a project's delivery. Strategy should inform not only the macro decisions about what projects to undertake, but also the myriad small project decisions made on a day-to-day basis. The success of a strategy is not just in the few big decisions occasionally made, but in influencing all the small decisions made in a business every day. Let us have a closer look at this issue.

Consider the situation of a strategy to improve customer service. This may be partially implemented in major initiatives to give better customer service, such as improved customer service facilities and more customer service staff. However, to be successful the strategy must also be reflected in day-to-day actions of staff in the business. Operationally, it would be no good having 50% more customer service staff, in new buildings, with the best customer management systems, unless the staff behaved in a customer-orientated way, and their management continually motivated them to achieve this.

The same principles apply to projects. The project manager achieves strategic alignment not only by ensuring she is managing the right project, but also by managing the project in a way that is consistent with the strategy.

Consider the following examples of how strategic awareness can impact a project. From a project perspective, strategy has an effect on

- o *Project strategy*: It is the general approach project managers adopt to achieve a project's desired outcome (Portny et al., 2008). Project strategy is not a term all project managers use or recognize, but the activity of defining an overall approach to a project prior to detailed planning as commonly understood. Deciding on a general approach to planning a project must consider more than strategy, but strategy will often have an influence on project strategy. Factors such as strategic objectives and strategic metrics will influence approaches to project delivery and the definition of project objectives and project metrics.
- o *Requirements selection*: The deliverables from a project are defined in detail by a set of requirements. Unless there is unlimited time and money a project will never deliver a universal and exhaustive set of requirements. There has to be a choice between different requirements, which can be influenced by strategy.
- o *Day-to-day project decision-making*: There are many decisions on projects which affect the final outcome in terms of what is delivered, how much the project costs, how long it takes to deliver and so on. These decisions should at least be partially shaped by strategy.

This is shown in Diagram 2.5. Let us look at the last two points in a little more detail.

A portfolio aligned to the strategy will ensure that a business only executes projects aligned to the strategy, and in the order of priority suggested by the strategy. There is a mass of detail below this high level which shapes the actual deliverables from projects, which is defined in project requirements. Depending on the nature of the project the requirements may be more or less complex.

Consider the following example to understand how strategy can influence requirements selection. In a major systems development project there will be thousands of requirements. Each requirement will take some time and cost to fulfil. Any one project cannot normally fulfil all of the possible requirements, and they have to be reduced in number.

A typical process to reduce the requirements starts by reviewing all requirements and categorizing them as

- o *Mandatory*: has to be included in the project delivery. If these requirements are not fulfilled the project will have failed.

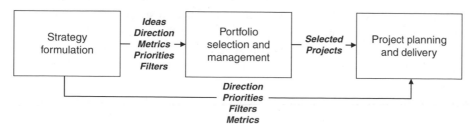

Diagram 2.5 *The impact of strategy on portfolio selection and project delivery*

- o *Important*: requirements which should be included, but not at the expense of mandatory requirements. Most important requirements should be fulfilled. Individual important requirements may be excluded only if they are particularly difficult or costly to implement.
- o *Nice to have*: may be included, but not at the expense of the mandatory or important requirements. The amount of resources allocated to fulfilling the nice-to-have requirements is usually minimal, but if they can be delivered without significant impact on time or cost then they will be included.
- o *Not required*: should be filtered out.

Other terms may be used such as *core* and *non-core* or *critical* and *non-critical* requirements. Whatever names are given to the categorization of requirements the principle is the same. Someone has to review the collected requirements and determine what category each requirement falls into. This decision should be based on the relationship of the requirement to business need. This decision should be informed, where relevant, by the strategy. If the strategy is to improve customer service, then systems requirements that support this should be given priority over those that do not. A requirement which has a detrimental impact on customer service should be excluded.

It would be naïve to suggest that the decisions over such requirements are made solely on a strategic basis. There are other valid considerations – cost, time to deliver etc. Also, at the detail level there is a significant risk of personal bias. Whilst a critical decision is usually subject to scrutiny, less significant decisions, such as the inclusion or exclusion of one requirement amongst thousands, are not. (The challenge of requirements development is discussed in detail in Chapter 5.)

Beyond requirements there are numerous decisions made on projects on a daily basis. Consider the *iron triangle* introduced in Chapter 1. As explained there project managers are always trying to balance between time, cost and quality of a project. Any trade-off decisions between these criteria should be informed by strategy.

A company's strategy could be to seek differentiation in the market place by having the broadest range and highest quality of products. In this situation, the focus in new product development will be on speed-to-market to get the widest range of products. It will also focus on the quality of the developed products. The business is less likely to be concerned with cost. If a project manager is presented with a delay on a project that can be overcome with some additional expenditure, he is likely to choose to spend the extra money. On the other hand, a competitor with an alternative strategy to provide the lowest-cost products, will tend to manage projects in the lowest-cost way. A project manager, in this situation, presented with a delay on a project that can be overcome with more money, is more likely to accept the delay and hence avoid the additional cost. (Decision-making on projects is explored in Chapter 8.)

The fact that project managers often make decisions contrary to strategy is a sign of a lack of strategic alignment in an organization, and a failure in the achievement of strategy. The consistency of application of strategy by project managers to micro-level decisions is dependent on the effective communication of the strategy, ongoing management direction to follow the strategy and personal motivation to do so.

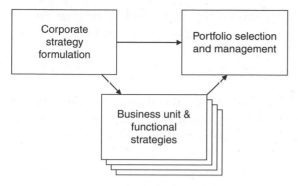

Diagram 2.6 Multiple strategies and project management

A multiplicity of strategies

This chapter so far has shown the relationship between strategy and projects. In practice there are multiple strategies in existence in most large organizations as shown in Diagram 2.6.

There will remain a direct link from the corporate strategy to project management, but also a separate link from business unit and functional strategy. A function like IT will have its own strategy that may require many projects to achieve. Business units will often have their own strategies concerned with activities such as what new products to launch, what customer segments to target and how to be different from the competition.

One of the challenges of portfolio management is prioritizing between projects which have originated in different strategies. (Prioritization is described in Chapter 3.)

Other influences of strategy on project management

Project management as a core capability

A different way to look at the relationship between strategy and project management is to consider how project management is viewed strategically as a core capability or competency of a business.

In the 1990s a prominent development in strategy theory was core competencies and capabilities (see e.g. Stalk, Evans and Shulman, 2002 or Hamel and Prahalad, 1994: Chapter 10). This is still an important concept in strategy formulation. The central idea is that businesses that thrive achieve success via the selection, deliberate enhancement and leverage of core competencies and capabilities.

Core competencies and capabilities vary, and examples include great logistics capabilities, skills in micro electronics, or ability to bring innovative products to market rapidly. Core competencies and capabilities provide differentiation and hence competitive advantage. Such competencies and capabilities are deeply engrained into an organization and cannot easily be copied by competitors.

Project management is not generally presented as core competency or capability. For a company that has as its core business running projects, such as a construction business, it may seem obvious that there needs to be great project management skills. But being good at something is not enough for that to be a core competency.

Yet an argument can easily be made that in some situations project management should be considered as a core competency. In a fast-moving market in which competition is won by innovation and *speed to market* then great project management skills will be important. In any situation in which businesses thrive by executing strategies which require successful project delivery, project management skills are core.

A strategy which has identified project management as a core competency would consider how this competency can be leveraged and developed. (Developing and enhancing project management capabilities is discussed in more detail in Chapter 12.) However, for project management to be a true core competency in a business it is not enough for it to support the execution of the strategy; it must add to the organization's ability to achieve sustainable competitive advantage.

There is a major issue with project management as a source of sustainable competitive advantage. Much of the development of project management is about standardizing best practice. By simple logic, for something to offer competitive advantage it must not only be effective, but must also be better than competitors and differentiated from what competitors do. Few, if any, firms have achieved this. Project management as a core competence is also in conflict with the practice of project management accreditation and standardization. By its very nature, standardization cannot lead to sustainable competitive advantage.

Green offers a possible solution in the development of Star Project Leaders (Green, 2006). Star Project Leaders work beyond the normal boundaries of project management to find creative and flexible ways to deliver projects that add business values beyond the constraints of normal project management. Other research indicates that intangible project management assets (knowledge-based assets) can be a source of temporary competitive advantage (Jugdev et al., 2007).

Sourcing of project managers

Strategy influences the allocation of resources and decisions about whether skills should be retained in-house or outsourced (or sourced offshore). Sourcing strategies start by considering which competencies are core, and hence should be in-house, and which are non-core and can be considered for outsourcing.

Most businesses do not consider project management skills as core, but they have an ongoing need for projects and access to project managers to run them.

Firms often rely on third parties, either independent contractors or consultancies, to provide them with some of the project managers they need. This is especially prevalent in project management as the demand for project managers tends to fluctuate. Assuming a business decides that project management is not a core skill, but something that needs to be available and provided to a high standard, it can be outsourced. There are many factors to consider in sourcing of skilled people like project managers, but it is feasible to outsource the provision of the resource.

Case study **2.1** **THE IMPACT OF STRATEGY ON THE PROJECT PORTFOLIO**

The following example is based on a multi national corporation, but it has been adapted and anonymized at the request of the company.

This organization provides a range of products to the health sector. It has factories in several countries, and sales operations across the world. The company is split into several autonomous divisions, the most important of which are

- *Division A is a large division producing and selling a complex range of typically low-margin products. The division operates in a highly competitive market and the divisional strategy is to compete on the basis of cost leadership.*

- *Division B is of smaller scale than division A. It provides lower revenues, but significantly higher margins, and its contribution to overall company profitability is greater. Although Division B also operates in a competitive market, it is not commoditized. There are ongoing opportunities for growth in both revenues and margins. Division B aims for market differentiation with products with a richer set of features than competitors' products. This requires continual innovation. There is also pressure to reduce costs, but it is less strong than in Division A. In addition, the division has started to develop a line in value-added customer services supporting its products. The aim is to provide a managed service offering to its customers.*

- *Division C is the smallest. Currently, it has very limited revenues and runs at a loss. It is investing in a radical new product range. The range is not yet launched. The products are protected from competition by a series of patents. The potential profits from the products are very high. However, to be successful the company has to convince a conservative group of buyers. They will take some time to be persuaded of the value of the new product.*

The corporate strategy was to invest in divisions B and C, and to minimize expenditure on division A. The company has been looking at divesting division A, and a corporate project is underway to look for potential buyers. This reflects itself in the product portfolios of the three divisions whereby

- *Division A's project portfolio consists of a large number of cost reduction initiatives and ongoing relocation of production facilities to lower-cost countries. There is also significant work in outsourcing non-core functions and much of the production. There is a very small set of projects working to improve existing products. These improvements are only those that are unavoidable for products to stay acceptable to customers. There are many price reduction initiatives and sales offers so that each runs for a short period of time.*

- *Division B's project portfolio contains a range of new product development projects, mainly focussed on enhancement activities with a few completely new products. There is also work on improved production and logistics management systems, and work on finance systems to increase understanding of customer and product profitability. The managed service offering is being developed as a project. Currently this project is in a customer trial phase with a small group of customers. The managed service offering is expected to expand soon.*

- *Division C's project portfolio reflects that most of division C's resources are allocated to bringing the new product range to market. A project is also being started to provide volume production capabilities as the product's sales start.*

At the time of writing the corporate strategy is being reviewed.

It has been identified that although the margins in division A are low they are complementary to the move of division B into services. In addition, division A has a much larger customer base, who can be used to target division B's service sales towards. The impact of this is expected to lead to stopping the divestiture and changes in division A's project portfolio. There is even consideration at a corporate level to buying some smaller competitors to fill out division A's product range. There will continue to be cost pressure, but additional resources are being allocated to broaden the project range, so division B's service offering can provide a 'one stop shop' for products in the area of this business.

This is summarized in Table 2.1.

Table 2.1 Strategy and portfolio link

	Strategy	Project Portfolio	Revised Strategy	Revised Portfolio
Corporate	Divest division A Invest in B and C	Sale of division A	Invest in division A to support B Invest in B and C	Closer integration of divisions A and B Identify complementary organizations to buy
Division A	Compete on the basis of cost leadership	Relocation to lower-cost countries; Outsourcing; Minor unavoidable product enhancements	Support division B's move into managed services	Continue cost reduction work; Enhance range of products by purchasing small competitors; Provide mechanism for division B to leverage division A's customer base
Division B	Compete with products with richer features than competitors' products	Significant product enhancements; Improved understanding of customer and product profitability; Improved production and logistics management	Move into managed services	Develop managed service offering using products from both division A and B
Division C	Compete on the basis of new and novel innovation protected by patents	Product innovation; Patent management; Provide volume production capabilities	No change	No change

From project management to strategy

Project and portfolio management are concerned with strategy, because it helps in both selecting and delivering projects. The reverse is also true.

Strategy can be influenced by project management. This is what Srivannaboon and Milosevic refer to as the reciprocal relationship between project management and a business's strategy, when they show how project management can impact business strategy, based on the specific situation of projects in an organization (Srivannaboon and Milosevic, 2006).

The influence of project management on strategy is dependent on the style and approach to strategy. A very linear, command and control, directive strategy will tend to be influenced less than an emergent strategy, which by its very nature is influenced by how things turn out.

Either way, project management can support and influence strategy in the following stages of strategy formulation and implementation:

- During strategy formulation
- In the creation of a plan for strategy execution
- As a strategy is executed
- In reviewing strategy

Project management and strategy formulation

Strategy is a continuous process. Strategy evolves, grows and is modified as a response to changing conditions and the effectiveness of strategy implementation. However, there are specific phases in the development of a strategy that are fixed-time activities with a start and end point. For example, strategy often has to be updated prior to completion of the annual budget round, so that it can be taken account of in developing next year's plans and budgets. Although it is not usually considered a project, the creation or an iteration of strategy can be considered as a project and managed as one.

Project management and execution planning

A more important role for project management, or at least for using the skills of senior programme managers, is in the development of the plan for strategy execution. A strategy that is formulated but not capable of being executed is of no value. Strategy has to define how it will be achieved; if it does not, it is not complete.

Strategy execution is preceded by the development of a high-level plan, which will include a project roadmap. Determining strategic options often requires assessing timescales, risks and costs of different options. For relevant options, determining this information at a high level is the skill of a programme manager.

For a business to be able to execute any strategy it has to have the resources available to undertake any resulting projects. Effective portfolio management is able to give an understanding of the organization's capacity to provide resources and to absorb any changes proposed by the strategy, to put this into the context of other projects and changes underway and hence determine whether the organization is over- or under-resourced in terms of the planned changes. A strategy that does not consider an organization's ability to implement it is of very limited value (Bossidy, Charan and Burck, 2002).

Project management and strategy execution

If strategy has to be executed, who does the execution? The team who create strategy may have a role to play, but usually the responsibility for strategy execution falls on the wider management community of a business.

Project management is core to the execution of many strategic ideas. It provides a mechanism for delivery of any strategic change that can be structured as a project. (It should be noted that not all strategic changes are ideally structured as projects; this is discussed in Chapters 9 and 13.) Good project management reduces the risk in strategy execution. In addition, a project structure provides a way to monitor and respond to any unintended outcomes during delivery of a strategy.

One issue that is given little consideration in theories and methods for strategy formulation and execution is assessing how usable a specific strategy is. If a strategy is going to be effective in directing an organization at both the macro and micro levels it must be usable by everyone who has to make decisions based on strategy during execution.

For the output from strategy formulation to be effective it should be

- o *Aligned to the projects that are initiated*: This requires the strategy to be communicated in a way that is meaningful to project managers. The mission, strategies, objectives and metrics need to be accessible and understood by the project management community. Moreover, the strategy management community want that understanding to be consistent with the original intentions.
- o *Unambiguous and without conflicting requirements*: (Or, if it contains conflicts, makes clear the priority.) A core part of project management is to achieve clarity over objectives, scope and requirements. The clearer the originating strategy the easier this task will be.
- o *Executable*: This sounds obvious, but strategies are sometimes proposed such that an organization does not have the competency to deliver.
- o *Realistic*: A strategy should be realistic in terms of resource availability to deliver the projects and in terms of the organization's ability to cope with the resultant changes. Resources include both human resources, and also budgets. Projects often get stuck between strategic aspirations and budget realities. A tight budget and high aspirations can drive creative and innovative thinking. It can also mean that outcomes are limited and a strategy is not achieved.

Strategic alignment of the project portfolio is a dynamic activity. Work to align the portfolio should continue during project execution as well as at project startup (Srivannaboon, 2006). As projects evolve, many aspects can be subject to change. Project objectives, scope, plans and requirements can all get modified. Plans may be wrong, and projects may take longer or cost more than expected. Unless this process of modification is managed and regularly checked back against the strategy, there is a real risk that projects incrementally drift away from strategic alignment.

A more difficult issue to manage is the evolution of strategy during a project's life. This is a significant problem for larger projects with a longer timescale to deliver. Strategies adapt and modify as a result of evolving competitive threats and the appearance of new opportunities. A project that may start out being aligned to strategy may, on completion, be less relevant to a business. The willingness to review projects as strategy evolves, and, if necessary, stop projects that are no longer relevant, is an important part of robust portfolio management.

Project management and strategy review

The final role that project management and project managers can play in supporting strategy is to provide feedback. This can be done most constructively at project initiation and at completion.

At project initiation there is an opportunity to ensure strategic alignment before resources are committed. Access to resources for a project should be subject to ensuring the project is aligned to the strategy. (There will always be exceptions, but they should be limited.) There should also be an assessment at a portfolio level, with feedback to strategy management, if too many projects are being initiated which are contrary to the strategy.

At project closure feedback relates to project outcomes: Was the project successful or not, and if not where does this leave the strategy?

Another form of feedback centres on project managers as users of strategy. Project managers have to be able to understand and use the strategy. They should have the opportunity to provide feedback into the strategy function on how well the strategy works in practice, at least from a project perspective. Are there any conflicts or ambiguities inherent in the strategy which project managers need resolved? Is the strategy actually executable from a project perspective?

More importantly there should be feedback at the project portfolio–level in terms of overall strategic compliance and portfolio outcomes. The sort of questions that a review of a project portfolio should answer for the strategist are

- o Does the entire portfolio meet the goals of the strategy? For example, if the strategy requires removing £100m of cost from a business, does the set of projects in the portfolio do this?
- o Does the portfolio meet the goals of the strategy in an acceptable way? For example, is the cumulative resources or budget required acceptable? Is the level of risk in projects acceptable to the business?
- o What contingencies are there if goals are not reached? There is an inherent degree of risk in projects: they may overrun, require extra budget or simply fail to deliver the expected benefits. How is this risk to be managed? In addition, budgets may be reduced due to wider issues in a business. Projects seen as discretionary are often the first items to be removed when budgets are tightened. How will this impact strategy realisation?

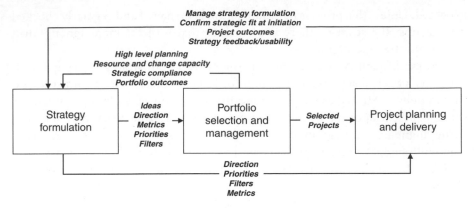

Diagram 2.7 *The two-way relationship between strategy and project management*

The reciprocal relationship between strategy formulation, portfolio management and project delivery is shown in Diagram 2.7.

Other influences on portfolio selection

Many text books show all activities in a business as being derived from strategy. This is rarely true.

There is often a difference between the strategy as espoused by an organization, and what exists in practice. For example, a firm may say its strategy is to be customer-orientated and delight its customers, whilst in practice be orientated towards cost cutting. These two may not conflict initially, but they probably will at some point. The reality is that businesses do not always implement the most important projects, or the ones with the best strategic fit. Often the projects that are best supported and argued for, or those for which there is the most urgent pressure to undertake, are the ones selected.

The fact that activity is not strategically aligned may or may not be a good thing, but it is something that someone managing a project portfolio has to deal with. The project and change agenda for a business in practice is broader than the strategic agenda.

Projects can be identified and initiated as a response to a whole range of non-strategic factors. Important examples include

- o *Exceptional tactical opportunities*: Although a business may desire to be strategically aligned, an opportunity for significant revenues or cost reductions may present itself which is too good to ignore. Depending on the culture of the organization the tendency to pursue such opportunities will vary, but from time to time most organizations will be tempted to seize opportunities which do not align with the strategy.
- o *Regulations and legislation*: Legal and regulatory compliance is not usually a strategic imperative and may not even be given strategic consideration. However, most businesses will comply with regulations and this will often require investment in projects.
- o *Operational performance problems*: Performance issues will occur regularly. From the need to replace a broken machine on a factory floor to the need to improve a failing sales force, potential project activities will arise as a normal part of management of a business.

- *Politics and personal whim*: Good company governance should reduce the allocation of resources to ideas that are being pursued for political reasons, but it would be naïve to say this always happens. (One tool to improve the chances of this happening is the business case. By formalizing the assessment of costs and benefits, business cases should remove pet projects. But business cases do not always remove the pet project, and can occasionally exacerbate the problem. Sometimes, projects which are identified as "strategic" have an easier set of business case criteria to meet to be accepted. Occasionally, simply being labelled as "strategic" is good enough for a business to invest in a project. Projects may be spuriously identified as strategic because by being labelled as such, the required rigour in business case is less.)

A different issue is a project starting out being strategically aligned, but by the time it completes is no longer so. Strategy evolves: there is a time lag between formulation and complete execution. It may take months or years for a new strategy to permeate an entire organization. During this time existing projects continue to be run and completed, making changes to the organization. A project that starts off being strategically aligned may end up being no longer strategically relevant.

This is shown in Diagram 2.8.

What can the project management community do about the existence of non-strategic projects? It is not the role of the project manager to undermine decisions made by more senior managers, which may have been made for perfectly valid reasons. Even if it was, project managers are not normally empowered to refuse to complete work that is not strategically aligned.

In reality, all a project manager, a programme manager or the project portfolio management function can do is

- Assess whether projects are strategically aligned
- When they are not, ensure that the implications of progressing with the project are understood by sponsors and customers

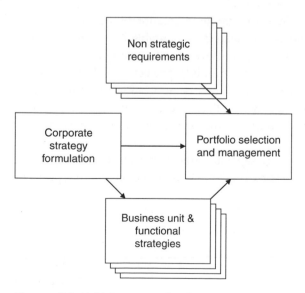

Diagram 2.8 Multiple sources of projects

o Accept decisions once made with a full understanding of the implications

o Continue to verify the desire to complete the project through its lifecycle and especially at any stage gate reviews.

How many portfolios?

This chapter has presented the relationship between strategy and project management through the project portfolio as if there is only one portfolio. From a conceptual basis this makes the description easier, but in reality, there may be more than one portfolio in a given business.

Portfolio management and resource management

The initial driver for introducing portfolio management into an organization is often the urge to resolve resource contentions and to ensure resources are allocated to strategically the most relevant projects.

In terms of resource management, where there are separate resource pools there may be independent project portfolios. A typical example might include a portfolio of IT projects which is separate from a portfolio of new product developments, the logic being that as these are worked on from separate resource pools they can be effectively prioritized separately.

Sometimes prioritizing projects in separate portfolios is effective, often it is not. Although it may suit the IT department and the product management department to have their own prioritized set of projects, the prioritisation is often illusory. Most new products will require IT development work and hence must be listed in both portfolios. If these are managed as separate portfolios with independent prioritisation mechanisms then there is a risk of wasted time and resource. For example, some components of a product may progress in one portfolio as a high priority. Other parts of the product may be delayed by being set at a lower priority in another portfolio. The end result is delay, as a project's true priority is the lowest priority any component part is delivered.

Multiple portfolios also present a risk of diluted accountability. If components of a project exist in multiple portfolios, who is accountable for overall delivery? Normally, it is the programme manager. But even the best programme manager will struggle to pull together effectively multiple projects into one coherent programme when inter-dependent parts of the organization involved in the programme treat their parts of delivery with differing levels of importance. A good programme manager will attempt to have common prioritization, and even lobby for a combined portfolio.

It is possible to effectively manage separate project portfolios, but only where there is a high differentiation between the resources required on different projects.

Portfolio management supporting strategy and change

There is a more sophisticated way to use portfolio management. By bringing together information about all projects, an organization can move beyond using portfolio management as simply a resource allocation mechanism. Rather than just looking at what inputs projects require, portfolio management provides the opportunity to look at optimizing the outcomes from projects.

An assessment of all the projects in a portfolio can provide the information to

o ensure that the results from projects in totality meet the strategic goals – by ensuring all the projects, the constituents of the portfolio, meet the optimal set of objectives.
o understand cumulative change across all projects, and use this as a basis to determine whether the organization can absorb the change.

Achieving this requires a single portfolio view across an organization.

Conclusions on the number of portfolios

Ideally an organization will have a single view of its project portfolio, but there are practical limits. For the largest of organizations it is questionable whether it is possible in practice for a single group of people to review, filter and prioritize between all the possible projects. In addition, where a business is split into autonomous divisions with limited shared resources there is less value in a common project portfolio.

Who is responsible for alignment?

This chapter has identified the web of interactions between strategy and project management. It is a conceptual view rather than dealing with the mechanics, which will be presented in Chapter 3. However, even at this level it is worth considering roles and responsibilities at a high level.

There are essentially five groups of people with the main responsibilities for linking project management and strategy. A breakdown of responsibilities is

o *Corporate Governance*: The Association for Project Management clearly links the responsibility with overall corporate governance and gives the responsibility to the board, to ensure "A coherent and supportive relationship is demonstrated between the overall business strategy and the project portfolio" (APM, 2004, p. 6). Corporate governance is the responsibility of a business's board of directors, though detailed control of an activity such as reviewing a project portfolio may be delegated.
o *Strategy management*: Beyond the responsibility for strategy formulation the strategy team should ensure that the resultant project portfolio is consistent with the strategy, in terms of both the individual projects and the cumulative effect of the portfolio. The strategy function should seek appropriately competent support from the portfolio management function and programme management community for developing a high-level plan for strategy execution. The strategy team should also be interested in the effectiveness of the strategy, namely how well the project management community understand and can use it.
o *Portfolio management*: It has a core role in ensuring strategic alignment. Portfolio management should analyse the portfolio and ensure the strategy team understands the degree of alignment, and understand the cumulative impact of the portfolio in terms of achieving strategic goals. The portfolio management function should use the strategy to support filtering and prioritization of projects in the portfolio.

- o *Project manager*: Individual project managers are unlikely to have the remit, influence or power to affect the strategy. However, they should seek to have sufficient clarity over the strategy to make daily decisions on the project and to ensure requirements selection fits the strategy. They also have a role in providing feedback on whether the strategy is presented in such a way as to be understandable and usable.

- o *Programme manager*: They have not been mentioned in this chapter so far, and they have a different role than project managers. Typically, programme managers have more experience and operate at a higher level of seniority than project managers. Depending on their specific role and programme of work they may have the ability to directly interface into strategy departments and support business-wide planning for strategy execution.

Case Study **2.2** **WHAT ARE THE CHALLENGES OF IMPLEMENTING STRATEGY THROUGH PROJECTS?**

Terry Goh is an experienced strategy manager. He has worked both as a strategy consultant and in senior-management positions in a number of major corporations. His work involves both strategy formulation and execution. The case study shows Terry's comments on implementing strategy through projects.

Terry Goh

*I have to answer that by starting to think about the strategy itself. What do we mean by strategy? Often people will point to a slide pack as the strategy. To be honest, it's easy to do a high-level plan and put a few ideas into a PowerPoint presentation. But, to be executed the strategy has to have backing and belief. We can all nod and agree about some grand-sounding high-level concepts. The acid test comes when the question "will you put money into **this**" has to be answered. If no one is willing to invest in a strategy it's worthless, and you won't get to implement any projects from it. Money won't come just from a presentation. Getting money allocated needs a strategy with some detail, something people think they can touch and can understand what it is selling. If strategy remains as an ethereal vision it won't get off the starting board. The first challenge is therefore to make the strategy real and meaningful.*

Once you have a fully concrete and agreed strategy, then if it is well-defined, the practical steps of delivering it are relatively straightforward. That's the job of the project manager. I value the skill, and as long as I've concretely identified what is required in the strategy, I'm confident that competent people will deliver what I need.

So, if the high-level stuff is straightforward and delivery is also straightforward, what's the problem? The difficult bit is moving from the high-level vision to a concrete set of undertakings with clear objectives.

*One of the challenges in creating a concrete set of undertakings with clear objectives is linking between strategy and delivery people. A classic conversation between these two groups goes from the strategist **asking "what** can you deliver, what are the **options"** **and the** delivery **person saying "what** do you **want?"** These are incompatible questions and lead to poor answers or never-ending conversations. If the strategist is to develop* a meaningful and implementable strategy, he needs support from delivery people in terms of what is possible. From the delivery manager's viewpoint the strategist has to really think through what is needed. Strategy development should be a dialogue between forward-looking strategists and practical-minded delivery people. For this dialogue to be effective requires good people who can see where each other is coming from.

Of course another problem is that everyone thinks strategy is his or her job – or everyone wants it to be his or her job. So the role of the corporate strategist overlaps with that of the business unit strategist, telling him what products are required – and the delivery people often think they can do the product strategy better than the business unit strategist! Everyone starts playing in everyone else's domain.

The easy answer to this is to think that you should clearly separate the roles with absolute role boundaries. But that is not a good answer as it generates silo thinking. If you box people in too much, you get a corporate strategy thrown over the wall to business unit strategist, who in turn throws his ideas over to the delivery people. No one worries whether the next part in the chain interprets the strategy correctly and can do what was asked for. This leads to misalignment – or worse, people ignoring the strategy. So, the answer is that a bit of overlap between roles is required, but not everyone trying to do everyone else's job. The solution lies in lots of constructive dialogue. For this to work well, you need experienced people with mature relationships who value what each other does.

In the end, there has to be very tight linkages between the strategy and the projects it needs. Once I've defined the projects I need, I just want them delivered. A big problem for me in getting projects delivered is 'scope creep'. I want something and what I get has a whole load of bells and whistles added, and takes forever to complete. The way to avoid this is to ensure the project starts with a small set of very clear objectives derived from the strategy. Then every requirement in the project must be tied to those objectives. Any additional requirements, even those we might think are worthwhile but are not related to the strategy, are rejected. Unless this degree of rigour and discipline is put in place, projects drift.

Finally, delivery people are always asking about the strategy. When they do this what they are really asking is **"why am I doing this?" That does not need strategy** to answer. It's back to those clear objectives. Give the delivery team clear objectives and a definition of the concrete outcome expected, and it will happen.

So to summarize, strategy is often implemented through projects. The challenge is in making the strategy concrete, definite and clear enough to scope out and run well-defined projects, and to make every part of those projects link to the strategic objectives.

MAIN LEARNING POINTS FROM CHAPTER 2

- Projects are one of the main mechanisms for the delivery of strategy. A strategy is successfully executed if activities in the business, including projects, are aligned with it.

- Projects are affected by strategy in two ways. First, in terms of the selection of projects. Strategy provides ideas for projects, directions which may be interpreted into projects, filters which remove projects from consideration and priorities which can be applied in selecting projects. Second, strategy impacts the day-to-day management of projects and the decisions a project manager makes in managing a project. This requires the strategy to be explicit to and understood by the project manager.

- Strategy in turn can be influenced by the outcome of projects and benefits from the application of project management skills, for example, in testing achievability of and creating a resource plan for implementing a strategy.
- Portfolio management assists in the delivery of strategy, and can help assess whether the portfolio of projects will achieve the desired strategic goals or not.
- The relationship between strategy, project management and portfolio management is multi-dimensional and bi-directional.

REVIEW QUESTIONS AND EXERCISES

1. Use your own knowledge of a real business to describe its strategy at a high level. What actions can be derived from this strategy? Which ones should be implemented as projects and which ones should not? Why?
2. Do you think strategy is a meaningful concept? Why? What are the implications for project management?
3. Define what the term *strategy* means and present a simple process for strategy formulation and execution. Where does project management fit in your process? If an organization does not have a clear strategy, in what ways does that ease the challenge of project management and in what ways does it make it more difficult?
4. Do you agree with the model of strategy presented in this chapter? How would you improve on it?
5. When is it reasonable for a strategy manager to ignore project and portfolio management? What are the implications of working in this way?
6. Do you agree that organizations undertake projects that are not aligned to strategy? Why? When is this reasonable and when is it not? What does this tell you about strategy?
7. How, in your experience, does the model in this chapter differ from what happens in reality? How can the two be reconciled?
8. Review the comments of Terry Goh in Case Study 2.2. How does this match with your experience? What do you agree with and what do you disagree with? Why?

Suggested reading

Two texts are suggested for those interested in exploring the relationship between strategy and project management further. The first is specifically concerned with this topic and contains several detailed case studies. The second is a broader description of an approach to strategy execution.

- *Translating Corporate Strategy into Project Strategy: Realizing Corporate Strategy through Project Management.* Peter Morris and Ashley Jamieson. Project Management Institute, 2003
- *Making Strategy Work: Leading Effective Execution and Change.* Lawrence G Hrebinak. Wharton School Publishing, 2005

Bibliography

Alexander Lord, M. "Implementing strategy through project management". *Long Range Planning.* Volume 26, Issue 1, February 1993, pp. 76–85.
APM (Association for Project Management). *Directing Change, A Guide to Governance of Project Management.* Association for Project Management, 2004.

Bossidy, L., Charan, R. and Burck, B. *Execution: The Discipline of Getting Things Done.* Random House, 2002.

Cooper, R., Edgett, S. and Kleinschmidt, E. "Portfolio management for new product development: Results of an Industry Practices Study". *R&D Management.* Volume 31, Issue 4, 2001.

Crawford, L., Pollack, J. and England, D. "Uncovering the trends in project management: Journal emphases over the last 10 years". *International Journal of Project Management.* Volume 24, Issue 2, February 2006, pp. 175–84.

Dietrich, P. and Lehtonen, P. "Successful management of strategic intentions through multiple projects – Reflections from empirical study". *International Journal of Project Management.* Volume 23, Issue 5, July 2005, pp. 386–91.

Green, S. *Strategic Project Management: From Maturity Model to Star Project Leadership.* 20 October 2005 (Published in PM World Today, March 2006).

Grundy, A. "Strategy implementation and project management". *International Journal of Project Management.* Volume 16, Issue 1, February 1998, pp. 43–50.

Hamel, G. and Prahalad, C. *Competing for the Future.* Harvard Business School Press, 1994.

Hrebiniak, L. *Making Strategy Work. Leading Effective Execution and Change.* Wharton School Publishing, 2005.

Jugdev, K., Mathur, G. and Fung, T. "Project management assets and their relationship with the project management capability of the firm". *International Journal of Project Management.* Volume 25, Issue 6, August 2007, pp. 560–68.

Longman, A. and Mullins, J. "Project management: Key tool for implementing strategy". *Journal of Business Strategy,* Volume 25, Issue 5, 2004, pp. 54–60.

Manning, T. *Making Sense of Strategy.* American Management Association, 2001.

Morris, P. *Managing the Front End: How Project Managers Shape Business Strategy and Manage Project Definition.* Proceedings of the PMI Global conference 2005 – Edinburgh, Scotland.

Morris, P. and Jamieson, A. *Translating Corporate Strategy into Project Strategy: Realizing Corporate Strategy Through Project Management.* Project Management Institute, **Newtown Square, Pennsylvania** 2003.

Pellegrini, S. and Bowman, C. "Implementing strategy through projects". *Long Range Planning.* Volume 27, Issue 4, August 1994, pp. 125–32.

Portny, S., Mantel, S., Meredith, J., Shafer, S. and Sutton, M. *Project Management. Planning, Scheduling and Controlling Projects.* John Wiley & Sons, 2008.

Srivannaboon, S. and Milosevic, D. "A two-way influence between business strategy and project management". *International Journal of Project Management.* Volume 24, Issue 6, August 2006, pp. 493–505.

Srivannaboon, S. "Linking project management with business strategy". *Project Management Journal.* December 1, 2006, pp. 101–106.

Stalk, G., Evans, P. and Shulman, L. "Competing on capabilities: The new rules of corporate strategy". *Harvard Business Review.* 1 March 2002.

Teague, T. "The gulf between strategy, projects and reality". *Project Manager Today.* February 2005, p. 14.

Whittington, R. *What Is Strategy and Does It Matter?* Thomson Learning, 2000.

3

selecting
projects and creating
the project portfolio

There are many aspects of projects that organizations have to understand and be able to deal with. Critical issues, such as how to manage an individual project, how to direct a series of inter-dependent projects or how to ensure benefits are achieved from projects, are faced by organizations all the time. But before any of these issues have to be considered the first challenge is to decide what projects to undertake.

Organizations have the opportunity to pursue a huge variety of projects, and any one project usually has many different possible variations. Every organization has finite resources, and so can only do a sub-set of the possible range of projects. The decisions that determine which projects to invest in and which ones to reject are some of the most important choices managers have to make on a regular basis. A range of current assets and competencies, such as the ability to sell, excellence in operations, and good products and services, is what creates a business's success today. But it is the choice of projects and the resulting changes that will determine, to a large extent, how successful an organization will be in future.

The process of selecting which projects to invest in can be a rather haphazard activity with little concept of best practice or formal guidance. But it need not be so. With experience, some organizations have developed formalized processes for selecting and managing portfolios of projects. The project management community has created an increasingly rich set of approaches to, standards on and best practice in portfolio management.

This chapter provides an understanding of the front-end processes of project management – selecting projects to create the project portfolio. It starts by presenting a brief description of portfolios and portfolio management. Next, the chapter presents the process of portfolio management and describes each stage of the process. Then, there is a brief overview of the relationship between portfolio management and budget processes. Finally, the chapter discusses some practical issues that often are the real challenges in portfolio management.

Portfolios and portfolio management

The terms *project portfolio* and *project portfolio management* are of increasing prominence in project management literature and amongst the project management community. Usually, they are shortened simply to *portfolio* and *portfolio management,* as in the context they are used the word *project* may be assumed. Occasionally, additional adjectives are added, and phrases such as *strategic portfolio management,* or *enterprise portfolio management* are used. Irrespective of the specific terms chosen the meanings are largely the same.

There are two ways in which project portfolios are defined: first, in relation to the inputs to the portfolio – that is the resources used in delivering the projects; second, in terms of the objectives projects achieve in an organization.

As per the first definition, the way to look at a portfolio is as a collection of projects that are in contention for the same resources. Portfolio management is a way to manage this contention by controlling which projects get access to which resources in a prioritized order. If an organization has 1000 people available to work on projects, the aim of portfolio management is to ensure that projects are selected so as to optimize the output from these 1000 people.

Senior project or programme managers often use the term portfolio to refer to the set of projects they are responsible for and must deliver with the resources allocated to them. This is a subset of the total portfolio. In this book the term portfolio refers to the diversified set of projects and programmes that are delivered from all the project resources in the organization. In other words, the portfolio is the complete set of projects undertaken by an organization. (There are some caveats which are discussed below in Section "Identify Potential Projects".)

Another, more powerful, way to consider a portfolio is as a collection of projects designed to achieve a set of organizational goals. At its most general a portfolio is the set of projects that achieves that portion of overall business objectives which is to be accomplished by projects. For example, if a business needs to cut costs by £50m per annum, it may ask line managers to reduce their budgets collectively by £20m and achieve this through business as usual operational management. The other £30m of savings will be achieved through various projects. The portfolio is the set of projects aiming to achieve £30m of savings, and portfolio management is about ensuring the set of projects achieve £30m of saving. Often a business will have a series of objectives like this.

The difference between the first definition of portfolio management and the second is important. In the first, portfolio management is a specialized form of resource management for projects. In the second, projects will still be in contention for resources, and optimizing the selection of projects relative to the resources remains a core aspect of portfolio management. However, the role of portfolio management is broader, and the more important aspect of the portfolio is what it achieves. Portfolio management seeks to ensure that the total set of projects achieve strategic and operational goals, and adequately contribute to the organization's overall objectives.

A definition of portfolio management is given below. This definition is from the context of new product development, but would be equally applicable to any project portfolio:

> Portfolio management is a dynamic decision process, whereby a business's list of active new product (and R&D) projects is constantly up dated and revised. In this process, new projects are evaluated, selected and prioritized; existing projects may be accelerated, killed or de-prioritized; and resources are allocated and re-allocated to the active projects. The portfolio decision process is characterized by uncertain and changing information, dynamic opportunities, multiple goals and strategic considerations, interdependence among projects and multiple decision-makers and locations. (Cooper, Edgett and Kleinschmidt, 2001)

Alternatively, portfolio management has been defined as

> the activity of aligning resource demand with resource availability to achieve a set of strategic goals. (Archer and Ghasemzadeh, 2004)

Whichever definition is used portfolio management is an approach to selecting projects for the portfolio, and managing the portfolio during the life of the various projects in it. Levine (2005) presents the portfolio as a never-ending pipeline of work and neatly divides portfolio management into two main components:

- o Selecting projects for the pipeline
- o Maintaining the project pipeline

This chapter focuses primarily on the first component, namely, selecting projects for the pipeline.

Portfolio objectives are unique to each organization. However, it can be generically said that portfolio management sets out to

1. Maximize relevant benefits from the investment in projects (where relevancy is based on the business's strategy and objectives)
2. Achieve an optimal balance between different objectives (e.g. a balance over time – between short- and long-term objectives such as tactical opportunities and strategic needs – or a balance between objectives such as customer-facing versus cost reduction)
3. Ensure the projects undertaken are strategically aligned
4. Ensure that the right number of projects are undertaken relative to the resources available
5. Ideally, provide a degree of flexibility and optionality to support risk management and the ability to respond to unknown future needs and opportunities

Project, programme or portfolio management?

There can be confusion between project management, programme management and portfolio management. One way to develop an appreciation of portfolio management is to understand the evolution of project management into programme management, and then the subsequent development of portfolio management.

This also helps in understanding the differences between project, programme and portfolio management.

Programme management grew out of project management with the emergence of increasingly regular complex and large-scale endeavours that required a series of projects to complete. Such endeavours face management challenges that extend beyond those faced by individual projects; for example, the management of complicated inter-dependencies between projects in a programme. Programme management provides additional tools and processes to overcome these challenges. Programme management still requires the use of project management principles and tools, and can be thought of as an extension to project management. Programme managers are usually chosen from people who are experienced project managers.

Portfolio management has developed as yet another layer of management beyond both project and programme management. It has grown from the realization that organizations need more than project and programme management, because successful delivery is more than completion of individual endeavours. Competent project and programme management will ensure that an endeavour is successful. Neither, though, really sets out to ensure that the *right* endeavours are undertaken, and they do not provide a management framework to control and direct a complex array of projects and programmes. This is what portfolio management sets out to achieve.

Although portfolio managers often have a project management background, this is not necessary. Successful portfolio management requires a deep appreciation of projects and programmes, but it is different from project or programme management as will be shown in this chapter. (The relationship between project, programme and portfolio management is shown in Diagram 3.1.)

An analogy can be made with driving. If project management can be considered as analogous to driving a car to complete a specific journey, then programme management is analogous to driving a lorry or controlling a fleet of cars to make a series of journeys, to deliver some set of goods for a common reason. Portfolio management is analogous to assessing the road network, agreeing which vehicles are allowed on it, controlling the flow of traffic, and ensuring that the outcome meets a defined set of transport needs. Performing this function requires a good understanding of the nature of driving, but is not in itself about driving.

The objective of portfolio management is different from those of both project and programme management. Project and programme management are about delivery of defined pieces of work. Programme management goes beyond project management in terms of scale and complexity, also often in taking responsibility for achieving business benefits and business change, but in the end it is still about delivering a piece of work. In contrast, portfolio management is not concerned with the management of individual activities, but sets out to ensure that

- The right sorts of projects and programmes are being undertaken according to business needs and business strategy;
- The optimal volume of projects is underway relative to the resources available;
- The projects and programmes that are underway are being done in the optimal sequence;

o The outcome from all the projects and programmes will deliver the necessary business benefits and objectives; and

o A suitable governance framework is in place to make decisions about projects and programmes.

In this chapter an organization is presented as having one portfolio of projects. In practice, a company with several divisions may have several portfolios, but the principles of operation are the same.

The portfolio manager

A range of managers and executives will be involved in and be responsible for different aspects of portfolio management. Decisions such as the portfolio objectives and the priorities of projects belong to a cross-section of senior management in an organization. In this book such a group of senior managers is titled the *leadership team*. However, the portfolio management process in itself needs management. This responsibility lies with the *portfolio manager*.

Depending on the scale of the organization and the range of projects undertaken, the portfolio manager may be anything from a part-time role for one person to the shared responsibility of a dedicated team. Often the responsibility lies with a central programme office function.

Portfolios and programmes

Portfolio management is more than the selection of the right projects. It is also about the management of the live set of projects. This chapter is primarily concerned with project selection. Management of the live set of projects is summarized in this chapter, but is developed in more detail in Chapter 8.

Portfolios are made up of both projects and programmes. The differentiation, in most situations, is irrelevant to understanding the principle portfolio management activities. In this chapter the terms project and project management should be seen to encompass programme and programme management. Where there is an important difference in handling of projects and programmes, it is explicitly noted.

Selecting a portfolio of projects – an overview

The main activity in portfolio selection is choosing the projects to undertake in comparison to the resources available, but selection is also about optimizing the complete set of projects and ensuring they meet organizational goals. This section provides an overview of the challenges of portfolio selection, which are then explored in the remainder of the chapter.

The steps in selecting a portfolio of projects are

o Determining portfolio objectives and metrics.

o Understanding project options; in other words, which projects should be considered for delivery. As projects are explored some prequalification will be done, and projects are eliminated without thorough assessment.

o Understanding constraints upon delivery and the resources available. This allows the questions how many and what combinations of projects can be undertaken to be answered.

- Understanding and applying selection criteria, filtering out or eliminating unsuitable projects and prioritizing those left. The intention is to match optimally the projects undertaken to the resources available.
- Reviewing the complete set of projects in the portfolio and matching this with the portfolio objectives.
- Responding to the dynamic nature of an organization and its ever-changing needs and situations.

Project portfolios are often compared to investment portfolios. In an investment portfolio choices are made about which set of investments to make to meet the objectives of a set of investors. Typically, investment portfolios are managed according to factors such as the funds available for investment, the level of risk the investor is willing to take, and the investment requirements. Considerations include issues such as whether an investor wants to maximize short-term returns, minimize risks, make an income or capital growth, and has any favoured or disfavoured sectors for investment. Similarly, in a project portfolio decisions are being made about which projects an organization should invest in, relative to the resources available, to meet a set of organizational goals. These goals should be derived from the organization's strategy.

The first challenge of portfolio management is to determine what the objectives of the portfolio are. Although this can seem obvious, the question "what is the portfolio setting out to achieve" is often forgotten. Portfolio objectives should be aligned closely to strategy. Examples of portfolio goals could be to maximize the return from the available project resources; to ensure alignment of projects with strategic intent, for example, ensuring that projects are contributing to a strategic objective such as increasing customer satisfaction; or to achieve specific targets, such as revenue growth of £100m, cost savings of £250m, headcount reductions of 500.

Having determined what the portfolio objectives are, the next step is to establish what the choices of projects are. This is often a rather haphazard process, as different departments or divisions generate their own ideas for projects and submit them for consideration. As was identified in Chapter 2, project ideas may come directly from strategy, may be generated by departmental or divisional strategies, or may be non-strategic.

The ideas for projects ideally need to be collected in a way that will ease comparisons between alternatives. Information has to be gathered on each project, often in a standard document. Information that helps size and categorize the project ideas is useful; for example, what will the project achieve? what resources will it use to achieve this? what degree of risk is there in achieving this?

In an unconstrained world an organization could pursue all the projects it could identify which have a positive business case. But organizations have constraints in terms of human resource, money and time. These constraints place limits on the projects which can be undertaken. Sometimes other factors such as space in a factory or time on an expensive piece of machinery are also resource constraints on projects. Like an investment manager needing to know the funds available to invest, before projects can be effectively selected the amount of resources available must be assessed.

The fact that resources constrain the decision as to what projects may be undertaken is not the only factor limiting the number of projects. All projects result in change in an organization. Change causes disruption, and an organization can only absorb a certain amount of change at any one time. The capacity to execute projects is also a function of the capacity of the organization to accept and absorb the resultant change. For instance, a project may successfully develop a great new IT system, but unless the department the IT system is intended for has the time to test, learn and generally get used to the new system, it will not be successfully implemented.

Once the constraints are understood, the next stage is to select projects. Selecting projects consists of two activities. First is filtering, that is, the removal of some projects and the creation of a shorter list of projects for further review. Filtering asks two questions: is a project desirable? and is it feasible? A project is desirable if it contributes to the objectives set out in a way that is acceptable to the organization. A project is feasible if it can achieve its goals within the resources available and with an acceptable level of risk. Only if a project is both desirable and feasible should it be accepted for consideration. Following filtering, the second stage is then to prioritize the projects that remain. Prioritization is the basis for sequencing the order the projects will be done in real life. The higher the priority the sooner the project will be done; the lower, the later it will start. Often the lowest priority projects will not be done because of resource constraints.

A problem with selecting projects is that developing and collecting the information to assess and compare projects uses the same scarce resources that work to deliver the projects. Ironically, there may not only be contention between different projects for the same resources; there may be contention for resources to assess projects with. It is not unusual for organizations to struggle with assessment of projects simply because all the people to do the assessment are busy on projects. To ease this it can be helpful to have a prequalification to remove projects which are irrelevant or unworthy of further analysis without doing detailed data gathering. This relies on management judgement, but it is often possible to reduce significantly the overall number of projects without detailed assessment.

Once projects have been selected and prioritized, the highest priority projects can be initiated. The portfolio manager has an ongoing role in governing live projects, but the main activity of delivery can be handed over to the appointed project manager.

To ease comprehension of the portfolio selection process, the activities of project ideas generation, understanding resources and selecting between options are shown in this chapter as a linear series of steps. In practice it is highly iterative. For example, several projects may be given high priority. However, it is possible that once analysed, the projects may in total use more resources than is available. In this case prioritization has to be visited again.

Portfolio selection also has to consider the relationships between different projects, and the risk associated with them. Some projects have inter-dependencies, and there is no point choosing one unless all the projects it is dependent upon are also chosen. In contrast, some projects conflict mutually, and it is only sensible to do one or the other.

Project and programme managers will manage the risk on their individual endeavours. But a portfolio has a cumulative set of risks. A well-designed portfolio can balance risk, mitigating high-risk projects with some low-risk ones. A poorly designed portfolio can magnify risk.

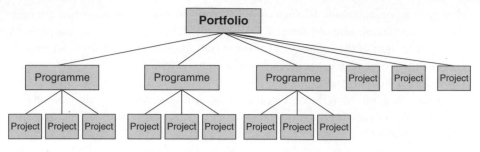

Diagram 3.1 Projects, programmes and portfolios

Portfolio selection can appear to be a static activity that is done now and again. It is not. Organizations are subject to continuous change. What was a critical issue when a project was selected, may cease to be critical before a project is completed. New ideas, opportunities and competitive threats arise all the time and have to be responded to. These may require different projects, which need the portfolio to be regularly reviewed and amended.

Maintenance of a project portfolio is like managing an investment portfolio. An investment manager does not select assets and then leave the portfolio alone. The investment portfolio is constantly tweaked as market conditions evolve and the returns from different assets change. Assets will be sold and different assets added. This is true of a healthy project portfolio as well. Projects may be eliminated and new projects added. However, a project portfolio is very different from an investment portfolio in one aspect: the concept of liquidity. Projects are not liquid assets that can be traded like investments. Often a decision to stop a project will require the complete write off of the investment made in the partially completed work.

The final stage in portfolio selection is ensuring that the result from all the projects in the portfolio will meet the portfolio objectives. So, for example, if an objective is to achieve £250m of cost reduction and £100m of revenue increases from projects, the portfolio manager must ascertain whether the projects across the portfolio will achieve this. This should take account of the risk of different projects, in the same way that an investment manager will take account of the risk of different assets.

What if the portfolio does not meet the objectives? It needs to be changed. Projects with a greater contribution to the objectives must be added, and those which do not achieve enough should be cancelled.

The next few sections in this chapter present each of the above steps in detail. Diagram 3.1 provides a simple process flow for portfolio management.

Define portfolio objectives and metrics

Portfolio objectives define the overall goals to be achieved by an organization's project portfolio. Having defined objectives helps in shaping the constituents of the portfolio and in deciding whether the results from the entire portfolio will meet the full needs of the business. A portfolio may contain a value-adding set of projects, but that does not mean it is the right set of projects that will meet business needs. If there are no clearly defined objectives, an organization cannot be certain whether the set of projects it is investing in will meet its needs. Setting portfolio objectives is similar to setting objectives and targets for any department in a business. They define the value the business will receive from its investment in the portfolio, and seek to motivate the portfolio manager to improve and maximize the benefits.

Portfolio objectives may contain both quantified objectives as well as qualitative objectives to give general guidance and direction. Both are useful in shaping a portfolio and reviewing it against the needs of the business. Objectives should be treated as guidance not as absolute rules. There will be occasions when projects need to be introduced to a portfolio for expediency, or for reasons not foreseen when the objectives were set, but these occasions should be exceptions (or the objectives need to be revised).

The nature of the portfolio objectives will vary greatly from business to business. Examples of possible objectives include

1. To maximize the return from the project resources available
2. To keep all resources utilized
3. To balance between meeting short-term and long-term objectives
4. To balance between customer satisfaction and cost reduction projects
5. To ensure alignment of projects with strategic intent of increasing customer satisfaction
6. To achieve specific targets, such as revenue growth of £100m, cost saving of £250m, headcount reduction of 500
7. To ensure that changes resulting from projects is spread across the year and avoids any peaks in the business cycle

The responsibility for ensuring that portfolio objectives are defined belongs to the portfolio managers. However, the actual decisions on what objectives are to be accepted should lie with the leadership team of an organization.

The identification of portfolio objectives should start with a review of an organization's strategy. Portfolio management is a key tool in the implementation of strategy, and the way this is achieved is to align portfolio objectives with the strategy. If the portfolio objectives are derived from strategy, then the resulting selected projects should also be aligned with the strategy.

Determining portfolio objectives requires analysis of needs, followed by debate by the leadership team. The debate is about both refining the specific objectives and understanding the role of the projects in the organization and the opportunities and risks they expose the business to. The debate on project portfolio objectives is an important part of organizational governance (APM, 2004).

Debate on portfolio objectives should ensure not only that the most appropriate set of objectives is selected, but also that there is a thorough understanding of the implications of them. There is a risk that portfolio objectives can be defined without a full understanding of the implications. For example,

- o The following objectives may at first glance seem both reasonable and compatible:
  - To maximize the return from the project resources available
  - To keep all resources utilized

In reality, keeping all resources fully utilized and maximizing returns from resources are different and sometimes conflicting goals. (This is discussed in Chapter 4.)

- The following objectives are about finding a balance in a portfolio:
  - To balance between meeting short-term and long-term objectives
  - To balance between customer satisfaction and cost reduction projects
- Without such a view there is a risk that a portfolio may become overly focused on a specific type of projects, such as those that show the best short-term financial returns.

Once the objectives have been debated they should be agreed on. This agreement should be made at the most senior levels in the business. Agreeing on strategy is accepted to be something done by the most senior managers in a business, whilst its implementation through specific operational decisions will be delegated. Similarly, the selection of specific projects can be delegated, but the setting of portfolio objectives should not be.

Portfolio objectives should be documented by the portfolio manager. If they are not documented it is not possible to be sure that the different management stakeholders understand what they are and have agreed to them. Often this does not happen, and there is a reliance on a general awareness of them, without necessarily a consistent understanding of what the objectives are. Having documented objectives makes it easier to ensure compliance, and if exceptions occur they are explicit and authorized. Also a documented set of objectives means that they stay consistent through the life of a portfolio, unless changed deliberately.

Portfolio objectives should be reviewed periodically to ensure they continue to meet a business's needs. A typical cycle time is to set them annually with quarterly reviews. If there are modifications in strategic direction, portfolio objectives will need to be adapted accordingly.

Identify potential projects

To populate the project portfolio an inventory of the proposed projects must be collected. If portfolio management is being introduced for the first time then this inventory should also include an assessment of all projects that are already running. This can be a significant undertaking, but it is an essential basis for effective portfolio management.

The inventory should collect enough information on each project to enable the following to be determined:

- The implications of the project for the business
- The implications for other projects in the portfolio
- The implications of including the project on the whole portfolio
- Desirability of the project
- Feasibility of the project
- The appropriate priority (order) to execute the project

The minimum information that will be required to make this assessment consists of

- The objective of the project – what is it setting out to achieve and why is this important to the business
- The deliverables from the project – what will be created that will achieve this objective

- The benefits the project will deliver – what the project will contribute towards short-and long-term objectives of the business. This is typically done in the form of a business case.
- The amount and type of resources the project will require, with an indication of the schedule of using these resources
- The level of risk associated with the project
- The change impact of the project upon the organization, when implemented
- The relationship and any inter-dependency of the project to other projects in the portfolio.

It is useful to have standard templates or forms, which are available across an organization, for the collection of this information. Ideas for projects will be generated regularly in organizations, and this is a continuous process.

There are a number of practical challenges in collecting this information. These include deciding on the level of granularity of information to collect; determining what counts as a project for consideration in the portfolio; and understanding the level of risk of a project and the implications of this risk for the portfolio and the business.

Granularity of information

When information is collected on anything it can be at differing levels of detail or *granularity*. One of the challenges in portfolio management is to decide the level of granularity to keep with regard to information about projects. Set the information at too low a level of detail and it will take excessive time and resources to collect, decision-making will be ponderous and control is overly centralized. In addition, very detailed information often becomes out-of-date by the time the collection process is completed. There is an inclination therefore to collect high-level information. However, set the information at too limited detail, and the accuracy of decision-making and the level of control provided by portfolio management is limited.

The practical answer, therefore, is to collect information at a level of detail related to the importance and risk associated with a specific decision, and to vary the amount of information collected depending on the scale of the project. The largest programmes, requiring significant investments, have to have enough information to provide confidence to management about the decision they are making. It can take months to collect the information about a major programme, and the collection of this information is effectively a project in its own right. Small projects may require relatively simple information that can be defined on one or two pages of text by a knowledgeable specialist.

Normally the understanding of a project will improve as the project progresses. For very large programmes, spread over months or even years, the understanding of the programme objectives and deliverables will be significantly greater at the end of the programme than at the beginning. This is an example of progressive elaboration. By linking different levels of portfolio approval to stages in the project lifecycle, portfolio management is able to vary the granularity of information as the project progresses.

What counts as a portfolio project?

Another challenge is agreeing which types of projects should be included in the portfolio and which should not. Theoretically, all projects should be included. Cooper *et al* claim that an effective portfolio must contain at least 80% of projects (Cooper, Edgett, and Kleinschmidt, 2000). What counts as a project? It may be obvious that a 500 man-year endeavour to develop a major new IT system is a project. Common sense indicates that whilst completing a 30-minute task can logically be thought of as a project, it benefits little from being considered as one. There is a grey area between these two extremes. Activities which take a few days, or even a few weeks, for a small group of people need control and management, but there will be thousands of such activities in a large business.

Very small projects gain little from being reviewed in a portfolio, and if too many day-to-day change activities are included the portfolio becomes unwieldy. In addition, subjecting small activities to portfolio management will slow down progress. It may require more management decision-making time to select between large numbers of small initiatives than is required to actually complete the activities. When portfolio management is applied to even the smallest of projects it is not unusual to see tasks that would take only a few days' effort to complete waiting for weeks or months to be accepted and prioritized.

Therefore, in practice there should be a threshold size for a project to be included for consideration in the portfolio. This throws up a subsequent problem. A small initiative that takes a few days to complete may be unworthy for consideration by a portfolio management process – it uses too small an amount of resources, has limited benefits and has a minimal change impact. However, organizations usually undertake thousands of small changes that cumulatively may have more impact than even the largest of programmes. Moreover, small initiative does not always mean small business impact.

One way to resolve this is to manage a portfolio at a programme level. Projects can be bundled into programmes, either because they really do form a single programme, or because they relate to a common area of the business. So, all projects impacting the sales department can be bundled together as the sales change programme. This programme overall can then be prioritized and resources allocated. The programme manager subsequently resolves more detailed prioritizations within the scope of the programme. This is not a perfect answer, as the resource and benefit estimates from a broad bundle of projects with limited definitions are usually inaccurate, but it can provide a pragmatic balance between extremes.

There is no right or wrong answer about the size of projects to be managed by a portfolio. The decision depends on the culture of the organization and the relative delegated levels of authority. It also depends on the relative levels of change and amount of resources available. An organization with comparatively little change and more available resources can afford to prioritize only the largest of programmes. An organization with significant resource constraints and many possible changes will need to consider even small projects for prioritization. Thus, for example, organizations in financial difficulty will place significant constraints upon project activity and may require authorization and prioritization for even the smallest of projects.

Risk

One of the main components in the management of any project or programme is understanding and managing risk. There are many tools and approaches for assessing and managing risk within project and programme management. Risk also should be managed at the portfolio level.

The aim of portfolio-level risk management is to ensure that the organization understands the cumulative risk from the portfolio, that this level of risk is acceptable to the organization, and that it can be managed so that the portfolio achieves its objectives.

Risk across a portfolio is complex. Risk arises in project portfolios not only as a result of the risk from each individual projects, but also because of the inter-relationship between different projects. Inter-dependency between projects, whether at a resource or activity level, means that different projects are linked by a web of risk. A project that is delayed or fails in a task will subsequently delay any other project which requires the same task completed. In addition, if as a result of the delay people work for longer on a project, then they cannot work on other projects requiring the same person, which are therefore also delayed. Any project which is delayed knocks onto other projects.

Risk has many effects. The level of risk on an individual project affects the likelihood that the project will be successfully completed. Risk though permeates beyond the confines of a project and impacts the business as well. A business's results may depend on the completion of a specific project. Targets may be set, and commitments made based on the assumption of successful project completion. Moreover, business operations may be put at risk as a result of the change a project brings about.

Portfolios can magnify risk. However, a portfolio also offers a mechanism to mitigate project-level risks. Depending on the level of risk from a set of projects, additional projects may be included to provide alternative ways to achieve a goal. In the same way that an investment manager accepts that some investments in a portfolio will decline in value, and is mainly concerned with the value of the overall portfolio, a portfolio may be managed to balance risks. This is achieved by selecting a broad range of projects with different risk levels, and by assessing benefits in relation to risk.

Important factors in understanding portfolio-level risk are

- Risk changes, and needs to be monitored on an ongoing basis.
- Projects present risk in terms of the likelihood of whether a specific series of activity will be completed, but also in terms of whether the activities will achieve the expected business benefits. Hence a portfolio may fail in its objectives either because projects fail to be completed or because even if they are completed they fail to achieve the objectives they were set out to achieve.
- Projects affect each other and the risk profile is affected by the inter-relationship between projects.

Risk is discussed in more detail in Chapter 11.

Perform pre-qualification

During project identification, and whilst the detailed information on projects is being collected, it is helpful to have a pre-qualification stage. Pre-qualification eliminates projects which do not have a realistic chance of being selected before detailed assessment is done. Pre-qualification reduces the potentially significant analysis overhead in generating information on project ideas and lessens the management overhead related to selecting projects.

Depending on the situation of the business pre-qualification provides different levels of filtering. For a business with significant resource constraints it is efficient to try and eliminate as many projects as possible during pre-qualification. Of course, this does result in the risk of eliminating potentially valuable projects prior to detailed assessment. For businesses with fewer resource constraints pre-qualification can be a less strict activity.

Pre-qualification works best when there is clear guidance or standard rules for rejecting projects. Typical reasons for removing projects prior to complete assessment include

- The project will be of too large a scale for the organization.
- The project will not deliver sufficient benefits in a timeframe acceptable to the business.
- The project will have too high a risk profile for the company (which includes consideration of competencies and capabilities to deliver new or unusual types of projects).
- The project's concept is inconsistent with the organization's strategy or direction.

Understand constraints

The limitations or constraints on the range of projects that can be undertaken in an organization at any one time, is determined by two factors: what resources are available to undertake projects (these include typically budget and people, but may include other scarce resources); and the rate of change the business is capable of accommodating.

When deciding which projects should be selected there must be at least some understanding of these constraints. This is one of the most complicated parts of portfolio management, and only an overview is provided here. There is more detailed discussion in Chapters 4 and 9 respectively.

Tools for assessing resource constraints vary from the simple to the very sophisticated and complex. They fall into one of three general categories:

- The least sophisticated approach is to start by ignoring any resource constraints. Projects are started in priority order until there is no capacity to do anymore. Whilst it may never be explicitly stated, this is effectively what many organizations do. Such an approach can initially ease the activity of project selection. However, it is often an ineffective and inefficient way of managing resources, and it is unlikely to lead over time to the optimal project mix.

- The most complex way to deal with resource constraints is to attempt to understand the workload for all resources in detail. This is possible in small organizations, and sometimes in specialist companies such as consultancies where determining whether someone is busy or available for more work is relatively simple. For large organizations the overhead of trying to manage a project resource pool like this is often too great. It requires continuous collection of data on every person on current workload and future commitments. Determining if a specific resource is available for projects or not is often complex. Projections on individual availability are subject to error. The resource pool is not fixed, as many resources are available for projects only in some situations. For example, staff in operational functions may work occasionally on projects only in certain situations.

- A compromise is to identify specific scarce resources which typically cause bottlenecks on projects. Usually organizations are not constrained on every type of resource, and it is only some specific resources that determine the number of projects that can be undertaken. This can be a practical and effective way to assess resource constraints.

The understanding and management of resources is discussed in detail in Chapter 4.

The second limiting factor on an organization's capacity to deliver projects is the rate at which change can be implemented into and effectively absorbed by operational departments. Understanding the level of change a business can undertake is complex. Factors which determine the rate at which change can be implemented include

- The number of projects or other changes being performed in parallel. Implementing one change is usually straightforward; implementing many changes on the same group of people or area of a business can be unmanageable.

- Events or specific times in the business cycle. For example, in the retail business there is normally a surge in activity prior to a sale and prior to Christmas. The ability of such organizations to undertake change when they are working at full capacity is limited. In addition, even if there is some capacity for change at such times, the risk to peak sales from change is usually unacceptable.

- The level of competency in change management and familiarity of the organization with change.

The solution is to manage change as a deliberate activity across projects. For every area of the business that is going to be subject to change it is helpful to build a map or plan of change impacting the area over time, and phase projects so that only a manageable amount of change is implemented in any one area at one time. (This is described in more detail in Chapter 9.)

The rate of change which will result from projects is often not factored into project selection by organizations. This is because it is usually not a problem at project initiation. Whilst insufficient resources delay projects from the start, change constraints do not. Change constraints limit the ability to implement the deliverables from projects.

If change constraints are not considered in project selection it is likely that one or more of the following will occur regularly:

- o The rate of change in the organization will be uneven, with occasions when there is more change happening than can be accommodated.
- o Projects may start on time, but the end is delayed as projects effectively queue up to implement their deliverables. This is inefficient in terms of resource usage and may delay benefits realization.
- o Project implementation is sub-optimal. Projects end on time, but the resulting change is not fully achieved in operational departments. This results in reduced benefits.

Select projects

Having gained a view of the possible projects an organization must choose which ones it will do. This is a two-step activity. Projects will be filtered out, that is, some will be completely rejected from further consideration. Having filtered the projects and reduced the options, the next stage is to prioritize the remaining projects. (Pre-qualification is also a form of filtering; the difference is that pre-qualification is done with limited information.)

Prioritization is used to determine the order in which projects are implemented. In principle the higher the priority a project has the sooner it should be started. However, scheduling projects is not as simple as mechanistically applying prioritization. For example, sometimes lower-priority projects are not in contention for resources with higher-priority ones so can start earlier than or at the same time as a higher-priority project. There will be situations in which a high-priority project has a dependency on a lower-priority one. The lower-priority project must be started sooner than it would be otherwise to enable the dependency to be met.

The outcomes from filtering and prioritization are often referred to as *keep, kill* or *delay.*

Filtering projects

Choosing what to reject from a project portfolio is as important as the prioritization of what will be accepted. Rejection is achieved by filtering out projects. Projects are filtered according to two criteria:

- o *Undesirable*: A project is undesirable if it has an unacceptable business case, such as not meeting minimum financial returns. Alternatively a project is undesirable if it does not meet the objectives of the business, or goes against the strategic direction of the business.
- o *Unfeasible*: A project is unfeasible if it cannot be completed successfully or will not achieve the planned outcome. Occasionally a project is clearly unfeasible, but often it is less apparent. Determining whether a project is unfeasible is a judgement best made by someone with experience. Factors to be considered are the scale and novelty of the project; the skills and competencies of the business relative to the needs of the project; and the level of project risk. For more complex situations it is necessary to run a feasibility study.

An effective way to filter projects is to develop a standard checklist of yes/no questions, for example, whether a project meets a minimum financial hurdle rate. Projects can be checked against this list, and only if sufficient questions are answered *yes* they are taken forward for prioritization.

Feasibility studies

For complex projects there may not be enough information to make an accurate decision on a project's feasibility. Decision-makers may require more information to make a decision. Feasibility studies, which seek to research into unclear areas about a project, provide this information.

Feasibility studies take many forms, but whatever shape they are in, they reduce the risk of incorrectly accepting or rejecting a project. Although feasibility studies can be considered as a stage in a project's lifecycle, they can be managed as projects in their own right. The feasibility study relating to a large programme may be a significant project in itself. Feasibility studies have a cost and absorb resources, so in turn must be reviewed and prioritized.

Feasibility studies can struggle to produce a viable business case in their own right, and so can be hard to prioritize. A feasibility study usually delivers limited tangible value to a business other than information and knowledge about a project (which in turn may deliver value). The decision whether to undertake a feasibility study is a trade-off between the cost and the value of the information determined. Whilst good information undoubtedly has great value to a business, quantifying it is often difficult or impractical.

Feasibility studies should be designed to provide the specific information needed to determine whether a project should proceed. Examples of the sort of information that can be determined include

- Technical feasibility to determine whether a project will successfully create the expected deliverables
- Commercial feasibility to determine whether a project will achieve its business case
- Market feasibility (usually in the case of new products) to determine whether the business's customers will buy the product
- Organizational feasibility to determine the operational impact of making the change resulting from a project successfully.
- Exploring requirements and designs to produce more accurate plans, costs and resource profiles for a project.
- Exploring project options. In some projects there is a known problem to overcome, but multiple possible solutions. Feasibility studies can explore different project options, to evaluate the alternatives and select the best solution.

A feasibility study can be run in different ways, using various levels of resources and taking different lengths of time. There is no direct link between scale of feasibility study and quality of information. However, typically, if a feasibility study is well-designed, the more resources applied and the longer it takes the better the information it will provide as to the feasibility of the resultant programme – and hence the reduced risk of making a wrong decision about a project. The size and scope of a feasibility study should be determined by the level of risk involved in and the investment required by the resulting project or programme.

Prioritization

Prioritization is more complicated than filtering, as it is not only about the merits of an individual project, but also about its comparative value to the business in relation to other projects. Although prioritization primarily determines the order of projects, it is effectively a further stage of filtering as well. There will often be more projects prioritized than can be completed, and the lowest-priority projects may never be started. The results of prioritization decide the sequence of accepted projects, and also may result in decisions to accept projects for a later date and put them on hold.

Prioritization should take account of various types of projects. It needs either flexibility to account for differences between different types of projects or explicit rules to ensure that the portfolio is not unbalanced in favour of one type of project over another. Examples of project types, with different profiles that are not easy to compare with each other include

- o *Must-do projects*: for example meeting legislative requirements or fixing a major operational problem. In reality there are very few real "must-do" projects, but there will be some. Projects, such as conformance to regulation may have to be done, but determining their priority relative to a significant revenue opportunity can be problematic.
- o *Maintenance projects*: enhancing existing business processes, infrastructure or systems. Such projects typically reduce costs or improve throughput, and normally have a moderate level of risk.
- o *Revenue growth projects*: such as launching of new products. Such projects normally have easily identifiable budget impacts and hence simple business cases. The level of risk will vary significantly.
- o *Transformation*: major or long-term business change programmes. Such transformations can radically change cost base or direction of a business and offer significant business improvement opportunities, but often have a high risk profile.

There are many ways of deciding the priority of projects. The simplest ways are

- o *First come first served*: literally starting projects in the order in which the idea for them arises. This is not really prioritization, and usually this is an ineffective way of selecting a series of projects that will meet the portfolio objectives. However, there is an element of this in selection, as initial projects started will usually be those available for review, and there will be a bias in favour of project ideas that are generated soonest.
- o *Urgency*: some projects are often prioritized high simply because they are urgent. Resolving immediate business problems or taking short-term opportunities are often too great a temptation for managers to resist. Prioritizing based on urgency rarely provides the optimal selection of projects as some of the most important and value-adding projects may not be urgent.

- *Management subjective*: a review of the options by senior managers and a subjective judgement of the best choices informed by the portfolio objectives. Although this risks individual bias associated with limited information, it can be fast and effective, especially for smaller portfolios and with a leadership team having a detailed understanding of the business.

More objective ways of prioritization are based on some quantified or objective criteria. These criteria should be aligned to the portfolio objectives. Criteria that can be considered include

- *Financial*: a review of financial criteria, such as Internal Rate or Return (IRR) or Net Present Value (NPV) and the selection of the projects with the best financial return as the highest priority. Such criteria provide a clear-cut and objective decision-making process. Financial criteria alone are usually not completely effective, as some projects must be done irrespective of financial returns (e.g. legal compliance). Also some projects have very clear financial cases (e.g. launching a new product), whilst alternative investments (e.g. improving staff satisfaction) may offer better opportunities but struggle to assess financial benefits with any degree of accuracy. Pure financial criteria should only be used if the only portfolio objectives are financial. Businesses that use financial measures alone tend to have poorer portfolio performance than those that use other factors (Cooper et al., 2001).
- *Strategic alignment*: selecting projects based on their alignment to the strategy and the degree of achievement of strategic goals they offer.
- *Multiple variables*: the variables will include financial, strategic alignment and other portfolio objectives, and can include others such as
  - Probability of technical success
  - Probability of commercial success (for new products etc)
  - Probability of operational success (for business change etc)
  - Impact on specific operational measures
  - Skills development opportunities

Assessing multiple variables can run from simple weighting and scoring systems to complicated tools such as Analytical Hierarchy Process (AHP). Graphical representations, such as bubble charts, are useful for showing how a set of projects balances between different business objectives.

Typically, prioritization is achieved through a combination of management judgement with some supporting analytical information across multiple variables. A degree of pragmatism must exist, as whatever system is devised there will usually be important projects which do not fit the normal criteria for prioritization.

It is less common to apply more advanced techniques derived from investment management, such as *Real Options*. Real Options provides a way not only to value the known costs and benefits of a project, but also to include a value of the options or flexibility that a project provides a business. For example, consider a business that buys property for expansion. The property includes additional land that may be built on at a later date. The new offices have an immediate value to the business, but the land also has value to the business in terms of flexibility for future expansion. It is this flexibility that Real Options helps to evaluate, and provides a way of valuing.

Real Options approaches a project in terms of the decisions that may be made to redirect a project, rather than a fixed plan that will deliver a specific already-known set of deliverables only. Looking at projects in terms of options creates an understanding of the value of flexibility. This can lead to more phases in projects and programmes. Instead of large committed plans that lock an organization into a predefined future path, Real Options favours breaking projects and decisions into stages, as that gives flexibility.

An approach like Real Options arguably provides a better basis for decision-making than standard financial tools, such as NPV, and in many situations reflects the reality of projects. However, Real Options are complex and many organizations do not possess the competency in this technique.

Another more complex technique for portfolio optimization is *Efficient Frontier*. Efficient Frontier is normally applied to financial portfolios. It shows the possibilities and options for optimizing a portfolio and the trade-offs associated with them. As with Real Options the application of such a technique to project portfolios is rare and requires specialist skills.

There are two common mistakes that are often made in prioritizing projects in a portfolio: confusing urgency with importance and not considering the dependency between projects.

There will always be short-term problems or opportunities in a business that are perceived as urgent. For example, a sales opportunity may exist only if a business can respond in the next four days. This is urgent. Businesses are often very much aware of the urgent problems and opportunities, and there is a tendency to prioritize any projects associated with them higher. But, urgent situations are not always the most important. A bigger sale may be available, but only with more work in some months' time. The danger with an excessive focus on resourcing urgent issues is that it crowds out the ability to pursue the more important opportunities.

Projects may have an inter-dependency at a resource level (i.e. a person with a specialist skill can work on one project or the other), or activity (i.e. a project can only complete when a different project has completed some of its work). Where projects have an inter-dependency this has to be taken into account when determining prioritizations.

Portfolio prioritization is an ongoing process. Although there tends to be peaks and troughs in project volumes because of the annual budget cycle in a business, there will be a continuous stream of requests for projects. A typical effective process is to review, filter and prioritize new projects on a monthly basis. Portfolio selection is fundamentally concerned with making trade-off decisions between options, and there will be many views in an organization. Unless the organization is highly centralized with a strong command and control culture, successful selection therefore is collaborative and based on open debate and decision-making.

Case Study **3.1** **HOW DO YOU GO ABOUT SELECTING THE PROJECTS IN YOUR PORTFOLIO?**

Jayne Cockill is an experienced programme and team manager. She has been responsible for a range of projects and programmes ranging from launching products, developing software and supporting business change. She has an in depth knowledge of AGILE methods.

Jayne Cockill

Let me set the scene for you. I was working in a fast-paced, project-orientated business. It had about 180 staff and 200K customers. Staff number was kept low through very high levels of business process automation, and automated customer self-service. Customers included both individual consumers and businesses. Although it was fast-paced it was more reactive than proactive as our ability to predict future needs was limited.

Customer demands and the market situation were continually evolving. At best we could predict needs up to three months ahead. We had experienced the situation of regularly kicking off projects, but as the projects progressed requirements would change and sponsors would change their minds. Consequently, projects regularly were abandoned before completion. Although we started a lot of projects, we completed many fewer. Internal stakeholder needs were not being met. Stakeholders were dissatisfied and lacking in confidence in our ability to deliver.

To resolve this problem I took a step back. What was the problem? Although the market was very dynamic, there were lots of things we knew we would have to do irrespective of what happened in the market. When I looked at the way we prioritized work it was based on "he who shouts loudest". This meant that the most important projects did not always get started, and prioritizations were volatile. I decided we needed to completely re-think the way we prioritized and the way we delivered projects.

The starting point for my re-think was to understand the company direction, and to review what had gone wrong in the projects we had failed on. The company direction was based on automating as much of our processes as possible, so that as the company grew it did not need to significantly increase headcount. We were a business focussed on projects – whether they were delivering new products for our customers, or continuing to develop our own internal systems. Because we were so project- and software-orientated, project and software development skills were important to us – and all such staff had to be kept as busy as possible. High utilization was important both because there was a lot to do and also because project staff could be capitalized when working on projects. For financial reasons, it was important to achieve high-capitalization rates.

I decided we needed some more structure in the way we selected and prioritized projects, without creating a complex bureaucracy. I put a simple template in place to define projects. It captured what the project broadly was; what the project gave to the business; and what needed to happen to make the project occur, and noted whether it was mandatory for legal or regulatory reasons. The definition of what the project gave to the business was related to the company's business model and captured the project's expected impact on metrics like cost savings, customer satisfaction, increased customer numbers or customer revenues and any opportunity to automate (as this was the company's strategy).

As the information was put into tables in the business case template it would apply a weighting system to give the project a score. This score was the input to prioritization. This paper-based form was soon replaced by an intranet system which was visible to everyone in the business, and which anyone could add to.

The score for a project gave an indicative prioritization, but the final prioritization was determined by a board. Given the importance of projects to this business the board was formed of the CEO and CTO plus representatives of key divisions who needed projects – such as the Director of Customer Services. They discussed and applied judgement before deciding which projects to do and what order to do them in. In some situations a project sponsor would be asked to attend this board meeting to describe and justify a project. At the end of the meeting a prioritized list of projects was produced.

The prioritization meeting was held monthly. Initially it was held every three months. The prioritization board meetings were then aligned with quarterly shareholder meetings. Shareholders could also add projects that they felt were important to the progress of the business. For example, following one shareholder meeting, a project was started to buy and merge a competitor into our operations.

The project board meeting was re-scheduled to monthly as three-monthly was not responsive enough for our business. Most of our projects could be delivered within a month as we applied an AGILE approach to all projects (Jayne's approach to project delivery is explained in the case study in Chapter 6). Delivery could take anything from two days to six months depending on the project, but the vast majority were completed in a month.

Applying this structured-prioritization process significantly improved our throughput of projects and enhanced our internal stakeholders' levels of satisfaction. Although no one got everything they wanted because the combination of good prioritization and rapid delivery meant we could work on around 20 projects in parallel with 7 completing every month, stakeholders could see we were making progress and delivering value. This raised confidence generally in our ability to complete projects.

Review the project portfolio

Once an organization knows the projects it is going to invest in, it is time to review the complete portfolio to optimize it. This stage is often missed out, but it is important, and it can be what differentiates the most successful portfolio management from the less effective. It changes portfolio management from being a useful way of allocating resources to being a true strategic tool and one which adds significant value.

The review starts where prioritization finishes. Prioritization is essential, but prioritization of projects alone is a crude mechanism to select a portfolio. Review sets out to ensure that

- The complete portfolio meets the defined portfolio objectives, including the need to balance between different objectives.
- The portfolio does this in an acceptable way (cost, risk etc).
- Changes are made to the portfolio if the objectives will not be reached in an acceptable way.

Reviews are even relevant where complex modelling and application of optimization algorithms have been applied. Such optimization will be affected by the errors that will exist in input data, which is often built from assumptions and estimates (Nawrocki, 2000). Therefore, there is at least the need for a "common sense" review of the priorities defined.

There are several issues in choosing projects without considering the portfolio as a whole, which can be rectified by a review:

- *Disregarding relationships between projects*: There are various levels of dependency between projects that must be considered to enable successful delivery.
- *Using project projections (time, resource, benefits) as facts without considering risk and human error*: Project estimates are prone to error and risk that change through a project's life. Making commitments based on a project portfolio without consideration of levels of risk is likely to lead to missed targets.
- *Taking no account of impact of change on the business*: projects result in change, and business departments can only absorb a certain amount of change at any one time. Giving high priority to projects which will result in unmanageable levels of change in one or more departments is counterproductive. The impact of change is determined by the complete set of projects.
- *Ignoring portfolio objectives*: The objectives are not about starting as many projects as possible, but getting the most value delivered, however that is defined in a specific organization. Not considering how the portfolio as a whole meets business objectives is a common failing.

Thus there are four areas that should be considered in reviewing a project portfolio to overcome these four issues:

1. Project inter-dependency
2. Change profile
3. Risk profile
4. Portfolio objectives

The remainder of this section looks at each of these issues in turn, and then discusses the process of portfolio review.

Project inter-dependency

Projects are not completely independent items in a portfolio, but have relationships. In reviewing a portfolio the following relationships should be explored to optimize the portfolio:

- *Activity*: Are the projects prioritized in such a way that any inter-dependency at an activity level is consistent with the prioritization? For example, does prioritization ensure that no high-priority project is dependent on a lower-priority project?
- *Resource*: Look for situations in which too many projects will require the same resources at the same time which will result in unscheduled delays in projects.
- *Deliverables*: Some deliverables are complementary; others will conflict. For example, a project to reduce headcount is unlikely to be complementary to

a project to increase staff satisfaction. In addition, there can be opportunities to gain efficiencies by combining projects producing similar or related deliverables, and hence remove duplicated efforts (though this can impact benefits realization, which is discussed in Chapter 10).

Change profile

Portfolio review should examine the timing of changes resulting from projects relative to the departments that the change is being implemented in. The objective is to avoid situations in which too much or too complex change will be implemented in any one area at the same time. Overloading change typically results in either delayed projects or reduced benefits or both.

Change is described in more detail in Chapter 9.

Risk profile

Each project in a portfolio has a range of risks associated with it. The portfolio will accumulate risk across projects, but also has the opportunity to mitigate risk. For example, a highly risky project to launch an innovative new product, may be balanced by a project to enhance existing products in case the new product is not successful.

Risk is discussed in more detail in Chapter 11.

Portfolio objectives

The final component of portfolio review is to assess the outcome from the projects in the portfolio in comparison to the original portfolio objectives. The core questions to ask are

- o Will the portfolio meet its objectives? (This includes ensuring that the portfolio has the right balance of projects to meet different objectives, for example, short-term projects versus longer-term investments.)
- o Is there sufficient contingency in the portfolio to take account of risk and still achieve the portfolio objectives?
- o Is there sufficient optionality in the portfolio to take account of unknowns or key decisions pending?

Responding to a portfolio review

Assuming that a portfolio review results in one or more issues with the selection of projects, it should result in some action. Possible actions to overcome the issues raised are

- o Alter the priority or phasing of one or more projects
- o Modify the scope of one or more projects
- o Change the combination of projects in the portfolio by adding or deleting projects

Frequency of portfolio review

Portfolio review is an ongoing process, which should be aligned to the normal business cycles. A high-level review should be held every time significant new projects are added to the portfolio, normally on a monthly or quarterly basis. A more thorough review should be undertaken on an annual basis, or whenever significant business events resulting in changes to portfolio objectives happen.

Projects are prioritized and accepted into the portfolio when they are started. Good portfolio management also requires projects to return at key stages in their lifecycle to ensure both it is still sensible to progress with the project and that the prioritization remains optimal. Such a review should consider changes to the project and to the portfolio, as well as any wider business changes.

The annual budgeting and target-setting processes

The portfolio selection process described is impacted by budgets and budgetary processes. Most organizations work to an annual budget and target-setting cycle. There is a two-way relationship between portfolio selection and management, and this cycle: budgets determine the availability of funds and impact the choice and timing of projects; and projects contribute to the achievement of committed targets embedded within budget predictions.

Budget cycles and availability of funds

The budget determines the availability of funds and therefore the total sum available for projects. In some cases a budget will permit, or constrain, specific large programmes of work which require significant budget spending. (This means initial project projections need to be completed in the prior year's budget to allow budget estimations to be included.)

The nature of the annual budget cycle impacts the timing of projects. There is a tendency for a peak of projects to start at the beginning of the budget year when funds become available. There is also often a desire for projects to complete within a budget cycle. Where this is not possible or projects are late, decisions on whether to roll over projects or to stop them must be made. This affects decisions on project-related accruals.

Budgets are also impacted by changing projections on costs and benefits as projects progress.

Achieving targets

Annual targets will depend to some extent on the successful completion of projects and the realization of their expected benefits. Due to the inherent level of error in project estimates, actual benefits delivered will vary from targets as projects complete. Portfolio management has a role to play in ensuring the project risk to committed targets is understood, and where possible that there are contingency projects to make up for any under-achievement.

It is not only the absolute level of benefit from projects that matters, but from a budgeting perspective, the timing is also critical. If a project is late, it becomes progressively harder to achieve expected financial targets. For example, if a project is meant to deliver £1m per month in savings at the end of the second quarter of the year, it will deliver £6m in-year-savings. However, if the project is 3 months late it will only deliver £3m of in-year-savings, or to achieve £6m would have to deliver savings equalling £2m per month.

Achieving benefits is discussed in more detail in Chapter 10.

In-life portfolio management

Portfolio management can appear as a static activity in which an organization decides on which projects to do, and then simply does them to achieve the expected benefits. But real life is dynamic and outcomes are rarely as expected. In-life portfolio management checks to ensure that the projects in the portfolio should stay because they are still adding sufficient value to the business.

The circumstances in which a project portfolio operates change in the following ways:

o *Project outcomes differ*: Projects can take longer or use different resources than what was planned. One project may have a knock-on effect on another. Projects regularly achieve benefits different from original expectations and at times different from the original commitments. The assessed risk in a project changes as the project progresses and becomes better understood, and the corresponding risk profile of the entire portfolio also varies over time.

o *The operational situation constantly alters*: Problems arise in business operations that need emergency responses which remove resources from projects. Operational departments can find themselves less able to support projects or accept the resulting change from projects due to unexpected peaks and troughs in workloads.

o *Business-needs change*: The competitive, regulatory and social environment in which a business exists constantly evolves. Business needs and strategy are derived from this environment, and portfolio objectives are in turn derived from the business needs. Portfolio objectives need periodic review and updating. In addition, knowing that needs will change makes the need for optionality in a portfolio higher.

The result of all of these factors is that the portfolio should be adapted over time. What may be the optimal portfolio at one time, may not be at a later date. Some projects can get added; others may need to be removed; individual project scopes and priorities may be altered; and the overall project mix may need to be modified. In-life portfolio management ensures that decision-making concerning project approval is not simply a one-off process at project initiation, but is revisited as projects progress and is in consideration of the whole balance of the portfolio.

If a portfolio is not adapted as the context evolves it risks being no longer relevant to the business. On the other hand, if projects are continually abandoned as the situation changes, no value is ever delivered.

In-life portfolio management is a process of regularly reviewing the situation, and making recommendations on alterations to the portfolio. The leadership team then decides whether to act on these recommendations. In-life management of portfolio should work hand-in-hand with the previously described portfolio reviews.

To do this successfully the portfolio manager must have access to good information on the business and the status of projects. Tracking projects is discussed in more detail in Chapter 8.

The regular review should also account for changing situations in the business and as projects develop. There is a tendency to finish projects once they have been started, but situations change and the value of projects can decline. There is an opportunity cost in keeping any project going, and there must be a willingness to stop projects, even late in their lifecycle, if they are no longer going to deliver sufficient value to a business. However, there must be a balance. Constantly tweaking priorities so that different projects are regularly stopped or started risks very little ever being completed.

In-life portfolio management should also ensure that a suitable governance and decision-making framework is in place. In-life portfolio management is also discussed in Chapter 8.

Portfolio selection – practical considerations

The process shown in Diagram 3.2 and described through this chapter is logically straightforward and easy to understand. In practice, problems must be overcome by the portfolio manager at every stage of this process. Successful portfolio management is as much about overcoming practical issues as it is about implementing the ideal process.

Typical problems in practice include

o The lack of an explicit strategy on which to base portfolio objectives, as well as the lack of information on the balance of objectives

o The inability or unwillingness of senior management to spend time in determining portfolio objectives.

o An unwillingness of senior managers to act as a team, and when making portfolio choices a tendency to act in their own or their function's interest inhibiting or slowing decision-making.

o Sub-optimal information, for example, in initial definitions of projects or understanding resource availability. This is a classic management problem of making decisions based on imperfect information. It is usually possible to get more information, but there is a point at which the time and effort to get it is

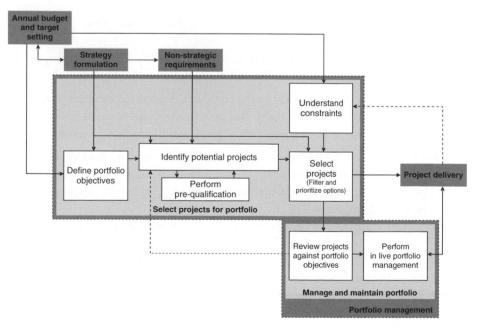

Diagram 3.2 Portfolio Management Process

disproportionate to the benefits. In addition, because it is a highly dynamic situation, once collected, the information often becomes out-of-date.

o The difficultly of comparing the merits of different types of projects with differing types of benefits, for example, comparing operational improvement projects and a new product development, or comparing a project to fulfil a major customer sale and one to ensure regulatory compliance.

o Excessive scrutiny or disproportionate information requirements delaying project selection and progress.

o Unwillingness to spend appropriate amounts of time in deciding project priorities. It can be complicated and time-consuming, and senior managers are usually pressed for time.

o The tendency to continually start new projects without completing projects already running. This places excessive demands on critical resources, and will delay progress as individuals continually swap between projects. Continually starting new projects is often driven by a lack of vision in general management of the impact of adding more projects or reducing the number of projects. Individual stakeholders will often try to add more projects, as it is in their interest, and they may not suffer the consequences. There are various other factors at play. The level of resources is not absolute and can flex to some extent. Also other projects can be incrementally slowed down, but this may not be visible or have an impact upon individual managers adding extra projects.

o The lack of understanding of the impact of high levels of parallel-working on timescales. Twice as many projects running in parallel may be assumed to take twice as long to complete, though often they will take far longer (parallel working is explored briefly in Chapter 4).

o A lack of willingness to stop any running projects and to use portfolio management to add projects only once existing projects complete. There is often great hesitation in stopping projects that are live, even if this means that better opportunities cannot be pursued.

o Lack of project- and commercial-risk information, leading to over-optimistic judgements about the likelihood of portfolio success.

These problems can be exacerbated by the fact that the portfolio manager often does not have the full visibility of all projects. This makes any decisions about prioritization and assessment of the portfolio against objectives sub-optimal. This happens because

o Managers holding their own budgets and resources may covertly start projects if they are not given adequate support or priority in the organization's portfolio. This can absorb resources that were expected to be available to projects in the portfolio.

o Specialist teams and groups (e.g. IT) often manage a separate portfolio of work.

o Some activities which are projects may not be identified as projects and are treated as business-as-usual initiatives.

o Some activities are too small to be in portfolio, but the cumulative impact of large numbers of small activities is large.

To mitigate and even overcome such issues the portfolio manager should

- Explain the value of portfolio management to the leadership team in terms of optimizing outcomes relative to resources available. This will increase support and reduce the likelihood of insufficient time spent in decision-making.
- Make sure the process and its requirements are understood and accepted by the leadership team and other senior managers.
- Educate the leadership team as to the implications of decisions; for example, decisions which result in very high levels of parallel working or allow projects to run outside of the portfolio.
- Act as an honest broker without bias not favouring one area of the business over others, to facilitate optimal decision-making.
- Help the leadership team by minimizing the overhead on them. This can be achieved by making suggestions and recommendations rather than simply presenting huge numbers of options. It can also be helped by ensuring that the leadership team are involved only where necessary, and decision-making is delegated where appropriate to managers with more time to allocate to portfolio management.

Cooper, Edgett and Kleinschmidt (2001) identify four factors that distinguish those businesses with the best performing portfolio management from the rest:

1. Senior management understand the importance of portfolio management.
2. The organization has an explicit portfolio method.
3. The best tend to rely less on pure financial models and lets business strategy allocate resources and decide the portfolio.
4. The business applies multiple methods for portfolio selection and prioritization, acknowledging that no one method gives the correct results all the time.

Portfolio management is a relatively simple concept. It can become complex because of the large volume of volatile information it has to process, and due to a lack of real understanding of it amongst the leadership team. But portfolio management has significant value to a business and the practical problems it exhibits are worth overcoming.

Case Study **3.2** **PROJECT SELECTION IN A LARGE ORGANIZATION**

In this case study Dave Keighley discusses how projects are selected when working within an operational environment. Dave is an experienced executive and entrepreneur. He has a background in engineering and technology development, has been responsible for major operational departments and runs his own businesses. This case study relates to Dave's time at leading the operational functions of a major corporation, where he was responsible for over 5000 staff and a budget of over £400m.

Dave Keighley

A key factor to understand in general about operational departments is that they are very fast-moving. Things are constantly changing, issues arise and problems occur that have to be solved. When a problem arises we have to find a solution. When the solution is found you have to rapidly determine whether it can be fixed as part of the day-to-day work of a department using the existing resources, or should it be taken away to be run as a project.

Projects arise in operations, because there is insufficient time or resource within the current department to deliver an idea. To deliver some ideas we need to separate out resources and give it more dedicated time to deliver. What happens is that a problem arises and we find a solution, or perhaps we identify an opportunity we can take advantage of, but no one can make it progress on top of day-to-day work. This idea is the seed of a project.

No one person normally comes up with a fully fledged concept for a project. An idea arises which is bounced around the management team for a while. It gets shaped into something we buy into. Normally, we have to jump to the end of the project and think about what we really need, what the success criteria will be for implementing this idea, and what it will be like once the idea is implemented. If, after doing this, we still have something we like, we go back and define the scope for a project. It is really only at this stage that it starts to become formally like a project; until now it has just been an idea we have been kicking around.

In operations there seem to be hundreds of ideas arising all the time. Everyone thinks their ideas are great, and everyone thinks their ideas will help the organization to be successful. But we cannot implement them all, and we have to filter through until we get to a small set of initiatives we have the capability to deliver.

The first stage of filtering is informal and based on commonsense. Which ideas are really valid? Which ones are truly feasible? Which ideas will actually result in improved performance? Thinking through questions like these enables you to remove some of the less realistic ideas.

Next we have to get into more structured analysis. We have to quantify the benefits of each of the remaining ideas. This is a huge challenge. Anyone can fill in a business case which shows some significant benefit from implementing an idea. The question is whether the business case is true. Everyone has biases. I don't mean people deliberately manipulate the situation, but our individual beliefs shape how we see things and influence the business cases we create. Most people put forward ideas for what they think are the right reasons. Often their reasoning is wrong – although this may not be their fault. Commonly, it is due to a failure to articulate the current strategy in a way that is meaningful to staff.

Determining which projects to invest in is not simply a function of what benefits they deliver, but also when they deliver them. The importance of timing in benefit realization is closely related to strategy and shareholder needs. Some businesses are short-termist and therefore are only interested in benefits that come about quickly. Others can take a longer-term view.

Ironically, in contradiction to what most text books would present, my experience is that senior managers are more interested in the short-term than are junior staff. It is not that junior staff are wrong in taking the long-term view, but they may be naïve and often do not understand the context of the business and the pressures exerted for quick returns by some shareholders. You see many great ideas in a senior operational role, and end up thinking if only we had the time and the money. But you are there to run a business to the needs of the strategy, not to dream! So, you end up rejecting many ideas which have too long a payback. Junior staff often do not understand this.

Whenever an idea for a project is rejected you need to explain to staff why it has been rejected. If you don't do this no one will ever really understand the direction of the business. Also rejection can lower motivation, and if repeated can stifle innovative thinking. That is the last thing you want to do. People should be thanked and praised for great ideas, even if they are not carried forward. Staff appreciate understanding the logic for why what they perceive as a great idea is rejected.

Once you know the benefits, the timescales to deliver, and the resources required, you can prioritize the projects. This is much easier if the project is contained within the operational functions. As soon as a project requires cross-functional resources from other areas it becomes much more complex. Getting an apples-for-apples type of comparison for projects from very different parts of a business is hard.

There is a tendency to start too many projects. We want to do 20 things so we start 20. The reality is that a project at priority 20 is going to wither on the vine and never finish. Staff may do some work, but at that priority the project is never going to get the resources it requires to complete, and we waste what limited effort we spend on it. The priority 20 project just gets in the way without ever delivering benefit. We need to be brave up front and make the decision to filter down to a very small number of projects we can really do. Again, we should communicate back to staff every time a project is rejected.

What is left in the project list will now progress. However, even at this stage it is worth setting expectations. The world changes very quickly. If we start a project we currently mean to finish it, but we may find in a few months time that things have changed so much that it is no longer the right project to be doing. Telling people now itself that starting a project does not mean it will finish can save a lot of problems later on.

MAIN LEARNING POINTS FROM CHAPTER 3

- Portfolio management is concerned with selecting and managing the projects an organization undertakes. It has several objectives including ensuring strategic alignment of projects, maximizing the returns from project investments, ensuring that the set of projects undertaken is optimal relative to the resources available, and balancing the resources allocated to achieving different corporate goals.
- Portfolio management starts by defining the portfolio goals, usually derived from strategy.
- Selecting projects requires an understanding of project options and resource constraints, as well as the definition of filtering and prioritization criteria.
- Portfolio management requires an inventory of projects. The challenges in creating such an inventory include understanding what projects exist, the level of detail to keep in collecting information on projects and deciding on the scope of the portfolio.
- Portfolio management prioritizes projects into an optimal order considering business needs, resource constraints, change capacity in an organization, risk levels and dependencies between projects.

- Risk management is essential at a portfolio level. A well-designed portfolio will reduce project risk, a badly designed one can magnify it.
- Portfolio management is ongoing and must respond to the dynamic nature of reality as project outcomes will differ from those planned, business needs will change and the operational situation will alter. In addition, there will be a constant stream of new project ideas.
- Portfolio management links closely to strategy, governance, resource management, and the annual budgeting and target-setting processes.
- Successful portfolio management requires a supportive and well-educated senior management who understand their roles with regard to it.

REVIEW QUESTIONS AND EXERCISES

1. Consider two different businesses that you are familiar with. How would you broadly define their strategy? How would you relate this to portfolio objectives? Are there other portfolio objectives you would include not related to strategy?
2. Create a structured form to collect information to analyse different projects. Select a project you were familiar with from your work experiences and complete the form for this project. What information do you think is easy to collect and what is more difficult?
3. What do you think are the main constraints on a business's ability to implement projects? How would you develop and maintain an understanding of these constraints? How easy is this to do? How would you apply this knowledge in practice?
4. In your experience, are portfolio objectives defined? What are the implications of this?
5. Using the information in Case Studies 3.1 and 3.2, as well as any information from your own experience, define what you see as the main problems in implementing a portfolio management process in a complex organization.
6. What are your objectives in studying the course you are currently undertaking? Consider the course as a series of projects with each subject as a project. Assume you have only two resources to invest – time (for lectures, tutorials, course work and study) and money (for textbooks and other materials). How are you going to prioritize access to these resources for different areas of study? Will this enable you to meet your overall course objectives? What other activities in your life use these resources and what problems does this create in achieving your course goals? How will you overcome these problems?

Suggested reading

There are two texts suggested for those interested in exploring the relationship between strategy and project management further. The first was written by an experienced practitioner and provides an accessible and thorough coverage of this topic. The second provides a series of tools and techniques for assessing and reviewing project portfolios.

- *Project Portfolio Management: A Practical Guide to Selecting Projects, Managing Portfolios and Maximizing Benefits.* Harvey A Levine. Jossey-Bass, 2005
- *Connecting the Dots: Aligning Projects with Objectives in Unpredictable Times.* Cathleen Benko and F Warren McFarlan, Harvard Business School Press, 2003

Bibliography

Akalu, M. M. "Re-examining project appraisal and control: Developing a focus on wealth creation". *International Journal of Project Management*. Volume 19, Issue 7, October 2001, pp. 375–83.

APM (Association for Project Management). *Directing Change, a Guide to Governance of Project Management*. Association for Project Management, 2004.

Archer, N. and Ghasemzadeh. "Project portfolio selection and management". *The Wiley Guide to Managing Projects*. Wiley, 2004.

Baugst, J. "The Value of flexibility in total project life – Real option applications". *Project Perspectives, Periodical of Project Management Association Finland*. Volume XXVII, Issue 1, 2005, pp. 12–9.

Beaujon, G., Marin, S. and McDonald, G. "Balancing and optimizing a portfolio of R&D projects". *Naval Logistics Review*. Volume 48, 2001, pp. 20–40.

Benko, C. and Warren McFarlan, F. *Connecting the Dots: Aligning Your Project Portfolio with Corporate Objectives*. Harvard Business School Press, 2003.

Brache, A. and Bodley-Scott, S. "Decisions: Which initiatives should you pursue?" *Harvard Management Update*. October 2006.

Cook, W. and Green, R. "Project prioritization: A resource-constrained data envelopment analysis approach". *Socio-Economic Planning Sciences*. Volume 34, 2000, pp. 85–99.

Cooke-Davies, T. "Portfolio management, delivering business strategy through doing the right projects". *Project Manager Today*, February 2002, pp. 15–17.

Cooper, R. and Edgett, S. "Portfolio management for new products: Picking the winners". *Product Development Institute Working Paper No 11*. 2001.

Cooper, R., Edgett, S. and Kleinschmidt, E. "Portfolio management for new product development: Results of an industry practices study". *R&D Management*. Volume 31, Issue 4. 2001, pp. 361–80.

Cooper, R., Edgett, S. and Kleinschmidt, E. *Portfolio management – Fundamental for New Product Success*. The Product Development Institute, 2000.

Dye, L. and Pennypacker, J. "Project portfolio management and managing multiple projects: Two sides of the same coin?" *Proceedings of the Project Management Institute Annual Seminar and Symposium*, September 2000.

Gardiner, P. *Project Management, A strategic planning approach*. Palgrave Macmillan, 2005.

Levine, H. *Project Portfolio Management. A Practical Guide to Selecting Projects, Managing Portfolios and Maximizing Benefits*. Jossey-Bass, 2005.

Martinsuo, M. and Lehtonen, P. "Role of single-project management in achieving portfolio management efficiency". *International Journal of Project Management*. Volume 25, Issue 1, January 2007, pp. 56–65.

Michelman, P. "Decisions: Which projects get top billing?" *Harvard Management Update*. April 2004.

Morris, P. and Jamieson, A. *Translating Corporate Strategy into Project Strategy: Realizing Corporate Strategy Through Project Management*, Project Management Institute, 2003.

Nawrocki, D. "Portfolio optimization, heuristics and the butterfly effect". *Journal of Financial Planning*. February 2000, pp. 68–78.

Puthamont, S. and Charoenngam, C. "Strategic project selection in public sector: Construction projects of the Ministry of Defence in Thailand". *International Journal of Project Management*. Volume 25, Issue 2, February 2007, pp. 178–88.

4

project
resources and
resource management 4

The ability to undertake any task is dependent on access to the resources necessary to do the work. Projects, programmes and portfolios with their wide-ranging tasks require a variety of resources. The availability of suitable resources is one of the central factors in successful completion of projects, and is also one of the main constraints that limits the scale and scope of an organization's project portfolio.

Successful project resource management requires three, apparently simple, questions to be answered:

o What resources are required to complete the chosen projects?
o What resources are available?
o What work can be undertaken?

The conceptually simple activity of providing the resources required for projects is in practice complicated, involved and time-consuming. Accurately understanding the resource needs for an individual project is difficult due to the inherent uncertainties and risk in planning and estimating. Aggregating the overall resource requirements across multiple projects is complex due to the volume of data and its highly volatile state. Choosing the best resources for a specific project is associated with understanding the various skills and capabilities of a large number of individuals. Managing resources in-life on projects is impacted by the effects of uncertainty, risk and change on projects.

Experienced project, programme and portfolio managers will be familiar with the constant challenge of gaining access to the right resources and the ongoing competitive jockeying between projects for scarce resources. Project managers are involved in a continuous search for available resources. In many business situations resources are kept fully busy and the only way to free up resources for one project is to take them from another, thus delaying the latter. This can result in project schedules regularly changing and expectations having to be continually reset.

Managers spend a significant proportion of time making trade-off decisions between projects for access to resources and regularly reviewing and amending prioritizations. This often results in a short-term focus rather than on complete project lifecycles. Allocating and optimizing resources is the primary challenge of managing projects in the multi-project environment (Engwall and Jerbrant, 2003), typical of most businesses. Yet many project and even portfolio management books gloss over this subject.

This chapter aims to give a comprehensive appreciation of the involved problem of project resource allocation and management. In addition, it sets out the steps in project resource management. As with other topics in this book, the level is sufficient for managers to support resource management, but there are many detailed processes and issues which occur in specific situations and which are beyond the scope of this book.

A comprehensive appreciation of resource allocation and management requires a good understanding of prioritization (Chapter 3), and planning and estimation (Chapter 6). Similarly, effective portfolio management, and planning and scheduling of project activities, cannot be done without a good understanding of what resources are available. For readers who are using this book purely to enhance project management skills it may be appropriate to read Chapters 5 and 6 before this chapter. For those readers interested in portfolio management, development of project management capabilities or improving an organization's portfolio it is preferable to read this chapter before Chapters 5 and 6.

Categories of project resources and associated issues

Project managers define the resources required for a project by planning and estimating the project and producing an initial ideal resource requirement. Then they determine what resources are available and revise the schedule to take account of this. In doing this, project managers seek both to gain the resources they need, and to understand any resource bottlenecks which will determine the critical path of their projects. Managing and overcoming bottlenecks is one of the key tasks for project managers on a daily basis.

So, what are the resources that project managers require? There are many varieties of resources that are required for different projects, but they can be grouped into four main categories:

o Money or finance, in the form of a budget
o Human resources
o Equipment or facilities
o Consumables

These are now described in the order presented here. At the end of this section there is also a sub-section on different levels of resource management.

Money

Money is an apparently homogeneous commodity. One pound is equivalent to every other pound and so, conceptually, as long as a project manager has access to a budget with sufficient funding to pay for a project, there should be few problems from a finance perspective. In practice, dealing with project budgets is complicated because of the impact of many factors. Project managers regularly underestimate the complexity of successfully managing a project budget within a business.

Important examples of issues facing project managers with regard to budgets include

o The effects of budget and financial-reporting cycles. Projects have to report financial status in line with the standard reporting cycles in a business, which may not match directly with definable stages in a project. Dealing with a business's financial year is even more involved. This impacts projects which cross accounting periods. Issues such as projects spanning financial years, especially when projects are delayed and unexpectedly cross financial years, can be significant problems. Whether it is possible to make accruals from one year to another needs to be understood. In some businesses it is simple to cross accounting years; in others it is complex, and planned spend in one year must be made in that year or the budget is lost.

o The ways in which finance departments track expenditure and progress compared to the way that projects managers do. Typically these are quite different. For example, an accounting system will often interpret that a project that has completed half of its elapsed time and spent half of its budget is on track. A project manager may know that whilst half the time has elapsed, the actual amount delivered is different from this. (Earned Value Analysis is one method to understand how much has really been delivered.) A project manager will usually note money as committed when a contractor is engaged and starts working, whereas accountants usually recognize it when the contractor's invoice is received. Additional problems include the phasing of cost allocation to budgets. It is not uncommon for project managers to find that though they feel they have successfully completed a project within a budget limit, they later have unexpected cross charges for indirect costs allocated to the project which pushes them over budget.

o Approval processes to spend money within a budget. Even though a budget exists a project manager may not be able to spend against it without approval for individual expenditures, especially larger items above the project manager's authority level. Such approval processes have to be included in a project plan if the schedule is to be accurate. Project managers regularly underestimate the time to get approvals to spend money. Beyond the approval process there will be potentially time-consuming procedures such as those associated with raising purchase requisitions (PRs) and purchase orders (POs).

o The desire to implement unbudgeted projects. Budgets are set out at the start of the financial year when there is usually only an imprecise understanding of the projects for the year. As the year progresses business needs and the understanding of needs will change. As this happens, the range of projects in the portfolio will be modified, and new unexpected projects may be required. It is always more difficult to gain approval for unbudgeted items which require either additional budget to be allocated or budget to be transferred from other projects.

o The accounting treatments and the associated implications for different types of budget categories (e.g. opex and capex). Depending on the financial state of a business it may be relatively easier or harder to incur operational expenditure (opex) versus capital expenditure (capex), and this will affect the type of projects possible.

o Having to handle both direct (those directly related to the project) and indirect costs (e.g. overhead, general and administrative costs). Indirect costs may be uncontrollable by and even invisible to a project manager, yet can impact the budget she is responsible for.

o Multiple budgets and the need to allocate project costs across different cost centres. This can raise the issue of how such an allocation is to be done, and can increase the complexity and extend timelines of approvals to spend money.

o Accounting practice in terms of what is and what is not expected to be accounted for in a project. (e.g. does a business charge for the time of internal staff on projects or not?) This has a significant impact on the size of budget required, approval processes, and the information the project manager has to track.

All of these issues can be compounded by project manager's lack of understanding of budget processes and principles.

Human resources

In contrast to money, human resource is definitely not homogeneous. Projects not only require people to work on them, but they require both the *right* people as well as *different* people for various tasks. Consideration has to be given to differing skills, capabilities, interests, attitudes, productivity and availability in comparison to the work on hand. The difference in the effectiveness of the best choice of staff for project roles and the worst can be dramatic. The most highly skilled and motivated staff will often be several times as productive as the least. A poor choice of project staff is likely to lead to project failure, whilst the best can overcome complex and high-risk projects.

What resources are available is determined not only by the individuals an organization employs, but also the organizational structures of a business. Organizational boundaries, relationships between different parts of the business and role definitions all impact which people are actually available for projects, as opposed to who may be available in principle.

Consideration has to be given not only to the individual resources on a project, but also to how they will interact and work as a team. Usually it is not individuals who deliver projects, but a combined team of people. The chosen staff should be capable of working as a productive team.

In addition, in many businesses projects are used not only as a way to achieve a specific goal, but as an environment in which staff can learn and acquire new skills. Hence, project managers often have to consider who are the staff who most need the opportunity to develop on a project instead of who are the best suited for the project.

A large programme requiring hundreds of people with differing skills from an organization of many thousands of people requires to collect, assess and maintain a complex set of information on human resources.

There are different categories of human resources that can be selected for projects, including

- o Dedicated project professionals, such as project managers or business analysts
- o Specialist resources who work predominantly on projects, for example, staff involved in new product development
- o People who are available for project work only for a proportion of their time. An IT programmer may spend 50% of his time on software development projects and 50% on maintenance of existing systems.
- o Operational people who are normally not available for project work. Operational staff may be allocated to projects from time to time, because of subject matter expertise in an area of the business relevant to the project. In many organizations the majority of employees are operational staff. Operational managers are often loath to provide staff to projects, as it reduces capacity for their own work. This is compounded by the fact that projects often require the most valuable, highly skilled operational staff with a current understanding of operations.

Each of these categories of staff creates different challenges in allocating and managing projects.

Project staff may be employees of the business or can be external resources contracted to work on a specific project. The productivity and effectiveness of external staff is impacted by additional factors beyond those which impact internal staff. What is the nature of the contract – is it to provide resource for a fixed amount of time, on a time and materials basis, or is to complete a specific task irrespective of time? The relationship between the supplying and buying organizations also has a significant impact. Relationships can vary from simple supplier relationships (pay X and receive Y resource) to more complex partnership and risk–reward situations.

There is obviously a relationship between budget and human resource availability on projects. This is clear-cut with external resources which typically must be paid for from a project budget. With internal resources the relationship between people and budget is less definite. Obviously, the cost of employing people who work on projects must be borne by a business. However, depending on the accounting practices in a specific business individual staff working on projects may or may not be re-charged to project budgets. If they are to be re-charged, mechanisms must exist for tracking the time they work on a project.

It is best practice for all staff time on projects to be tracked, as this enforces good discipline in using resources and provides a way to measure project progress and cost. However, such practice will increase the overall amount of information to track and manage.

Often consideration has to be given to whether staff costs can be capitalized or not, which depends on the nature of the project and the company's accounting policies.

Project plans often rely on the buildup of a team of people. Where these people are to be recruited on a permanent basis the time to achieve this is often extended.

It can take several months to recruit the right individuals. Not only is permanent recruitment relatively protracted, it is often slower than planned. The often sluggish pace of permanent recruitment increases the tendency to use contract resources in projects with tight deadlines.

In all businesses there are limits to human resources. Therefore effective allocation of staff is dependent on prioritization. However, project prioritization is not a panacea for all resourcing decisions. Resource models often support decision-making as if the only options were choosing between different projects. Many of the people involved have business-as-usual operational tasks to do, which may be more critical than projects. Business-as-usual tasks are usually not formally prioritized relative to projects.

Equipment and facilities

Equipment and facilities needed for projects can be as simple as building access passes and desk space for project staff or as scarce as time on highly specialist machinery. Access to such resources is often assumed. For example, in most situations project staff will require PCs, and most will have them. If the provision of PCs is managed as an overhead cost in a business, a project manager does not need to be concerned about finding, funding for and allocating PCs.

However, there are situations in which specific equipment and facilities have to be explicitly planned and managed for a number of reasons.

First, access to some equipment or facilities takes time. For example, contractors working on a project require building access passes. In some situations these can take several days to be approved, created and distributed. This can impact project time lines.

Second, access to some equipment or facilities limits the capability to do project work. For example, in technology projects there may be a requirement to access specialized testing equipment. If availability of this equipment is limited and multiple projects need access to it, then this equipment may become a constraint and projects schedules need to be planned around access to this equipment. Another example could be access to specific facilities such as large meeting rooms.

Third, usage or provision of some equipment will be charged to a project budget. Therefore usage or consumption must be tracked for financial reasons. For example, although PCs are generally universal in most businesses, contract staff may require a PC configured to a business's specification, and a PC configured as such may be re-charged to a project.

Consumables

The final resource category is consumables. In some cases consumables are managed through a budget, and as long as a project can pay for all consumables it requires, there is no limit or delay in getting the resources required. Many consumables are effectively unconstrained; for example, it is unusual to find a project nowadays that has problems regarding access to paper or photocopying facilities. However, there may be more specialist consumables that have to be scheduled and budgeted. Examples include providing cables in a network expansion project or building materials in a construction project.

In some situations consumables are in limited supply, or are purchased centrally and allocated to projects on a priority basis. In either situation the project manager has to manage these consumables as a scarce resource and include consideration for gaining access to them in the project schedule and budget.

The levels of resource management

Resource management happens at a number of levels. Project managers are concerned with gaining access to and managing the resources required for their individual projects. Programme managers have a similar focus, with the added complexity, and in some cases advantage, of having resources working on multiple projects in the programme. Programme managers have the ability therefore to balance and adjust resources across projects to some extent. This requires them to make local prioritization decisions within the scope of the programme. Portfolio managers are less focussed on the *ins* and *outs* of getting tasks completed and are more concerned about making sure the right projects are getting access to resources, and that the necessary prioritization decisions, in the situation of bottlenecks, are made.

Whilst project and programme managers typically are concerned about resources on their project or programme, a portfolio manager is more concerned with aggregated resource demand and availability across a business.

Overview of resource planning and management

Resource planning and management is a process that is complicated in implementation and goes through many iteration, but is relatively simple in terms of the stages in the underlying process. It is a good example of progressive elaboration in projects, as typically at the start of a project the estimates for resources are very broad and subject to an acceptable large degree of error. As projects progress the estimates become more accurate, although the only time resource estimates are 100% accurate is when a project completes, and it is no longer an estimate!

Diagram 4.1 represents the basic steps in resource planning from the viewpoint of an individual project manager. A project manager may have to go round this loop of activities several times until an acceptable plan is developed using levels of actually available resources.

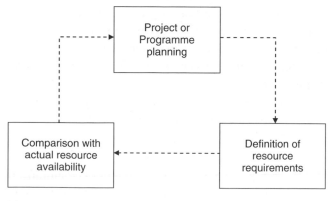

Diagram 4.1 The resource planning cycle

In reality, resource planning is more complex than Diagram 4.1 suggests. Resource planning and subsequent resource management happen at different levels, and are linked to or part of several other business processes, including

- The annual strategy- and budget-planning process in a business. This includes decisions about what strategies to follow in the coming period and results in budgets being set. Although there is a tendency to assume that a similar amount will be spent on projects each year, as is typical for operational budgets, this often leads to inaccurate estimates. Project budgets cannot be set in the same way as operational budgets because project estimates are unique. Operational budgets are typically determined on the basis that they will be the same as for last year plus or minus an agreed percentage. True zero-based budgeting is rare for operations, but is what should be done for project budgets.

- The portfolio management process for periodic approval and prioritization of projects (typically monthly or quarterly). The only reason for prioritization is allocation of scarce resources. One of the core roles of portfolio management is to ensure that there is the right number of projects for the resources available (Cooper et al., 2001).

- Regular modifications to strategy and other business change which alters the project portfolio. Although budgets are typically set at the beginning of the year changes to the budget drivers will occur which result in additions and deletions to the project portfolio. In turn this will impact resource needs and prioritization.

- The programme or project management process for the planning and initiation of new endeavours. Planning provides an understanding of both the resource needs and the schedule of those needs. Unless a project is similar to a previous project, it is only when planning and risk assessment are complete that resource estimates can be considered as accurate.

- The programme or project management process for the ongoing delivery of projects, especially variations to plan as a project progresses. A plan is a projection of expectations, but is rarely absolutely accurate. Variations in progress and resource usage in reality versus what was planned will occur. Assuming a project has thorough risk management and contingency planning these variations may be invisible to anyone outside of the project as the contingency buffer will account for any excess needs. However, there will always be some projects for which variations are greater than contingency.

- Project change control to in-flight projects, resulting in modifications to project scope, objectives and requirements. Dynamic business needs result in alterations to live projects during delivery. This results in re-planning and adapting resource requirements.

- Finally, actual resource usage needs to be fed back into the ongoing financial reporting processes, and plans updated in line with real usage.

All of the above interactions are summarized in Diagram 4.2. The boxes shown in grey represent the increasingly accurate understanding of resource needs from left to right across the diagram. (Diagram 4.1 is represented by the third column from left in Diagram 4.2.) The dotted lines represent feedback loops requiring repeated iteration of the activities shown. Each of these processes is highly iterative.

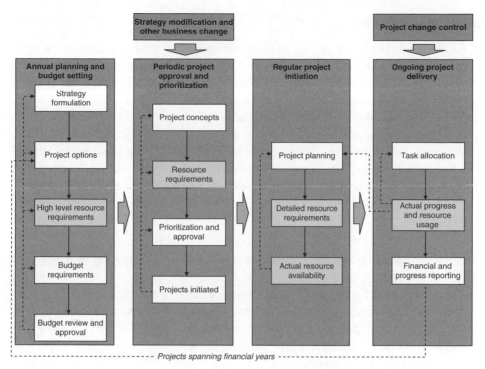

Diagram 4.2   How resource management fits into wider business activities

Resource management is a highly dynamic activity and needs the continuous involvement of management. Engwall and Jerbrant (2003) identify four key reasons for the need to constantly manage resource allocations:

- Failing project schedules. On average it might be thought that across a large portfolio late projects are balanced by early projects and the resource load will stay the same. However, there is a tendency for more projects to be late than early. Resources are not homogeneous, so the fact that one project releases resources early may not help another unless the latter specifically needs that type of resources.
- Over-commitment. This is rife in many businesses, and there is a tendency to keep piling on more projects until a crisis point is hit.
- Management accounting systems which tend to be dysfunctional for projects by typically not accounting for internal labour, which is therefore "free" to individual projects. This tends to exacerbate the tendency to over-commit.
- The behaviour of project managers. Opportunistic project management push projects to crisis points to gain higher priorities, and keep key resources busy on non-critical tasks simply to keep them available for the project.

In addition, the behaviour of line managers who "own" resources can complicate resourcing decisions. Managers may not actively support overall project prioritization and allocate the expected resources, especially if such resource allocation impacts their ability to achieve their own performance targets.

Resourcing objectives

Resource management can be understood simply as a way to ensure the right resources are applied to the right projects. However, resource management can be performed to achieve different objectives, such as choosing between the quickest or the cheapest project delivery. Before resources can be effectively managed, it is essential to understand what the objectives of resource management are. Often there are inherent and unquestioned assumptions about how resources are to be allocated – for example, many managers assume that keeping all staff fully utilized is a universally good situation to be in. In many situations it is not. It is better to challenge these assumptions and make resourcing objectives explicit.

Examples of different important objectives that resource management can support are

o Optimizing the delivery of projects versus maximizing staff utilization
o Maximizing the throughput of work versus maintaining flexibility to respond
o Managing the delivery against resource constraints versus managing delivery against time constraints – or managing delivery against time constraints versus managing delivery against cost constraints
o Optimizing completion of project work versus minimizing impact of resource drain on operations.

Let us look at each of these in turn.

Most businesses operate with staff at very high levels of utilization. In some such as consultancies, where staff are charged to client projects on a day-rate basis, profitability is a function of staff utilization. In this situation high utilization is the goal of the organization as it maximizes profitability. In most businesses high staff utilization is not an objective in itself, but is an outcome of large numbers of projects. In reality high utilization of all staff does not always result in the maximum amount of benefits delivered from projects. In some situations, project delivery is more effective and efficient when some staff wait for tasks rather than being kept artificially busy on non-critical activities.

Businesses have some predictable workload and some unpredictable. Keeping staff highly utilized reduces the opportunity to respond to unpredicted events and unforeseen opportunities. On the other hand, maintaining a pool of under-utilized staff to respond to project opportunities can be inefficient. The optimal balance between flexibility and utilization depends on the business's needs. There are some situations in which flexibility is essential. In a volatile sales environment there is often a requirement to keep some resource free to respond rapidly to new sales-led projects. If there is a continuous stream of work that needs immediate response there must always be a degree of buffer or "fat" in headcount levels.

At the simplest level a project manager can determine what resources are available and set the schedule to this constraint. Alternatively, she can determine when a project is scheduled to finish and define the resources required. In most situations there is a trade-off between these two extremes, but there are some where the time or the resource constraint is absolute. Projects with time-critical due dates, such as a consumer product launch prior to Christmas, need whatever resources are required to meet the date.

Organizations often choose to manage projects against the time constraints or against cost constraints. For example, to meet a pressing schedule contract staff can be brought in to speed up a project at some cost. In-house staff can also be asked to work overtime to speed up delivery, though again at some cost. Alternatively, costs can be minimized by using in-house staff only for their normal working (contracted) hours. Although such decisions will vary from project to project there are usually some trends across a portfolio. A cash-constrained or low-margin business is generally more likely to be focussed on cost constraints than time; a high-margin business is more likely to be focussed on time than cost. (Project trade-offs are discussed in more detail in Chapter 6.)

Project managers tend to view the allocation of resources as an issue of competition between projects. In reality, aggregated project resource is often a small proportion of total organizational resources. There may be large amounts of resources within operational departments which is not usually available to projects. This resource is not made available as releasing the staff for project work will have a detrimental impact on business-as-usual operations. In some businesses daily operations are treated as sacrosanct and projects must minimize all impacts on them. Alternatively, decisions can be made to compromise operations by allocating more resource to projects to enhance project delivery for the longer-term benefit of a business. Project-induced outages to customer service centres is an example where there is a trade-off between completing a project and impacting operations versus maintaining high levels of customer service and delaying a project.

Management information for human resource management

The way resource management processes are defined and the supporting information captured can support a range of different management decision-making. There is a substantial overhead in capturing detailed resource plans and actual resource usage, so significant thought should be given to what management information is required. For example, resource management information can be used for

- Tracking costs and resource usage on projects. Understanding the full cost of projects is good management practice. It is essential in some situations, for example, in cost-plus contracts.
- Supporting juggling or balancing between projects as situations change. Accurate resource information enables the impact of such decisions to be understood. This includes resource smoothing or levelling within and across projects.
- Giving reliable commitments on project delivery dates. More accurate project planning enables greater levels of business commitment. Most businesses value predictability. Being able to make future commitments requiring resources confidently is of significant value to some businesses.
- Understanding individual staff workloads. From a line management perspective it is helpful to simply know what each member of staff is doing.
- Business planning. Medium- to long-term planning is helped by forward resource plans.

Understanding resource needs

There are two ways that the resource needs for a project can be understood both top-down and bottom-up.

Top-down are summary estimates made by looking at the complete project. Such estimates are based on familiarity with the type of project. Hence a builder is able to accurately estimate without detailed planning, but based on knowledge of previous projects, the resources required to build a house of a certain size. Similarly a specialist in management reporting may be able to reasonably accurately assess, based on similar reports previously produced, the time to deliver a management reporting project. Top-down estimates are sometimes called *comparative estimates.*

Bottom-up are estimates derived from a detailed review of all tasks in a plan. Understanding the resource needs of a project from a bottom-up perspective is linked with the activity of project planning and estimating what is required to complete each task in the plan. The resource requirements are determined by the resource needs for every task in the work breakdown structure.

The mechanics of bottom-up and top-down estimation are described in more detail in Chapter 6.

There are advantages and disadvantages to each approach. Top-down tends to be quick to achieve, but requires experience, and unless the project is very similar to previous projects will only give rough estimates of resource requirements. Such estimates may be sufficient for budgetary purposes, but are often insufficient for business-case approval or to actually manage project delivery.

Bottom-up estimates are often more accurate, but can take more time to produce. The accuracy of bottom-up estimates is dependent on the precision of the project plan. Such estimates are inherently risky, as there are usually a degree of uncertainty and unknown in all plans. This can be mitigated by the use of contingency.

There are other ways of creating bottom-up estimates through some assessment of a measure-of-scale of a project (sometimes called *parametric estimation*). For example, in software development there is the concept of function points. A function point represents one function a software programme has to be able to do. By determining the total number of function points a heuristic can be applied. There are heuristics that give estimates of the time and resources required to develop the software.

In some critical situations both top-down and bottom-up estimates are used. By using both, the different estimates can be compared to give confidence in the resource estimates. Where there is a high degree of correlation the confidence increases; where the correlation is poor the confidence reduces, and it is necessary to revisit the estimates.

Where real accuracy is required, or when a programme is complex and difficult to estimate, it is sensible to run a feasibility study. Feasibility studies can be used to improve on bottom-up project planning estimates. By exploring what a project is trying to achieve and how this can be best implemented, feasibility studies can both test assumptions inherent in many plans and so reduce risk, and also provide a way to learn more about the tasks required in a plan.

Different types of projects have differing levels of difficulty in estimating. In Chapter 1 the paradigm of *soft* projects was introduced. Hard projects are typically easier to estimate – and to reduce uncertainty – than soft projects (Atkinson et al., 2006). Some projects are clearly definable at the start. Others are more emergent in nature, and a real understanding of the tasks required is only possible as the project evolves. For such emergent projects, resource estimates are likely to vary as the project progresses.

As part of planning a project there is the option of performing resource levelling. When a plan is first produced it will often show large variations in resource needs. Thus a project may need 10 people for a few weeks, then only 2 people for some time, and then finally 15 staff in the project team. It is usually more efficient for a business to try and remove this lumpiness in resources and attempt to develop a plan such that a more constant level of resources is required. A formal approach to achieving this is *resource levelling*.

Resource levelling seeks to spread the resource requirement over the life of a project by analysing peaks and troughs in resource consumption. Most planning software offers resource levelling functionality. Resource levelling will ensure no resource is loaded at over 100%, which planning can sometimes result in. Resource levelling generally tries to keep resources at around 100% utilization. There are a number of different resource levelling algorithms which can produce different changes to a project plan.

It is important to avoid generic definitions of resource requirements. It is better to be specific. For example, many projects identify that they need IT support. In a large organization there may be hundreds or even thousands of staff in the IT department. Superficially, it can therefore seem as if it should be simple to find one or two people to support a project from such a large resource pool. IT departments are not though full of staff with the same skill-set. There may be very few staff with the specific IT skills a project requires. Unless the requirement is clearly specified in terms of the specific skills needed it is likely to lead to poor resource planning and over-optimistic project planning.

Finally, whatever resource plans are created by a project they should reflect the objectives at both a project and portfolio level. Thus, if a specific project is required to be completed by a set date irrespective of cost, it should be prioritized and resourced that way. Alternatively, in a cash-constrained business, in financial difficulties, projects typically must be resourced in the most cost-efficient way possible.

Understanding resource availability

Developing an understanding of resource availability can require a significant amount of volatile data to be collected and regularly maintained, the most difficult part of which relates to human resources.

For some resources there are systems and processes in all businesses that will help with understanding resource availability. Finance is tracked through the budget and accounting processes. Finance systems allow views of supply and demand of money to be presented in many different ways. Businesses have developed accounting systems and finance processes. Sometimes these need adaptation or interpretation for projects, but the processes for financial management are usually more mature than those for project management. Consumables can be tracked through stock-holding levels. For equipment and facilities that are in short supply, but regularly required by projects, a schedule of availability can be set up. This schedule requires some form of allocation of the equipment or facility to projects, ideally based on project priority. Except in specialized situations, this is normally straightforward and is often as simple as a diary booking system.

The remainder of this and the next section focus on human resources which usually provide the greatest challenge in understanding availability across an organization.

The available human resources for a project in a specific business is a function of the number of employees, their skills and their availability for project work. The internal pool of people is expandable by contracting temporary staff or consultants. With the exception of rare specialist skills the external pool is effectively unlimited to any one business. It is though constrained by the ability and time to locate, contract, and pay for staff.

Understanding human resource availability requires the collection and maintenance of data on staff's current utilization and utilization into the future. To be useful for project planning the data needs to be sorted by skill group categories. Not all staff are available, or available for 100% of their time on projects. Human resource can be broken into the following general profiles:

o Dedicated project resource, 100% available to projects
o Specialist resources available for a fixed percentage of time (e.g. IT developers 50% on project work and 50% on maintenance)
o Non-project resources (e.g. operational departments may be expected to provide 5% of their resources to projects at any time. This level will vary from department to department.)
o External resources (depending on the nature of the contract may be available for a time period, or until they have completed a specific series of tasks)

There are different ways to manage human resource availability. The choice of approach alters the information that must be maintained. Each approach has varying strengths and weaknesses. The three main alternatives are

o Resource limits
o Resource capacity analysis
o Resource capacity analysis for key resources only

Human resources can be managed to resource limits by allocating resources from the pool of available resources without detailed analysis of availability. Projects are initiated on a priority basis until there is no capacity left. This removes a significant overhead in not needing to maintain databases of staff utilization (although skills databases are still required to identify which staff are suitable for which project roles). Such an approach does suffer from a number of weaknesses. The main one is the issue that determining when an organization has enough project work is not easily identifiable without some understanding of capacity and project demand. Working this way risks over-commitment.

Alternatively human resources can be managed using a capacity analysis. This requires maintaining detailed understandings of all project resource availability and allocating resources to projects on a priority basis. In principle, this is the most thorough way of understanding resources. This approach's weakness is that it is very intense in terms of gathering and maintaining up-to-date information. Organizations such as consultancies, where there is a strong culture of time sheet and forward utilization reporting (probably, because of its link to company profitability), are often best at this.

Human resource capacity analysis can be simplified by performing it for key resources only: The theory of constraints shows that the capacity of any system is limited by the size of the bottleneck in it and that there is only one bottleneck at any one time (Goldratt, 1997).

Hence to understand the capacity of an organization it is not necessary to understand total resource availability, but only the availability of the scarcest staff who are causing the bottleneck. This eases the information and analysis requirement significantly, as only the constrained resource needs to be tracked. However, it suffers from the issue that the bottleneck may regularly change. Even so it is normally possible to identify a small group of key skills that create the constraint most often and so need to be tracked. Some organizations create an artificial bottleneck, for example, by limiting the number of project managers. Project management becomes one simple pool of resource to be managed. In managing this team the overall amount of work underway is limited and hence the total human resource capacity as well.

In an effort to avoid the complexity of resource management, managers and business leaders may allocate a project manager to a project and ignore other resources, assuming that the project manager will find what he or she needs. This is a line of thinking to avoid, unless project managers are the bottleneck resource in a business. Inefficient resource usage, resulting from over-commitment, happens when projects are continually initiated by allocating more and more project managers to start projects. The project managers will start their projects, and, in doing so, be competing for the same pool of organizational resource as all other projects. This simply results in continual swapping of resources between projects, ending in elongated and unpredictable timescales for projects. Such a situation is symptomatic of poor or failing portfolio management.

Matching needs and availability to allocate resources

Having developed an understanding of both resource needs from individual projects and resource availability across an organization, it is conceptually simple to match demand with supply. In practice, as with much of resource management, this theoretically simple activity is complicated. The problems of resource allocation contribute to the overall difficulty in resource management, and that is why it is one of the most intense and time-consuming activities for project, programme and portfolio managers working in businesses operating many projects.

The first issue to consider in allocating human resources is that different people have varying levels of skills, capabilities, needs and motivations for a specific project. The outcome of a project not only depends on allocating sufficient human resource, but also on allocating the right people. Project managers will often have significant experience of individuals and make use of large amounts of anecdotal information on people's performance on projects. There can be a tendency to try to stamp out such thinking, but usually if project managers are to be held accountable for the work on projects it is best to allow them to provide some input on choice of resources for the project.

Resource needs and availability are highly volatile. Project needs change on a daily basis. Staff availability also continually gets modified. Hence any records for supply and demand start to accumulate errors as soon as they are created.

There is a tendency for key people to become involved in high levels of multi-tasking, both at a project or programme and at a portfolio level. Individuals end up working on multiple projects and have to keep swapping projects regularly. The theory of constraints shows that multi-tasking for constrained resource should not be done. It is more efficient to allocate constrained resources to tasks sequentially.

Projects do not need all of their resources at initiation, but will have a profile of usage related to the project plan. Often therefore key resources are not allocated at the start of a project, but only when the project needs them. This increases the risk in project plans, for two reasons. First, new projects may be added to the portfolio, which means that resources that were expected to be available at a future date are no longer available. Second, one project using resources ahead of another project may overrun on its schedule. This overrunning will then delay the second project waiting for the resource.

The marginal impact on resources of adding one more project is often invisible to the sponsors of projects. The impact is felt by the individual or the team the resource comes from, rather than the person asking for the project. This leads to pressure to over-commit resources continually. An important role of prioritization in portfolio management is to overcome such pressures.

All of these issues contribute to the need for resource information to be regularly updated as situations change, and resourcing decisions and trade-offs to be made on a regular basis. This is a core feature of operating a dynamic project portfolio typical of most businesses.

Because of the ongoing work and risk involved in securing resources for projects, project managers do have a tendency to hoard resources. Individuals are kept artificially busy so they will be available when required. Project managers build up "squirrel stores" of equipment and consumables that they require. Doing this benefits an individual project and project manager at the cost of overall portfolio efficiency and should be discouraged.

The availability of external contract and consulting resources means that the apparent resource pool is expandable, in practical terms, without limit. Although it is not always true, contract resource is generally more expensive than internal staff. There are some situations where it is essential to use external staff as the skills do not exist in-house, but in many project situations contract staff are simply used as an extension of the in-house staff pool.

There is a tendency for the highest-priority projects to be given first access to internal resources. Lower-priority projects, if they are to run, have no choice but to use external resources. This can result in the lowest-priority projects having a higher cost base than the highest-priority. This in turn can lead to more problems justifying lower-priority projects. Whether or not this is a problem depends on viewpoint. On one hand the lowest-priority project having the highest resource cost seems intuitively wrong. On the other hand, it means the chance of a lower-priority project starting is reduced, and this is a reasonable result of effective prioritization.

Case Study **4.1   RESOURCING A CHANGE PROGRAMME**

James Edwards is a project manager with Enixus Limited, a specialist consultancy, providing project and change managers to businesses mainly in high-tech industries. In 2006–2007 he was involved in a large-scale business change programme within a leading provider of telecommunications services. This case study covers his experience of resource allocation for this change programme.

James Edwards

At the start of the programme we ran some workshops which defined what our objectives were. The programme objectives were defined in terms of improvements in customer service as well as cost reductions. The workshops were really great, and the programme started with a fanfare of high expectations and a buzz of excitement. Senior management saw the programme as highly beneficial and a real opportunity for the business.

Following the workshops I started to develop a plan for the programme. However, the nature of this type of business change work is that it is very difficult, and possibly counter-productive, to be prescriptive in terms of a detailed work breakdown structure and task allocation. This meant it was initially difficult to be precise about what resources were required.

I therefore started by requesting a small team of subject matter experts in the business to work together to identify what could really be changed, and how this could be achieved. It took me a couple of weeks to get this team, but I was fortunate in getting some really good people who were willing to give the programme 100% of their effort.

The initial team progressed intensively for a few weeks and came back with a plan and a request for additional resource. The resource required was a combination of specialist resources such as project managers, Six-Sigma black belts and business analysts, as well as a larger team of operational staff with experience and detailed understanding of the operations of the business. Most of the specialist resource was to be found externally.

A budget was allocated with sufficient funds to recruit contract team members, and operational managers were requested to provide experts from their areas of the business to support the project. As it was a business change project, operational staff were essential to design practical changes; to explain current operational problems; and to identify potential problems in implementation. There was little problem recruiting the necessary external resource, but operational staff were provided in very small numbers and often only on a part-time basis. Although operational management supported the programme, their view was that having had their staff budgets cut recently they had too few team members already without having to hand over some of their best people to a large programme.

The project team worked the best we could with the resources we had. But I realized there simply was not enough expertise in the team. All the consultants and specialists in the world cannot drive business change without sufficient involvement of people who really understand the details of the business. I had to escalate this problem to the COO.

Fortunately, the COO and the CEO were very supportive of the programme, and they gave their backing to allocating more resources to it. This was helpful and did significantly increase the numbers of operational staff on the programme. However, it was from such a small base that even with this increase we were still struggling to achieve progress at what seemed like a reasonable rate. Although the COO supported us, his backing did not always turn into action by the operational directors to provide the resources we needed.

At this time the project team also started to throw up some relatively simple IT requirements from our programme needing the support of IT and the management information team. We needed some simple reports set up, and a basic database. The reports required someone from the business's management information team. I requested someone and got no one. I remonstrated with the manager of this team and indicated that we were prioritized as one of the most critical programmes in the business. He was sympathetic, but his priorities were set independently of the project portfolio, and his team worked to a completely independent schedule. However, with some serious horse-trading I was able to get someone allocated after a few weeks to create our reports.

Gaining IT resource was even harder. The one programme in the business with a higher priority than ours was a major systems re-development programme, which was happening just following a cost-cutting programme in IT. This meant that although the IT department had almost 1000 staff, there was no one available with the skills we needed. The irony was that the IT re-development programme would run for another 18 months, whilst our project needed someone for 10 days work at most. I could not contract externally as the job needed familiarity with our internal systems. Again, with some difficult negotiations I got the resource we needed, but only after some time and by trading one of my project managers back to the IT department in return for the analyst-programmer we needed. (The portfolio management team don't really like it when you do bilateral deals like this between programmes, but sometimes it's the only way to get resources you need.)

The operational experts on the programme team continued to increase, but remained below optimum; especially as the programme progressed, the project team started to identify a whole new range of activities we could do to improve the business. At this time I took a hard decision. We had some great specialists, but, frankly, without good operational people to work with we were wasting money. So, I chose to reduce our specialist resources (project managers, Six-Sigma black belts, business analysts). Although we could afford to keep them on the programme there was no point without the backing of sufficient operational resource.

Although we did not have enough resource, we were making progress. In fact, it was good progress relative to the resources we had, even if it was less progress than we had originally envisaged. As we had carefully managed expectations the business was generally happy with what we had achieved – and having got rid of some of the external resource we were running below budget. We worked on like this for about four months making steady, reliable progress.

Getting the right resources continued to be a major headache, and I spent a fair proportion of my time in meetings with managers convincing them to provide staff to support the programme by doing some task or the other. Some departments were more helpful than others. On some occasions the negotiations to get staff for the programme took longer than the task requiring the resource needed!

In the last quarter of the year although the programme was starting to be seen as a success, our budget was cut. The business was not thriving and it needed to reduce costs quickly. Most discretionary budgets were cut. Although our programme was reducing costs, our timescales were too slow and the business needed to cut costs quickly.

In response to the reduction in our budget I reduced our external specialist resources further still, and let go of several good team members. This had an impact on the programme. Ironically, at the same time some of the operational departments started to provide more resources for the programme. I think this had less to do with support for the programme, and was more to keep all their people busy to avoid redundancies that were happening as part of the business's cost-cutting. Nevertheless it was helpful, and I mitigated the loss of external resource by using internal resource. Although their skills were not quite as good, with some rapid training they were helpful to the programme.

Currently, the work is ongoing and will continue into the next year. It has been a good, if at times frustrating and difficult, piece of work. My main challenge as the programme manager has been finding and allocating sufficient resources, and regularly re-planning based on the resources allocated. This has been a daily challenge. At times the team has been unbalanced with too many of one type of skills and not enough of another. In the end I have found it helpful at times to let people go, rather than hoard them, though as the programme manager I was always uncomfortable doing this.

I have learnt a lot this year!

At the time of writing this, James was preparing a budget and plan for the programme to continue in the next financial year. He was optimistic that with his knowledge of the programme now he could develop a realistic plan, scaled to whatever budget is actually allocated to the programme for the following year.

More information on Enixus can be found at www.enixus.co.uk

Managing resources through project or programme lifecycles

Ensuring a project has the right resources when it is initiated is only the starting point of resource management for project and programme managers. Resource planning, allocation and management are dynamic activities that must go on throughout the lifecycle of a project.

Specific issues which cause changes to resource requirements during a project's progress include

o Alterations in allocated resource availability. Staff may become sick or be pulled onto new higher-priority projects. The same can happen with equipment or consumables. Budgets can be reduced as a result of overall business pressures. Project managers regularly have to manage such situations.

o The impact of other projects on to-be-allocated resources. A project may be waiting for a resource to be made available once another project completes a series of tasks. If these tasks are delayed for any reason, then it is likely that availability of the resource will also be delayed.

o Variations in actuals versus planned. Plans are estimates and as such subject to uncertainty, unknowns and risk. For many reasons plans can be wrong, and this will knock onto the resources required to complete a project. (This is discussed in more detail in Chapter 6.) Different types of projects are susceptible to variations and amenable to risk reduction in plans to varying extents. *Hard* projects are typically more amenable to uncertainty reduction than *soft* (Atkinson et al., 2006).

o Changes in business needs. The requirements, objectives and scope of a project are liable to change any time, as business needs adapt to the ever-changing competitive and regulatory environment a business operates in. Any change to requirements, objectives or scope is liable to have a subsequent impact on the resources required by a project.

All of these issues are manageable to some extent with the use of risk management, which is described in Chapter 11.

When it comes to human resources there is another challenge for project managers, and that is the issue of motivation. Even the most highly skilled person will deliver little on a project with insufficient motivation. Human motivation tends to fluctuate depending on a large range of factors. Not only the staff need to be motivated to complete a project task efficiently, but the motivation needs to be maintained throughout the life of their involvement in the project. Maintaining a motivated project team is an important skill for project managers.

Resources: solution and problem

Resources are always required on projects, and insufficient resource will result in delay and, in some cases, in project failure. It is important to understand that the provision of resources is not a panacea that will resolve all project problems. Often junior and inexperienced project managers will look for more resources to solve project problems they have. Senior management can exacerbate this tendency by offering more resources to projects that are perceived to be late or in difficulty.

In many situations providing additional resources will speed up project progress and may help to overcome problems that arise on projects. But more resource is not always the solution.

For more resource to be a solution to project delay the problem the project is grappling with has to be dividable into multiple work streams. This is not always possible. If one person is completing a task too slowly a second person may be brought in to assist, but this will only have an effect if the work can be broken into two parts. (Project managers frequently quote the following anecdote as an example of this: *one woman can have a baby in nine months, but nine women cannot have one in a month.*)

Even if a problem can be subdivided into the work of multiple people, additional resource brings its own issues. New staff brought into a project take time to learn what a project is about and take time to become productive. New staff can initially slow down progress, as they often require the time of otherwise productive project team members to explain the project to them. In addition, the larger the project team the more complicated the management challenge becomes. A project manager capable of delivering a project with 20 team members may lose control if he is suddenly confronted with 50 or 60 staff. As early as 1975 Brooks identified that extra resource on late-running software projects tends to make them later rather than speed up progress (Brooks, 1995).

As one manager at a multi-billion-pound enterprise formed from several mergers once lamented:

> *It used to be we had very little resource. So we just had to get on, make decisions and do things. Now we have loads of resource, we spend our whole time in analysis and choosing between options and it takes ages to get anything done.*

Responsibilities for resource management

One of the complicating factors in resource management is understanding who is responsible for it. In many organizations there are split responsibilities which makes resource management complex. For example, a project manager will be responsible for sourcing the resources required for a project, but usually will not have any dedicated team of his own. Conversely, a line manager who has a team may not have any project responsibilities and may not perceive providing resources to a specific project as her problem.

A typical spread of responsibilities includes

- *Project or programme manager* is responsible for defining resource needs, seeking commitment from line managers to provide resources according to the planned requirements, adjusting plans according to resource availability, and managing resources to the plan, once allocated to a project.
- *A central project function* (this may be a project office or the portfolio manager) aggregates resource demands and identifies constraints across the business where prioritization decisions will need to be made.
- *Portfolio manager* provides prioritization, and facilitates decision-making on allocations when bottlenecks occur. Ideally resource allocation will be based on prioritization. (In practice, it is not always possible to mechanistically apply prioritizations. For example, it may be sensible to provide a scarce resource for one day to enable a lower-priority project to complete when the higher-priority project the resource is working on will not deliver for at least another six months. This can only happen occasionally or else the higher-priority project will start to slip.)
- *Line management* is responsible for day-to-day management of resources, and commitment of them to specific projects based on agreed priorities. But line managers will also have separate objectives which sit outside and may conflict with the objectives of projects.
- *HR* is responsible for the development of resource pool to meet project requirements over time, as well as the provision of suitable information and tools for resource management.
- *Equipment or facilities management* is responsible for the provision and scheduling of access to scarce equipment and facilities required by projects.
- *Procurement* supports the provision of consumables and any contract or temporary resource.

Resource management tools

This chapter has introduced the complexity of resource management, which is associated with a large amount of highly volatile information. Various software vendors understand this issue and have developed a range of tools to support this work.

The main tools, from a human resources perspective, are

- Planning and estimating tools, which often incorporate resource levelling algorithms. It is important to understand that there are different algorithms which achieve different resource outcomes implemented by different vendor's software.
- Databases of what resources exist and their skills and capabilities. Such information needs to be easy to update and maintain. Ideally, it should also include factors such as performance levels. Information on people's skills and capabilities needs interpretation. Project managers tend to rely on or be supported by anecdotal information owing both to limitations of systems and to unwillingness to put certain information into a system.
- Aggregated resource demand and supply profiles which may or may not be linked to planning tools.
- Timesheet systems which are often linked to forward-looking resource utilization, and hence can be used to identify resource availability. Timesheet systems also support verification of what work staff are actually doing. There is often some sensitivity in introducing timesheets as it can be interpreted as only being useful because management do not trust staff.

From a finance and budgeting perspective project managers often maintain their own spreadsheets for finance tracking. There are many project accounting systems available. These can be stand alone or part of a business's overall ERP system.

The functionality for resource management can exist in many different parts of a business's software systems. It is often a challenge to draw these together cohesively into an effective integrated solution. (A difficult project in its own right!) Adding to this complexity, some of the components will probably be designed without project needs specifically in mind, and there are often overlaps in functionality between different systems. Nevertheless it is possible to pull together effective resource management systems.

Functionality to support project resource management exists in

- *ERP systems*, especially those components associated with HR information, and also project accounting systems
- *Stand alone HR systems*, if the HR system is not an integral component of the ERP
- *Specialist resource planning systems*, especially those components associated with aggregating resource demand and time sheets
- *Project and programme management tools*, especially those components associated with planning and estimation, as well as resource modelling and levelling
- *Portfolio management tools and professional services automation (PSA) software*, including timesheets, resource aggregation and prioritization support

Case Study **4.2   HOW DO YOU MANAGE THE RESOURCES IN YOUR TEAM TO DELIVER THE COMPLEX SET OF INITIATIVES YOU ARE INVOLVED WITH?**

Marie Dutton is a head of department, responsible for the successful implementation of change across the operations division in a major corporation. She leads a team of change managers who have a hybrid skill-set bringing together project and change management skills as well as knowledge of operations.

Marie Dutton

Right now is an interesting time to answer that question because we are in a state of transition. The business as a whole has a new leadership team and a new divisional structure. This is creating a significant pressure for change. As a result we have been working on a new strategy for the operational departments, which has had a real impact on what my team is doing.

Having said that, in one way it's the same as ever, as it's never really stable!

With the new leadership team coming in place we had to revisit all the work we were doing. All the change in the division has been combined into a single portfolio of work called ADEPT.

To begin with, ADEPT was just a list of ideas. It was a brain-dump, a set of everything anyone might want to do. We did not really have an impression of what the whole thing looked like. So, my team were given one month to shape, scope and develop a resource plan for ADEPT. Our first role was to tease out from our senior managers what they really want delivered.

There was a huge number of potential projects in ADEPT. With our level of resources we realized we could not do them all. So, next we developed a scoring system to assess all the projects and determine which ones we would focus on. This gave us a smaller set – but it was still 61 initiatives. Seven of these were large programmes in their own right, with several projects in each of them. As we did the assessment our senior stakeholders would change their minds, so we had to be very responsive in adding and deleting projects.

In the first month we assessed the projects, prioritized them and estimated the man-days and skill-sets required to do them. Determining skill-sets is important, though in reality you don't always have the option of putting the people with the right skills on a project, and you have to allocate the person who is available. At the end of the month we did a sense-check and a review with the managing director. This was more like asking "does this feel right" than a detailed assessment. With a few more tweaks we were ready to start implementing ADEPT.

In the first two weeks of implementation we had to include ten new projects in ADEPT without any additional resource. To accommodate this we had to stop other projects. At this rate within about two months we would have changed every project in the portfolio. I had to work with senior stakeholders to try and manage the rate of change to the portfolio. I have to be flexible, but they have to be realistic. Already the work of five people from my team was stopped, and they were moved onto other work. So within two weeks we had wasted fifty man-days of work.

The reasons for the ongoing modification to the portfolio are two-fold: first, we do work in a dynamic business, and as such we have to be responsive to the market; and second, as we have a new leadership team their thinking is not yet stable.

In terms of converting the work into a resource plan, I can, on paper, predict what people I need; what can be done with the people I have; and who will do what. In practice, this is always more volatile and messy. Most of my time as the departmental head is spent on resolving resourcing issues – "here is a new piece of work, who shall I allocate to do it?" I should be spending more time on resolving real project and change issues, but right now they feel like a distraction from the problem of simply finding people to do the work we have been allocated.

When a new project comes around I have an immediate thought – "how possibly can I resource this?" but then we find a way. I have a central planning manager who goes through what options there are for resourcing every piece of work – which team members are not fully busy, where can we free up time, can we juggle the order of anything, what choices have to be made and so on. My planning manager is valuable. Personally, I think for a team of ten people upwards a line manager needs some kind of resource planning function, even if it is a part-time role.

As well as dealing with the projects the planning office has to account for staff availability, considering factors such as holidays and training. For holidays there is a simple rule – only so many people can be on holiday at any one time. For training, it's harder to plan as there is a tendency for training to be delayed and delayed until everyone goes at the same time – at the end of the business year.

Loading is a matter of judgement. Some people with specialist roles on large projects may be allocated to nine or ten projects in parallel. Others with more central or bigger role on a programme may only be able to handle one or two things at a time. The sizing of each piece of work is not scientific; it is based on experience. However, we do have a way to continually improve our estimates.

Everyone completes time sheets once a week and I can see who has been working on what. This has many advantages. One of them is that I can see how many hours are actually spent on each piece of work, and compare it with our estimates. This gives a feedback loop that builds an ever-improving picture of how long different types of work really take. When I add on my gut feel of how long a piece of work should take we normally have a pretty good idea of what resources we need for every project. We don't resource plan from detailed bottom-up estimates of project tasks – it takes far too long, and we don't have enough information about the project when it starts.

Timesheets are useful. They provide information, although it does need some interpretation as different people have different ways of filling them in. They also provide a way to ensure no one is overloaded. I try not to use timesheets to spy on the team or as a stick – this is counter-productive. But I do use them to identify who is overloaded and then we can find a way out of that situation, and determine what we can do for people when we are asking them to work too many hours.

From the timesheets I have a monthly utilization report. I review this with my direct reports. We check where we are against plan and what changes we have to make taking account of up-to-date resource availability.

Whatever processes, forms and databases are used for managing resources, have to be pragmatic. People in my team aren't paid to fill in a timesheet, but to deliver change. Bureaucracy must be minimal.

What makes someone successful in a role like mine? Three things I think: being passionate and focussed when it comes to delivery; being very organized, there is constant juggling and this can't be done if you are not organized; and finally, having credibility both with customers and with the team.

MAIN LEARNING POINTS FROM CHAPTER 4

- Resource availability determines the scope and boundaries of an organization's project portfolio.
- For an individual project, resource needs are theoretically determined by the project plan, but in reality the plan is constrained by resource availability. Planning and resource estimation are inter-dependent and iterative activities. An important planning tool for the project manager is resource levelling.
- Four types of resources have to be considered in planning projects: money, human resources, equipment and facilities, and consumables. People are the most complex to manage, and it is often the availability of staff that determines a project's timelines. The categories of resource are not independent – for example, the availability of budget affects the level of human resourcing possible on a project.
- Resource management is highly dynamic. Information on resource needs and availability is subject to progressive elaboration and continuous change. Estimates for resources are subject to error and regular updates. Project needs regularly change. Staff availability, motivation and productivity fluctuate.
- Resource management can achieve different long-term objectives – maximizing staff utilization, maximizing project output, or maintaining flexibility to respond to new demands. Often there is an attempt to try and achieve all three objectives, but they are incompatible.
- The effects of poor resource management are most obvious to project managers on a short-term basis, with continuous balancing between over-commitment and stock-piling.
- There is a tendency to plan resources to multi-task on many activities at once – this is usually inefficient and leads to extended delivery timescales.
- Project and portfolio managers often have to trade-off effective resource management with practicality. The management information for resource management can become a major resource overhead in its own right. One way to provide an effective and practical level of resource management is to maintain a capacity analysis of utilization and availability only for key bottlenecked resources.

REVIEW QUESTIONS AND EXERCISES

1. Case Study 4.1 provides an example of resourcing a specific project. How does this match with your experience of gaining resource for project work? How easy did you find it to gain the resources you needed? How could businesses improve the way resources are allocated to projects?
2. What are the strengths and weaknesses of the following: to run many value-adding projects in parallel, or to run them sequentially? Which alternatives are better in which situations? Why?
3. Consider the requirements for a database to store information on staff for projects. What tasks will this database support? What data would you want to keep? What are essential and what are nice-to-have? How would you collect and maintain this data? What problems can you foresee?
4. Select three different organizations which you are familiar with. Broadly how would you define their strategy, competitive situation and financial position? What would you expect their resource management objectives generally to be, and how would you expect this to be reflected in project progress?

5. Imagine that you are the head of a programme management function in a large business. You are being asked to support the annual budgeting process by providing input on the budgets required for programmes and projects in the following year. How would you approach this challenge? Are there any particular issues you would be cautious of?

6. How do management accounting systems and processes help project managers, and in what situations are they a hindrance?

7. Consider a project you have been involved in. Write a brief definition of the project's scope and objectives. How would you determine the resources required for this project? What are the risks and issues in the approach you have chosen and how will you deal with them?

8. How do you see the relationship between a project manager who needs resources, and an operational manager who has a team? How would you advise a project manager to approach gaining resources from an operational manager?

Suggested reading

Most good project management primers will cover resource management to a limited extent (e.g. Levine, 2002). At the other extreme there are books which go into significant details of subjects such as different resourcing algorithms (e.g. Schwindt, 2005), which are usually only relevant to individuals who want to specialize in these areas.

Brooks' book *The Mythical Man Month and Other Essays on Software Engineering*, although based on some relatively old work, and written about software development, still provides an interesting read for those wanting to understand the pitfalls in resource management (Brooks, 1995).

Bibliography

Atkinson, R., Crawford, L. and Ward, S. "Fundamental uncertainties in project and the scope of project management". *International Journal of Project Management*. Volume 24, Issue 8, November 2006, pp. 687–98.

Brooks, F. *The Mythical Man Month and Other Essays on Software Engineering*. Addison Wesley, 2nd edition. August 1995.

Cooper, R., Edgett, S. and Kleinschmidt, E. "Portfolio management for new product development: Results of an Industry Practices Study". *R&D Management*. Volume 31, Issue 4, 2001, pp. 361–80.

Engwall, M. and Jerbrant, A. "The resource allocation syndrome: The primary challenge of multi-project management". *International Journal of Project Management*. Volume 21, Issue 6, August 2003, pp. 403–409.

Goldratt, E. *Critical Chain*. The North River Press, 1997.

Levine, H. *Practical Project Management. Tips, Tactics, and Tools*. John Wiley & Sons Inc, 2002, pp. 117–75.

Patrick, FS. *Programme Management – Turning Many Projects into Few Priorities with TOC*. National Project Management Symposium, Philadelphia, October 1999.

Schwindt, C. *Resource Allocation in Project Management*. Springer-Verlag Berlin and Heidelberg GmbH & Co. K, June 2005.

Treble, S. and Douglas, N. *Sizing and Estimating Software in Practice: Making MK II Function Points Work*. McGraw-Hill Publishing Co. May 1995.

5

exploration and definition of
requirements
and designs

A project starts with an idea. The idea may be a pure creative insight; it could be generated from a need to respond to competitive pressures or the identification of a new opportunity; or it may derive from the desire to overcome an operational problem or inefficiency. Whatever the source, the spark of an idea is essential, but ideas are not enough to define projects in such a way as to ensure the outcome is as required.

Projects require a thorough definition of the outcome desired. This definition has a number of labels in project management, and terms such as *scope, objectives, requirements, constraints, critical success factors* and *deliverable definitions* are some of the tags used. Reference can be made to documents such as *project definitions, project charters, specifications* and *project scoping documents.* The precise terminology used varies from situation to situation. As long as there is clarity in understanding what terms are used in a given context, and as long as the underlying principles of what is required of a project is appreciated, the variations in terminology should not cause problems. This chapter provides such clarity. It defines the terms it uses and encapsulates the entire definition with the word *requirements*, though also makes reference to *scope* and *objectives.*

The process of defining requirements is characterized by an ongoing tension between the free-wheeling thinking associated with pure creativity, and the more prosaic desire and need of a project manager to tie down projects to concrete deliverable specifics. It is also characterized by the difficulty for many organizations in really understanding their needs in an unambiguous and communicable way. Even where needs are fully understood and definable, they are subject to the pressures of ongoing change and evolution.

Scope, objectives and requirements are the source of many issues and problems within projects. They are subject to ambiguity, misinterpretation and a lack of understanding. They may be insufficiently defined when a project starts, and still subject to ambiguity when a project completes. In some cases they may be indefinable. As a project progresses they can change, and yet they are the foundation a project is built upon.

The nature of requirements and the terminology used vary from context to context. In some situations, such as IT development, there are very formal definitions of requirements and processes for their capture and use. This is usually because the requirements are complex. There may be many thousands of requirements in a major software development project. On the other hand in business change programmes requirements may be rather vague. In some projects requirements are truly limited and can be documented in a few sentences. This chapter assumes some complexity in requirements to enable a full understanding of the range of issues associated with capturing requirements. The chapter has been influenced by the approach to requirements in typical business projects such as IT and new product developments.

This chapter provides an appreciation of requirements and the processes for their collection. It aims to provide the reader with an understanding of the importance of requirements to projects and ways to avoid some of the pitfalls in requirements collection. It starts by introducing some of the terminology and builds a basic linear process for requirements. By considering the relationship between requirements, planning and solutions design, different project lifecycles are explored.

Understanding requirements has developed into a complicated topic, with many specialist concepts only of relevance to expert practitioners. However, requirements management should be of interest to all managers, and some general level of understanding is useful. In complex projects, such as large-scale IT systems, the work involved in requirements collection can form a significant proportion of the overall timeline and resource consumption of the project. Whilst individual requirements are generally of limited interest to senior management, the overall quality of requirements is important. Poor analysis and understanding of requirements have caused the failure of many projects. Finally, depending on the nature of the requirements very different types of project approaches will be required. Management need to be supportive of different lifecycles for different situations.

Understanding and delivering requirements is associated with a number of other components of project management which are discussed in other chapters. Requirements underpin and shape the project plan (see Chapter 6). Errors and unknowns in requirements are a major source of project risk (see Chapter 11). The ongoing elaboration and modification of requirements is the major reason for the need for change control (see Chapter 8).

Objectives and scope – the why and what

The definition of a project starts with a summary description of *why* a project is to be undertaken, and an overview of *what* the project will consist of and deliver. These are referred to as *project objectives* and *project scope*.

A project starts with one or more objectives. The objectives define why a project is being pursued, and what the benefits to the business of doing the project are. Objectives are high-level statements, often no more than one or two sentences, which shape and direct the project. Examples of objectives for a project are

- This project will improve our competitiveness by reducing the cost of customer services by £100m per annum on an ongoing basis.
- This project will prepare the organization for future needs by increasing the number of trained and experienced change management professionals in the organization.
- This project will launch a new product into our core customer segment and increase revenues by £5m per annum.

Arguably, a project can progress without objectives. It could be assumed that a project manager needs to understand what to deliver, not necessarily why he is delivering it. This is generally short-sighted. Objectives provide an overall sense of direction for a project, as well as a reference measure for success at the end of the project. Objectives also help to shape the scope and detailed requirements on a project. As projects progress, a range of decisions need to be made which are influenced by an understanding of objectives.

Where objectives define *why* a project will be undertaken, the scope takes this further and defines *what* the project will be. There are many related definitions of scope. For example,

A description of the sum of the products and services to be provided by the project (PMI, 2004)

Scope describes what you expect to deliver to your customers when the project is complete. Your project scope should define the results to be achieved in specific, tangible, and measurable terms. (Gray and Larson, 2006)

The collection of information you need before you can go on to develop a meaningful activity and resource plan for your project. (Newton, 2005)

Scope contains several different types of information. It contains definitions of the boundaries (what is in and what is out) of the project, deliverables and critical success factors. It should also contain project priorities and constraints to support the trade-off decisions between time, cost and quality. Project priorities are not the same as portfolio priorities, which relate to a project's prioritization versus other projects, but are instead the relative priorities of different aspects of the project, such as whether it is more important to be completed on time or for a certain cost. Constraints are more specific. For example, a constraint may be that a project has to be complete by a certain date, or completed for a maximum cost, or cannot detrimentally affect some other activity in the business. Scope should contain a definition of how the project's success will be assessed (see Chapter 7). Scope also contains the project strategy. The project strategy is a simple summary statement of the general direction the project will take to achieve its objectives. (Scope is often defined to include objectives, but they are separated for clarity in this book.)

The information to define the scope exhaustively can be enormous. Successful project managers are pragmatic about defining scope. For example, the definition

Diagram 5.1 A simple project lifecycle

of what is not in the project only needs to include those things that must be explicit because they may otherwise be assumed to be included. Good project managers recognize the importance of defining the scope of a project, but will do so at a practicable level of detail.

Scope can usually be defined in a few pages of a standard format document. Larger or more complex programmes tend to have longer scope definitions. What is more important is that the scope is correct and comprehensive, rather than it is written in enormous detail. Defining the scope for a project well can take time, but that time should be spent in exploring the implications of scope and clarifying all assumptions rather than worrying about excessive detail. A boundary is usually made between scope which is defined before a project can really start, and *requirements* which contain much more detail and are generally defined as part of the project execution.

As the scope is fundamental to project success, project managers talk of *scope management*. Scope management is the process of determining and then managing the scope definition. It should define the procedures for updating the project definition. A description of scope management is

> *Scope management is the process by which the deliverables and work to produce them are identified and defined.* (APM, 2006)

The objectives and scope form the definition of the project. Where it is possible to define objectives and scope in an exhaustive way it can lead to a simple project lifecycle as shown in Diagram 5.1. The definition phase leads to planning (which in this simple diagram includes resourcing), and then to the execution stage when the deliverables are created and implemented.

Requirements

In many situations objectives and scope are not sufficient to fully define the outcome wanted or deliverables from a project. To deliver the project to meet the needs of the customers of the project, the project team must also understand the project's requirements. Requirements describe the nature and features a project's deliverables must conform to, to achieve the objectives of the project. The APM defines requirements as

> *Requirements are a statement of the need that a project has to satisfy, and should be comprehensive, clear, well structured, traceable and testable.* (APM, 2006)

Unlike scope which is normally defined pragmatically in sufficient detail to enable planning and resourcing to go ahead, requirements need to be exhaustive and define unambiguously all features of the project's deliverables. The collection of requirements is often considered as a stage in project execution. However, it is only after

| Define scope and objectives | | Initial plan | | Requirements analysis | | Detailed plan | | Execute |

Diagram 5.2 Expanding the project lifecycle to show requirement analysis

requirements have been agreed on that a project plan can be developed in a detailed and accurate way. This produces a project lifecycle as shown in Diagram 5.2.

There are different types of requirements. A useful breakdown, often used in IT projects, is between *functional* and *non functional* requirements. Functional requirements define the actual functionality of a software system, that is, what it must be able to do. Non-functional requirements contain a whole host of other factors such as quality and performance characteristics. How fast it must operate, and what availability it must achieve are examples of non-functional requirements. Another important category of requirements is *validation criteria*. Validation criteria are used to check conformance of deliverables to the requirements when the deliverables have been created.

Requirements are usually defined as a specification of need, not of solution. So "I need a way to transport 1000kg of materials on a daily basis from the factory to the sales point" is a valid requirement that defines a need, whereas "I need a Ford Transit van" is not – this is a definition of a solution. Requirements are the formal communication and boundary between the customer and the designer of a solution. By defining requirements as a need, rather than a solution the project stakeholder who defined the requirement does not unnecessarily constrain the project.

Understanding requirements

Project management processes and lifecycles typically show the definition of scope and objectives as part of the project management process. Having defined the scope and objectives, a project manager can create a work breakdown structure (WBS). If more detailed requirements are needed, then a task has to be included in WBS for requirements analysis. In contrast, software development lifecycles, which can be considered as a specialized and extended form of project management process, show requirements analysis as one of the fundamental steps in the process.

The term *requirements management* and *requirements engineering* are used to describe the activity of understanding and implementing requirements. From a project management perspective, the APM defines requirements management as

> ...*the process of capturing, analysing and testing the documented statement of stakeholder and user wants and needs.* (APM, 2006)

All project managers require to some extent the ability to collect and document requirements. Making sense of needs is part of a project manager's role. However, this is just one part of a project manager's role, and in many cases they do not have the full range of skills required to perform requirements analysis. There is a separate, well-recognized discipline for understanding requirements called *business analysis* performed by *business analysts*. A business analyst or even a team of business analysts is a valuable addition to a project of any complexity. Project managers need to work hand-in-hand with business analysts. High-quality project management is often dependent on good business analysis (Lyneham-Brown, 2001).

There are many different processes for requirements management and approaches to business analysis. A typical requirements management process includes the following steps:

o Identify stakeholders
o Elicit requirements
o Analyse requirements
o Document and create requirements specification
o Accept requirements

Understanding requirements starts by identifying the stakeholders in a project. Who can be accepted as a valid stakeholder of this project, and who therefore can place requirements upon the project? These are not, as it may first appear, trivial questions.

Depending on the choice of stakeholders, and their views of requirements, a project can vary significantly in terms of scale, complexity and the direction it takes. Stakeholders can include project sponsors, other managers with an interest in the project, users of the deliverables once the project is complete, subject matter experts, customers of the project – both internal and external to a business, financers and budget holders, suppliers and staff representatives, and anyone else affected by the project.

A project team can usually quickly identify a large group of people who may put requirements onto a project. To ensure the requirements collection can be completed in a sensible amount of time this group has to be kept to a manageable number of individuals. Peripheral stakeholders may be ignored, and individuals are sought to represent groups of stakeholders to reduce the overhead of talking to large numbers of people. The number of acceptable stakeholders will depend on the scale, importance and sensitivity of the project. A small project may have only one stakeholder representative, a major programme may have tens or even hundreds.

Having identified the stakeholders, it is necessary to elicit their requirements. Although simple in principle, the activity of elicitation is beset by all the normal problems of human communications – misinterpretation, misinformation and ambiguity of meaning. People often do not really know what they want or cannot express it in a clear or meaningful way. This can be a major problem with non-functional requirements, especially those associated with defining the quality of deliverables. Business analysts are trained in various ways of collecting requirements. These include structured interviews, group sessions, consulting and workshops, as well as the use of example deliverables and prototypes to encourage thinking. (The use of prototypes is described later in this chapter.)

After eliciting requirements the business analyst must review and check them. Different stakeholders may put forth conflicting requirements. Such conflicts need to be resolved. The requirements must be checked to ensure they are of suitable quality (see next section). Requirements must be clear and understandable. Requirements must be desirable and feasible. Feasibility relates not only to individual requirements, but to the total set. Often more requirements will be generated than can feasibly be delivered in a reasonable amount of time, leading to the need to prioritize requirements and filter out some of the less essential ones.

Finally, the requirements are documented into a form that can be referenced, and signed off or approved by the project sponsor. There are a number of software tools for documenting and referencing requirements.

Collecting requirements is not simply about capturing and cataloguing them – it is also a communications exercise. At one level, this communication exercise is about developing and checking understanding, but at another it is about creating understanding. Through questioning and discourse needs, issues, problems and solutions are explored. The dialogue, debate, compromise, negotiations and decision-making associated with creating a definition of requirements is not merely an overhead that has to be borne to collect requirements, but is the essential activity in creating, understanding and making sense of needs.

Quality requirements

The quality of requirements is critical to successful project delivery. There are two ways of considering quality with regard to requirements:

- What is a quality requirement (i.e. what does a requirement have to conform to, to be of a sufficient level of quality to be acceptable)? What is a quality set of requirements (i.e. do all the requirements together meet needs)?

(There is a third way in which the term 'quality requirement' may also be used. This is defining what quality requirements a project has. Are there specific stakeholder requirements related to quality? This is an important set of requirements, but is not considered in this section of the chapter.)

Quality requirements are documented in such a way as to be *understandable* and *unambiguous*. Requirements may have to be understood by a wide range of people involved in the project, and the way they interpret the words in the requirements specification should be consistent. A requirement should be *correct*, in that it is an accurate representation of need. Each requirement should be *testable*. Once a project is complete it should be possible to test whether the requirement has been met. If a requirement is not testable it will not be possible to be sure if it has been achieved or not. Finally, requirements should be *traceable*. Traceability enables a requirement to be linked back to the originating stakeholder, through the design and implementation process and into the final deliverables of the project. Traceability provides an audit trail to show linkages between the final output and the original requirement. Ideally requirements should be traceable back to the objectives of the project. Requirements which do not link to the project's objectives should, arguably, be removed.

As well as each requirement meeting quality criteria, it is also necessary to ensure that the complete set of requirements also meets a suitable level of quality. A quality set of requirements is *complete*, and *meets needs*. A set of requirements should completely fulfil the project objectives, and meet the needs of the sponsor and customers of the project. It should be possible to link back every requirement to the original objectives, and ensure that every aspect of these objectives will be met by the requirements.

There is a trade-off between the variety and richness of the requirements and the speed and cost to deliver a specific project. It is often necessary to make compromises over the overall quality and completeness of requirements to achieve a deliverable project within the agreed project constraints. As long as this trade-off is an explicit and understood decision by a business it is not a problem.

At times requirements can be added opportunistically by sponsors, because they want them fulfilled irrespective of their relevance to a specific project's objectives. Requirements should be relevant to the objectives of the project and not be included simply because it is possible for them to be delivered by a project.

When considering the role of the project manager with respect to requirements there is a possible ambiguity. A project manager's role may be to deliver what is defined as required, or alternatively it may be to deliver what is needed (which may not be what is defined). This ambiguity lies at the heart of many project problems, and it is essential for project managers to clarify the expectations with regard to their responsibility before progressing with a project. Often a project manager is responsible for delivering whatever requirements are defined, whereas a programme manager may also be accountable for the quality of the requirements and ensuring they meet the programme's objectives.

From requirements to design

Requirements are a definition of need, not the description of a solution to fulfil this need. But a deliverable from a project often needs to be designed. A requirement is a definition of need. The design describes the solution to this need. Project deliverables are designed to meet the defined requirements by a specialist in the domain, whatever, of the project.

This is best explained with a couple of examples. A simple example could be when a backpacker has a need or requirement for a portable shelter. The solution is a tent, so the *design* is the design of a tent meeting the backpacker's requirements. A more complex business example is an IT system to provide a single system for customer service agents to access all the systems they require to resolve customer issues. A requirement collected by a business analyst from an end user could be that the system must be accessible 24 hours a day, 7 days a week. A software engineer must then design a computer system that meets this requirement.

Solutions design can be identified as a separate stage in a project's lifecycle. This results in an extension of the project lifecycle from that depicted in Diagram 5.2 to the one detailed in Diagram 5.3. Diagram 5.3 also shows how the project plan is updated and detailed throughout the project as understanding improves. Two inter-related streams of work for the project manager emerge – managing the process of delivery, shown as the top set of activities in Diagram 5.3, and the ongoing development of the plan as shown in the lower set of activities.

Project stakeholders do not always find it easy or possible to understand or describe requirements simply because they have asked for them. To gather requirements from stakeholders it is often helpful to be shown an example of a solution and then to be questioned on whether it fulfils their needs, and if not what has to be changed. Such an example could be as complex as a working prototype or as simple as a sketch on a piece of paper. Any object that provides improved understanding of what the final solution will look like can be helpful.

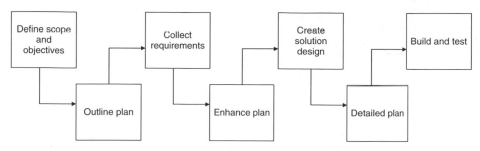

Diagram 5.3 An extended project lifecycle showing the solutions design phase

Papadimitrou and Pellegrin apply Vinck and Jeantet's term *Intermediary Objects of Design*, or *IoD*, to cover any objects such as prototypes, initial designs, pilot implementations and descriptive documents which represent this intermediary form of solution design used in projects. The term IoD is useful as a generic term to cover a variety of situations in which some example is used to help to extract requirements from stakeholders. Their research shows how IoDs are used to make sense of project needs. (Papadimitrou and Pellegrin, 2007; Vinck and Jeantet, 1995.)

The concept of an IoD is best explained through examples. A simple non-business example might be when someone wants to decorate a room. They know they want to paint it yellow, but cannot describe which colour. By showing a colour chart with different shades of yellow it is much easier to define the requirement. A more complex business example could be a business defining its needs for a new office. Representatives of the business can define their requirements – but it is only when they see a plan of the new office, or even a model of it, that they are able to really define all their requirements and confirm that what they have said is really what they want.

The concept of an IoD can be used to create an extension of the design process from that shown in Diagram 5.3 to the one shown in Diagram 5.4. Rather than creating a design following requirements, an initial design is produced in an IoD, which in turn helps to generate fuller requirements.

In some situations the IoD is discarded, the same way that a plan of a house can be discarded once the house is built. It was merely an aid to reaching the final solution, and has no value once that solution is created. However, in other situations an IoD may be iteratively refined in an ongoing dialogue with stakeholders until it becomes the final solution. This is shown in Diagram 5.5. Such an approach is only suitable for certain types of deliverables. Some component IT systems are developed in this way, for example, certain user interfaces.

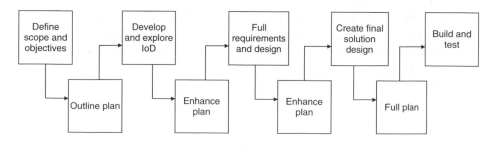

Diagram 5.4 A project lifecycle using an IoD to make sense of requirements

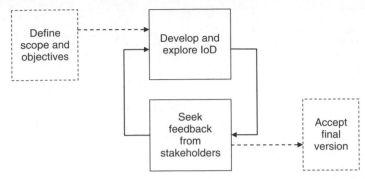

Diagram 5.5 Using an Intermediary Object of Design to create a project's final solution

Testing and assessing conformance to requirements

A quality set of requirements may exist, but that does not mean that the end deliverables will conform to them. Misinterpretations may occur in the design of a solution. Designers may deliberately or unconsciously make compromises to speed up the development of a design. Errors may come in during the activity of building a solution. In many complicated developments it is not possible to ensure without formal checking that all requirements have been met.

Checking whether deliverables conform to the original requirements is called *testing*. Testing is a formal activity carried out following a *test specification* or *test script*. The test script defines precisely which tests are to be performed and presents *validation criteria* for the different tests. Validation criteria define what the outcome from a specific test should be. Another term in use is a *test case*. A test case is the definition of an individual test including precise instructions on how the test is to be performed and what the outcome should be. A test consists of many test cases.

Often there is a need for a series of tests. The nature of tests and the stages of testing depend on the nature of deliverables. A typical series of tests, based on a technology development project, are

- o *Functional test*: Do the deliverables perform the functions that they were meant to perform?
- o *Integration test*: When the deliverables are integrated with other technologies that they are meant to work with do they still work in the way expected, and without adversely impacting the other systems?
- o *User acceptance test*: When the deliverables are used by user representatives are they satisfied that the deliverables meet requirements?
- o *Systems test*: When the deliverables are implemented into a live technical environment do they still work in the way expected, and without adversely impacting the other systems? Are the defined non-functional requirements, such as performance levels, achieved?
- o *Operational test*: When users of the systems start actively using the deliverables, do they work the way the users expect and in a way that is acceptable to the users?

There may also be separate tests to check with customers new deliverables or changes in a business. Such tests are often called *trials*.

Testing requires acceptance by those members of an organization who are involved in using the deliverables once the project is complete. So, the user acceptance test is an important stage when formal sign-off on the deliverables is achieved.

Of course, tests may fail. If they do, some parts of the deliverables need to be improved or changed. Depending on the nature of the failure this may require re-work. The need for re-work is a driver of the desire for quality throughout the project delivery process. The later in this process an error is found, typically, the more expensive it is to rectify. It is far easier and cheaper to fix and error in requirements collection than in solutions design, and in solutions design than in solutions build.

Testing is not a foolproof process. Designing tests to ensure compliance with all requirements is complex and time-consuming. In addition, some requirements – especially non-functional requirements and those associated with defining the quality of deliverables – may not be economically testable, or testable in a sufficiently short period of time. Designing tests is typically a trade-off between the completeness of the testing, and the time and cost it requires.

5

Case Study 5.1 HOW DO YOU COLLECT REQUIREMENTS AND WHAT COMMON ISSUES DO YOU HAVE TO DEAL WITH?

Sauming Pang is an expert in product development, with a specialization in service development and service design in the telecommunications industry. She is the author of Successful Service Design in Telecommunications: a comprehensive guide to design and implementation, published by John Wiley.

Sauming Pang

The way to collect requirements does depend on the situation. I work with new products, and the people I collect requirements from are usually product managers and customers.

Put simply, the way to collect requirements is by asking open questions. When collecting requirements for a new product I will start by asking who are the customers for the product, what they want it for, and how they will use it. Understanding the business context and the objectives of the product is the best starting point. Having ascertained that I move on to ask more specific questions, such as what features and functions do they want. As the information expands I will ask more and more detailed questions.

There is not an exhaustive set of questions that will help you understand all requirements, but there are some obvious ones to start with, for example,

What type of customers (business or retail) will be using the service? What is the sales forecast for the service? Will the customers be expecting a 24 × 7 customer service?

If you go into a garage to buy a new car the salesman may have a set of standard questions because he is trying to steer you towards one of a limited number of choices. With a new product it's not like that, there is usually no pre-defined answer and so there is no complete set of pre-defined questions.

So far this is simple, but there are a number of problems that occur whilst understanding requirements. The first problem is that people don't actually know what they want. They have a vague picture in their head, or some general idea, but that is not enough to define requirements. When I ask "what do you want", they reply "what have you got"! There are various ways around this problem. In collecting requirements I am as much helping them to understand what they want as am extracting information from them. I can use more structured questions, make suggestions, go through user-cases or scenarios, show prototypes, run workshops and so on.

Prototypes are really helpful. They help to make ideas concrete, as requirements are quite abstract. Having a prototype that roughly does what someone wants, based on a few requirements and a designer's interpretation of what this means, is extremely useful in developing a much better understanding of requirements. The prototype can be very simple, and does not have to be correct, as long as it helps the customer to think through what they want.

In specifying requirements people often stipulate solutions and not requirements. This should be prevented if possible. It can't always be, and sometimes they are adamant that a specific solution should be used. If possible, it should be avoided as often customers or product managers don't have sufficient knowledge or expertise to choose a solution. The solution they have chosen may be sub-optimal.

Of course, occasionally the opposite happens, whereby we have a solution we want the customer to choose, and we need to try and steer the requirements to make them fit this!

It is common for customers to put forth requirements that are not possible or are in conflict with other requirements. The answer to this is to give choices. It is not necessary to tell them they cannot have a requirement met. Very few things are truly impossible; it's just they are not possible within time or cost constraints. This can effectively be done by offering them a choice such as "you can have A, but it will cost you £1m, but if you are happy to compromise with B we can deliver it for £50K". Most people, given such a choice will accept B!

If two different customers are putting forth conflicting requirements then this must be resolved. The easiest way is to determine who is the more powerful or influential person in an organization. I'm afraid seniority rules here. If that is not possible then a sponsor or a senior person must be asked to choose between the options. Unfortunately, conflict is not normally clear-cut. There may be different ways of looking at the same problem which can produce multiple requirements for the same problem.

Often customers will raise meaningless requirements; for example, these are common with reporting. "We want a report which shows X", is the style of requirement. But when you look at X, you can see the information is not available, will not be meaningful, and will not enable any form of management decision-making. It can take considerable effort making someone understand that a requirement is not meaningful. One way to gain an understanding is to ask why they raise this requirement.

Another area of difficulty is with non-functional requirements. Asking someone whether a product should do A or B is normally straightforward. Getting them to define factors such as how many customers will use the product, how many at any one time, what is the required response time of the system, what fault rate is acceptable, and what service level is needed is much harder. The starting point for non-functional requirements has to be convincing customers or product managers that they are even necessary. Telling a customer something like "is it ok to wait five minutes between responses to key strokes?" normally makes them understand the need to be as specific with non-functional requirements as with functional. Once this understanding is achieved, it's back to the same process of gradually more detailed questioning. Questions like how many, how fast, how reliable or how accurate are the basis of non-functional requirements.

There are other areas of requirements that are often forgotten as well, such as reporting or management information.

The next problem to deal with is that as requirements are collected there can be too many. If there are too many, a project to deliver them will never finish and cost too much. This has to be resolved by categorization, and then prioritization based on categories. I think that there is no point having more than three categories – category 1, which must be included, category 2, which should be included and category 3, which are nice to have and will probably be left out. If you break into more categories it can soon become meaningless. If you have five categories and you know that all of category 1 and 2 will be included, and all of 4 and 5 will be rejected you might as well consolidate to three.

The final common problem is not knowing how to make sure requirements are complete. In one way requirements are never fully complete, so the goal is for them to be complete enough. What analysis can be done to ensure requirements are complete? This is a judgement based on experience. In some situations, such as when there is a known solution and the requirements are to tailor it to a specific context, it is possible to have a reasonably exhaustive set of questions. Even when you know in what areas requirements are needed it is not a foolproof way to know you have the complete set, as having a requirement for a part of a solution is not the same as having the right or best requirement!

As well as problems with customers, analysts themselves can make mistakes. One to avoid is not collecting or documenting enough supporting information on a requirement. Requirements have a number of attributes beyond the statement of need. Most of the attributes support the management of requirements, and are important. A requirement contains a unique ID, the definition of need, some form of categorization to understand where it fits, a priority, information to enable traceability known and the requirement source, a flag for compliance – will the product meet this requirement or not – and perhaps a phase if the product will be delivered in a multi-phase programme and so on. One may choose to use a requirements management tool to manage all the requirements. Requirements management tools are extremely useful when it comes to testing and assessing the compliance of requirements.

Amongst these attributes traceability is particularly important. Traceability is essential to manage requirements, to resolve conflicts, and to understand when requirements become obsolete due to a change in business drivers. If a solution becomes non-compliant with a requirement the originator of the requirement has to know. Also if two requirements are in conflict, traceability enables the analyst to understand who needs to be involved in choosing between the options.

Understanding requirements can be complex and time-consuming, but it lies at the heart of the delivery of any project.

Managing requirements across multiple projects

The collection and implementation of requirements has been described in this chapter as if it is a sub-component of an individual project. Requirements are defined as a step in the project, the project is managed to deliver those requirements, and finally some checking and any necessary re-work are performed to ensure conformance to requirements.

Requirements are often managed like this, but requirements management can be considered as a process that sits outside of a project lifecycle, and which interacts with it and the lifecycles of other projects. It may have to be considered as 'outside' the process of an individual project because

o Within a programme, requirements may not be fulfilled within an individual project, but may be stored for later phases of the programme.
o Requirements may be excluded from a project or programme, but need to be captured for consideration in other projects in the portfolio.

Compromises often have to be made on the scale and variety of requirements to meet time and cost constraints in projects. Individual requirements which have only limited effect on meeting objectives, or those which are particularly hard or expensive to achieve, may be left out of a project.

Programmes will often have several phases of delivery. Programme managers can structure their work so that each phase delivers progressively more of the requirements. A typical approach may be to have an initial project which delivers only the absolutely essential and easiest-to-implement functionality. Further projects within the programme are run to meet additional requirements. A *requirements catalogue*, which contains all the requirements across the phases of the programme is set up.

Requirements will be rejected from even the largest of programmes with the most comprehensive phases of projects. From a portfolio perspective it is worth considering what happens to valid requirements that are rejected and for which there is no project or programme delivering them. The requirement can simply be forgotten about, but if it is a valid and potentially value-adding requirement it should be captured and stored in a requirements catalogue to be considered for inclusion in future projects.

From the perspective of an individual project all requirements should link back to the original objectives. This ideal was noted earlier in the chapter. However, from a corporate- or organization-wide perspective this is not always optimal. A project that is working on a set of deliverables, which may have use for another part of the business, can have additional requirements added for expediency or efficiency. For example, in a business expansion project to create a new customer call centre a new building is found and is being fitted out for the new call centre. What if the marketing department, is also growing and requires additional space? Rather than setting up a separate project, they may ask for some building space to be created in the new building. Although the project objectives relate to providing more room for an enlarged customer services centre, the marketing department's requirements could be included for expediency.

There is a risk, however, with adding requirements to projects that do not contribute to the project's objectives. This is the risk of *scope creep*. Scope creep is the term used by project managers to describe the situation in which the scope, objectives and requirements on a project expand. If this happens without control, then there is a danger that project timelines, budgets and risk levels increase – sometimes to the state at which the project is no longer achievable, or cannot be achieved within the constraints or expectations of the business. *Change control* is the a mechanism to manage scope creep (see Chapter 8).

Difficulties of the classical approach and alternatives

The outline process which takes a project from scope and objectives, through requirements collection, solutions design, and solutions build, and finally into testing works for many types of projects. The terminology will vary for different types of projects depending on the expertise of those involved, but the fundamental stages will be the same. Examples of projects that usually can be undertaken following such a lifecycle include

- o Software development
- o Launching a new product
- o Building new facilities

The typical involvement of stakeholders in such projects is at the start and end of a project. At the start stakeholders define requirements, and at the end they are involved in testing and acceptance of the deliverables.

Not all projects though fit into these categories. In some projects there is not a clear requirement that can be specified up front, and even when it is known, there is no obvious solution to it or the solution is so innovative and unknown that a plan cannot be built with an acceptable level of certainty about it. Projects that fall into this category include

- o Projects which set out to explore options rather than to deliver a specific solution; for example, a project with an objective to improve a business's understanding of how it could reduce its carbon footprint.
- o Projects which explore the use of technology advances. Projects traditionally start with a statement of need and then define solutions to meet this need. In some situations a solution exists, but needs to be explored for possible application. Such a project does not have a clear schedulable series of activities.
- o Many business-change activities. For example, general performance improvement, cost reduction or cultural change programmes. These do not deliver tangible and easily definable deliverables.
- o Volatile situations, where project stakeholders cannot specify their requirements in a sufficiently consistent way, or where the requirements are not static long enough to deliver. Some IT developers argue that this is actually the reality of much of software development.

There is no single lifecycle that will suit the delivery of such projects. In these situations the roles of the project and the project manager change. The project is not to deliver a set of known requirements, but is a sense-making endeavour to take some less determined needs and intentions and shape them into a desired outcome. In the most extreme examples the outcome or deliverables can change up to the point at which the project itself is complete. Deciding when the project is complete becomes more a matter of judgement than of black and white assessment against objective criteria.

The approach to such projects must be more iterative and needs to have a much greater level of involvement from project stakeholders. Rather than departing at the point at which requirements are complete to return at some future date to inspect and check final deliverables, the stakeholders must remain involved throughout the project. They are there to be involved in the ongoing dialogue and to make continual decisions on change and direction.

Approaches such as that shown in Diagram 5.5 are one way of facing challenges like this. Iterative and incremental software development approaches stressing the need for short series of development rather than large projects produce a lifecycle as shown in Diagram 5.6. The difference between this and the original lifecycle in Diagram 5.1 is that stakeholders are continuously involved; change and debate about it are encouraged; and the individual iterations of the project are of limited duration. Durations as short as one day are sometimes used, but more typically they are a few weeks long. Approaches such as AGILE are based on lifecycles like this.

Let us return to the original simple process shown in Diagram 5.1. Instead of considering the three activities of definition, planning and execution, as sequential process steps, think of them as a series of inter-related activities with a continuous feedback loop between them. A project still initiates with a step of definition. Planning commences as soon as the definition is sufficient to allow planning to start. Definition and planning then continue in parallel. As the definition expands, this is fed into planning. As the plan evolves the implications are fed back to definition stage in terms of cost, time, resources and so on. This in turn is assessed and further feedback occurs depending on the acceptability of this information.

Similarly, execution of the project starts as soon as sufficient planning is done to instruct what tasks must be initiated. Planning and execution continue in parallel. As the plan evolves it shapes the tasks that will be executed. As the tasks are executed the reality in terms of outcome, time to complete, cost and so on is fed back into planning. This ongoing loop of instruction and feedback continues until the programme is complete. The process is shown in Diagram 5.7.

What are the implications of the evolving process for project and programme managers? It does make their roles more complex, but it is unavoidable in many situations. It also means that the only time a project manager can be certain of the timescale and cost to complete a project is when it is complete – or by forcing an end date by time-boxing the work (see Chapter 6).

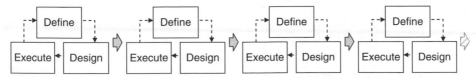

Diagram 5.6 *Rapid iterations of projects*

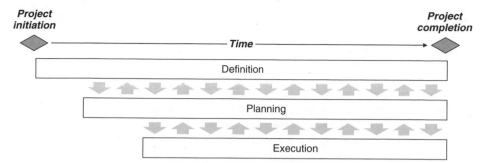

Diagram 5.7 *Simultaneous definition, planning and execution*

Choosing a lifecycle is not an issue of right or wrong lifecycles, but one of choosing the most appropriate lifecycle for a specific situation. Project management often gives a sense of confidence and control. Often this is a valid perception, but it is an illusion if scope, objectives and requirements are not understood, or are indeterminable. The boundary between requirements collection, design and execution blurs. In these situations success has less to do with the project management process itself, and more to the skills and experience of the individual project manager.

Case Study 5.2   HOW DO YOU PLAN AND MANAGE YOUR PORTFOLIO OF WORK – TAKING ACCOUNT OF CLIENT REQUIREMENTS?

Steve Oliver is the co-founder and a director of Abritas. Abritas is an innovative systems supplier focusing on the social housing sector. Their core product Nova-HX is the market leader in its sector. It has modules to support local councils in areas such as housing register, homelessness, choice-based lettings, temporary-accommodation management, rents (expenditure tracking) and e-Government & CRM.

Steve Oliver

That's a good question, and a good time to ask it, as right now we are busy like crazy having won a number of new contracts recently.

Our workload is split into three components: delivering solutions for new clients; providing support and upgrades for existing clients; and the development and enhancement of our core product, Nova-HX. These are very different workloads. Historically, we have tried to manage them as a single combined portfolio and allocate resources according to priority. The problem is that these are such different types of work that it is difficult to allocate resources commonly. In addition, the nature of our business is such that work resulting from new sales is always urgent, and being urgent it can overtake other important but not as time-critical projects, such as the ongoing development. The danger is that we always end up doing the urgent sales, and never the other important projects. So we now split this work into three components, supported by three separate teams.

We have been providing solutions to councils for a number of years now, but we are still a relatively young business. What that means is of the three components of work we have, delivering solutions for new clients is currently our biggest and most important stream of work. Let me talk about that in some more detail.

Our new customer projects are started as a result of winning a sale. The sales cycle can vary: sometimes it can take several months, on other occasions it is very quick. Given that we are working with local government a lot of our sales are won in response to tenders, which may require a commitment to a delivery deadline.

The client may buy our whole system or sometimes just some of the modules. The modules need configuring to the client's specific needs. So, the first piece of work we have to do post-sales is to agree on what configuration is required and produce what we call a configuration specification. We allocate a project manager to each client we win, and this project manager is responsible for working with the client to develop the configuration specification.

Once we have a completed and agreed configuration specification we do the necessary development work. The development work is done by one or more of our software developers working under the project manager. Development is followed by a systems test and then a customer acceptance or UAT. The chunks of work in a specific project are always the same – configuration spec, development, systems test and customer acceptance.

So, all our projects for new customers follow the same steps. In some ways this makes the challenge of managing a portfolio of projects easier, but there are many complicating factors. First, unlike a normal set of projects we have very limited freedom to juggle their order. Having won a sale we cannot avoid doing the work or delay it. We have to complete all the projects we get as we have made commitments to clients. Simply delaying projects by prioritization does not work for us. Second, although the steps in each project are largely the same, they are not predictable. Third, we have a fixed resource pool, or at least one that can only expand slowly. It's our policy to only use permanent staff, and recruitment takes time. Peaks in workload have to be managed by our current in-house staff, unless they are predicted sufficiently far enough in advance to allow recruitment to take place. As our project workload increases we have to be continually recruiting, and supporting recruitment for projects has evolved from an occasional to a continuous task.

How do we manage our workload? We start in the sales process. When a sale gets to a certain point we alert our central programme manager who maintains a plan of all the projects in the business. We want him to start preparing for an imminent sale, but we also want his feedback. Do we have the resources, or should we try to manage the sales process to complete a sale at a certain date, or to manage customer's expectations about when we will be able to do the work for them? At this time the programme manager builds the future work into his overall plan and can start to think about cumulative resources required and so on. Our programme manager's plan at this stage is built around a standard project, taking standard lead times.

We roughly know how long a sale takes and what percentage we win (which is high). But, there's a big difference between an average and what happens in practice on an individual project: we win sales we did not expect to; some sales complete quickly; others drag on for ages. So, we are always juggling resources in response to what happens in reality. This means planning is more art than science, as we can't know absolutely which sales we will win until the sale is complete.

Once we have won work we then start to work with the customer on the configuration specification. We know this typically takes four weeks. Some clients are very responsive, and the work is done quickly. In some situations, developing the configuration specification can take a lot longer as customers don't allocate enough resource, or cannot make up their minds as to what they want. We have planned for a project manager to be supporting this activity for four weeks and then for development to start. If it takes longer than four weeks our plan is wrong. The problem then is that this has a knock on effect on other work.

Sometimes during the creation of a configuration specification we do a little development work, so we can show the customers what the system could look like for them, and to try and encourage their thinking about the configuration they need.

At some point the configuration specification is complete. This is the first time we really know what the customer wants. It is when we see and understand their requirements we are able to ascertain the amount of development work we need to do. At this point we can produce a final plan. If this is significantly different from our initial plan then we may have to juggle resources around.

We tell the clients up front a rough timeline to complete the project, but we don't commit to the timeline until we have completed the configuration specification. Whilst we are very clear about this, in truth clients don't always hear it. People hear what they want to hear, so it can be a surprise if we go back with altered timelines based on a particularly complex set of requirements. Expectation management and negotiation skills are core to making this work!

Once we have an agreed configuration specification the work is fully in our control, and I am quite confident about our ability to stick to our plans from this point until we involve our customers again in the acceptance phase. Occasionally, between winning a sale and completing work we have to reset customer's expectations, but this is rare.

The final stage is the User Acceptance Test (UAT). This is the first time our clients have used the system in anger. Not surprisingly, it can sometimes be slightly different from what they expect, even if we have stuck 100% to their specification. So, we get asked for changes. If the changes are small we try and do them then and there – and we don't charge. That is all part of building a strong relationship with a customer. Of course, sometimes the changes are significant and will require more work. In that case we have to quote for the work, and it is best if the client lets us finish the current implementation and do those enhancements as a second phase.

Overall, the process works well, but it requires a lot of juggling at times. One thing our customers don't always understand is that deadlines are like a two-way street, and they have work to do as well. This impacts the sales process, developing the configuration specification and UAT. These are all joint activities. When our work is complete, the customer may have lots more to do, as a system like ours can bring a radical change for some parts of their organization.

More information on Abritas can be found at **www.abritas.co.uk**.

MAIN LEARNING POINTS FROM CHAPTER 5

- The definition of a project starts with an understanding of objectives (why a project is to be pursued). Following this a scope is developed which defines what the project is. The scope is often insufficient to define all aspects of a project, so more detailed information is defined as requirements.

- Scope is controlled by *scope management,* and requirements through *requirements management* or *requirements engineering.*

- Requirements are teased out from project stakeholders, usually through a process of structured questioning. Typically, this requires a dialogue rather than a simple question-and-answer session. Requirements are often subject to progressive elaboration. Business analysis is the discipline which specializes in determining requirements.

- Requirements may be functional or non-functional. It is often non-functional requirements that are hardest to define, especially those associated with the quality of deliverables.
- Requirements often suffer from misinterpretation, ambiguity and the stakeholder's lack of ability to define them. Project stakeholders can be helped to understand requirements by the use of prototypes or Intermediate Objects of Design.
- Quality requirements are understandable, unambiguous, testable and traceable. A full set of requirements should be complete and meet the project's needs.
- A requirement is a statement of need. This is converted into a solution via the process of design. Design and development of solutions are not fully reliable processes, and therefore project deliverables should be subject to testing to ensure conformance to requirements.
- Different project lifecycles can ease the process of requirements collection and design of solutions. Lifecycles range from waterfall lifecycles to iterative lifecycles typified by AGILE or Extreme project methods.
- Requirements management links directly to project planning and is closely linked to change control.

REVIEW QUESTIONS AND EXERCISES

1. What are the differences in meaning between the terms *objective*, *scope*, *requirement* and *design*? Write down three statements that are examples of each.
2. Write down five examples of each of the following types of requirements:
   - Functional requirements for a new document management system
   - Non-functional requirements for a document management system
   - Requirements defining the business change needs associated with implementing a new document management system
3. What examples of IoDs can you think of in everyday life? What examples being used in business have you come across? In what way do IoDs help – and what might be the dangers of them?
4. When would linear approach (as in Diagrams 5.1–5.4) versus a more iterative approach (Diagram 5.5) versus a continuous approach (Diagram 5.6) be most relevant? List an example of a project that would suite a linear, an iterative and a continuous approach?
5. Consider a project to develop a new system to help manage the scheduling of all the different courses in your institution? Who are the stakeholders for this system? Is the stakeholder group sufficiently competent to define requirements? Is it manageable as a project? What do you see as the issues in managing such a group?
6. How would you manage the activity of prioritizing requirements on a project? What criteria would you consider for prioritization? How would you involve stakeholders in this process and what problems would this create? What do you think is the role of the leadership team in such a process?
7. Why do people sometimes have difficulty expressing what they require from a project? How do you think an understanding of needs develops? What ways can you use to help people understand what they want when they cannot define it clearly?
8. What is a quality requirement? How do you ensure individual and a complete set of requirements are of an appropriate level of quality?

Suggested reading

There are many books on requirements and requirement analysis. They are specialized books and are not aimed at the general management market. The most comprehensive tend to come from engineering disciplines such as software engineering, for example,

- ○ *Requirements Engineering: A Structured Project Information Approach.* Elizabeth Hull, Ken Jackson, Jeremy Dick. Springer-Verlag London Ltd, August 2002

Truly generic approaches to requirements that are valid for all project types and deliverables are probably not possible, but try

- ○ *Project Requirements: A Guide to Best Practices.* Ralph R Young, Management Concepts, Inc. March 2006

Bibliography

APM (Association for Project Management). *APM Body of Knowledge*, 5th Edition, 2006.

Davis, A., Hickey, A. and Zweig, A. "Requirements management in a project management context". *The Wiley Guide to Managing Projects.* Wiley, 2004.

Gray, CF. and Larson, EW. *Project Management: The Managerial Process.* McGraw-Hill International Edition, 2006.

Ivory, C., Alderman, N., McLoughlin, I. and Vaughan, R. "Sense-making as a process within complex projects". *Making Projects Critical*, Palgrave MacMillan, 2006.

Lyneham-Brown, D. "Business analysis and project management – roles and inter-relationship". *Project Manager Today*, March 2001.

Maylor, H. *Project Management.* FT Prentice Hall, 3rd edition, 2003.

Newton, R. *The Project Manager, Mastering the Art of Delivery.* FT Prentice Hall, 2005.

Papadimitrou, K. and Pellegrin, C. "Dynamics of a project through Intermediary Objects of Design (IODs): A sense making perspective". *International Journal of Project Management.* Volume 25, Issue 5, July 2007, pp. 446–57.

PMI (Project Management Institute, Inc). *The Guide to the Project Management Body of Knowledge*, version 3, 2004.

Pressman, R. *Software Engineering: A Practitioner's Approach.* McGraw-Hill Higher Education, 6th edition, June 2004.

Robertson, S. and Robertson, J. *Mastering the Requirements Process*, Addison Wesley, 2nd edition, March 2006.

Vinck, D. and Jeantet, A. "Mediating and commissioning object in the socio-technical process of product design: A conceptual approach". *Management and New Technology: Design Networks and Strategy.* Cost social science series, Bruxelles, 1995.

Young, R. *Effective Requirements Practices.* Addison Wesley, 2001.

Young, R. *Project Requirements: A Guide to Best Practices.* Management Concepts, March 2006.

6 planning projects

One of the ways that project management differs from other forms of management is the rigour with which it approaches and uses project plans. It is not that other management disciplines do not develop plans, but they are different. When an operational manager talks about plans he usually means forecasts of output from and resource requirements for his department. A project manger uses the word plan to mean a detailed description and schedule of activities that will be undertaken by the project team.

The importance and centrality of planning to project management cannot be overemphasized. The first activity that a new member of staff is introduced to on his or her first day of working as a project manager is planning. The items that senior managers ask to see when they talk to project managers are plans. A plan sits in the centre of a project the way that a spider sits in the middle of her web. It is a tool for exploration and understanding, a way of communicating, and the basis of control and management of a project.

The plan is a representation of the project strategy, defining how a project will be realized. Planning is what converts objectives into actions. Without a plan objectives are just desires; with a plan there is an explanation of how they will be achieved.

Many people have an image of a plan as a chart with some bars on it showing a schedule of tasks. This is one aspect of planning, but project plans are more than this. Planning results in an understanding of tasks, a schedule, resource requirements (people, budget etc) and also the allocation of tasks to people. Plans show how long a project will take and provide an understanding of what resources will be used and how much the project will cost. Plans are a tool for project managers to manage projects successfully, and they also enable many business commitments to be made.

Various terminologies are in use with different project managers. In this book the term planning is used to cover understanding the activities in a project, estimating resource requirements, scheduling as well as providing information to measure and manage project progress.

This chapter describes the activities associated with planning and also presents alternative views to the classical planning approach. The topic lies at the heart of project management and accordingly is the subject of large amounts of debate, views on best practice, theory and research. Every aspect of planning – whether it is the best way to understand activities, techniques for estimation, or different ways to schedule tasks – has been the subject of hundreds of papers and books. This chapter aims to provide sufficient information for a project or general manager to gain a solid appreciation of planning and the range of issues that have to be considered. By reading the chapter the reader will learn a variety of project planning terminology and be able to understand and investigate a project plan better.

The plan is the central tool in project management, and links to almost every other aspect of projects. The plan and the schedule are built upon the project's requirements (Chapter 5) and the resources available (Chapter 4). The plan is both a key source of risk and also a tool for managing risk (Chapter 11). Planning links closely to change control (Chapter 8).

An overview of planning

Planning is dependent on an understanding of the desired outcome from a project. This is specified in the project's objectives, scope and requirements. With no information on objectives or scope it is not possible to plan in any meaningful sense. However, the information does not have to be complete, and planning can begin as soon as objectives and scope start to become clear. As was shown in Chapter 5, there will be several iterations of a plan in increasing detail as the definition of the project becomes more precise.

The term "plan" is used to refer to two types of definition in projects: First, the plan is a definition of the steps required to complete the project in the order required. This is the use of the word plan to refer to a schedule, cost and task breakdown. Second, the term plan is used to describe guidance documents for how the project is to be managed and how the project team should work on the project. In other words, plans are also used to describe the process for managing various aspects of the project. For example, a project may have a communication plan, a risk management plan, a quality management plan and a configuration management plan. These respectively provide the project team with guidance on how to approach communications, risks, quality and configuration on the project. This chapter focuses primarily on the first usage of the word, but there is a section at the end of this chapter which explores the second.

A project plan is created, based on the project's strategy, and then maintained throughout the life of the project. This section starts by describing the uses of plans and then reviews the main stages of planning.

The uses of project plans

Project plans are powerful, multi-purpose tools, used by a variety of audiences other than project managers. The main purposes that plans are used for are

- o Providing the project team with guidelines to approach certain aspects of the project (e.g. communications, risk, configuration and quality)
- o Providing an understanding of the activities involved in a project
- o Exploring what resources will be required by a project, and consequently sizing and budgeting projects
- o Communicating and explaining the project to project stakeholders and project team members
- o Allocating work to project team members, and providing a measure to check progress against
- o Supporting wider business planning and management commitment making. Most businesses value predictability, whether it is telling customers the date of the launch of a new product, committing cost reductions to shareholders, or advising staff of improved facilities. Plans provide improved levels of predictability.

To meet these various needs, and to optimize the benefit from planning, requires different plans, or alternative representations of the same plan. The information collected in creating a plan has to take account of these different needs.

Define the project strategy

Planning starts with the project strategy defined as part of the project scope. The project strategy is the choice of a general approach to delivering a project and meeting the project's objectives. The project strategy sets an overall direction and boundaries for the tasks within the project plan.

Examples of project objectives and strategies are

- o *The costs of raw materials will be reduced by re-tendering with all our current and alternative suppliers.*

   In this case the objective is reduction of costs of raw materials, and the project strategy to achieve this is to re-tender with current and alternative suppliers.

- o *The efficiency of the factory will be improved by selecting and implementing a new production management system.*

   In this situation the objective is to improve factory efficiency, and the project strategy to realize this is to select and implement a new production management system.

- o *A better understanding of the opportunities to exploit the new product will be reached by trialling the new product with different customer segments in various parts of the country.*

   The project objective, in this example, is to identify ways to exploit a new product, and this will be accomplished through a project strategy of performing a series of trials with different customer groups.

- o *The problem with the high rates of faults in the products will be explored by workshops with every customer-facing department in the business.*

   The project objective is to explore the high fault rates in products, and the project strategy to attain this is to run a series of workshops with all customer-facing departments.

Create the plan

Plans are developed through a series of steps. Creation of a project plan cannot be done by sitting at a desk for a few minutes and simply writing it down. It requires concentrated effort and usually takes several attempts. It needs information from various project team members. The plan will be refined as scope, objectives and requirements become clearer.

The steps that have to be undertaken to create a plan are

- Defining the activities to achieve the needs
- Identifying linkages between activities
- Estimating duration and resources required for each activity
- Reviewing the resources available and the schedule of availability
- Scheduling the activities taking into consideration the linkages, duration and resource availability
- Reviewing the plan against objectives and constraints and ensuring it is consistent with them. If it is not, revising the plan and adapting it until it does conform to objectives and constraints. This includes consideration of time, cost and quality constraints and critical success factors.

Creation of a plan is both an analytical and a creative exercise. Each of the activities in creating a plan will result in a range of choices and decisions for the project manager. Depending on the choices different plans are possible. Consider the simple activity of making a sandwich. Even for an activity as trivial as this there are choices about the tasks and the order of them: select bread first or the filling, what filling, what bread to use, how thick to cut it and so on. For a complex project the range of choices is obviously orders of magnitude greater.

The scope of activities in the project plan includes both those activities involved with the development and delivery of the project's deliverables and also the activities associated with management of the project itself. For example, many projects have significant communications- and operational-readiness activities to support the business change aspects of a project, or projects contain risk management actions. Such communication and risk management actions are not directly linked to the creation of deliverables, but are still essential parts of a project and need to be included in the plan.

One of the choices in planning is the level of detail to create the plan at. Too little detail and the plan will not provide sufficient understanding or ability to control a project. Too much detail and the plan will become unwieldy and inflexible. Deciding what is the right level of detail is a judgement best made with experience.

Planning requires significant amounts of information: what tasks should be done; how long will they take; what skills are required and so on. To collect perfect information is probably impossible and certainly impractical. A plan is a working tool, and as such its creation cannot take an unreasonable amount of time or effort. Successful planning is not about perfect information, but sufficient information. Practical planning with sufficient information requires judgement, estimates and making assumptions. These are sources of risk. To manage that risk requires an explicit understanding of the assumptions being made.

The effort expended in creating a plan is dependent on the scale and complexity of the project and the familiarity of the project manager and project team with the type of project. It is also linked to the quality of the plan required. The quality needed in a plan depends on the implications of getting it wrong and the risk to the business. For a small low-risk project planning can be completed quickly in a few hours by an individual. For a major programme, requiring significant investment or exposing a business to high levels of risk, creating a reliable plan may be the subject of months of a team's work.

More detailed plans are often perceived to be better plans. Detail facilitates accurate estimating and control. However, the most detailed plan is not necessarily the best. If the planning assumptions are wrong or the understanding of domain of project is limited, then the plan will be wrong no matter how much detail is provided. More detailed planning may simply lead to more precise, but equally erroneous, descriptions – with the added danger that precision may give the impression of accuracy and credibility. When there are many unknowns, excessive detail may be harmful, as it can give spurious levels of confidence. It is often better for a project manager to spend additional time ensuring the assumptions in a plan are right than to delve into greater detail.

The culture of an organization can also impact the level of detail in plans. Organizations with a culture of control tend to prefer more detailed plans than do those with a more decentralized and delegated structure of management.

The responsibility for developing the plan lies with the project manager. The project manager will need the support of many of the project team members to understand the activities to perform specialist tasks, or to estimate their length. On larger projects there may be a dedicated *project planner* who, working for the project manager, creates and maintains project plans. Such specialized project planners often have advanced skills and knowledge in specific planning techniques and tools.

From plans to action

A project plan is a statement of intention. The activities defined in the plan will not occur simply because the plan has been created. Action has to be taken to make the plan happen. Starting a project is called *project mobilization*; it may alternatively be referred to by phrases like *project initiation* or *project kick off*.

The objective of mobilization is to brief and motivate the project team and to start them working on the activities in the plan. A mobilized project team should have common expectations of the project. Mobilization may also involve project stakeholders and try to ensure that they are supportive of the project and will actively engage with it.

The specific activities involved in mobilization are dependent on the context. A typical mobilization starts with a group briefing for the entire project team to ensure the team members understand the project's objectives and scope. The briefing includes presentations from the project sponsor on the importance of the project to the business and the project manager talking about how the project will be approached. Then more detailed explanations will be given to smaller groups of the project team so that they understand their roles in the project and the expectations of them.

Planning is often seen as an activity that is done as a project commences, but planning is ongoing throughout the project's life. Planning starts at the beginning of a project and only ends when the project is complete.

Plans require modification to take account of:

o Improvements in understanding as the project progresses
o Decisions to alter approach
o Actual progress to complete tasks which will often be different from what was originally envisaged
o Changes in needs

But the plan cannot be constantly altering or else it loses its value as a mechanism for controlling a project. Hence, there are procedures for deciding when a plan is to be updated. (These are described in the Section *"In-life management of plans".*)

The creation and maintenance of plans can be supported by a range of software tools: from the well-known MS-Project, through to a large number of vendors' packages which contain project planning functionality and support other project management activities. Different software packages have different advantages and weaknesses. Irrespective of which software is used, it helps significantly in managing plans and their associated data. Planning software makes plan presentation and scheduling easier, and can provide support with planning-related algorithms such as resource levelling. However, the software does not create a plan; it merely stores and manipulates data input by the project manager. It cannot help with the data creation and deciding the relationship between data in the plan such as dependencies.

Information is the core of planning. Creating and collecting the necessary information is the focus of this chapter.

Understanding project activities

The basis of planning is the idea that complex activities can be understood through the reductionist concept of *decomposition.* Decomposition is the division of a project into smaller and smaller chunks of work until a point at which each chunk is of sufficient simplicity to be understood. Understanding is achieved when an estimate of the size of each chunk, the resources required, and any prerequisites to completing it can be determined. These chunks are called *activities* or *tasks.*

Project managers do not simply decompose activities in a random fashion, but create a hierarchy of activities. The name for this hierarchy is *Work Breakdown Structure* or *WBS.*

The WBS can categorize the project in a number of ways. The three most common ways of creating a WBS are by decomposing one of the following:

o *Deliverables*: a breakdown based on the deliverables and their components. This is often useful for complicated engineered deliverables made up of separate components.

- ○ *Activity*: a breakdown based on the activities that typically have to be performed to create the deliverables. This is a common approach for a wide variety of business projects.
- ○ *Project lifecycle or process*: a breakdown based on a standard process or lifecycle. This is similar to a functional breakdown but uses pre-defined lifecycles or processes as the basic components of the hierarchy. Such an approach is often the starting point for work like new product and software development which have well-defined lifecycles.

As an example, the WBS for a project to fit some new PC hardware into an office using each approach to decomposition is shown in Table 6.1.

The different types of WBS are suited for different situations. There is no perfect choice, but the WBS should be complete, with each task existing only once in the hierarchy. The WBS should be chosen to minimize the dependency between tasks.

There is no rule defining the optimal level of detail in a WBS. The level of detail and the number of layers in the hierarchy of a WBS are the project manager's choice. The detail must be sufficient to support

- ○ Estimation of task duration and resource requirements.
- ○ Allocation of activities to teams or team members. If an item in the WBS cannot be allocated to one identifiable organizational unit then the decomposition is not sufficient. The level of decomposition at which tasks can be allocated to teams or team members is called a *work package* or *work assignment*. Ideally work packages are independent of all other work. Work package exists only once in a plan. Size varies considerably.
- ○ Control of tasks in the live project. Control may require further decomposition below work package level. If a work package is an activity that will take three months to complete, a project manager may have insufficient opportunity to measure and manage progress. The work package is then divided further still into tasks and sub-tasks. A typical level of detail suitable for sufficient control by a project manager is 1–2 weeks in duration. A programme manager may be satisfied with less detail, assuming the detailed planning is still done within the constituent projects in the programme. (This is a very rough guide only.)

WBSs are typically presented as lists. The levels in the hierarchy are shown by differing degrees of indentation. The more indented an activity, the lower level it is. In addition, tasks in a WBS are numbered. Top-level activities are numbered in sequence 1, 2, 3, 4 etc. The next level of decomposition below the activity numbered 1, is labelled in the form 1.1, 1.2, 1.3 etc. Further layers can be added as required following the same convention. (WBSs may also be presented as a diagram in the format of an organizational chart. Activities are shown as a hierarchy of boxes. Lower-level activities are shown as boxes "reporting into" the higher-level activity.)

It is important that any breakdown of activity into lower-level tasks is complete. Whenever a work package is broken into tasks, or tasks into sub-tasks, the lower level of decomposition must consist of all the activities required to complete the higher level. An example of both an incorrect and a correct breakdown is shown in Table 6.2. The right hand-side breakdown is incorrect as there are tasks missing

Table 6.1 Different decompositions for a simple project

Deliverable	Activity	Project lifecycle or process
Hardware	Understand requirements	Initiate project
PC	Select equipment	Develop business case
Processor	Review hardware and software	Gain approval
Hard drive	options	Prioritize project
Screen	Choose best options	Understand needs
Peripherals	Choose suppliers	Develop plan
Printers	Review possible suppliers	Execute plan
Software	Short list suppliers	Selection
System	Collect quotes	Installation
Operating System	Select supplier	Test
Utilities	Install solution	Train users
Applications	Test	Close project
Office applications	Train users	Handover all deliverables to
Specialist	Handover to users	support teams
Training		Perform project review

Table 6.2 Complete and incomplete WBS

Correct WBS	Incorrect/incomplete WBS
1 Initiate project	1 Initiate project
1.1 Develop business case	1.1 Develop business case
1.2 Gain approval	2 Understand needs
1.3 Prioritize project	3 Develop plan
2 Understand needs	4 Execute plan
3 Develop plan	4.1 Selection
4 Execute plan	4.2 Installation
4.1 Selection	4.3 Train users
4.2 Installation	5 Close project
4.3 Test	5.1 Handover all deliverables to support teams
4.4 Train users	5.2 Perform project review
5 Close project	
5.1 Handover all deliverables to support teams	
5.2 Perform project review	

from lower levels of the WBS hierarchy. The top level task "initiate project" requires more than just "develop business case", and the top level task "execute plan" is incomplete without performing a test.

Of course, for a project with any degree of innovation or novelty, it is impossible to be certain that all the necessary tasks are included. (Tasks may be missed because understanding is incomplete at the start of the project. Hence the project manager must be open to enhancing the plan as understanding improves as the project progresses.) Missing tasks is a significant factor in the risk involved in the project. Risk management should consider the degree of novelty of a project and from this assess the likelihood that the WBS will be incomplete.

Numbering enables project managers to track tasks, and enables plans to be *rolled up*. The following WBS has three levels of decomposition, but it can be presented in a rolled-up fashion as shown in Table 6.3:

Table 6.3 Rolling up a WBS

Full WBS	Partially Rolled Up	Fully Rolled Up

1 Hardware
  1.1 PC
    1.1.1 Processor
    1.1.2 Hard drive
    1.1.3 Screen
  1.2 Peripherals
    1.2.1 Printers
2 Software
  2.1 System
    2.1.1 Operating System
    2.1.2 Utilities
  2.2 Applications
    2.2.1 Office applications
    2.2.2 Specialist
3 Training
	1 Hardware
	  1.1 PC
	  1.2 Peripherals
	2 Software
	  2.1 System
	  2.2 Applications
	3 Training
		1 Hardware
		2 Software
		3 Training

Rolling up is useful for communication to different audiences, as well as budgetary and control purposes.

There are different approaches to identifying tasks in a plan. The different approaches are not exclusive, and often a project manager will use a combination of methods. The main methods are listed below:

- *Top-down and decomposition*: analysing each activity in turn and determining a suitable breakdown until sufficient granularity is achieved.
- *Group effort and workshops*: techniques such as brainstorming to identify all the possible tasks in a plan. Following such a session the project manager sorts and structures the activities into a plan. This can be a helpful way of initiating planning.
- *Adaptation of previous plans*: reviewing a plan for similar projects that have been done previously. By this method it is often possible to speed up the process of planning. Care has to be taken in ensuring the relevancy of the old plan to the objectives and scope of the new project.
- *Expert input*: input from a specialist in a specific part of the project. Often, identifying the task breakdown for a component of a plan requires expert input.

Milestones

Projects do not exist as structures simply to perform activities, but are created to achieve an outcome. Achievements happen through the life of a project. In addition, various important events happen at points on projects, whether it is holding a kick-off event for a project, or presenting to senior managers about the project. Key events and achievements are called and shown on a plan as a *milestone*.

There is a variety of milestones that can be included in a project plan. Milestones come about as a result of

- Natural check points in delivery, for example, when a major component of a deliverable is due to be complete.
- Project lifecycle events. Key events in project lifecycles are *gates*. Gates are the decision points between moving from one stage of a project to the next. Crossing

a gate requires authorization to proceed. A typical situation is a decision whether to proceed with a project following the completion of a feasibility study.

o Events associated with wider business reviews. Dates associated with portfolio reviews or budget processes may have to be built into the plan.

Which milestones to include in a plan is another decision for a project manager. Milestones are included in a project plan because the achievement or event is important to the project. The inclusion of milestones helps to ensure that a project is not only focussed on completing activities, but also motivated to achieve goals and outcomes from a project plan.

Milestones are not representations of activity, but the result of activity. Therefore, whilst they have a date associated with them, they should not have any duration or resource allocated to them on a plan. Milestone titles represent an outcome, such as *project mobilized*, *approval achieved* or *first stage deliverables complete*.

Assigning ownership for tasks

Once a project manager has a sufficient work breakdown structure, consideration has to be given to responsibility for performing and completing the activities shown in it. A project manager may do this by working through each task and allocating ownership. A more structured approach is to use an Organizational Breakdown Structure or OBS.

An OBS provides a decomposition of a hierarchy in the same way that a WBS does. However, instead of dealing with the activities in a project, an OBS is concerned with the business functions involved. An OBS is normally presented in the form of an organizational chart.

The relationship between an OBS and WBS is at the level of work packages. Work packages exist within the WBS, and are allocated to an organizational unit on the OBS. An organizational unit in an OBS has one or more work packages allocated to it. (This may be used as a project cost centre for project budget purposes.)

There is a requirement to allocate all tasks to organizational units so the project manager can determine which areas need to provide resources to the project. As the project progresses, the tasks should be allocated to named individuals responsible for ensuring that they are completed. A task may need more than one person to complete the work involved, but there should always be one named individual responsible to the project manager for ensuring that the work is completed to the necessary level of quality.

Estimation

Estimation is the part of project planning that many project managers dread most and often is one of the major areas of risk. With a systematic approach and with experience it is usually possible in most plans to produce an adequate work breakdown structure and to identify which area of the business is responsible for completing a certain task. Estimation of what resources will be required to complete a task is more difficult.

It is almost impossible to avoid some errors in estimation. In reality, the challenge is not to remove all error from estimation, but to provide an estimate that is accurate enough with a level of understanding of the degree of risk associated with it. In this way the project manager can then manage a project with an understood level of risk, and where appropriate a commensurate level of contingency built into the plan.

To understand why estimating is so tricky think about a task you are familiar with. How long does it take to drive to your office? You can probably give a reasonable estimate. But how sure are you? Something might go wrong – there may be a traffic jam on a specific day. If you had to commit to a time what would you say? Make it more complex; it is not a drive to your office, but a drive to somewhere you have never been before. Now, let us make it more difficult still; you have to go somewhere you have not been before using a mode of transport you have not used before and carrying a parcel of indeterminate size. Of course you can provide an estimate, but what assumptions have you made, and how certain are you of the timing?

There are two types of estimates, which are inter-related. The first is *the resource requirement*. That is the required resource to complete an activity. The second is the *activity duration*. That is how long an activity will take, which is often dependent on the level of resources allocated. Estimates may be required for a variety of resources, but the most common are budget and human resources. There are specific issues with estimating for different resource types (see Chapter 4).

Estimates can be developed in one of several ways:

- *Top-down and comparative estimates*: a summary estimate at the total level for a project based on the assessment of an experienced practitioner. The experienced practitioner can make comparison with similar projects.
- *Bottom-up*: using the WBS and estimating the resources required for each activity in the WBS, and then totalling across the project.
- *Expert input*: support and advice from an expert in one or more areas of the project. Normally projects managers have to manage the development of estimates. However, on a project of significant complexity they may not be able, personally, to estimate the length and resource requirement for every task.
- *Parametric*: using a sizing algorithm or heuristic for a type of work. The most common in a business context is the use of function points to size IT developments. Similarly, building companies will have rules of thumb for how many bricks a brick-layer can lay in a day, or how many square metres of plastering a plasterer can do.
- *Template*: completion of a template or form, which lists some pre-defined characteristics of the project and has rules of thumb for scaling each characteristic. The rules of thumb are based on experience, and can provide a reliable way to size a project. This is an extension of parametric, but using several dimensions rather than one. Many businesses have developed such templates. Such templates can exist in the form of spreadsheets or databases.
- *Risk-based*: including a consideration of risk in project estimates. There are different ways of doing this. For a simple example, consider PERT. PERT is an acronym for *Program Evaluation and Review Technique*. PERT estimates are a variation on bottom-up estimating, but instead of using one best estimate, PERT relies on three: the estimate of the most optimistic time to complete a task (a), an estimate of the expected time (b), and an estimate of the most pessimistic (c). Task length is then worked out using the formula $(a + 4b + c)/6$. The thought process behind a PERT estimate is that at the point in time at which estimates are made, it is impossible to confidently determine an error-free estimate, but by taking account of the range of possible estimates PERT attempts to reduce the risk from error.

To reduce the likelihood of error in estimations multiple techniques can be used and the results compared. A common way to do this is to do a detailed bottom-up estimate and then compare it with a top-down estimate for a "common sense" check. Alternatively, multiple people can estimate the resource requirements separately and compare the results.

In estimating durations for human resources in projects, clarity has to be achieved to differentiate between the *task length* or *elapsed time* to complete a task and the *effort* required. Effort is the actual working time in hours or days required to complete a task. Elapsed time is the total length of time between starting working on a task and completing it. A task may take only a few hours of effort, but may have a task length of several weeks if it is only worked on for 20 minutes a day.

Additional considerations such as the actual availability of staff versus a theoretical level must be factored in. There are 365 days a year, but the average person only works on 240 of them. Taking account of various issues, productive time on a project is typically a maximum of 200 to 220 days a year. There are other complicating factors, such as levels of motivation and differences in productivity of different individuals.

Determining the order of tasks and creating the planned schedule

Knowing the resources and durations for each task provides critical information in planning a project, but it is not enough on its own to create the project schedule. Consider the situation of a project that consists of ten one-week tasks. How long will it take to complete? It is not possible to say without additional information. It may take one week if all tasks are done in parallel, ten weeks if all tasks are worked on in series, or between one and ten if there are dependencies between some tasks. It could actually take over ten weeks if there is a dependency on some event external to the project.

Task order is determined by the precedence of tasks. The basic question is *what has to happen before this task can start or complete?* Precedence creates an order in which tasks must be completed. Precedence is determined by

- o *Activity-level dependency*: when a task requires something else to have happened before it can be started or completed. A business presentation cannot be given until the presentation is created. The activity of giving the presentation is said to be *dependent* on the activity of creating the presentation.
- o *Resource dependency*: project activities having to wait for the availability of resource. This can be human resource, where an individual is responsible for completing several tasks but can only do one at a time. Alternatively a resource dependency may arise owing to the availability or access constraints to consumables or equipment and facilities.

There are other factors, which whilst not formally constituting *precedence*, directly impact and even control the schedule of a project:

- o *Business processes*: for example, a business's decision-making and approvals processes. Frequently, activities in projects, and especially moving through a *gate* between one stage in a project lifecycle and the next, are subject to management approval. Budgets have to be approved; project initiation has to be approved; decisions may be required on project direction; and various documents, such as a requirements specification, must be signed off. These activities take time, and are not always within a project manager's control.

Some activities may happen at fixed times in the management calendar of a business. For example, it is not uncommon for significant budgetary expenditure to have to be approved at periodic meetings when all major expenditures are reviewed, and approved or rejected. Such events are often shown as *milestones* on project plans. For instance, a milestone *budget approval achieved* is included in the plan. All activities that are dependent on achieving budget approval cannot commence until such milestones are passed.

o **Date commitment**: having specific dates for activities to be complete. This can force the order of tasks. Projects often have to complete prior to the end of a budget year, or before national events such as Christmas or the start of the Olympics. Alternatively, there may be times of the year when work is not possible, like national holidays or during factory downtime.

Where resources are constrained most project management software will automatically present a schedule of tasks taking account of that constraint. The software will also take account of any periods when project work cannot be completed, such as weekends and national holidays. Other dependencies, including those related to business processes, have to be built into plans.

Dependencies can affect the order of tasks in different ways according to the type of the dependency. The most common type of dependency is where one task cannot start until another is completed. This is known among project managers as a *finish-to-start* dependency. Another type is *start-to-start*. A start-to-start dependency is where two or more tasks must start at the same time. A variant on this is where the start times are linked, but with some form of delay. So a task may be able to start two days after another task has started. The third type of dependency is *finish-to-finish*. A finish-to-finish dependency occurs where two or more tasks cannot finish until they are all complete. A variant is where the end times are linked, but with some form of delay. So, a task may only be able to be completed one day after another task has completed.

Diagram 6.1 shows these graphically:

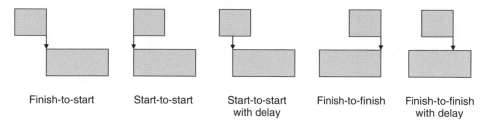

| Finish-to-start | Start-to-start | Start-to-start with delay | Finish-to-finish | Finish-to-finish with delay |

Diagram 6.1 Types of task dependency

It is important to apply the right sort of dependency relationship in a plan, and not to assume that all are finish-to-start. If all dependencies are included as finish-to-start then the schedule will be unnecessarily long.

A dependency may exist between activities in a project or between an activity in the project and an activity happening elsewhere, such as in another project. These are known as *internal* and *external* dependencies respectively. External dependencies are discussed in the Section *Programme and portfolio planning* later in this chapter.

Scheduling combines the data on activities, activity length and precedence to produce a timeline for a project. The timeline shows the duration of each task, the sequence of tasks and the duration of the overall project.

Once a schedule is developed the duration of the project is determined, and the resource requirements at different points in time along the project are known. The duration of a project is not a factor of the length of all the activities in the plan, but is determined by the durations of a specific set of activities called the *critical path*. Moving the start or end date of some tasks will not alter the end date for the whole project. However, moving the end date of some other tasks will – this is the critical path. This is shown in Diagram 6.2.

In Diagram 6.2 tasks A, B and C form the critical path, as delaying any of them will result in slippage to the project. Tasks D, E and F can be moved. However, if the task D is delayed to complete beyond the first dashed line shown, or F moves beyond the second, they will become part of the critical path.

Diagram 6.2 represents a very simple project. In more complex projects determining the critical path can take significantly more analysis, and project management software is very helpful. *Critical path method* or *CPM* analyses the critical path of a project by reviewing the project twice: once in a *forward pass* from start to finish, and then in a *backward pass* from finish to start. The forward pass determines earliest start and finish dates for each activity. The earliest start date for any activity is when any preceding dependency is complete. The backward pass determines the latest start and finish for each activity. The latest finish date for any activity is when it must be complete in order not to alter the critical path of the project. In Diagram 6.2, the earliest task D can start is at the beginning of the project, as it has no preceding dependency. The latest it can finish is when task B is due to start on the critical path. If D finishes later than this it will delay task B and hence lengthen the project. The difference between the earliest and latest start/finish time is called *float* or *slack*.

The slack is a buffer of time, and a task's start and end dates can shift within this buffer. As long as a task is completed with zero or more slack left, it will not change the critical path for the project. The critical path is that series of tasks with zero float, and it is these tasks that receive the most attention from the project manager. She cannot afford for any of the tasks on the critical path to be delayed or the whole project will be delayed.

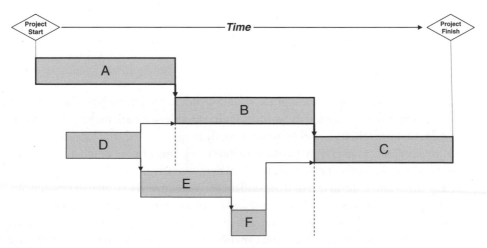

Diagram 6.2 The critical path (shown in bold lines)

Another technique used when a project's schedule is being created is *resource smoothing* or *levelling*. Resource levelling attempts to flatten peaks and troughs in resource demand across a project. Resource levelling may be applied to any type of resource, but it is most commonly used for human resources, and particularly for individual critical team members with scarce skill sets.

From a project manager's perspective the key aspect of resource levelling is to avoid any situation when a resource is required at greater than 100% utilization. In reality, this is not possible and so will create a delay in a project as an activity waits for resource. From a general management perspective resource levelling is usually used to try and move resources towards a steady state of approximately 100% utilization. From an overall business perspective 100% utilized resource is often perceived as the most efficient way to use resources. Resource levelling can be done to a limited extent manually and by experimentation. Most project management softwares offer support through resource levelling algorithms.

Reviewing plans

Project plans are fundamental to the way a project is managed. They determine the cost, timescale and risk levels of a project. As noted at the start of this chapter a plan is a choice. There are usually many alternative possible plans. Plans are also subject to error. As such, for a project of any importance plans should be subject to some level of review before finalization.

Reviews should consider the various information and ideas that have gone into creating a plan: for example,

- o *Approach*: Is the approach optimal, or can a better (quicker, cheaper, lower risk) approach be identified?
- o *Tasks*: Are the tasks complete and correct? Are there any omissions or unnecessary tasks?
- o *Estimates*: Are the estimates reasonable? Have they been developed in an acceptable way from acceptable sources?
- o *Resources*: Are the resources correct?
- o *Dependencies*: Are all the necessary dependencies included? Are all the dependencies included necessary?
- o *Risk*: Has sufficient consideration been given to risk? Is the right level of contingency included?
- o *Constraints and critical success factors*: Is the plan consistent with all defined constraints and critical success factors?

The plans of important projects are often subject to management assessment at a high level. However, this is less of a formal review and is usually more about providing challenge to the project manager. Project managers are regularly challenged to do projects cheaper and quicker. Such encouragement can provide the impetus for project managers to improve plans. However, if taken to extreme, this can create increased risk in plans as project managers may take short cuts to meet management requirements, for instance, by removing all contingency buffers to show a plan meeting a specific deadline.

Given the specialist nature of planning, an alternative and often better way to perform plan review is by a peer group of experienced project managers.

Responsive Load Ltd (RLtec) is a dynamic, visionary and ambitious company committed to improving the way electricity is supplied and consumed – reducing greenhouse gas emissions and reducing the overall cost of electricity supply. RLtec has developed a range of innovative technology, some of which can be used in conjunction with domestic appliances to help electricity grid operators manage periods of peak energy demands.

By monitoring the frequency of the electricity supply it is possible to determine whether the total load on the grid is normal, and when there are peaks and troughs in demand. By performing this monitoring real-time in domestic appliances such as refrigerators, and linking the results of monitoring to the behaviour of the device, it is possible to modify the device's power consumption to reduce power demand during peak periods. This in turn can reduce the need for the electricity grid operator to seek additional generating capacity.

In 2007, RLtec started to work with their first partner, one of the largest white good manufacturers in the world. The project was to trial RLtec's technology in the manufacturer's fridges. The objective of the trial was to demonstrate how the technology influences the behaviour of fridges to reduce energy consumption during peak-demand periods.

The first task the trial project manager was faced with was developing a project plan. Producing a plan for this project posed several problems, most notably,

- *The fact that this technology was innovative and had not been implemented before. Therefore there was limited knowledge of what tasks were required and how long the tasks would take.*
- *The involvement of two different companies (RLtec and the white goods manufacturer), who had different ways of working. Initially there was a lack of clarity of which party was responsible for which activities in the trial.*
- *The location of the people involved in the project across several European countries.*
- *The speed at which the project had to be completed to meet RLtec's and the manufacturer's needs.*

The work involved in the project required the creation of some software based on patented RLtec algorithms to be implemented on electronic controllers in the fridges. This had already been tested successfully on one fridge to ensure it had no adverse impact on food preservation. The trial project had to implement an enhanced form of the RLtec algorithm on 100 fridges with modified electronic controllers. These 100 fridges were to be connected to a specially designed power supply that could mimic the behaviour of a grid and hence initiate the required behaviour of fridges.

Another complexity was that the project had a number of dependencies on other activities on other RLtec projects, including

- *The development of modelling software to predict the behaviour of large numbers of devices in the grid*
- *Working with the grid operators to understand their needs and to develop contracts with them for the service provided*
- *The progression of commercial relationship and contracts between RLtec and the white goods manufacturer*

Although the project manager was not responsible for these tasks, each of them could impact the plan he was developing.

The project manager understood that he would not be able to create a plan without significant input from other members of RLtec with greater expertise than him, and from staff of the white goods manufacturer. However, he also realized that unless he had some form of plan it would be difficult to gather the information required to produce an accurate plan. He therefore developed the plan in a series of steps:

1. *First, he discussed the project with different members of RLtec. This enabled the project manager to form a picture of what was required and start to understand the range of tasks required. This information was essential for building the WBS.*
2. *Then he produced a first-version plan, draft 0.1. Draft 0.1 was based on the project manager's experience of launching new products. The objective of the draft 0.1 plan was not to show a correct plan, but to encourage thinking, debate and input to a better plan.*
3. *The plan was sent for review to RLtec team members, who gave feedback on the tasks and dependencies. This was done by e-mail, and a range of comments and input was received, enabling the project manager to produce much better draft 0.2, 0.3 and 0.4 plans.*
4. *Next he discussed the plan with the manufacturer. The plan was sent to various members of staff of the manufacturer, primarily engineers involved in the trial and commercial staff involved in developing the relationship with RLtec. This started to clarify who would do which tasks, and again improved the WBS, so a draft 0.5 could be produced.*
5. *Finally, he added timelines and durations to produce an initial schedule. There was limited information on task durations as many of the tasks had never been done before. A combination of known timelines, estimates based on experience, and judgements made by comparing to similar tasks enabled a draft 0.6 plan with a timeline to be produced. Dependencies on other RLtec activities were added to this plan.*

There were a few more iterations of the plan achieved over a series of meetings, phone discussions and e-mail feedback. Eventually a version 1.0 plan was produced to manage the project.

A plan has only one critical path, but given the level of uncertainty over some task lengths the project manager determined that there were two possible critical paths for the project. Given that there was a need to complete the trial quickly, minimizing the critical path was key to successful completion. Which set of tasks really formed the critical path required more information to determine and was impacted by small changes in planning assumptions. The two possible critical paths were

- *The creation of the revised fridge software and its implementation on 100 fridges; and*
- *Obtaining the power supply to mimic the grid. This was tailored on existing equipment, but a supplier had to be found and contracted to produce the device.*

The project manager therefore focussed on these tasks to allow the project to successfully progress.

More information on RLtec can be found on www.RLtec.com.

In-life management of plans

In-life management encompasses the ongoing use of the plan as a way for the project manager to manage and allocate tasks, and the checking of progress relative to the original plan.

The *baseline plan* is a formally accepted and approved plan that is used to guide and control activity. It is also the comparative basis for future performance assessments. Whether a completed project is late or not is determined in comparison to the baseline plan. Project managers track actual progress and maintain a record of this. The status of a project at any point in time is a comparison of *baseline versus actual*; differences between baseline and actual are known as *variances*.

Identifying variances requires tracking and understanding progress of completion of tasks. Measuring progress against a plan is not always straightforward. In the original plan development of activities are decomposed into tasks of sufficient simplicity to help an understanding of progress to be maintained. For a task such as laying bricks in a wall it is relatively easy to determine progress. When 50% of the bricks are laid, it is reasonable to assume that 50% of the task is complete. But, if the task was to create a design document, when is a design 50% complete? If the task is meant to take two months, determining after one month that the task is 50% complete and so on track is difficult and relies on a subjective view of design completeness.

To avoid this problem some project managers only accept completed deliverables as a proof of progress. An activity is only complete when a deliverable is produced or a milestone is achieved. Activities can only be at a binary state of 0% or 100% complete.

There are in-life situations in which the baseline plan does need to be updated. *Re-baselining* occurs when there is an accepted reason for a plan to change. Re-baselining is not done simply because a plan is shown to be in error, but it is normally done in response to a change in requirements and controlled by change control.

In-life project control and management is described in more detail in Chapter 8, Managing the execution of projects.

Plans and risk management

Projects are subject to risk. Unintended outcomes will occur. Project management provides a mechanism to deal with risk in *risk management*. Risk management should start as soon as the project starts, and project planning is a major part of risk management. The way a plan is created and what it includes affect risk, but plans also provide an opportunity to manage risk.

Risk exists because of the factors inherent in the project – for example, creating a new unknown technology, is risky. Risk may also be created by the project planning process – for example, omissions, unnecessary inclusions, and wrong assumptions in the plan. Risk is also a result of the behaviour of the project team and project sponsors – for example, insufficient effort may be put into planning; individuals' skills may not be adequate; and also the estimates may be influenced by management pressure to achieve goals within preset timeframes. Whilst it may be thought that on average some underestimates may be balanced by some overestimates, in practice many business environments create cultures that encourage consistent over or underestimation.

However, planning offers ways to reduce or mitigate risk as well. The main possibilities are

- Ensuring robust challenge and review of plans by skilled peers.
- Including specific activities to reduce risk.
- Making assumptions explicit. Assumptions are inherent in most activities, especially complex ones like projects. Assumptions are a source of risk, as they may be wrong. This can be managed if assumptions are explicit.

Assumptions tend to become more explicit through planning. Without planning many assumptions are implicit and therefore not exposed for consideration in risk management.

o Including contingency time and budget in the plan as a reflection of risk. The higher the level of risk associated with the project the more the contingency buffer required.

o Supporting projects by contingency plans. Contingency plans are additional activities that can be included in a project (and are described in more detail below). A contingency plan contains activities that are contingent on some event occurring. The event may be a risk happening, or may be as simple as a risk being identified. For example, in a project to run an outdoor event a hall may also be booked in case the weather is bad.

Contingency is not a random buffer for error. The amount of contingency is determined by a project manager. The level of contingency in a plan can be determined by a top-down assessment of risk, or from a bottom-up assessment of the risk inherent in every part of the plan. The level of contingency needs a degree of rigour, or it may become an excuse for bad planning. Contingency is included in a plan to deal with risk. Arguably, it is not included to account for changes in requirements. But, for political reasons and to support managing expectations, contingency may be used to provide the capacity to absorb a certain amount of change.

A *contingency plan* is the name given to additional optional tasks that are added to a project specifically to overcome risks. The plans are only implemented if some predefined event occurs. The predefined event may be a risk happening, it may be risk reaching a certain level, or it may simply be a date. Consider a project to develop a new toy to be in stores before Christmas. If the development slips beyond a certain date the stores may have a contingency plan to buy alternative existing toys so they are not without stock in the Christmas period. Alternatively, think about a project to provide a software suite of management reports. If the project is late the contingency plan may be to put some simple spreadsheet reports in place in the interim.

Risk is dealt with in more detail in Chapter 11.

Styles of plan

Project plans can be presented in different ways with varying levels of detail and alternative types of information shown on them. These various formats of plans fulfil different needs, and it is common in a project to make use of different formats at different times.

The most common formats are

o WBS view
o GANTT charts
o Milestone charts
o Network diagrams

The work breakdown structure is often thought as an intermediate stage in planning, but it can be presented as a plan in its own right. This format is helpful when explaining the nature of the work in a project, and the way it is organized. It can be helpful when communicating to different teams and individuals about their role in the project. Its use is limited though, as it shows no schedule information.

GANTT charts represent the format that many people think of as project plans (named after its originator, Henry Gantt). The typical layout consists of a list of activities from the WBS to be documented on the left hand side, with an axis across the page representing time. Bars are then used to represent the length of time different activities take. GANTT charts are helpful ways to communicate about projects to many audiences, especially those interested in project schedule. By varying the level of details they can be adjusted for audiences with different information needs.

Milestone charts are diagrams of timelines showing only the milestones on projects. Milestone charts are useful for explaining projects and project progress to audiences who are primarily interested in the outcomes from projects rather than the activities involved in them. Senior managers who are dependent on the results from a project, rather than are supplying any resource to it, and may, for example, be making commitments dependent on project outcome, can be communicated to effectively with a milestone plan.

Network diagrams are a more specialized form of project plan that can support various types of analysis. They are primarily of use to professional project managers. There are two forms of network diagrams, one called "activity-on-node", and the other called "activity-on-arrow" (or precedence diagrams). The difference is largely only of interest to professional project managers. Network diagrams show events (which are significant occurrences in a project which may be a milestone or deliverable), and they are linked by activities required to go from one event to the next. Network diagrams use *span time*, which is the elapsed time between events.

Diagrams 6.1 and 6.2 are based on a GANTT chart representation (usually considered as intuitive to understand). There are many detailed choices about what specifically is included in different plan formats and how they are presented. Diagram 6.3 shows a simple project using basic versions of the four different plan formats.

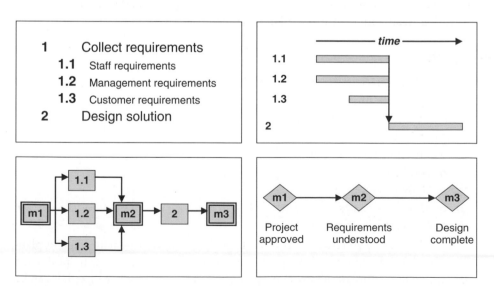

Diagram 6.3 Different plan formats. Clockwise from top left, WBS, GANTT, milestone, Network diagram (activity on node format)

Alternative approaches to planning

There are many alternative approaches or variations on the approaches to creating plans and managing projects. Examples of variants are

o Critical chain
o Goal directed project management
o Time boxing
o Right-to-left planning
o Emergent projects

Critical chain project management (CCPM) was created by Goldratt and based on his Theory of Constraints (Goldratt, 1997). In the theory of constraints (ToC) Goldratt shows how the throughput of a production system is determined by the constraint or bottleneck in the system. Goldratt argues that at any one time there is only one constraint and this is where focus of management must lie. CCPM applies the same thinking to project management.

CCPM is similar to normal project management in many ways except for the focus of the management on the *critical chain*, and not the critical path. The critical chain is the longest chain of tasks that considers both task dependencies and resource dependencies.

Features that differentiate CCPM from CPM are

o CCPM considers resource dependencies, makes them explicit, and provides tools in the form of buffers to manage them. (Normal planning uses resource dependency, but does not show it on most plan diagrams.)
o CCPM disallows *bad multi-tasking* for critical resources that are the constraints on project timescales. Goldratt shows how multi-tasking delays progress in almost all situations and should be avoided unless there is no choice. Bad multi-tasking is essentially unnecessary multi-tasking. If a resource can work on tasks in series this should be done, as it is better than working in parallel.
o CCPM does not worry about finding an optimal solution. CCPM recognizes that no method provides an absolutely optimal plan. It assumes that the difference between a near-optimal and a good-enough plan is less than the error inherent in plans because of the uncertainty in estimates.
o CCPM applies a vision of human behaviour. Goldratt claims that people always make estimates of task length to give themselves high levels of confidence in completing them. There is therefore hidden safety in most estimates meaning that project durations are longer than necessary. However, this safety buffer is lost because people tend to start tasks as late as possible (*student syndrome*). This means more and more tasks tend to drift onto the critical path. Moreover, although tasks can be done early on projects, there is often no incentive to do so.
o CCPM estimates are therefore based on most-likely time to complete a task (50% likelihood). This means on average that 50% of tasks will be late and 50% early. Rather than applying contingency buffers to each task, a central contingency buffer is held.
o CCPM plans backwards from the end date required of a project and starts tasks as late as possible.

o CCPM proposes the use of contingency, and applies buffers at project level and for critical resources, as well as feeder buffers. It does not have task-level buffers. Through the use of aggregated buffers the total amount of contingency is reduced.

CCPM is a variant on the classical approaches in the sense that planning is based on decomposition. However, Goldratt accepts that estimation is inherently inaccurate. CCPM does not see benefit in trying to optimize solutions as any advantage gained from optimization is lost in the scale of estimation error. Some project managers believe that they were effectively doing CCPM prior to Goldratt's book. Other commentators question the reality of one constraint in an ever-changing business situation, especially in the context of multi-projects. However, the book has been highly influential and has been successfully applied in many situations. CCPM advocates claim significant improvements in delivery reliability and reductions in time to finish projects.

Goal directed project management (GDPM) has a different emphasis in project planning (Andersen, Kristoffer and Haug, 2004). GDPM identifies a general failure in projects in their lack of alignment with the real business objectives. Normal planning focuses on the activity, whereas in GDPM the project manager is focussed on the goal of the project. GDPM also stresses that most (business) projects have Process, Systems and Organizational (PSO) components. GDPM is a way of managing projects as much as it is about an alternative approach to planning.

There are several components to GDPM, but a main point of difference is the strong differentiation between *what-planning* and *how-planning*. What-planning is at a milestone level, and how-planning is at the activity level, as usual in project management. By focussing on the milestone plan, based on achieving real goals, stress is kept more on outcomes than activity. To support this GDPM has some of its own plan formats.

The difference between GDPM and normal project management is one primarily of emphasis, as milestone plans exist in normal projects as well. Milestone plans are used in GDPM for communication and motivation. Also responsibilities are allocated at a milestone level as well as at a task level.

Another way to plan is by *time boxing*. A *time box* is a fixed period of time, for example, one day, two weeks or three months. A project is planned to achieve whatever it can within the time box. Rather than the length of a project being the result of how long activities are, the activities and deliverables are those that can be done within the fixed period of time. Some Iterative and Incremental Development (IID) approaches use time boxes. IID approaches often focus on activity and delivering improved solutions in short periods of time rather than on detailed planning. A typical approach is for a set of deliverables to be produced in a time-boxed period, and then the next time-boxed period starts to improve on them. Time-boxed projects rely on a specific mindset: the important thing is speed to deliver a working deliverable rather than richness or meeting every possible requirement. Richness can be developed over time.

Right-to-left planning is a form of time boxing. It starts by considering the end date of a project. This is typically a date by or a period within which something has to be achieved for organizational reasons, such as the date by which new regulation must be complied with, or the financial year within which a project must be completed. Right-to-left contrasts with the normal planning approach, which is *left-to-right*.

When a left-to-right plan is created on paper, it normally is developed from the left-hand side of the page, and the end point is determined as the tasks stretch to the right-hand side of the page. The date of the right-hand side is whenever all the tasks in the project are completed. Right-to-left works like time boxing and forces the project to complete by a certain date and plans to do whatever can be done in the time available. It starts on the right-hand side of the page and plans backwards to see what can be completed in the time available.

Emergent is less a different type of project planning, and more a mindset. In an emergent project needs and solutions are insufficiently defined at the start of the project and are subject to ongoing changes as the project evolves. Needs and plans emerge as the project progresses. The changes are not simply stakeholders altering their minds on requirements, but are a reflection of the dynamic and ever-moving environment in which businesses operate. A business does not shape its environment, but has to respond to it. The term *fluid reality* can be used to describe situations like this (Vaasaagar and Andersen, 2007). In such situations the project manager's role is dependent on his ability to make sense of reality. Project tasks change as project teams strive to complete them. The evolving and controversial approach of complex project management accepts the continuous change in projects. *Wave planning* has been proposed as part of complex project management as one approach to dealing with such complex situations (Dombkins, 2007).

Virtually all projects deal with a degree of unknowns at the start which only gets clarified as the project progresses. Everything is uncertain to some degree. The objectives, scope, requirements, resources, constraints, assumptions and features of the business environment may all get modified. This can normally be handled with change control and by making and verifying assumptions. Most projects exhibit a level of progressive elaboration where requirements and plans become more detailed as the project proceeds. So, it can be thought that all projects are emergent. In truth, whether a project is emergent or not is a matter of emphasis. Some projects are reasonably predictable – others are not.

Emergent projects take the lack of predictability to extremes which undermine the validity of an initial scope and plan as a reliable source of forecast. There is no single process to manage such situations, and in them arguably a project manager's role becomes increasingly like a normal line manager's role. Delivering such a project relies more on the skills, flexibility and innovativeness of the project manager than on the application of the project management process, tools and techniques.

Reducing plan durations

There is a regular pressure in business to reduce the time it takes to complete projects. From new product developments, where there is a desire to increase speed to market, to cost reduction exercises, where there is a need to meet shareholder expectations, time pressures are almost always there. Evidence shows that speed to market for new products and speed in identifying and taking advantage of opportunities that arise in competitive situations are significant drivers of business success.

A project's plan can be shortened and progress can be sped up in many ways, including the following:

o More focussed management, possibly combined with incentives for team members to complete work faster. Simply managing and motivating staff to tighter timescales can often reduce the time to complete a project.

o Speeding up decision-making. Whether it is gaining budget approval or prioritization in a portfolio, projects are subject to many management decisions and often have to wait on them. Speeding up decision-making in a business will usually reduce project timescales.

o Additional resources to speed up some project activities. In theory, if an activity takes one person ten days, then two people can do it in five days. In practice, it is more complicated than this as not all project tasks can be subdivided. Increased resource can speed up many projects, but it is not a general panacea. (See Chapter 4 – "Resources: solution and problem".)

o Removing Constraints from projects. Projects are subject to many constraints which can delay progress. From needing to wait for a management decision to limited access to certain facilities, there are constraints that can be removed and which will speed up progress.

o Reducing the scope or quality of a project. By focussing on the objectives and the desired outcomes from a project it is often possible to reduce scope or quality of deliverables and still meet the original goals. However, care is required in high-pressure situations. Even if there is not a desire to reduce scope or quality it may occur anyway. If scope and quality are not managed well, reduced quality or reduce scope can be the unintended outcome of an overfocus on reducing the timescale of projects.

o Phasing projects. Projects can be broken into a series of phases. Phases are shorter than the time it would take to deliver all project requirements and deliver a sub-set at any time. Although each phase only delivers part of the requirements, the business is able to start to generate value from the project as soon as a phase is complete. This is common in large programmes, and as well as increasing speed to value by simplifying project phases, it can reduce risk. Phases do, however, need to be well-designed.

o Time boxing. Forcing completion of delivery within a set period of time sets focus of the project team on the core aspects of a project. It can be very successful. This generally results in reduced scope, but can be an effective way of management.

o Parallel working. The schedule of a project is dependent on the sequence of tasks. If more tasks can be done in parallel, it will tend to shorten project times. The advantages of parallel working have to be balanced against more complex management and often higher risk.

o Applying special approaches to parallel working such as *concurrent engineering* or *simultaneous engineering*. As well as doing tasks in parallel, concurrent engineering makes use of multi-disciplinary teams. By using multi-disciplinary teams, which traditionally would have worked in sequence, progress and problem-solving is speeded up. Concurrent engineering has proved its value in many situations, but it can be complex to manage and may require changes in organizational culture in order to be successful. Similarly, CCPM has also been shown to reduce some project timelines.

- o Changing the project strategy or planning approach. A plan is just one approach to a project. Reviewing the plan and looking for simpler or quicker alternative ways often provides good results, especially if a project plan has never been subject to any review.

Programme and portfolio planning

This chapter has dealt so far with the issue of project planning. Consideration must also be given to programme- and portfolio-level planning. Although the principles of programme and portfolio planning build on project planning, there are some significant differences.

Programme planning

Programme-level planning has all the challenges and difficulties of project planning but on a larger scale. Programmes are usually bigger and more complicated than projects, so the corresponding programme plan is often more difficult to create and manage. Programmes are often higher in risk and more important than projects, so the emphasis on planning can be greater.

Programme managers recognize a number of areas that differentiate programme planning from project planning. As the boundary between projects and programmes is often imprecise these can be differences of emphasis. Key ones include

- o *Integrating plans across projects*: Programmes are usually made up of a series of projects. Each project has to create its own plan which must be integrated into an overall programme plan. There are various ways to integrate plans, which depend on the skills of the programme manager and her relationship with the project managers. Some programme managers consolidate all details of project plans into a programme plan. This will often result in a very complicated plan and does question the role of the project managers. Other programme managers will integrate rolled-up project plans, or even milestone plans, to create the overall programme plan. Integrating project plans into a programme plan may not result in a combination that achieves programme-level objectives. In this case the programme manager must ask for the projects to be re-planned.
- o *Dependencies between projects*: The individual projects in a programme often have a high level of inter-dependency. One of the areas of additional value a programme manager brings in is managing inter-dependency between different projects, which are beyond a project manager's remit to manage. Programme-level plans must show project inter-dependencies very clearly.
- o *Multi-phase activities*: Programmes are more likely to be broken into phases than are projects, if for no other reason than the scale of work involved. Early phases of programmes can be planned in great detail; later phases may only be planned on outline. Programme managers therefore regularly have to create plans with varying levels of detail, typically with later parts of the plan less detailed than the current.

Programmes also tend to have a higher level of accountability for benefits realization than projects.

Portfolio planning

Portfolio planning is different from project- or programme-level planning. The emphasis in portfolio planning is on looking across various aspects of the portfolio at an aggregated level. Portfolio planning is primarily about assessing the cumulative effect of projects and programmes.

Examples of areas where consideration has to be given at a portfolio level are

o Projects status relative to the portfolio management process
o Change impact of the portfolio
o Critical resource loading across a portfolio
o Aggregated benefits realized across a portfolio

Projects status needs to be assessed relative to the stages and decisions in the portfolio management process. A plan can be created showing all projects and their milestones relating to portfolio gates, such as project initiation, project approval and prioritization, and project closure. Such a milestone view is used to support the portfolio management process.

Portfolio plans also should provide summary views of change impact of the portfolio. Each project results in change in various areas of the business. To allow preparation for change, to ensure that individual areas of the business are not being overloaded with change, and also to support prioritization a diagram can be created showing which parts of the business will be subject to change and when. (See Chapter 9 – "Implementation: delivering and sustaining change".)

It is important from a portfolio level to understand critical resource loading across a portfolio. Each project and programme requires common resources, and it is often useful to see a schedule of demand, especially for critical resources in high demand to support prioritization and resource management.

Finally, portfolio managers should track the delivery of aggregated benefits across a portfolio. Portfolio managers often need to see the timing of benefits realization across business periods to ensure progress is being made towards portfolio goals. (See Chapter 10 – "Achieving and measuring benefits".)

There may also be a need for a summary view of progress across all projects in a portfolio. This is normally achieved by integrating rolled-up project milestone plans.

Case Study 6.2 HOW DO YOU RAPIDLY PLAN AND DELIVER PROJECTS USING A METHODOLOGY LIKE AGILE?

Jayne Cockill is an experienced programme and team manager. She has been responsible for a range of projects and programmes including launching products, developing software and supporting business change. She has an in-depth knowledge of Agile methods.

Jayne Cockill

I am going to talk about my experiences in a very fast-moving business that had to respond to constantly changing needs. Historically, projects were not terribly successful. We suffered from many started projects that never completed due to a combination of poor foresight and ever-changing needs. This was an ideal environment to implement an Agile development methodology.

As an example of our bad experiences, we had one project which took six months, and took considerable resources for a business of our size, to complete. At the end of the six months the project was completed. It fully met the documented requirements; but when the customer saw it for the first time they rejected it as they said it was not what they wanted. It was wasted investments like this that really triggered my search for a better approach. The better approach I chose was Agile.

Before we talk about Agile, it's worth adding that it was only one of our pillars of success – the other was having a simple but effective project prioritization mechanism. (Jayne's approach to project prioritization is described in Chapter 3.)

Once a project was approved and prioritized it was allocated to my team to deliver. I was responsible for a mixed team consisting of project managers and software development staff. As the bulk of projects were software development we sat within the software function – although many of our projects were broader than simple software development. My team was responsible for managing projects from beginning to end. The role of the project manager was to gain the resource required, develop the plan and make sure everyone knew what they were responsible for doing.

With Agile the customers are closely involved in the project. It was a project-orientated business, and fortunately therefore projects took priority. When resource was required to work on a project it was allocated. The fact that we needed regular time with our internal customers was not therefore a problem.

The first stage of a project was for all the involved project team members to meet in a room. The first meeting was used to drive the scope and requirements down to a sufficiently detailed level to design and plan the solution. The customer had to define the purpose of the project and what they wanted to achieve by it. They also had to define the key features – what was essential, what was desired and what was nice to have.

Unlike a traditional development methodology customer requirements were defined with the inputs of the software developer. This needs a developer of some experience who understands existing systems and their constraints. As the customer specified requirements, the developer tried to understand them and made suggestions as to how they could be improved. By bringing together the customer, developer and project manager at the end of the first session the aim is not only to understand what is required, but also to have a committed time to deliver it. For a simple change to a well-known process this first meeting might take only half an hour. For a more complex new development it could take half a day, or in the worst case a whole day. Compared to traditional development approaches knowing after half an hour, or in worst case one day, what will be delivered and when is a major improvement.

Having committed a plan to deliver the development activity would start. At least once a day the customer, project manager and developer got together to review progress and resolve any issues or risks. These meetings only took 15 minutes or so and were generally done standing up to ensure they were completed quickly. A guiding principle of Agile is cooperative working, but another is for meetings to be as short as possible. Sometimes, to ensure development was on track there might be two or three such meetings daily. Because of the intense involvement of the customer there were rarely any surprises, and at the end of the project they knew precisely what would be delivered to them.

At the end of the committed timeframe we generally completed the project to the customer's satisfaction. Because of the ongoing involvement of the customer they

could be accountable for what was delivered. As we were regularly meeting customers'
expectations, the business overall became more confident and supportive of our
development team.

In this business we found Agile to be a significant improvement on traditional
development approaches. It does not suit everyone, as it can be a very intense
environment to work in. Although we did lots of projects, none was individually too
large. Where projects were larger and/or more complex we would try to break them
down into smaller chunks and limit the changes so the work could be completed in a
phased iterative approach. Like all methodologies it needs to be set in the context it is
used in. I am never afraid of breaking the rules or guidelines if I think they do not work
in a specific situation. It needs to be applied intelligently and relative to the needs at
the time. If Agile is to work it needs to be implemented in a business that understands
what it means and is supportive of it.

Plans and the project management process

Early on in this chapter it was noted that the term "plan" is used in two ways within
project management. The first way has been considered in the previous sections of
this chapter, as a definition of the activities required to complete the project in a
scheduled order and the resulting resource requirement. However, the word "plan"
is also used to denote documents produced by the project manager which describe
various elements of the project management process.

The need for documented definitions of project management process depends
on the scale and complexity of the project, and the domain of the project. Examples
of such plans include

- *Communication plan*: defining the communication strategy, key messages
  for the project, communication activities and responsibilities
- *Risk management plan*: defining the approach to and processes for managing risk on the project.
- *Quality plan*: defining the approach to quality planning, assurance and
  control to ensure the project meets its objectives. Quality should be built
  into all project processes; however, there is often a need to define the ethos
  and approach to quality on a project.
- *Integration plan*: defining, for a large project of multiple workstreams or
  a programme of multiple projects, how the components of the project's
  deliverables produced by each part of the project or programme will be
  integrated into a coherent end deliverable.
- *Configuration plan*: defining the way in which the configuration of deliverables is recorded and managed as the project evolves and is subject to change.
- *Operational readiness plan*: describing the approach to preparing the
  operational departments for the change resulting from the implementation
  of project deliverables.

MAIN LEARNING POINTS FROM CHAPTER 6

- Project plans are one of the central tools in project management. The plan provides the basis for predicting the cost, timescale and outcome from a project – and how the project strategy will be achieved. The plan also provides a way to communicate the project details and allocate tasks to project team members.
- The steps in developing a project plan include
  - Define activities in the project in the form of a WBS
  - Estimate duration and resources required
  - Identify linkages at an activity and resource levels, and identify any external dependencies
  - Apply available resources
  - Develop schedule and budget
  - Add milestones to the plan
  - Review – ensuring it is conformant with objectives and constraints, is complete and correct, and entails only an appropriate level of risk.
- Plans can be presented in different ways. The different styles support different project management activities and communication of the plan to different audiences. GANTT charts are the most common form of plan presentation.
- Plans need ongoing management during the delivery of a project, with progress against the plan assessed and variances identified. In practice, assessing progress is usually a subjective judgement and is prone to error. The project manager will focus on the critical path – the series of tasks with zero float. Plans may be periodically updated during a project under change control.
- Project plans are a source of risk because of the inherent uncertainty and ambiguity in planning and the influence of organizational pressure. But plans also provide a way to understand and manage risks.
- Alternative approaches include critical chain and time-boxed planning.
- The term "plan" may also be used to refer to descriptions of project management processes, for example, for quality, risk, communications and configuration management, integration management and operational readiness.

REVIEW QUESTIONS AND EXERCISES

1. Identify a project you have good understanding of. This could be a project from work, or it could be an activity you have to complete as part of your studies.
   a. Create two alternative work breakdown structures of your choice.
   b. Determine how much resource is required for each of the WBS by estimating the resources for each task at the lowest level of decomposition you have created. Compare and contrast the estimates. Which one do you think is better and why?
2. Assume a working day has 7.5 hours in it. How many productive hours of work do you have for projects in a year? What assumptions have you made in determining this number?
3. For a project you have been involved in, how easy was it to accurately estimate the project by creating a work breakdown structure and determining the resources for each task? How did the understanding of task emerge as the project progressed? What were its implications for planning and risk management?

4. How would you know if a task is at variance with the baseline plan? If you find variances would this concern you or not? What consideration would you give to the critical path? How would you make use of contingency?
5. Consider the following groups of people in a large programme made up of a number of projects:
   a. Portfolio manager
   b. Programme manager
   c. Project manager
   d. Programme sponsor
   e. End customer
   f. Project team member

   What are the different information needs of each of these groups from plans? What format of plan, and at what level of detail, would you use for each group?
6. Which is better: critical path method or critical chain project management? Why?
7. What is the relationship between project planning and project risk management?
8. If you were asked to create a project's quality plan what would you include in it?

Suggested reading

Understanding the components that go into forming a plan, producing estimates and then scheduling are core parts of most project management books. Examples of reasonably thorough treatments of the subject are

- *Project Management*. Harvey Maylor. Third edition. FT Prentice Hall, 2005.
- *Project Management the Managerial Process*. Clifford F Gray and Erik W Larson. McGraw-Hill International Edition, 2006

For an example of an implementation of the critical chain method see

- *The Definitive Guide to Project Management: The Fast-Track to Getting the Job Done On Time and On Budget*. Sebastian Nokes, Ian Major, Alan Greenwood, and Mark Goodman. Financial Times/Prentice Hall, August 2003

Bibliography

Andersen, E., Kristoffer, G. and Haug, T. *Goal Directed Project Management, Effective Techniques and Strategies.* Kogan Page, 3rd Edition, 2004.

Cardinal, J. and Marle, F. "Project: The just necessary structure to reach your goals". *International Journal of Project Management.* Volume 24, Issue 3, April 2006, pp. 226–33

Dombkins, D. "Wave Planning". *PM World Today.* Volume IX, Issue X, October 2007.

Goldratt, E. *Critical Chain* The North River Press, 1997.

Gray, CF. and Larson, EW. *Project Management: The Managerial Process.* McGraw-Hill International Edition, 2006.

Ivory, C., Alderman, N., McLoughlin, I. and Vaughan, R. "Sense-making as a process within complex projects". *Making Projects Critical*, Palgrave MacMillan, 2006.

Kerzner, H. *Project Management: A Systems Approach to Planning, Scheduling, and Controlling,* 8th Edition, John Wiley & Sons Inc, 8 Rev edition, February 2003.

Lewis, J. *Project Planning, Scheduling and Control.* McGraw-Hill Education, 3 Rev edition, January 2001.

Maylor, H. *Project Management.* Third edition, FT Prentice Hall, 2005.

Vaasaagar, A. and Andersen, E. "On task evolution in renewal projects". *International Journal of Project Management.* Volume 25, Issue 4, May 2007, pp. 354–64.

7

defining project

success

It is self-evident that being confident of success in any activity requires a definition of what success is and a way of assessing the activity, measuring it against or comparing it with that definition. Projects should fit into this model; but in practice measuring success on projects is beset by confusion, ambiguity and often radically varying views.

Let us look at a typical situation when a large project or major programme completes. This is a time for celebration for project team members. It is a chance for reflection: what went well, what went badly, and what can be learnt for next time. A difficult and risky piece of work has been completed. A valuable set of deliverables has been produced and implemented within the operations of the organization. Benefits are being achieved. The project manager is feeling satisfied, and from his perspective, he has been successful. The work came in on time and to budget, and the deliverables seem to work as required. Surely that is a complete success?

The answer, in the case of projects, is that *it depends*. It depends on the meaning of project success which is often surrounded by confusion and the varying perspectives of different stakeholders. The budget holder, who paid for a project, may be happy, whilst, many of the users are not. A project team may consider they have done a brilliant piece of work, and yet the sponsor may be unsatisfied. Depending on who is asked, a project can be assessed simultaneously as a failure and a success, or even more confusingly as a partial success: to paraphrase an old idiom *success is in the eye of the beholder*. The situation becomes more complicated when time is factored in. A project may be considered a success at the moment of completion, but a failure six months later when expected business benefits are not achieved.

There is a lack of clarity not only as to what success is for each individual project, but also, more fundamentally, as to what success means generally for projects. Yet, without a definition of success, it is not possible to have confidence in the direction in which a project is going. Nor is it possible to determine with any certainty whether a project was successful or not. Projects consume significant amounts of an organization's resources and it is reasonable, even essential, for management to demand *was that project successful* or *is our investment in projects worthwhile*. Project managers invest time and effort in their careers and also want to understand whether they are being successful or not.

This chapter deals with the challenge of defining project success and shows how the concept of success can be ambiguous within a project environment. There is no single definition of project success – it is context-specific. It needs to be decided on in each organization, and to some extent for each project. The contents of the chapter will help in making such a decision. Project success can be defined, but choosing definitions should be approached carefully and thoughtfully. This chapter will help in taking the right approach.

Success criteria and success factors

Before exploring the concepts of measuring success in projects it is essential to differentiate between two phrases which are often confused:

- Success factors or critical success factors, also known as CSFs
- Success criteria, also known as success definitions or measures of success

CSFs are factors that have been identified to assist in making a specific project successful. Take the resources on a project. Having sufficient resources on a project is a critical success factor, as a project is unlikely to be successful if it does not have enough resources. The question, "will this project be successful", can be answered at least partially by "yes, it is likely to be because we have the right level of resources" or fully by "no, it will not because it does not have the necessary level of resources". There are other CSFs and a project will need to meet many CSFs to succeed, but sufficient resource is one among the range of CSFs. However, having enough resource is *not* a success criterion. The question, "was this project successful", cannot meaningfully be answered by "yes, because it had enough resource".

This chapter discusses success criteria, or more generally how success can be defined and measured. At the end of the chapter is a brief discussion on critical success factors and their relationship to success criteria.

Definitions of success

The starting point for defining and subsequently assessing project success appears simple. The objectives are set at the beginning of the project and balanced against some agreed constraints, usually in terms of time and cost limits. It may therefore seem an easy equation: as long as the project manager manages the project to achieve the objectives within the constraints, isn't the project a success? This view that success amounts to achieving a bargain between the project manager and the organization, in the form of "tell me what you want and if I deliver it, the project is a success", is an important, but unfortunately insufficient, definition of success in many situations.

This simple view of success does not encompass the variety of ways in which success is defined in business projects. Projects may be assessed against a wide variety of success criteria, where success criteria are

Key measurements, which, when achieved, are indicative of whether the task/ project/programme has accomplished what it set out to do (the stated objectives and benefits). (Williams and Parr, 2004)

Depending on the situation, a project may be assessed as successful if it did one or more of the following:

1. Used the expected level of resource in the expected way over the expected time period. This is success in terms of *meeting time and cost constraints and against an agreed plan.*
2. Created expected deliverables. This is success in terms of *meeting the speci- fication or requirements and the quality of output.*
3. Managed in the expected way the expected process. This is success in terms of the *approach and quality of work undertaken.*
4. Produced deliverables which resulted in the achievement of expected business benefits. This is success in terms of meeting a *business case* or *the achievement of business value by a project.*
5. Achieved stakeholder satisfaction. This is success in terms of *meeting the stakeholders' perceived needs as defined by their levels of satisfaction.*
6. Delivered what was expected or what was needed by the stakeholders, irrespective of what was planned. This is success in terms of *meeting the stakeholders' needs as opposed to rigidly holding to the defined specification.*
7. Proved that it was the right project to have been chosen. This is success in terms of *optimizing the choice of project.*

These are not mutually exclusive categories. Project success may be defined in terms of combinations or components of the points 1–7. Hence, an organization may consider a project a success if it meets a time constraint (point 1) and stake- holder needs (point 4).

Let's consider each one of these definitions of success, and helpful combina- tions of them, by referencing the numbers in the above list.

Success definition 1 should be relatively straightforward to assess for a project. There may be different balances in different situations between constraints such as time and cost. For one organization cost may be of paramount importance and for another, time. However, the principle exists that a project's success can be assessed by checking compliance to time and cost constraints, defined in an agreed plan. When definition 1 is combined with definition 2, they form the traditional way of measuring project success that most project managers are comfortable with. A project that is on time and to budget and has created the expected deliverables would be successful using these definitions. To some stake- holders the combination of definitions 1 and 2 is an ideal assessment of project success. To other people definitions 1 and 2 are an insufficient description of a successful project.

A project manager may consider himself as successful by meeting time and cost plans and delivering the agreed deliverables. In contrast, whilst a senior executive may be pleased that a project took the expected time, kept to its agreed budget, and produced the required deliverables, if the deliverables do not add any value to the business, that pleasure will soon turn to a view that the project was a failure.

The definition 3 of success is often thought of as a CSF rather than as a useful assessment of success. However, it may be important in some situations. For example, in organizations which value compliance to defined process, such as when ISO 2000 accreditation is important, success is measured according to this definition. Any project which jeopardises accreditation by not following agreed process is therefore a failure. To anyone interested or involved in such accreditation this may be a valid definition of success; to other stakeholders interested in the outcome of a project only, point 3 is an irrelevance.

Success measured against definition 4 starts to consider the needs of the wider organization beyond the project. The objective of any investment in a business is to add some value in one way or another. In many situations, a combination of success definitions 1, 2 and 4 provide a balanced set of success criteria. A project which is positively assessed against these definitions would be on time, to budget, have created expected deliverables and met the necessary business case. Most activities in a business which achieve this would be considered as successful. Unfortunately, life is not this simple! Stakeholders have needs which may go beyond achieving a business case.

Success as defined in points 5 and 6 brings a more complex, but potentially more realistic, view of business. Definition 5 introduces the concept of stakeholder needs, understood by achieving stakeholder satisfaction. How well a task was done and whether it achieved what it was expected to do are often less important than whether the person the task was done for is happy with the result. This is the basis for business performance metrics such as *customer satisfaction* and *customer advocacy* ratings. Projects impact a wider variety of stakeholders, all of whom may have different levels of satisfaction. In a project it is better to think of *stakeholder satisfaction* or *stakeholder delight* than of customer satisfaction or customer delight. Of course, satisfaction is partially determined by how well tasks are done and whether they achieve the expected results, but also by a whole range of personal and environmental factors which influence individuals' judgements. Issues such as honesty, reliability, demeanour and even the level of fun impact levels of satisfaction.

A project stakeholder may be satisfied as long as she is kept informed of progress, even though a project is otherwise performing badly. Conversely, a project manager may lower stakeholder satisfaction by not providing sufficient information on project progress, even though the project finishes on time and within budget. In either case, the provision of information has not actually changed the project outcome, but it has altered the level of stakeholder satisfaction. Factoring in level of satisfaction, whilst complicated to do, significantly enhances the judgement of success.

(I have used the terms *stakeholder satisfaction* or *stakeholder delight* rather than the more common terms *customer satisfaction* or *customer delight* as there may be stakeholders who are not project customers, yet whose view of success is important. Customers are stakeholders of the project, but not all stakeholders are customers.)

Definition 6 is a variant of success definition 5. It explicitly makes the point that achieving satisfaction may sometimes be at variance with creating the proposed deliverables. Wants and desires are broader than easily defined packages of deliverables, and are subject to change. What may be defined as the deliverables may not be quite what a stakeholder requires. Even if a deliverable is as required, it may not create satisfaction. Satisfaction is also derived from intangible aspects, like how someone was treated, or how well they were involved in project activities.

Many commentators assume that project managers primarily worry about technical factors such as time, cost and quality of deliverables, and largely ignore stakeholder satisfaction. This is increasingly not true. There is evidence that in reality project managers are more sophisticated than this and progressively more customer-orientated rather than technical (Iclemi-Turkel and Rom, 2001).

Success definition 7 looks at project success in a completely different way. It does not even assess the way a project was done or what it achieves, but asks whether it was the right project to do. This is akin to measuring the success of a business by assessing whether it has the right strategy rather than by looking at how well it operates. In a project context, this can be considered as a measure of *portfolio success* and an assessment of the decisions related to project selection. Portfolio success is discussed later on in the chapter.

These seven ways of defining success, or combinations of them, are common, but there are many other options. In an attempt to elicit the possible range of additional definitions of success, the author held a series of discussions with experienced project managers and project sponsors. They were asked the non-specific question "what does project success mean to you?" Although not a statistically relevant sample, it gives flavour to the range of alternative definitions of success. All of the following mentioned below are valid ways of assessing success:

o The organization learnt as a result of a project. This was especially true when the project itself was to implement a methodology, such as Six-Sigma.
o The project led to personal growth for project team members and project team satisfaction.
o The project dealt well with changes to scope and objectives. (If change is inevitable in a dynamic environment and is a major strategic challenge, then successfully handling change can be considered as one definition of success.)
o Business risk was minimized. The project avoided exposing an organization to potentially excessive risk.
o The project resulted in increased organizational flexibility.
o The project enabled business commitments to be made and provided a degree of business predictability.
o The project enabled a business to move towards its strategic goals. If projects exist to deliver a business's strategy, then project success is a strategic concept which should align project efforts with the short- and long-run success of the business (Shenar et al., 2001).
o The project resulted in innovation in the company. This could be technical, process or organizational innovation.
o The project produced a sustained change, rather than simple change at the point of completion.
o The project overcame situation-specific constraints or limits beyond those shown in the baseline plan – such as minimizing duration or hitting a specific date, minimizing cost or delivering to a specific budget, and maximizing benefits or achieving a specific target.

Again, like the first list of success measures these are not mutually exclusive factors, and a project may be assessed against several of them.

What conclusions can be drawn from this web of definitions? A project may be considered as having varying levels of success or failure from different viewpoints. One person may see a project that does not complete and does not deliver any measurable business benefits as a total failure and a wasted investment. Another, looking from the viewpoint of what an organization has learnt from such an experience may consider it a success and an essential stage in an organization's evolution. A definition of success can be created for a project, but there is no universal definition suitable for all situations. The way success will be assessed must be defined for each project and depends on the context. Identification of success measures should be done as part of the project's scope (Diagram 7.1).

Having built up an understanding of the range of possible success definitions it is easy to get lost in the complexity. To overcome this problem models can be created which group success definitions into simple categories. These models form useful and more easily applicable descriptions of project success.

In one piece of research four separate dimensions of project success were identified (Shenar et al., 2001):

- o Project efficiency
- o Impact on customer
- o Direct business and organizational success
- o Preparing for the future

Baccarini proposes an even simpler model and identifies two fundamental components of project success: project management success and product success

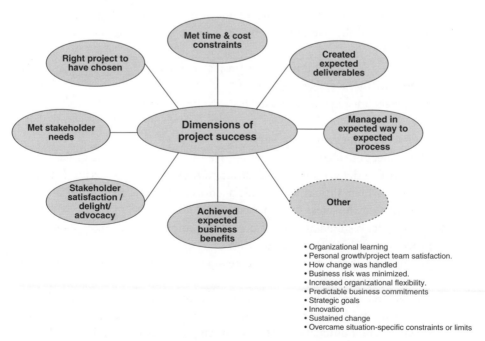

Diagram 7.1 The dimensions of project success

(Baccarini, 1999). Project success focuses on project process and the accomplishment of cost, time and quality objectives. Product success concerns the effects of the project's final *products*. Product, in this case is an alternative word for deliverable. He suggests that project management success is subordinate to product success and project management success influences product success.

Applying definitions of success

In the previous section the range of ways of assessing a project's success was discussed. This section explains why even if a project manager or project sponsor has a definition of project success it can still be difficult in practice to make an assessment.

Practical problems that arise when attempting to assess project success include

- Lack of clarity in objectives
- Change in objectives
- The limits and difficulties of measurement
- The differing views of various stakeholders
- The ambiguity between managing a project well and the outcome from a project
- The impact of cultural aspects in assessing success
- The effects of time
- Unexpected outcomes from projects
- Conflicts between different criteria.

Let us look at each of these points briefly.

According to classic project management theory objectives are defined at the start of the project. They provide a baseline guide to direct the project. Unfortunately, sometimes owing to poor project management or pressure from impatient stakeholders, objectives are not fully defined or agreed on at the start of a project. Project execution is started without fully defining scope and objectives. In some other situations, especially in those in which a project is an exploratory venture to gain knowledge, the objectives are inherently unclear and evolve with the project.

Objectives are only words, and words are subject to misinterpretation and ambiguity inherent in language. Business analysts are often aware of this risk, but project managers are not always. This risk is especially high when the project team has been created from people with different organizational or cultural backgrounds. Common business terms used to define success may be assumed to have the same meaning for different project team members, and yet in reality can have different interpretations. Words like *quality* and *satisfaction* have formal definitions, but have a variety of meanings to different project participants.

Even if objectives are well-specified, documented and agreed by all stakeholders, project and stakeholder needs evolve. What may have been identified as important to success may not be relevant when a project completes. This comes about both because organizations adapt in response to the environment in which they are in and also because projects create understanding and knowledge. As learning occurs through a project it is common to find that objectives need to be modified. Objectives may be overambitious or underambitious, or simply wrong, which is understood only when some of the project work is complete.

The ability to measure or assess objectively is limited with respect to some project objectives and constraints. This is especially true in softer projects, such as cultural change. When can a cultural change programme be deemed to be successful? Is it when the cultural change has occurred? But when can that be assessed in any meaningful and objective fashion? There are ways, but they tend to be indirect and subjective.

Even some of the bedrocks of project management are not that easy to measure. Reflecting on the iron triangle, it may appear straightforward to measure the time a project took or the amount it cost. This can often be more difficult to assess than it seems. Standard business processes do not always assist in measuring project times and costs. As an example, management accounts do not always facilitate data on project costs to be easily consolidated from a project perspective. But it is of course possible to measure time and cost in great accuracy with the right data capture.

Whereas measuring time and cost are usually surmountable challenges, factors such as scope and quality are far harder to measure. For instance, assessing whether an IT project has met its scope may be achieved partially by testing and ensuring that all the planned functionality exists. But IT project requirements often include non-functional measures such as performance criteria when a system is fully loaded, availability hours and reliability. These can be very difficult to assess at the point of project implementation.

Quality has several definitions, and often is interpreted in quite different ways by different stakeholders. Though there are some more formal methods, such as the proposed Earned Quality Method (Paquin et al., 2000), these are not commonly used, and it is questionable whether they have value outside of an engineering environment. Quality, therefore, tends to be subjectively evaluated. Subjective evaluations mean that different assessments will be made by various stakeholders reviewing the same project deliverables.

In addition, there are often significant differences between what should or what have been planned to be used as measures, and what are (Icmeli-Tukel and Rom, 2001).

Projects have large numbers of stakeholders. As individuals each stakeholder will have his or her own perception of success. This may sometimes be rational and based on published measures, but in other cases it will be a purely personal view based on their own experience or even irrational perspectives. The sponsor of a project will tend to consider it as a success if it meets its objectives. A budget holder may be more interested in the fact that it was delivered to cost predictions. Users will be mostly interested in how well the deliverables from a project work. Project team members are often most aware of how well the project was managed and whether it achieved its scope – or even what they personally gained from involvement in the project. Other managers may primarily be interested in the timing of project completion.

One of the key stakeholders in any project is the project manager. A project manager's opinion of success is usually based around a view of whether the project achieved what was required in the time, cost and to the scope defined. A broader stakeholder group may be more interested in whether the project met its business case and achieves sufficient value for the business.

There can be culture-specific measures of success that are only relevant in certain situations, or to specific groups of stakeholders. For example, Wang and Huang stress the importance of good relations or *guanaxi* to success in Chinese projects (Wang and Huang, 2006). Such a measure is unlikely to be often used, or even understood, in a Western European or American project.

Stakeholders' impact on project success is discussed in the next section of this chapter in more detail.

Assessments of success in projects are influenced by the passage of time. A judgement that a project is a success after completion is probably made based on a combination of meeting time and cost criteria and the general level of satisfaction of a set of stakeholders. Such a judgement may be revised 6–12 months later when issues arise associated with a lack of reliability of deliverables, or missing functionality. Alternatively, time may improve the success of a project. The London Dome was widely seen as a failure when it was built, but in a second life as a music venue it is generally perceived as a success. Whether senior stakeholders do actually link back to projects completed in previous time periods is questionable, and it may be that functional problems are only visible to more junior staff. Senior stakeholders may perceive a project as a success because detailed problems are not visible to them. Their staff who have to work with the detailed problems may be less positive about the project.

For some very large programmes it is not practical to wait until the end of the work to assess success. Management needs ways to assess and quantify success during progress and through the passage of time.

Time is also necessary to achieve business benefits. Benefits may arise as projects progress, but many projects complete before delivering the planned benefits. Benefits accrue over time. For example, a new IT system may achieve efficiencies and hence cost savings. The project may have ended and the project team disbanded at the point of systems implementation. The efficiency and savings will occur only in the months and years following implementation. An initially successful project can therefore change into a failure if benefits are not achieved. This may not be due to project management failure. Achieving benefits over time may be dependent on factors outside a project's control. For example, business assumptions may be wrong; strategy may change resulting in decreased usage of deliverables; regulations may be altered requiring re-working of a project's designed processes; and social views may change meaning that a new product delivered by a project is no longer acceptable. (Benefits realization is discussed in Chapter 10.)

Many projects, especially complex business transformations, often result in unexpected outcomes. In a survey 46% of projects resulted in unexpected side effects, split almost evenly between desirable and undesirable effects (White and Fortune, 2002). How should these be assessed and valued? Business-change projects are particularly prone to unexpected outcomes because of the difficulty in reliably predicting the response of people to change.

Having reached this point in the chapter the reader will understand that assessing project success can be complex, and is almost certainly multi-dimensional. The final difficulty is assessing success is when different dimensions of success conflict. Considering even the simplest dimensions of success – the iron triangle of time, cost and quality – it is easy to imagine situations in which these are in conflict. Corners may be cut on a project to meet time or cost criteria, but resulting in poorer quality; resource consumption may be reduced to lower the costs, but resulting in extra time; and quality may be enhanced, but this may knock on into time and cost. Unless there are clear guidelines as to the relative balance between such different criteria, or a process to make balancing decisions as progress is made, such conflicts will occur. A project that is considered a success by one stakeholder because it was done quickly or cheaply may be considered as a failure by another for whom the quality of deliverables is too low.

Case Study **7.1**   **TECHCORP'S GAMBLE: SUCCESS OR FAILURE?**

This case study relates to the launch of a consumer technology–based product. The names of the involved companies have been changed to retain client confidentiality. In this case study the organization is referred to simply as Techcorp

Techcorp operated in a highly competitive market. The market had been changing as new competitors entered and others merged. At that time there were three main competitors to Techcorp. There were several smaller players trying to enter the market, but none had yet reached critical size, and they posed limited threat at this stage.

At the time of this project there was a leap forward in technology, which presented the opportunity to provide a radically enhanced level of service to customers, and based on this, new revenue streams. This was attractive as the business was highly capital-intensive and low-margin. Only one of the competitors was consistently profitable. Therefore any increased margin was welcome.

All businesses in this market planned to make use of the new technology to provide enhanced products and services to their customers. Techcorp was a well-run business, but was at that time the smallest of the four main companies providing the services. It was also the last to start a programme of work to make use of the new technology to upgrade its products.

Techcorp's strategic analysis showed it really had no choice but to invest in the new technology. With a successful investment the business could thrive. Without the investment Techcorp would become a marginal player in the business with a significant decline in revenues over the next 5–10 years. Investing in the new technology was therefore seen as a gamble that Techcorp could not avoid.

A programme was set up and a programme manager was appointed. The programme manager developed a plan and a budget for the work. The initial plan showed that the full design and implementation of the new technology would lead to a time-to-market of 18 months for new products. The programme would cost approximately £100m. This was some three to nine months behind Techcorp's estimation of the launch dates for competitors. Techcorp believed there was significant advantage in being relatively early to market.

Following several stages of presentation and decision-making the programme budget was approved in outline, subject to further board approval, but the timeline was not. The executive sponsor of the programme, who given the programme's importance to Techcorp was the CEO, asked for the programme to be completed in 12 months. By completing in 12 months the programme would be one of the first to market. In addition, the executive team were allocated an additional special bonus by shareholders if they could launch the product within 12 months.

The programme manager re-visited the programme plan and created a plan that could be completed in 12 months. To achieve this, a number of compromises had to be made, and there was an increased level of risk of programme failure. In parallel with the re-planning board approval was gained for the budget. Re-visiting the programme plan, and achieving final board approval for the project expenditure took two months.

There were a number of technical and commercial problems in the programme, but all of these were successfully overcome to deliver the project within 12 months from the start of the programme.

At the end of the programme there were various ways to assess the project's success:

- *The product was launched within 12 months of starting the programme. However, this was 14 months after the start time taking account of the 2-month re-planning and budget authorization delay.*
- *The product was second to market within two months of the first to market. This enabled Techcorp to capture a significant share and grow from the fourth to the third largest business in this market.*
- *The programme budget overran by approximately 5%. However it later emerged that budget tracking had not been very diligent, and many other unknown expenditures had not been included. Moreover, further invoices for work on the programme arrived over the next six months which pushed it up by a further 3%.*
- *Techcorp's share price rose significantly as a result of the launch of this product.*
- *The executive team received their special bonus. All staff also received their full bonus payments that year, for the first time in five years.*

Twelve months after the launch of the product

- *Two competitors had merged to form the largest player.*
- *One of the smaller marginal players had surprising success and their revenues were now almost as big as Techcorp's.*
- *Techcorp's product had a significantly higher fault rate and resulting complaints than expected. There was lower customer satisfaction, higher customer churn and higher operating costs than in the original business case.*
- *Techcorp had to invest in a series of product enhancement projects. These reduced faults, but competitors were also enhancing their products and Techcorp's level of customer churn remained high, and customer satisfaction relatively low.*

The stock market entered a period of uncertainty and stock prices fell. Techcorp's fell significantly more than average. There were varied opinions on the success of the project.

The stakeholder dimension: facts, viewpoints and perceptions

Projects have a range of stakeholders with interest in the project's success – and occasionally its failure. Even if stakeholder satisfaction is not to be formally included as a way of assessing project success, it will impact the way a project is perceived. Unless stakeholders agree that a project has succeeded there will be uncertainty. Unfortunately, stakeholders do not have the same perspectives, and the project manager has a balancing act to perform to maximize the level of satisfaction across the diverse group of stakeholders.

The many stakeholders in a project have different and often divergent interests. The budget holder will benefit from a project completed for a minimal amount of money, whereas users of project deliverables will gain from the highest quality output. These will often be conflicting needs. In addition, various users may have different requirements from the deliverables, and a choice such as what functionality to include in an IT system will satisfy some users more than others. The manager accountable for a project's business case may benefit from the fastest implementation to enable benefits to be accrued quickly, whilst an operational manager may want to delay implementation to minimize the impact on operations. The director of sales may have a completely different perspective from that of the director of engineering. Managing and balancing these types of tensions is core to successful project delivery.

The project manager and the project team are *internal stakeholders* in the project. Internal stakeholders are those directly involved in working on a project. They control how projects are run and are responsible for many aspects of a project's success, but internal stakeholders are not unbiased agents of delivery. They have their own needs from projects. On top of a general desire to be successful, project team members' interests include how enjoyable the project work is, how much they learn on the project and what the project workload is like. Beyond their own personal interests they often think that scope or quality is the most important success criteria. Whilst appreciating the importance of cost and time constraints, many internal stakeholders do not think these are complete measures of success.

External stakeholders, not directly involved in working on a project, are more likely to assess success in terms of the outcome of a project and its impact on the business. However, external stakeholders do not define success criteria based purely on business benefits. Some stakeholders' own performance will be influenced or assessed based on project outcomes. Such stakeholders are not independent and unbiased observers, but are opinionated judges with vested interests. This increases political and personal pressures on projects. Work may become easier or harder for the users of project deliverables depending on the quality of deliverables. Stakeholders may be judged on the quality of the project requirements they define. (A project may fail to meet objectives owing to poor project management, but also because stakeholders defined requirements wrongly.) Different managers may benefit more or less depending on the timing and scope of a project.

Therefore in assessing project success it is important to understand who or what is being assessed or measured and how this will influence their support for a project. When the topic *project success* is discussed what really is being assessed? A project is an artificial management construct that arguably does not actually exist. Therefore the question of whether a project was successful or not has limited meaning. In reality, the question of whether an activity was successful or not is a reflection of whether a person or group of people was successful in performing that activity and achieving the expected goal from it. In a project context this could be the project team, the project manager, the project sponsor or any of the other stakeholders.

It is easy to confuse project success with success of the project manager, but the two are not synonymous. The project manager cannot be held accountable for every facet of the project. What is it reasonable to judge the project manager against, as opposed to other stakeholders? Reflect on the issue of achieving business benefits from a project. Often project managers are not accountable for benefits, and if the benefits accrue long after the project is completed then it is probably impractical to judge them in this way. On the other hand, this can raise the concern that if project managers are not judged on business benefits might they give insufficient attention to them and instead only focus on factors such as time and cost which they are accountable for. One of the differences sometimes made between the role of a project manager and that of a programme manager is that programme managers have some accountability for business benefits, whereas typically project managers do not.

Other issues arise in judging the success of a project manager versus the success of a project. For example, can a project manager be held accountable for a problem resulting from a risk he has flagged to senior management or because of a delay in decision-making by the project sponsor? The answer will depend on the specific details of the situation.

Stakeholders have a mass of different viewpoints, interests and expectations each of which is subjective and evolves over time. The level of stakeholder satisfaction generated by a project is influenced both by the known facts about a project and by the subjective perception of a project. A project may be completely under control, but if an individual stakeholder does not receive a weekly status report he may perceive that the project is not. As is often said in business *perception is reality*. Whilst this is not literally true, it does inform the mindset required to understand and manage stakeholder satisfaction. Each individual has his or her own perceptions, and how the stakeholders perceive a project to have performed will become the de facto measure of success.

Perceptions can be influenced and manipulated, and they are not totally rational or based on fact. Perceptions change, and stakeholders' memories of them may not be reliable. A stakeholder may feel dissatisfied with a project forgetting they were satisfied previously and it was their direction that drove the project to its current state.

Project management provides two ways to manage the influence and needs of different stakeholders:

o Stakeholder management
o Expectations management

Stakeholder management is concerned with the identification and understanding of stakeholders, as well as the inclusion of specific actions to meet or manage stakeholders' needs. A typical stakeholder management activity will start with a brainstorming session to identify stakeholders. It is then followed by an assessment of each stakeholder according to his or her power or ability to influence the project, and his or her degree of support or opposition to it. The next stage is to define actions to make use of supporters and to counter or mitigate the actions of opponents. These actions are managed by the project manager. Stakeholder management is discussed in Chapter 8 in more detail.

Expectations management is concerned with maintaining the understanding and expectations of the stakeholders in line with what will actually be achieved by a project. Expectations management is an impressive term for something that is not a formal discipline or approach, but more an area of focus or awareness for a project manager. It can be considered as a part of stakeholder management.

Expectation management is important because there is a strong relationship between meeting expectations and the level of satisfaction that follows. If someone expects an activity to cost £100 and take 5 days, they are likely to be dissatisfied if it costs £1000 and takes 50 days and quite likely to be satisfied if it costs £10 and takes 1 day. The principle of expectation management can be summarized in two project management idioms:

Under-promise and over-deliver and *no surprises*

A stakeholder may desire a project to be completed in 6 months, but the plan may show it taking 9 months, and in reality it may take 12. There is obviously a conflict between these different states, and if no action is taken the stakeholder will be dissatisfied. Expectation management is about ensuring the stakeholders are not surprised by this, and ideally that they are satisfied when the project finishes. An approach may be to start informing the stakeholder that the project will actually take longer than 12 months. Although this will initially cause dismay, it does enable the stakeholder to take whatever management action is required to be ready for the late delivery. As the project progresses, the stakeholder is regularly updated and when it completes after 12 months the stakeholder is satisfied, as, although it took longer than they originally wanted, it was quicker than expected.

Of course expectation management is by no means fool proof, and views of its effectiveness are largely a matter of the anecdotal opinions of project managers. Expectation management is as much an art as a science and relies on many aspects of communication skills and relationship management. Good expectation management has resulted in many projects that were overbudget, late and underdelivered to be seen as a success. Poor expectations management has resulted in projects delivered to time, budget, scope and quality criteria being perceived as a failure simply because expectations got carried away and the project manager has never reined them in!

Determining success

This chapter has so far shown the complexity of assessing project success owing to three factors:

- o Multiple ways of defining success
- o Problems inherent in applying definitions of success in a project environment
- o The influence, perceptions and variations in stakeholders' views, needs and understanding

This complexity invariably leads to projects being assessed simultaneously as a success and failure. Whether or not a formal framework for assessing success is put in place, judgements will be made. But this is not sufficient for effective management. Management and executives have the right and the obligation to understand whether an investment such as a project was successful or not. It is better if this judgement is made against an agreed framework of definitions. In addition, putting a definition of success in place provides the project manager and the team with clarity and helps them in making the right decisions on how to manage and deliver the project.

The steps to a reliable definition of success are

1. Identify valid stakeholders. Many people will have a view on the project; only some of them are relevant for actually determining success.
2. As part of the scope definition, work with the stakeholders to define and agree how success is to be defined. This requires time spent with stakeholders to understand their views, to consolidate the opinions of the relevant stakeholders, and to resolve any unworkable conflicts.
3. Ensure success criteria are documented and explicit. If success criteria remain implicit, objectivity can be lost.
4. Prioritize across and balance between success criteria. When measures are in conflict it is necessary for the project manager to know how to choose what to do. Classic examples of this include making decisions to

meet time or quality criteria, and hitting budget versus satisfying users. It is difficult to develop a formal framework of prioritization of different success factors that works in every situation. Experienced managers explore the prioritization by asking simple what-if style questions of stakeholders. For example: "what if the project was running late, would you prefer it to stay late or to invest in extra resource to bring it on line?" By asking such questions the project manager can build a picture and rules of thumb to enable trade-off decisions to be made as a project progresses. It is also helpful for the project manager to appreciate limits to decision-making and to know when he or she should refer to senior management for a trade-off decision. For example, a sponsor could provide guidance in the form "if the project is late it is acceptable to spend more budget to add resource to bring it back on track; however, you must not spend more than 5% additional budget without the sponsor's approval."

5. Agree who is actually being assessed by each success criterion. Which internal stakeholder is accountable for each success measure? A typical breakdown will hold the project manager accountable for project measures such as time and cost compliance, and the project sponsor accountable for delivery of the business benefits.

6. Agree time frame to make the assessment. Success does not happen at one time in a project but is related to events and accumulation of outcomes over time. For example, project time and cost may be assessed at the point at which a project implements its deliverables, but there is typically no point trying to measure business benefits until deliverables have been in use or operation for some time following project completion.

7. Perform ongoing stakeholder and expectations management through the life of the project. The success factors should be subject to change control. As with many other features of projects there should be an expectation that the success measures will evolve through progressive elaboration and often will change as a project progresses.

There is a risk that project managers worry about stakeholders mostly at the front end of projects when ascertaining needs. The focus on stakeholders is naturally reduced as the project moves into delivery phases, when heads are down working to produce the deliverables. The danger with this is that without sufficient stakeholder and expectations management, needs and perceptions will change without the project manager or project team knowing. In this situation, whether or not a project has successfully completed according to the original definition, it risks being perceived as a failure by stakeholders. Stakeholder engagement naturally tends to vary in intensity at different stages of projects, but it is always important.

Programme and portfolio success

In many situations and in most organizations the success or failure of an individual project, amongst the hundreds running, is of limited relevance to anyone beyond the immediate project team and project sponsors. Of course, there are exceptions. Mega-projects and large programmes can expose a business to significant risk whilst offering huge returns. The success or failure of such an endeavour is of interest to the whole organization and even to external stakeholders such as shareholders, but normally success comes about through the simultaneous management and delivery of portfolios of projects, and the accumulation of project benefits over time. Success criteria aimed at a single project do not alone guarantee success at the organizational level (Dietrich and Lehtonen, 2005).

Programme managers typically look at success more broadly than do project managers. This is partially a reflection of the scale and long-term nature of programmes, and partially a result of the relative seniority and leadership roles of some programme managers in the organization's hierarchy, but it is also a result of the emphasis in programme management on owning accountability for business benefits. However, in principle the range of ways of assessing programme success is the same as for projects.

Portfolio-level success is somewhat different. If the project portfolio, or at least those components of it that will be delivered by projects, has been designed for achievement of the business strategy, then portfolio success is concerned with achieving business strategy. Unlike a project, a portfolio does not end; it merely changes its make up of projects over time. Measuring the success of a portfolio is therefore more like making an assessment of operational performance.

Terry Cooke-Davis neatly summarizes the various fundamental questions that can be asked to ascertain whether projects were successful or not:

o Was the project done right?
o Was it the right project to do?
o Were the right projects done right time after time? (Cooke-Davis, 2004)

The first question is an issue of project success (and only a measure of one aspect of project success). The second question is to do with project selection criteria and is therefore a more relevant question for portfolio management. The final question extends the second one and looks for successful selection of projects over time, and is therefore also a portfolio management question.

Dietrich and Lehtonen (2005) see multi-project success in relation to the achievement of strategy and via this to the achievement of sustainable competitive advantage. They measure multi-project success through the examination of how well

o Project objectives are aligned with organizational strategy
o Resource allocation across projects is aligned with organizational strategy
o Current portfolio of projects implements the organizational strategy

Taking these different perspectives, portfolio success is made up of

o *Selecting the optimal mix of projects versus resources*: At the most basic level portfolio management is a resource allocation decision process. The optimal mix is the correct level of projects for the resources, so that maximum value can be delivered from that resource pool.
o *Achieving the portfolio objectives*: Assuming the portfolio objectives were set with the right level of strategic and leadership input, this should ensure that the right projects were done time after time. Whatever a business strategy is, the measure of success is achieving this strategy.

However, differing stakeholder viewpoints and varying perceptions mean that stakeholder and expectations management are as relevant at programme and portfolio levels as at an individual project level.

Critical success factors and their relationship to project success

Critical success factors are the set of conditions that a project needs to operate within in order to be successful. Where the success criteria or measure of success is a statement of *what* a project has to achieve, the CSFs are descriptions of *how* a project should be managed to achieve this success. Whereas research and comments on success criteria are comparatively limited, those on success factors are significant.

Critical success factors can be thought of in three categories

- Factors which are controllable by project team, for example, the quality of project planning. As these are in the control of the project team, the team can ensure the project operates to these factors.
- Outside project team's influence, but still necessary for the project to be successful, for example, the effect of senior management politics on projects. A project manager is reliant on the project sponsor or other stakeholders to ensure the project operates to these factors.
- The inverse of CSF known as critical failure factors. Critical failure factors are not simply failure to meet CSFs. For example, choosing project team members who cannot work together constructively is a failure factor.

There are many definitions of the critical success factors for projects, and various writers in this area have proposed different sets. As an example, some of the classic studies on critical success factors by Pinto and Slevin (1987 and 1988) list ten areas that are critical to the success of a project and control:

- Project mission
- Top management support
- Project schedule and plan
- Client consultation
- Personnel
- Technical tasks
- Client acceptance
- Communication
- Monitoring and feedback
- Trouble shooting

Newer studies place increasing stress on human factors, and a significant proportion of modern writing on project management is on the importance of the human side of projects and the management and cultural environment of an organization (e.g. Gray, 2001). Dvir et al. correlate between project manager's personality types, categories of projects and project success. Their research suggests that projects will be more successful when managed by project managers whose personality profile matches the project profile, and conversely, that project managers will be more successful managing projects that match their personality profile (Dvir et al., 2006).

Most organizations run many projects in parallel, but less research exists which considers the CSFs for a multi-project environment. Fricke and Shenhar look at an example of a multi-project environment and find that additional CSFs exist beyond those necessary for single project success: for example, the way resources are divided and allocated across projects, prioritization, and the flexible customization of management to the specific project type (Fricke and Shenhar, 2000). Cooke-Davies (2002) describes the factors leading to consistently successful projects. In this context consistent project success is where projects lead to corporate success.

Individual CSFs do not have the same relevance in every project. CSFs are context-specific, and the balance between the importance of different factors varies from project to project. So a list of CSFs can only provide outline guidance, and it needs interpretation by the project manager. CSFs also change as projects are at different phases in their lifecycles. Take client consultation, for instance. The relative importance of client consultation varies at different stages of the project – it is core during scoping, but less critical during execution. It is also possible, within certain limits to have a degree of trade-off between different CSFs. For example, if the project mission was not absolutely clear at the start of a project, but there is strong management support, good client consultation and regular monitoring and feedback, this may not be an insurmountable problem and may be resolved as the project progresses.

There are many examples of high-profile projects which were perceived as failures. As this chapter has shown, some of this can be traced to differing views of success criteria, and different perceptions. However, no one will seriously argue that *all* project failure is a matter of perception. There are many projects which, whatever definition of success is used, will be measured as failures. This implies that there is insufficient linkage between the way projects are managed and the factors that create project success. In theory if the correct set of CSFs are chosen and adhered to, then level of success should increase. There is plenty of anecdotal evidence amongst project managers that this is true. However, whilst there is research on critical success factors in projects, it is less clear whether CSFs really link to the measures of project success.

Cooke-Davies (2002) provides some idea of the linkages between project success and success factors. He splits CSFs into three categories: factors that lead to project management success (defined as quality, time and cost predictability); factors that lead to success on an individual project (defined as achieving the objectives of the project and realizing benefits); and factors which lead consistently to project success (defined in terms of how projects support corporate success).

Jha and Iyer (2007) have proposed a linkage between the CSFs – such as commitment of project participants, coordination amongst project participants and the competence of the project manager and other stakeholders – and meeting the objectives of the iron triangle.

Case Study **7.2   MANAGING SUCCESSFUL PROJECTS**

In this case study Tony Collins discusses what makes a project successful. Tony is a highly experienced executive, with a background in civil engineering projects. He is currently the Managing Director of UK Water for Black & Veatch. Black & Veatch is a leading global engineering, consulting and construction company.

Tony Collins

In my 30 years in the construction I have worked predominantly on water and waste-water treatment delivering projects and solutions to the major Water Utility Companies in the UK. To understand what makes a project successful in today's market, it is useful to understand what has happened In the water industry over the last 20 years.

In the early 1980s a water client would have separately employed a consulting engineer to design the works; a civil engineering contractor to build it and an M&E contractor to install the M&E equipment. The client's own process team would have set about getting the plant to work before handing it over to the client's operations team. Each element would have been carried out in isolation and in linear progression, for example, the civil construction would have been completed before the M&E contractor was allowed to start on site.

The construction element would have been a traditional construct-only measure and value contract. The consultant's design drawings were issued to the contractor by the client. The contractor was paid for the work done at his tendered rates applied to the actual quantities of work done measured from the drawings. The risk of design changes and quantity increases remained with the client, and there was little opportunity for or advantage to the contractor to influence or improve on the client's design. In fact the contractor often benefited from design errors, omissions and changes. His job was simply to construct the structures and pipelines to the drawings provided, for the lowest cost. Success for the contractor was about making a good financial margin on the project regardless of the outcome for the client.

Different parties were responsible for different elements of the project, each one with a direct contract with the client. Nobody (other than the client) had overall responsibility for or an interest in the solution as a whole. Interface management was poor, and often there were lack-of-fit problems between the M&E equipment and the civil structures.

Each party had different objectives, so cooperation was poor and relationships tended to lack trust and be adversarial. Apportioning and avoiding blame became more important than solving problems. There were usually a number of claims against the client for additional time and money.

Timescales for delivery, quality of the finished product and final cost suffered. There was no single accountability for the overall solution, so even when the project was complete it did not necessarily perform as desired even though each party had fulfilled his contract obligations.

There was little connection between success for the designer or contractors and success for the client.

In the last 20 years we have moved to a completely different type of delivery model based on a team responsible for delivering a total solution to a client's business problem, with open-book costing and shared risk and reward. This change was driven primarily by the privatization of the Water Authorities in England and Wales in 1989 and the need for improvements in capital investment efficiency and asset performance.

The key changes are that we are now contracted to do the whole project (from design to handover of the operational works). We are fully responsible for the working solution. We are no longer solely civil engineers building someone else's design. We have a multi-disciplinary team with our own designers, including process, civil, mechanical and electrical engineers. We work in partnership with clients and our supply chain, and we look for long-term relationships with shared success.

We are usually paid the actual cost for the work we do (i.e. the amount it actually costs us) up to a previously agreed target cost, plus a management fee. If we deliver for less than the target cost then we share the savings with the client. If we overrun the target cost then we contribute to the cost overrun. This leads to open-book accounting which eases the relationship with our clients and improves the level of trust.

The focus of risk management is cost. In this type of business the margins are tight and we need to keep focussed on them. We keep a continuous track of predicted final costs, looking at the actual cost to date and the forecast to completion. We can use tools like Earned Value to verify the projections. When risks are realized we need to take action to overcome them. The easiest way to deal with risks is via a contingency pot of money or in some cases by passing the risk onto sub-contractors. This response is not really solving the risk; it is just removing the impact of it occurring. In a business like ours it's essential to really understand and overcome risks to improve the way we work and to eliminate them for the future.

The water utilities plan in five-year time horizons, because of the regulatory framework in the UK. This five-year period is known as an AMP or Asset Management Period (in England & Wales). We are currently in AMP4 (2005 to 2010). The amount to be spent by the water utilities on improvements during the AMP is agreed with the regulator and is related back to the charges the utilities can make to their customers. We now work with the utilities in a cooperative working style. In this we don't just sign up to do individual projects, but agree to carry out whole programmes of work over the five years of the AMP. At the start we know the investment programme the utility has set. We agree to help them achieve their five-year plan for a predicted cost. Of course we carefully manage each individual project, but we tend to focus more at the total returns for our business across the whole AMP programme. Some projects outrun the target cost, and we have to contribute to the overspent amount, but these are balanced by the ones that come in under budget. We take a programme view of risk and reward.

There are a number of essential factors that make cooperative projects successful. We have to understand our client's business drivers and how they work internally. No matter how well-managed a project is or how good a project manager is, if you work in ignorance of the client's business drivers you will be unlikely to succeed. For example, consider the acceptance of our project by the client's operators. The people we have been dealing with on a project, who we consider as the client, are in reality only one part of the client's organization. They are not usually operators, who are the end-users of the product. If we don't meet operational needs then the project will have trouble being accepted.

Clients often assume you understand their internal organization, but unless you really work with the client and get to know them, you will not. Only when client departments like operations are involved in the front end of the process can you understand what the project must achieve to satisfy them. Delivering successful projects is not just about delivering what you set out to do in the contract, but has to cover meeting the needs of all parts of the client. For instance, we are rarely delivering into a green-field site; whatever we deliver has to fit in and work, from an operational *viewpoint, with everything else that is already at the site. This may not be formally specified in a contract, but unless it is achieved our deliverables will be difficult for operations to use, and they will not be satisfied.*

As another example, we know that employers are required to carry out risk assessments for health and safety reasons. Everyone knows this, but unless you actually talk to the person who will perform the risk assessment on the work you are doing there can be complications. If you engage that person, and understand how she will do the risk assessment, you will get a much better outcome. Similarly, if you involve people with a stake in the project's outcome in risk reviews, you will get a much better understanding of all risks.

When projects in this field fail, it is usually because they have not been planned effectively. Planning has failed because there is not a real understanding of all the different needs of a client. The more you understand the better-planned the project will be and the less likely will it go wrong.

To deliver a "successful" project in today's market of strategic and long-term alliances the measure of profit generation and meeting of milestones is not enough. We must leave the client with a good to great experience, and by "client" I include the various internal stakeholders – asset owner, operator etc. If we leave our client with an unpleasant experience it will stay in his memory and we run the risk of losing future opportunities. Success is really measured on generation of future opportunities from today's performance.

To deliver a successful project the project manager must have a vision of the end product, which is shared by the rest of the team. If there are differences it will jeopardise the project's success. The shared vision of the end product must match the client's vision or surpass it.

More information on Black & Veatch can be found at www.bv.com.

MAIN LEARNING POINTS FROM CHAPTER 7

- There are multiple ways to measure project success, and various stakeholders will simultaneously assess success in different ways.
- There are practical issues in the measurement of project success, such as the clarity/ambiguity of different stakeholder's desires, the inability to measure some dimensions of success such as quality, and ongoing variation in views of relevance of different success measures.
- To ensure a project is perceived as a success, a project manager must understand the project stakeholders and their desires, and actively manage their expectations as the project progresses.
- Project success is not the same as the success of the project manager.
- From a portfolio perspective success is different from individual project success. Individual projects may be successful without the portfolio being a success. Portfolio success is concerned with ensuring the optimal mix of projects is undertaken and with achieving portfolio objectives.
- Measures of project success should not be confused with critical success factors or CSFs. Project CSFs aim to contribute to project success, but are not in themselves measures of success.

1. In what ways was the project in Case Study 7.1 a success, and in what ways could it be considered a failure? If you were the project manager would you be happy with the work you did or not? Why? Which other stakeholders could feel satisfied and which ones would not? Overall, what is your judgement on the project and how would you have improved the level of success? How would your judgement have changed over time from the start of the project to 24 months after completion?

2. Select some examples of major projects that you have read about in the national press over the past 5–10 years. Are these, in general, examples of great success or of failure? In what ways are the judgements of the press fair and what might the views of other stakeholders be?

3. Choose a project you are familiar with, or select one from the national press. Who are the main stakeholders for this project? How could they benefit from the project, and what would their concerns about the project be? How do you think each stakeholder would be satisfied, and how would each define success? If you were the project manager how would you approach the challenge of keeping stakeholders satisfied?

4. How often do you perform stakeholder or expectation management in the course of your normal work? How could you benefit from doing it more often?

5. What are the most important project success criteria? Why?

6. Consider a project which is complete and which you are familiar with. What went well on this project, and what went badly? What can you learn from this? Based on this project and any other sources define your own list of the top five critical success factors for projects. By complying with these factors how likely will a project be successful?

Suggested reading

Defining and measuring project success is a topic that is surprisingly absent or trivialized in many project management books, and thorough reference sources are rare, although Obeng is an exception:

o *The Project Leader's Secret Handbook*, Eddie Obeng. FT Prentice Hall, 1996, pp. 56–69

For further reading, more material is available in journals or project management magazines. Recommended articles include

o Project success: A multidimensional strategic concept, Aaron Shenar, Dov Dvir, Ofer Levy and Alan Maltz. *Long Range Planning*. Volume 34, Issue 6, December 2001, pp. 699–725

o The logical framework method for defining project success, David Baccarini. *Project Management Journal*. Volume 30, Issue 4, December 1999, pp. 25–32

o Consistently doing the right projects and doing them right – What metrics do you need, Terry Cooke-Davies. *The Measured*. Volume 4, Issue 2, Summer 2004, pp. 44–52

Bibliography

Agarwal, N. and Rathod, U. "Defining 'success' for software projects: An exploratory revelation". *International Journal of Project Management.* Volume 24, Issue 4, May 2006, pp. 358–70.

Baccarlnl, D. "The logical framework method for defining project success". *Project Management Journal.* Volume 30, Issue 4, December 1999, pp. 25–32.

Cooke-Davies, T. "The 'real' success factors on projects". *International Journal of Project Management.* Volume 20, Issue 3, April 2002, pp. 185–90.

Cooke-Davies, T. "Consistently doing the right projects and doing them right – What metrics do you need". *The Measured.* Volume 4, Issue 2, Summer 2004. pp. 44–52.

DeWit, A. "Measurement of project success". *International Journal of Project Management.* Volume 6, Issue 3, August 1998, pp. 164–70.

Dietrich, P. and Lehtonen, P. "Successful management of strategic intentions through multiple projects – Reflections from empirical study". *International Journal of Project Management.* Volume 23, Issue 5, July 2005, pp. 386–91.

Dvir, D., Sadeh, A. and Malach-Pines, A. "Projects and project managers: The relationship between project managers' personality, project types, and project success". *Project Management Journal.* Volume 37, Issue 5, December 2006, pp. 36–48.

Fricke, S. and Shenhar, A. "Managing multiple engineering projects in a manufacturing support environment". *IEEE Transactions on Engineering Management.* Volume 47, Issue 2, May 2000, pp. 258–68.

Gray, R. "Organisational climate and project success". *International Journal of Project Management.* Volume 19, Issue 2, February 2001, pp. 103–09.

Iclemi-Turkel, O. and Rom, W. "An empirical investigation of project evaluation criteria". *International Journal of Operations & Production Management.* Volume 21, Issue 3, 2001, pp. 400–16.

Jha, K. and Iyer, K. "Commitment, coordination, competence and the iron triangle". *International Journal of Project Management.* Volume 25, Issue 5, July 2007. pp. 527–40.

McKinlay, M. "A matter of perception". *APM Yearbook 2005/6.* pp. 10–12.

Oluwatudinu, A. "Managing expectations in projects". *APM Yearbook 2005/6.* pp. 16–18.

Paquin, J., Couillard, J. and Ferrand, D. "Assessing and controlling the quality of a project end product: The Earned Quality method". *IEEE Transactions on Engineering Management.* Volume 47, Issue 1. February 2000, pp. 88–97.

Pinto, J. and Slevin, D. "Critical factors in successful project implementation". *IEEE Transactions on Engineering Management.* Volume 34, Issue 1, February 1987, pp. 22–27.

Pinto, J. and Slevin, D. "Critical success factors across the project". *Project Management Journal.* Volume 19, Issue 31, 1988, pp. 67–72.

Shenar, A., Dvir, D., Levy, O. and Maltz, A. "Project success: A multidimensional strategic concept". *Long Range Planning.* Volume 34, Issue 6, December 2001, pp. 699–725.

Sillince, J., Harvey, C. and Harindranath, G. "Conflicting rhetorical positions on trust and commitment: Talk-as-action in IT project failures". *Making Project Critical.* Palgrave MacMillan, 2006, pp. 294–315.

Wang, X. and Huang, J. "The relationship between key stakeholders' project performance and project success: Perceptions of Chinese construction supervising engineers". *International Journal of Project Management.* Volume 24, Issue 3, April 2006, pp. 253–60.

White, D. and Fortune, J. "Current practice in project management – An empirical study". *International Journal of Project Management.* Volume 20, Issue 1, January 2002, pp. 1–11.

Williams, D. and Parr, T. *Enterprise Programme Management Delivering Value.* Palgrave Macmillan, 2004.

8

managing the
execution
of projects

At the point of mobilization a project should be a well-planned and properly resourced endeavour with a set of known requirements. Through the plan it is clear what activities are required, and as part of mobilization each member of the project team should know what is needed of them. If the plan is followed the requirements will be met.

Unfortunately, a project team cannot be left alone and expected reliably to complete the tasks in the plan. Team members need to be coordinated to work together. Unforeseen issues will arise that, if not resolved, will delay a project, and yet no one will feel responsible for overcoming them. Team members tend to drift away and lose focus on their project work under the ongoing demands of a large organization. On top of this, project customers want to know how the project is progressing, especially if they had justified the work or made a personal commitment to its completion. They want reports and updates. Executives also need to be chivvied into making decisions and releasing resources. Projects are simply too complex, fragile and beset by inertia to be left to themselves – they need to be managed and driven.

Of course in practice plans are never perfect, resources are rarely optimized and requirements are unlikely to be fully understood. And they never will be, because, every aspect of a project is subject to uncertainty and ongoing change. These facts add to the challenge of managing the execution of projects. For all of these reasons, and many more, projects need to be controlled as they are executed. This is, perhaps, the essential role of the project manager.

This chapter concerns the activities on a project following planning and mobilization of the project team until project completion. There are various names for this stage of a project depending on the context. Words like *execution, delivery, build, construction, manufacture* or *design and development* are used to refer to this stage of a project. It can be called a *live* or *active* project. This phase may also be called *implementation*, although that has a more specific meaning and refers to the phase of a project when the completed deliverables are moved from the stage of development to their live use in a business. Implementation is the point of business change and is described in Chapter 9.

There are different perspectives and various role types involved in managing project delivery. The central role is that of the project manager, and much of project management's value is achieved during execution. Scoping, requirements capture, resourcing and planning are all essential prerequisites to deliver a project, but it is in execution that projects succeed or fail. The project manager does not work alone;he or she is supported by a project sponsor. The sponsor provides overall direction to a project and helps to remove any barriers to project progress that can arise in an organization.

Projects are subject to all sorts of organizational pressures beyond those that the project manager and even the sponsor can control, and successful execution is impacted by many wider organizational considerations. Organizations do not simply deliver single projects, but have to execute many projects in parallel which requires additional management. The right balance and selection of projects should progress and the pipeline of work in the portfolio must be manageable, else individual projects will suffer. The capability to execute projects has to be developed and resources required made available. Within an organization there are usually senior managers or executives with a significant responsibility for developing the capability for project delivery. A typical example of this is the CIO or IT Director. Finally, success or failure in delivery is also dependent on the governance structure in a business and the overall management and leadership culture.

This chapter provides an understanding of what is required to control and manage a live project. It looks at the execution of projects from five perspectives:

- o The perspective of the project manager as the primary manager responsible for ensuring a project is delivered successfully
- o The perspective of the project sponsor in directing projects and generally helping them to be delivered
- o From the perspective of the activities needed to manage the whole project portfolio.
- o The perspective of senior managers or executives with a responsibility for delivery of projects and programmes – for example, the CIO or head of product development, who must ensure that the capability to deliver projects exists.
- o From the perspective of overall business and project governance. This links project management to the leadership of an organization from two directions: from the corporate governance of an organization, and the leadership role in developing an environment in which projects can thrive.

This chapter will enable the reader to understand the different aspects of project delivery and to develop a holistic view of the management activities. The scope of this chapter is shown in Diagram 8.1.

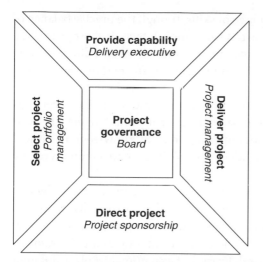

Diagram 8.1 *The building blocks of project execution*

The role of the project manager in project execution

The role of the project manager in the execution of a project can be simply summarized as *doing whatever is required to make the project happen*. Whilst this is a useful reminder of the breadth of a project manager's responsibilities, a more detailed definition is needed to understand the range of day-to-day work of a project manager.

Typical responsibilities of a project manager in the execution of a project are

- o *Initiating work*: allocating the tasks in the plan to the relevant members of the project team. Initiating work happens at the beginning of a project during mobilization, but also at intervals throughout the project.
- o *Driving progress*: managing and motivating the project team to complete the tasks allocated to them in an efficient and effective manner.
- o *Quality checking*: ensuring the quality of work completed is as required.
- o *Monitoring progress*: putting the necessary tracking and project control systems in place, and using them to understand how the project is progressing relative to the baseline plan.
- o *Overcoming existing or potential impediments to the project*: the identification and management of issues and risks as they occur.
- o *Maintaining the project*: taking decisions and actions based on project monitoring to keep the project on track.
- o *Communicating to relevant stakeholders*: keeping relevant stakeholders informed of progress, understanding and responding to their evolving needs, getting appropriate decisions on and support for the project, and managing their expectations.
- o *Maintenance of plans and budgets*: the ongoing adaptation of plans and budgets based on actual project performance, and taking account of any changes.
- o *Thinking forward*: ensuring the project is progressing towards its end goals, and the organization as a whole is getting ready for project implementation and change.

Project management calls on a wide range of skills, though the precise balance of skills will depend on the specific project. A three-month technical project with a team of four dedicated engineers working in one room will need a different style of management from that of a three-year business transformation programme with hundreds of participants from multiple departments based internationally, many of them allocated to the project on a part-time basis. However, it is possible to identify common skills and capabilities that project managers need to develop. The APM, for example, identifies 52 areas of knowledge in project management (APM, 2006). These include several skills that are common to any management role.

Project management is much more than everyday management and leadership skills. Project management approaches provide a number of specialist tools and techniques to help manage live projects, and execution brings together the full set of project management competencies. Some of these techniques are the same as those required in preparing projects for delivery, but execution can place different emphasis or require additional techniques, especially as a result of the ever-present fact of change on projects. Project execution requires the ability to continue with and manage change across

- o Resource and budget management (Chapter 4)
- o Scope and requirements management (Chapter 5)
- o Planning, estimating and scheduling (Chapter 6)

During project execution, project managers have to be aware of and plan for the later stages of a project. These are described in this book in later chapters, but are noted here for reference:

- o Implementation and achieving change (Chapter 9)
- o Benefits realization and value management (Chapter 10)

One of the bedrocks of project management is risk management. Risk management is concerned with the identification, assessment and appropriate management of risks in successful project conclusion. Risk management was introduced in Chapters 1 and 6, and is an essential part of managing project execution. Risk is a critical topic and is discussed in its own chapter (Chapter 11).

The remainder of this section looks at five areas of specific relevance to project managers during project execution and which are not dealt with in sufficient detail elsewhere in this book:

- o Progress tracking and project control systems, with a section on one of the most common project control methods: Earned Value
- o Issue management
- o Change control and configuration management
- o Team management
- o Stakeholder management

Progress tracking and project control systems

A helpful summarization of the role of a project manager during execution is the *plan–monitor–control* cycle (Portny et al., 2008). A plan is created, and action is instigated for the project team to follow this plan. As work progresses the project

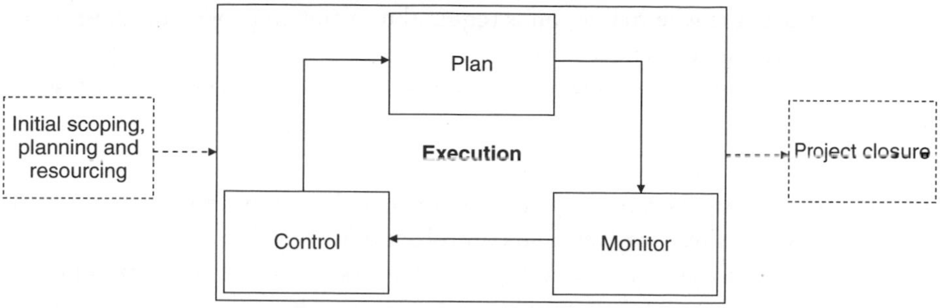

Diagram 8.2 *The plan-monitor-control cycle*

manager monitors progress and checks whether it is according to the plan. Where activity is not progressing according to the plan the project manager takes controlling action to attempt to bring it back in line. Even if monitoring shows activity is in line with the plan, the project manager may take controlling action. For instance, he may be tasked by the project sponsor with improving on the plan by reducing cost, reducing timelines or increasing quality. As a result of control action the plan may need to be updated. This is shown in Diagram 8.2.

This series of activities is an ongoing cycle throughout the life of the project. At its heart is the *control system*. The control system provides the project manager with the information he needs to manage the project effectively. There are a host of standard tools and approaches for controlling projects. Project management softwares can produce a large variety of standard information. Many organizations have accepted project report format templates. However, whilst the control system can be developed from standard components, it often requires tailoring for each project.

A control system may be completely paper-based, or can make extensive use of IT. Either way, the steps in designing, implementing and using a control system are

- Design and set up control system:
  - Decide what sorts of information is important for a project. This is typically cost, time (schedule) and quality, but it can include other factors depending on the success criteria. For example, information on stakeholder satisfaction may be required.
  - Determine what specific data is required. If cost information is required, the data may be actual monthly cost by workpackage and expected monthly budget spend.
  - Design collection mechanisms to provide the data in a timely and regular fashion. Information may be provided through regular meetings and periodic progress reports and collected from IT systems and informal sources.
- Use control system:
  - Collect the information on a regular basis.
  - Perform regular analysis on the collected information. For example, a comparison of the baseline plan against the actuals reported. The analysis may be done on different cycles. Some control information may be analysed daily and others weekly, whilst on a major programme some information might only be assessed monthly or quarterly.

- Determine whether action is required to maintain project progress and if so what action is necessary.
- Take the defined action and assess results. This includes plan updates.

Using the control systems is an ongoing process for project managers, and there are normally periodic cycles within in. For example, project team members may provide weekly reports, and project managers may have monthly sponsor review meetings. Each of these may result in control actions.

The project manager has to develop a control system that is practical: one that provides accurate or useful data without overloading the project team with work to create it, and without swamping the project manager with more information than he can handle. Inexperienced project managers often end up with too little or too much information.

An understanding of progress on a project can be developed by looking at the situation at a specific point in time, but is often more usefully gained by looking at the trend over time. Trends are particularly powerful. For example, tracking the schedule over time allows a project manager to understand the difference between blips in performance that can be resolved with some minor intervention versus a trend for increasingly delayed progress which may need a more fundamental revision in approach. A one day slippage on a major programme is not normally cause for significant concern, as with the right control actions it can usually be recovered. A one day slippage every week, on the other hand, should be a cause for concern, as this is a trend which will result in a 20% time overrun. Similar trends can be monitored and analysed for cost.

Typical areas under assessment in a project control system are

- Time: schedule of performance of actual task completion versus that shown in the baseline plan.
- *Cost*: cost of work effort and expenditures.
- *Quality*: this can be either or both of quality of work done (conformance to process) and quality of deliverables (conformance to specification). Quality is often a point of contention on projects as expectations can vary, and time and cost pressures can often result in compromises in quality.
- *Project management process measures*: areas like the numbers and trends in issues, risks and changes. By looking at the number of issues arising and the number being resolved a project manager can gain a view of whether the project is staying in control or has an increasing number of problems. A similar analysis could be done for changes or risks.
- *Benefits realized*: business benefits delivered during execution. Some projects will deliver business benefits as the project progresses, others only once the project is complete. If a project does deliver benefits during execution, these should be tracked.

Factors such as stakeholder satisfaction can be formally tracked using questionnaires and feedback, but are normally assessed in an informal way based on the feeling of the sponsor and project manager.

Project status is described in terms of actual progress compared to expected progress on the baseline plan. If progress is as expected, the project is said to be *on track*. A variance where a task is progressing less quickly or more expensively than expected is called *slippage* or *overrun*. Slippage is generally used in reference to time variances; overrun may refer to cost or time. (In contrast, when a project is progressing faster or cheaper than expected it is said to be *ahead of schedule*, or in terms of costs, *below budget.*)

Whether the metric being measured is time, cost or benefits, the assessment of whether progress is acceptable or not relies on making an estimate of how complete activities are. Let us look at the situation in which progress is measured for a weekly report every Friday. Many tasks will be partially complete on any one Friday, and so assessing how much progress has been made needs an estimation of how complete the task is on that Friday. Ideally, in such a situation, an objective measure of progress is required – in practice subjective views are often necessary. For activities like collecting requirements, or designing a solution, assessment of whether they are 10, 25, 50 or 75% complete relies on the opinion of the project manager or the person completing the task. If a task takes 5 weeks, theoretically it should progress by 20% each week. If it is judged to be progressing at this rate, then the project manager will consider progress as being on track.

Unfortunately this exposes projects to risk. Opinions on progress can be wrong. This may be simply because of misjudgement, but also because of deliberate manipulation. Performance management systems, social pressures in organizations, human psychology and management approaches can often bias project team members to give overly optimistic views on how complete a task is. Project managers need to be alert to this. Assessments of progress should not be taken on face value, but must be subject to review and questioning.

The later an error in estimation is detected, the harder it is to resolve. A 5-week task may be expected to progress at 20% per week. The project team may only make 10% of the necessary progress in the first week. This means that 90% of the task has to be completed in the remaining 4 weeks. Therefore to catch up, for the last 4 weeks the project team have to make 22.5% of the progress instead of 20% per week. This will often be achievable. However, if the slippage is not detected and the trend continues for another 3 weeks, after 4 weeks the task will only be 40% complete, instead of 80%. This leaves the often impossible workload of completing the remaining 60% of the work in one week, instead of just the last 20%. This is shown in Table 8.1:

Table 8.1 The benefits of early detection of slippage

Theoretical Planned Progress			Reduced Progress in Week 1 Detected and Action Taken			Reduced Progress Undetected Until End of Week 4		
% progress per week	Cumulative % complete at end of week	% of task remaining at end of week	% progress per week	Cumulative % complete at end of week	% of task remaining at end of week	% progress per week	Cumulative % complete at end of week	% of task remaining at end of week
20	20	80	10	10	90	10	10	90
20	40	60	22.5	32.5	67.5	10	20	80
20	60	40	22.5	55	45	10	30	70
20	80	20	22.5	77.5	22.5	10	40	60
20	100	0	22.5	100	0	60	100	0

The three columns on the left-hand side of Table 8.1 show the expected progress from the project plan. The three columns in the middle show the effect of poor progress in the first week on the work required in the following weeks. The three columns on the right-hand side show the impact if the slippage is not detected until week 5. The figures in bold italics on the bottom right-hand side of the table show the size of the challenge that is left for the final week, where three times as much work as was planned has to be done for the task to be completed on time. This may be impossible to recover. Alternatively, if the progress continues at the rate of 10% per week, it will take 10 weeks and be 5 weeks late.

Another problem with estimating the progressive completeness of a task is the confusion between *effort* or *duration of work* and *progress* or *output*. Effort is a measure of how many man-hours/man-days are spent on a task; progress is a measure of how complete it is. In assessing progress the project manager is primarily interested in how complete a task is. The project manager should be aware of effort – if tasks are generally taking more effort to complete than what the plan shows there is a problem, and the whole plan may be wrong. But simply measuring the hours someone has worked on a task is not a measure of completeness of the activity. A 2-week task may be thought of as 50% complete if a project team has worked on it for one week, but this is wrong. This simply means they have used up 50% of the time; whether they have actually made 50% of the progress is quite another matter!

One approach to reducing the risk from poor estimations of task completion is to accept progress only when a task is 100% complete. In this way a task is assumed to be 0% complete until it is actually finished, and then it is treated as 100% complete. This can lead to progress being measured in steps rather than in gradual increments.

Earned Value and other control systems

Earned Value is one of the most common project control methods and is included as a core part of project management BoKs (Bodies of Knowledge). Earned Value is especially prevalent in the construction and defence industries, but is applicable to almost any project. It combines monitoring of two dimensions – time and cost – into one set of measures, and is helpful because of this. Earned Value is based on the WBS and uses variances in cost and time against schedule. It works by assigning a monetary value to work completion.

Earned Value is conceptually simple, though can be somewhat involved to implement in practice, and is often confusing because of the set of acronyms it uses. Earned Value makes use of three pieces of information:

- What was expected to be done, called the *Budgeted Cost of Work Schedule* or *BCWS* or the *planned value*, derived from the baseline plan
- The budgeted cost of what has been done, called the *Budgeted Cost of Work Performed* or *BCWP*, or the *earned value*
- The actual cost of what has been done, called the *Actual Cost of Work Performed* or *ACWP*, or simply the *actual cost*.

Earned value tracks two measures:

- The *cost variance* or *CV*, which is the variance between the expected cost to date and the actual cost to date. Hence, if a project was expected to have spent £45k, but has only spent £30k, then the cost variance is +£15k. CV = BCWP – ACWP.

o The *schedule variance* or *SV*, which is an assessment of what activity progress a project has achieved versus what it was expected to have achieved. SV = BCWP – BCWS

Consider, for example, the BCWS at a point in time is £100,000; in other words the project is expected to have completed £100,000 worth of work. The ACWP is £100,000, or the actual amount spent is £100,000. This seems an ideal situation, as the cost variance is zero. It may appear that the project is on track with regard to budget. However, the BCWP is also £75,000, which means that the project has actually completed £75,000 worth of work. Therefore, although the project has spent £100,000, it has only actually completed £75,000 worth of work, and the schedule variance is – £25,000. Although the project has spent what it is expected to have spent at this point in time, it has not achieved as much as it should have. By providing these two measures Earned Value provides a powerful assessment of progress in terms of both cost and schedule.

Although Earned Value is useful, its title can be misleading. It is questionable whether Earned Value really represents a measure of *value*. For example, in a construction project, with a tangible output in the form of a building, completing half of the work can be assumed to have created half of the value. On the other hand, a project that develops an IT system, which results in business change through cost reduction, no value has actually been achieved even when the project is complete – the value, in terms of a cost saving, will accrue over time following the project.

Although powerful, Earned Value does suffer from two problems. The first is the same problem as ordinary progress control: it relies on accurate, but in practice often subjective, estimates of how complete project activities are. The second problem relates to its conversion of schedule into a cost. This can be misleading. Earned Value has proved its capability in cost-tracking and management. In businesses, such as construction work, in which company profitability is often directly linked to project costs, Earned Value is a popular tool. Earned Value can perform less well in helping project managers with schedule tracking. A better alternative may be *Earned Schedule,* which builds on Earned Value. It is somewhat more involved in implementation, but it shows schedule performance in terms of time, and not cost, and provides more intuitively useful measurements (e.g. see: Van De Velde, 2007). Earned Schedule is growing in acceptance, although it is still an uncommon technique.

More complex control systems are being proposed which assess other dimensions, such as quality and operational readiness (e.g. Rozenes et al., 2004), but these have so far failed to become common usage. It is questionable how applicable they are outside an engineering context.

Whatever control systems are used, they should have some features in common:

o The measurement system should be complete and relevant to the context of the project
o The data used should be reliable

- The system should be effective and improve the quality of decision-making
- The measurement system should be subject to continual improvement

(Cooke-Davies, 2004)

Issue management

As projects progress problems will occur, which were not foreseen initially. Predicted problems are dealt with either by actions already included in the project plan or through the risk management process. Unpredicted problems, known as *issues*, are managed through *issue management*.

Issue management is a structured approach to dealing with problems on projects. It is a useful term for all managers to understand if only because project managers tend to regularly refer to issues and issue management. Depending on the scale and complexity of a project issue management may be a more or less complicated activity, but the principles are the same. The typical steps in issue management are

- Issue identification
- Issue logging
- Issue assessment and identification of resolution
- Allocation of ownership for resolution
- Implementation of resolution
- Tracking and issue closure

There are various formal definitions of issue management. For example, the APM gives the following one:

> ... *process by which concerns that threaten the projects objectives and cannot be resolved by the project manager are identified and addressed to remove the threat they pose.* (APM, 2006)

In the APM's definition an issue is not any problem affecting a project, but only one that is outside of the project manager's direct control. Such issues have to be flagged to the project sponsor or other stakeholders for resolution. The assumption in this definition is that issues within a project manager's control will simply be resolved as part of the day-to-day activity on a project. In reality, many project managers treat all problems as issues and use issue logging and management as good discipline to ensure all issues are managed to resolution.

An issue should not be confused with a *risk*. Generally, the term risk is used to denote an occurrence which is uncertain, whereas an issue denotes one that has happened.

Change control and configuration management

Change control is one of most important processes in project management, as poorly managed change is the root cause of a high percentage of project failure. Change control is

> ... *the process that ensures that all changes made to a project's baselined scope, time, cost and quality objectives or agreed benefits are identified, evaluated, approved, rejected or deferred.* (APM, 2006)

Change control attempts to deal with the reality of projects. No matter how well a project is planned and resourced, and no matter how well scope and requirements were defined, they will change as a project progresses. Change is a result of both an improved understanding that happens as projects progress and also wider changes to businesses. Change is sometimes presented as a negative concept in project management literature, as it often makes completing a project successfully harder. But it is not negative in itself, merely a reflection of reality.

Although change control is important and developing an understanding of a specific change can be complex, the process is conceptually very simple:

o *Identify request*: This is the documentation of the proposed change in sufficient detail for it to be understood and assessed.

o *Analyze the request and determine its effect on the project*: This is the core part of change control. The effect on a project can be on the time, the cost, the resources required, the quality of deliverables, the scope or the benefits from a project.

o *Approve or reject the change*: Based on the information from the analysis, a change is either approved and accepted into the project or rejected. Changes may also be deferred, which means consideration is rejected until future times.

o *Update the plan*: If a change is approved, update the plan and implement it by allocating the necessary work to project team.

Changes come about because of both internal and external stimuli on a project. An external stimulus could be a stakeholder requesting a change to requirements, or it may be a line manager wanting to withdraw some resource from a project. An internal stimulus could be a project manager seeking permission to modify the baseline project plan which he has discovered is unrealistic.

Approval for changes comes from the project sponsor or sometimes a change control board made up of a group of project stakeholders chaired by the sponsor.

Change control should theoretically be used on any change in a project. But judgement can be applied. Changes with minimal impact on a project, or which have an effect within limited thresholds, may be accepted by some project managers without change control. For example, a change which results in a one day increase in a five-year programme may be accepted without change control. It is questionable whether this is good practice, as it can result in a lax attitude towards change. Problems on projects due to change are often the result of many small changes and are not always caused by a few significant changes.

In addition, project management theory shows all changes as requiring approval, and that the project will continue as it is until approval is gained. In practice, a change may be a matter of fact. For example, if project prioritization changes due to strategic shift or resources are removed due to current operational projects, the project team and sponsor may have no choice but to re-baseline the project. Approval is meaningless in this situation, as the impact is a matter of fact and not alterable. However, even in these situations, the discipline of assessing the impact and changing plans accordingly is important.

Although change control provides a mechanism to handle change, it has its limits. There are situations of such volatility or poor understanding that a project will become swamped very quickly with change controls. There is no simple answer to this problem. Some project management approaches, such as iterative and incremental approaches, try to limit this by running the project through very small phases. However, if a committed time and cost is required for a project, then there is little choice but to constrain requirements and subject them to change control.

The management of change on projects can often be an area of significant tension between different stakeholders. A typical situation is where a stakeholder wants additional requirements included, but this will delay or add cost to a project. Other stakeholders may be unhappy with the delay or the cost. Dealing with such issues, and managing stakeholder expectations with regard to change, is often a key factor differentiating senior and successful project managers from less successful colleagues.

One sign of poor project control is *scope creep*. Scope creep is a term used by project managers to describe the situation in which the scope of a project continually increases as a result of changes. There may be no single change that creates a problem, but the volume of changes and the cumulative impact of them means that the project's scope expands beyond a reasonable level. The danger of scope creep is a never-ending or at least extended project timeline, combined with a continually increasing budget requirement. An assessment that a project is suffering from scope creep is a subjective judgement. Unfortunately even robust change control may legitimately lead to this situation of scope creep – if each change is individually reasonable and justifiable. Avoiding scope creep takes vigilance on the part of the project manager and project sponsor. Preventing scope creep requires that each change is considered in terms of the cumulative effect of change, as well as its individual impact. Scope creep is a common project problem.

Change control should not be confused with *change management*. Change management is described in Chapter 9 and is concerned with implementing change to a business. Unfortunately the potential confusion can be increased by the tendency in some organizations to refer to change control as change management.

Configuration management is closely associated with change control. A configuration is the definition of the final deliverables. It is most commonly used with technical deliverables such as those in an IT system, where the configuration defines the functional and physical characteristics of the system. Configuration management is the creation and maintenance documentation or records of the configuration. Once created and baselined the configuration should only change as a result of an agreed change control. The configuration describes the existing planned deliverables from a project. The effect of changes are analysed by reviewing the configuration. When a change is approved, the configuration is updated in line with the change. For complex engineered deliverables configuration management can be a significant activity supported by a variety of tools such as a *configuration database*.

Team management

The project manager has a team management role over the project team. In many ways the requirements of this role are as for any other manager, and project managers need to exhibit a range of common management and leadership skills. All of the following tasks need to be performed by a project manager, and they are required at times by most managers:

- Defining roles and responsibilities
- Building a (project) team
- Leading and motivating a (project) team
- Making people accountable for their work
- Resolving team member issues
- Modifying management and leadership styles to context

This is not a book on general management, so the skills needed to perform these tasks are considered as outside the scope of this text. However, projects offer some unique challenges in terms of team management which project managers specifically must be able to deal with:

- Rapid and continuous forming and re-forming of teams
- Working outside of normal management chain
- Limited support from the performance management system

Let us look at each of these in turn.

Although most managers have to build new teams at some points in their careers, it is usually an infrequent activity. Project managers build a new project team on every project. Achieving this successfully is not simply about choosing resources with the right skills for the project, but is also about forming teams that work together well. Project managers should have an understanding of team dynamics and how team performance can be optimized.

Project managers usually do not have a line management responsibility for the project team members. They do not therefore have the formal power such position in an organizational hierarchy entails. Project managers may even be junior to some project team members. This is common with the involvement of specialists such as corporate lawyers in projects. The potential difficulty this entails can be increased in situations in which the line managers of project team members are not supportive of the project and want their staff to perform other tasks first.

Project management approaches will often stress the need to align project team members' performance measures with their role on projects. From a project perspective, ideally all project team members' performance will be assessed in relationship to their role on a project. This often works well in organizations such as consultancies, where staff spend most of their time working on projects. In many other organizations it does not.

For many reasons performance management systems may not be aligned with projects and project roles. Sometimes, especially if a project role is short-term, it is impractical to change annual appraisal metrics. In other situations, line managers may not be bothered, or actively oppose doing this, perhaps owing to a sense of loss of control of their own staff. The performance management system may not be easily adapted for project-based assessment. Whatever the reason, project managers have to learn to adapt to situations in which they do not have the lever of control an organization's performance management system offers.

There are various ways that project managers can resolve or mitigate the problems of limited formal power and lack of control of performance levers. First, whilst a project manager may be junior, she can to some extent inherit the power associated with the approvers or sponsors of a project. If a powerful manager is sponsoring a project, a project manager can make leverage of this to convince people to work hard on projects. In addition, project managers can formally and explicitly gain commitment from line managers to allocate their staff to projects for specific periods of time. This reduces the likelihood of staff being removed or project work interfered with. Finally, project managers often develop influencing skills to persuade people to complete work even though they have limited formal power to do so.

These issues are discussed in more detail in Chapter 12 on developing a project management capability.

Stakeholder management

Projects have a variety of stakeholders who have an influence on the progress of a project and will make judgements on the success of a project. (Chapter 7 reviewed the role of stakeholders in determining project success.) Stakeholders are involved at all stages of projects, and are essential to the completion of many tasks. This is an important community for the project manager, and a project manager cannot assume that they are a passive group.

The objective of *stakeholder management* is to positively influence stakeholders so that they both actively support the project and also have a positive perception of the project. Of course, in certain situations some stakeholders will never be positive advocates of a project. For instance, in a cost-reduction programme, staff who will lose their jobs as a result are unlikely to ever be favourable towards the programme. In that situation stakeholder management is concerned with mitigating any influence or negative affect such stakeholders may have on the programme.

Stakeholder management is closely aligned to communications, and relies on the use of appropriate communication to understand, inform, deal with concerns of and influence stakeholders. A major part of the communications on any project is to deal with stakeholder management.

There are many approaches to stakeholder management. Some project managers, especially those on larger or more contentious programmes, may have training in communication skills, influencing skills and even techniques such as NLP. A typical stakeholder management process aims to

- o Identify stakeholders
- o Concentrate on those stakeholders with a relevant view on success or ability to influence project outcomes
- o Understand stakeholders' levels of power or influence
- o Understand attitudes of stakeholders to the project. This may be complicated as a stakeholder may not have a single view about a project – she may be positive about the goal of a project, but negative about the way a project is addressing this goal.
- o Determine how best to utilize the support of positive stakeholders and mitigate the result of actions of negative stakeholders.
- o Take action and assess the result.

Stakeholder management is sensitive. It makes use of often subjective assessment of individual stakeholder views, which can cause political problems if communicated in an inappropriate way.

The role of the project sponsor in project execution

Project managers execute the projects required by an organization. However, successful delivery is not simply a result of good project management; it also requires the support of the wider management hierarchy of an organization. In an operational role management support is provided by a line manager. In a project situation, this support is provided by a *project sponsor*.

The role of the project sponsor is discussed in three sub-sections:

- o *The project sponsor's role*: describes the main responsibilities of the role.
- o *Understanding projects*: describes how the sponsor can maintain an understanding of a project sufficient to perform her role, especially if she is not a specialist in project management.
- o *Performing the role of project sponsorship*: looks at how this role can be put into practice.

A sponsor may be a group or a committee, but in this section is assumed to be an individual. The role performed in practice varies considerably, and the role required also differs depending on the context and the role that the project manager and other stakeholders perform. This section applies a standard view of the role of the project sponsor.

The ability to be able to sponsor projects effectively is of importance to all senior managers, as most will end up involved in projects at some time in their careers irrespective of whether or not they have a project management background. Whereas project management is a specialist discipline, most managers should develop the skills to sponsor projects successfully.

The role of the project sponsor

The role of project sponsor is to direct and support the project manager. Without sponsorship a project is reliant on the authority, personal skills, influence and power of the project manager. In reality without sponsorship a project will often not get far in most organizations, and it becomes questionable on what authority a project is being pursued. The seniority of a project sponsor will vary between organizations and projects, but irrespective of seniority there is always a link between the leadership team of an organization and the management of a project.

The precise split in responsibilities between sponsor and project manager will depend on the situation and the personality and skills of those involved. Typically, the project sponsor is required to:

- o Identify the business need for a project, and act as an evangelist for the project. Provide senior support to a project during execution. That can involve accessing resources, overcoming problems and decision-making such as approving baseline plans, budgets and changes. The sponsor has an important role in communicating about a project and retaining enthusiasm and support for a project within a business. Project managers are dependent on sponsors' power and authority, and their influencing skills.
- o Set the business context for a project, the project manager and the project team, answering questions like why is the project important, and how does it fit into the organization's strategy.

- Ensure that the project manager is managing the project in a competent fashion.
- Take accountability for delivery of business benefits, which may accrue after project completion.

There are tangible aspects to a sponsor's role, such as gaining support for resources or taking accountability for benefits. There are also less tangible components and differences in emphasis of outlook between the sponsor and project manager. When the project is in delivery stage, the project team and project manager are often heads down getting the job done and less aware of the wider organizational context. The sponsor needs to make sure that objectives are not forgotten in the pressure to complete planned tasks. Rather than heads down delivering, the sponsor should be focussed on achieving the desired outcome and on managing the relationship with external stakeholders, especially those in senior positions.

A senior project sponsor adds credibility to a project within organizations. Without sponsorship a project will have difficulty gaining traction within a business, as businesses are typically conscious of status, power and authority in an organizational hierarchy.

In theory, the project sponsor should exist prior to the project and the project manager. In practice projects often start as a result of a business need and the influence of a group of stakeholders. In this situation it is normal for a project manager to request for a sponsor of suitable seniority to be appointed.

Unless the project is of major significance or size, a project sponsor is normally a part-time role and may spend only a few hours a week on project-related work. Some senior managers may have to sponsor several projects in parallel. There is usually no conflict in sponsoring multiple projects other than the availability of the sponsor's time. It is important for the sponsor to have sufficient time to allocate to each project.

It is not unusual for sponsors to be unsure of the requirements of their role. Project managers are often trained in project management, but sponsors are rarely trained in project sponsorship. Such training exists, but it is seldom taken up. The role tends to be learnt by practice, and managers often assume it is obvious what is required. It is not, and it is often reliant on the project manager coaching the sponsor as to the needs of the role. Given the project manager's generally lower position in the organizational hierarchy, this may be difficult. The result is that the project manager cannot always rely on all aspects of project sponsorship to be fulfilled and may end up "filling the gaps".

Understanding projects

Fulfilling the role of project sponsor requires an understanding of the project and its status. It is a challenge for many sponsors to get a good grasp of what is happening in a project in sufficient detail to enable them to fulfil their role. In some ways this is the challenge that any manager has with any task being performed for them. This challenge is enhanced when, as is often true, the sponsor does not have a project management background. Unless the sponsor has such a background, he may not have the expertise to understand all aspects of a project. There is a risk from a sponsor taking on face value what he is told by the project manager. Moreover, often a sponsor has only limited time to allocate to understanding and supporting a project manager.

Knowledge and competencies that are helpful in understanding projects are

o *Familiarity with project management concepts and terminology*: A good project manager will translate project language into business terms, but it is still helpful for the project sponsor to be able to talk on and understand project issues in project terminology. In ensuring a project is being well-run, the sponsor is assisted greatly by an ability to review plans and to understand other tools such as risk assessment.

o *Recognizing the relationship between sponsor behaviour and project success*: The behaviour of the sponsor will have an impact on project success. The ability to speed up or slow down decision-making, the type of resources allocated, the support for stakeholder engagement in a project and so on all affect the ability to deliver a project successfully.

o *The ability to probe and question successfully*: This can be difficult for a manager with limited experience of projects. It can be at least partially resolved by having sponsor or executive checklists to probe the relevant areas of the project. If an insufficient answer is forthcoming, the executive must request action to get the project team to a point where they can answer the question satisfactorily. The questions need to be asked at periodic intervals and vary depending on the stage of project. Asking too many questions will simply result in data overload; ask too few, and insufficient information is gathered (Knutson, 2001).

o *Willingness to spend sufficient time understanding project status*: Managers are always under time pressure, and if project sponsorship is only one amongst many tasks there can be a tendency to limit information gathering and to request very simple status reports. Sometimes the information can be reduced to a single piece of data as typified by traffic-light reports. A traffic-light report uses the analogy of traffic lights to show the status of a project – if it is green, all is OK; if it is amber, there are some concerns; if it is red, then action is required to bring it back on track. With such a limited understanding of status it may be impossible to take the right supporting actions. The opposite trap should also be avoided in which masses of detailed information is requested by the sponsor. Managers often assume that detailed information is accurate information. An erroneous plan or status report is still erroneous even if it is in great detail.

o *Willingness to take information from multiple sources*: Project managers will produce status reports, but a true understanding of status can often be enhanced by a willingness to gather information from other sources, including informal conversations with project team members and stakeholders. An understanding of status is often gained best by correlating information and testing any conflicting data. Multiple views help in identifying error and subjectivity in reports.

Project sponsorship is helped by a good relationship with the project manager and trust, based on a track record of reliability, in the information he or she provides the sponsor.

The work of the sponsor cannot simply be described in a tick-list fashion anymore than the work of the project manager can truly be understood through a short list of responsibilities. This section aims to give a flavour of how a sponsor can perform his or her role.

An early task of the sponsor is to ensure the project manager is driving the right project and proposing to do it in the right way. The sponsor should have input on and verify scope and objectives of the projects. She should check the structure and approach of the project, and make sure the project manager has an adequate control system in place. This should include periodic reviews of project tools such as the plan, issues log and risk assessments and change logs.

During project execution the sponsor should request information on and review status and performance through regular reports. The sponsor should also perform gate and milestone reviews. Project sponsorship faces the universal management challenge of balancing between too much and too little delegation. When a sponsor micro-manages a project manager it achieves little. Micro-management can actually delay projects as project managers spend too much time with the sponsor. In contrast, overly hands-off styles of management can lead to unexpected project failure.

As the project progresses, the sponsor should provide support to the project manager. There are many decisions and issues that a project manager does not have the influence, seniority or authority to resolve. Typical areas where support is required are resourcing, prioritization, problem solving and dealing with senior stakeholders. Factors outside of a project manager's control, such as power and politics or other environmental issues in the organization, need a sponsor's support to resolve.

In performing these activities the sponsor should be alert to the needs of the project and take guidance from the project manager. There is a reciprocal relationship between the sponsor and project manager. Although the sponsor provides management guidance to the project manager, he is also a member of the project team – and needs to be willing to take direction from the project manager. The project manager should alert the project sponsor when decisions or support is required. The tasks of the project sponsor can be managed like any other task in a project.

The sponsor can help the project manager to understand and work within the culture of the organization by providing guidance on what is important, what are the most appropriate styles of interaction, and how to approach different stakeholders.

The sponsor should provide constructive challenge to the project manager. The purpose of challenge is to expose weaknesses, errors and risk. In providing challenge the sponsor should be seeking to see whether the project can be done in a better way. Can the project be done quicker or cheaper? Is the project producing the right quality of deliverables? Will the business benefits be realized? Critically, is the project exposing the business to a level of risk that is acceptable?

However, challenge is not simply to give a project manager a hard time or for a manager to achieve personal goals, such as reducing cost to meet a budget constraint. Every time something in a project changes as a result of challenge, a sponsor should ask *has the project improved because of this challenge* and *is the level of risk still acceptable*? A senior sponsor acting in an overly assertive manner may achieve agreement from project managers to all sorts of project objectives and the development of very optimistic plans. However, assertiveness in itself does not actually make achieving targets any more likely. There can be a tendency to pressurize for reductions in cost and time, without understanding the impact on the quality of deliverables or the risk of the project. It is as important for a sponsor to ensure that plans are not overly optimistic and risky, as it is to try to reduce time or cost.

The sponsor's role is core to ensuring the project will achieve the outcome and business benefits expected. This requires checking that business cases and objectives will be achieved as projects change. There is a tendency to make a split between project approval and project management (Levine, 2005). Yet, as a project is a dynamic process business case, time, cost, scope and quality are subject to change. A project that starts with a valid business case can, through the process of change, end with one that is no longer acceptable. Therefore the sponsor should not assume that simply because a project was approved to meet a business case it will continue to do so. The validity of the business case should be reviewed regularly throughout the project.

Sponsors should also be the people who decide whether a project needs to be stopped or *killed*. If a project cannot meet its goals in an acceptable fashion, or if the business case deteriorates to a situation in which it is no longer worthwhile, the project should be stopped. This can be a difficult decision for sponsors. Managers are often reluctant to close projects down. There are several reasons for this including personal motivations, organizational social pressure, organizational inertia, politics, and culture (Straw and Ross, 1987). If projects that should be killed off are not done so at the right time, then significant resources can be wasted.

Finally, a sponsor should insist on reviews and learning from all project situations to ensure the project manager and the project team's competencies improve.

A note on programmes, programme management and programme sponsorship

The primary focus of this book is on projects, project management and on overall portfolio management. Programme management is not emphasized. It is not that programmes are not important: they are; but much of the difference between a project and a programme is one of emphasis. Programme management is different from project management, but the difference is primarily of interest to professionals in the field. However, it is worth looking briefly at sponsorship in the context of programmes.

In most cases the principles and responsibilities of project management and project sponsorship also apply to programme management and programme sponsorship. Programme management can be thought of as a super-set of project management.

There are differences in the usage of the terms programmes and programme management between organizations, and between different project management professionals. However, if they are to be useful terms, programmes should not simply be considered as big projects, and programme managers as not just senior project managers. In addition, programme management is not simply a layer between project management and portfolio management in a hierarchy.

Differences between a project and a programme relate to the breakdown of a complex endeavour into a series of typically inter-dependent projects with a common goal. During execution programme managers, on top of the areas of management project managers should consider, must concern themselves with managing the schedule of several projects, inter-project dependency management and the outcome of the programme or benefits.

The relationship between the programme manager and programme sponsor tends to be slightly different from that between a project manager and project sponsor. The individuals involved tend to be more senior, and the emphasis on responsibilities changes as a result of this. Given programme managers' focus on benefits delivery and business change, the programme sponsor can be more externally focussed on stakeholder management and decision-making. However, every situation is different.

Where a programme has a sponsor, the individual projects within the programme usually do not require separate sponsorship. However, in some situations, to minimize the overhead on the programme sponsor, projects within a programme may have a less senior sponsor as well as the overall programme sponsor.

Case Study 8.1　HOW DO YOU KEEP CONTROL OF ALL THE PROJECTS IN YOUR BUSINESS?

Steve Oliver is the co-founder and a director of Abritas. Abritas is an innovative systems supplier focusing on the social housing sector. Their core product Nova-HX is the market leader in its sector. It has modules to support local councils in areas such as housing register, homelessness, choice-based lettings, temporary-accommodation management, rents (expenditure tracking) and e-Government & CRM.

Steve Oliver

We are a relatively small business, with less than 100 employees. Even so, we have lots of projects ongoing at any one time and keeping track would be a problem if we did not have strong controls in place.

Each of our projects has a project manager on it. A project manager may be running one or several projects. Every week the project managers produce a weekly status report on each project he or she is responsible for. We keep it fairly simple, but it has to be enough for us to reliably understand status. The reports contain key dates, some free-form comments on the project, any significant changes or slippages in progress and an overall traffic-light status summary. There may be more detailed reviews from time to time, but these reports are enough for us as a business to keep an overall understanding of projects.

The project manager's reports are collated by our programme manager. He does an excellent job of summarizing all the projects and producing a consolidated report for me and the other directors. One of our strengths is that because we have such a reliable programme manager we can trust what is in the report and don't have to spend too much time testing and probing it. It's not that we have never had any surprises. We had one project that threw up a whole series of unexpected surprises, caused probably by an inexperienced project manager. But of course you learn from such mistakes, and they are becoming increasingly rare.

Occasionally, project managers feel they are too busy to complete the reports. Sometimes in the past we haven't received them, but we have now built the habit into the organization, so producing a weekly report is an automatic task.

We are helped by the fact that as most of our project work is about developing our core system, Nova-HX, each project follows the same lifecycle: sale, configuration specification, development, systems test and user acceptance test. Of course each project varies, but they have the same basic series of steps. This makes management and control easier.

We have tried to monitor projections of cost of our projects as well as time to completion. With time we are pretty accurate. We have had less success in projecting total costs, which are primarily staff time on projects. We always know what a project has cost to date, or what a project has cost when it is completed as we keep timesheets tracking hours spent on different projects. However, projecting costs forward is harder. The nature of our projects is such that this is not a major problem.

The critical milestone I like to track and to see not slipping is User Acceptance Test (UAT). As long as we hit the start of UAT on time I am comfortable, knowing that the project will be completed on time. When we get into UAT and implementation, we are dependent on our customers providing resource and completing actions, which is outside of our control.

In the course of classic project management processes we also manage risks and changes. Risks are flagged up by project managers as and when they are identified. If they are significant they will likely be escalated, and we will take the necessary actions. Changes do not arise much during our development process, but they do arise in UAT. When a customer becomes involved in UAT, it is often the first time they really see the system in use for them. Of course, not everyone can envisage what the system will be like when we have configured it to their changes. When they do see it, sometimes it does not precisely meet their expectations. So, then we have changes. If they are small we will just implement them straightaway. For larger changes we need to re-plan. We try to push any larger changes into a later phase of delivery.

All in all our control processes work well. Like any projects ours do not always go exactly to plan, but with good information and a good team we are able to resolve problems as they occur and regularly complete projects successfully.

More information on Abritas can be found at www.**abritas.co.uk**.

In-life portfolio management

Good project management in an environment in which critical success factors are met should ensure the successful execution of individual endeavours. But, as was shown in Chapter 4, project management alone will not ensure that the right projects are undertaken, and that the whole portfolio continues to be optimized for an organization's benefit as the projects in it are delivered.

There are a number of reasons why information must be consolidated across projects to support the management of the organization's portfolio. Reasons include the need to summarize information for reporting purposes to senior managers and executives, who are often more interested in the general picture and overall view than they are in details about an individual project. There is also a requirement for information on projects to enable decisions to be made about portfolio management issues such as prioritization and trade-offs between project options. Finally, there are cross-project issues such as resourcing and achieving benefits.

The cost and complexity of a portfolio of projects is such that it requires a control system capable of collecting several distinct, but often inter-dependent, sets of information, yet not overloading decision-makers with information, and which is practical to maintain. Many organizations struggle with getting this balance right. This is the responsibility of the portfolio manager, although there will be overlaps with delivery executives (see below).

In terms of in-life management of a portfolio there are two separate, but related, tasks:

- o The management of work flow through the pipeline:
  - The management of decision and review points, such as project gates and project control processes, including change control boards
  - Ensuring the balance of the portfolio continues to meet objectives at an acceptable level of risk
  - Resource levelling and ensuring that the forward project workload is optimized against resource availability
- o Monitoring and taking action at a cross-project level, which requires summary and consolidated information from across the project portfolio. Examples of important information are
  - *Resource allocation and availability*: aligning capacity with what is being done on an ongoing basis
  - *Benefits accumulation*: ensuring the total benefits that are being achieved are in line with needs and cumulative to meet the overall objectives
  - *Risk to business*: ensuring that the cumulative risk across the portfolio is acceptable for the business
  - *Business change and implementation schedules*: looking at the degree of change that will occur as a result of project implementation across the organization, and, where necessary, adapting project schedules so that business operations are not overloaded with change at any point in time

The aim is to have a portfolio that is achieving company objectives and is optimized relative to the resource base. Good portfolio management should positively be able to answer these questions: Is this the best set of projects that can be delivered? And, are the projects progressing as required to meet objectives?

Projects, programme and portfolio execution – the role of delivery executives

There are some senior managers who have, as a core part of their role, an ongoing responsibility for the delivery of projects. For example, the CIO may have a significant operational responsibility, but also has an important ongoing project role for IT applications development. Similarly, a role like the head of product development, running a series of new product developments and product enhancements, is a senior delivery manager or delivery executive.

These roles are particularly important in the delivery of projects. The role of a delivery executive in the execution of projects varies from situation to situation, but essentially involves

- Provision of the capability and resources for delivery of projects. This includes project and programme managers, but may also include the project staff such as business analysts and engineers. In addition, it often encompasses the portfolio management capability.
- Provision of the infrastructure required for projects to be successfully managed in terms of approaches, processes and tools including project and resource management software.
- Encouragement of an appropriate management and leadership framework. This includes performance management approaches and HR policies which support project managers and associated roles.
- Encouragement for the ongoing improvement in project approaches, and to enhance knowledge over time.
- Support for portfolio management and ensuring that the projects being undertaken by the function are in line with strategy and adding value to the business.
- Support and guidance for other executives in the management and delivery of projects, and encouragement for the development of a suitable project governance framework.

Such an executive may also have responsibility for portfolio management, and the portfolio manager may be a direct report of such an executive. Developing a project management capability is discussed in Chapter 12. An example of a delivery executive's views is given in Case Study 8.2.

Projects, programme and portfolio execution – governance of project management

In the last few decades there has been increasing emphasis on the need for good corporate governance, primarily as a result of many high-profile cases of corporate failure. There are several descriptions of corporate governance, but for the purposes of this book the straightforward definition given in the original Cadbury Report is adequate. In this influential document corporate governance is defined simply as the system by which companies are directed and controlled (Committee on the financial aspects of corporate governance, 1992).

The objective of corporate governance is to ensure that the company has objectives in line with various stakeholder needs (especially those of shareholders); that achievement of those objectives is monitored; and that action is taken to see that those objectives are attained. Corporate governance is the responsibility of a company's board of directors.

A significant proportion of investment in companies is in projects, and one of the main mechanisms for achieving company objectives is projects. There are probably even more cases of high-profile project failure than there are of corporate failure. Projects individually and cumulatively subject businesses to high levels of risk. For all these reasons, it is appropriate that projects are brought into the corporate governance spotlight.

However, corporate governance guidelines do not normally have sufficient detail to describe approaches to projects, and hence the concept of *project governance* has arisen. Project governance links the realms of project management to the corporate governance of a business.

The definition and understanding of project governance is often applied in a vague and ambiguous fashion. However, there are formal definitions. The APM has documented a description of project governance in *A Guide to Governance of Project Management* (APM, 2004). In this publication project governance is shown as overlapping with and as an extension to corporate governance. It consists of

- Portfolio direction effectiveness and efficiency
- Project sponsorship effectiveness and efficiency
- Project management effectiveness and efficiency
- Disclosure and reporting

As with corporate governance, the APM places responsibility for project governance at the door of the board of an organization, arguing that project governance overlaps with corporate governance (APM, 2004). The guide contains compliance checklists for each of these areas. The guide reflects the importance of the portfolio in achieving business objectives, the key role sponsorship plays in successful project delivery and especially the achievement of the business case, and the importance of project management. The fourth item, disclosure and reporting, identifies the need for timely, relevant and reliable information to support the decision-making processes in a business.

A board needs to be aware of major individual programmes that subject a business to any combination of significant costs, risks or opportunities. However, in general, project governance has less to do with control of individual endeavours and more with progress towards strategy and creation of an environment in which achievement continues to be made and in which projects can be executed.

A board should approve portfolio objectives and ensure that the way prioritization is applied is in line with these objectives. The board should also ensure that the capacity of the organization matches the work being undertaken. The board should also ensure the effectiveness and efficiency of project sponsorship. (It is interesting to note that amongst the project management community, project sponsorship is seen as of such importance that it is included as one of the main pillars of governance.)

The board should encourage the development of a culture that supports the delivery of projects. Factors which influence this culture include HR practices, performance measures, leadership actions, structure and strategy (Suda, 2007).

Much of governance involves setting a framework in which the right things are done, rather than detailed definition or control. Part of this should be defining what is important and setting the framework for projects. The definition of what is important should be based on the organization's strategic drivers and supported by relevant measures and metrics. In some situations it could be cost that is the primary driver; in others it may be quality; or it could be a balance between such factors. In addition, a perspective on the appetite for projects and risk should exist. It is not helpful for project sponsors to be constantly proposing £10million projects if the board has no intention to invest in endeavours with budgets of greater than £1million.

The board should create an environment in which killing projects off is possible. An unwillingness to stop projects in execution can lead to significant wasted investment. During execution it may become apparent that a project is not feasible, or business needs may change making the project irrelevant. The sensible decision in these situations is to stop the project. However, there is a common tendency to resist stopping projects once they have started. Reasons include manager's and sponsor's concerns about being seen to have failed and the associated risk to their careers. Another common problem is simply the lack of information on projects and their ongoing relevance. The board can help to overcome this by reducing the risk of failure on individuals, by not (overly) penalizing individuals for choosing projects which later have to be stopped. They should also insist on reliable and timely information on projects and risk levels. Finally, the board can separate decision-making about project continuation from project originators (Straw and Ross, 1987).

Executives need to understand the impact of decision-making on projects in terms of the general way they make decisions and the implications of specific decisions. The critical bottleneck on a project portfolio can be the unwillingness or incapability of executives to make decisions. Unless decision-making is responsive to project timescales, delays and overruns are likely. Moreover, specific decisions can unintentionally have an adverse impact on the portfolio. For example, any decision to add another project impacts existing projects in the portfolio. The overall number of projects needs to be kept to an optimal level. It is very easy to continually agree to start more projects. Too many projects is not only weak decision-making – it is bad management. Adding even one more project than is optimal can significantly delay all projects in a portfolio.

Case Study 8.2 PERSPECTIVE OF THE EXECUTIVE RESPONSIBLE FOR DELIVERY

Howard Watson is the CTIO of Virgin Media, a major integrated telecommunications and media company providing services to millions of customers in the United Kingdom. In this case study, he provides his views of the major challenges he faces as the executive responsible for the delivery of most projects and business change in the organization.

Howard Watson

As the CTIO I face many of the issues that any executive faces. In my role with responsibility for delivering change in the organization there are five specific challenges I identify as real problems:

1. ***The conflict between the medium-term portfolio management and the annual budget cycle:*** *My team is responsible for the delivery of many of the projects the business requires. There is a trend whereby our projects take longer than a budget year.*

   Obviously projects take different lengths of time, but a typical project could take two months in planning, six months in delivery and then four months in test and implementation. There is a tendency for all projects to be started at some point in the first quarter of the year with the new budget. What this means is that many enter implementation in the third quarter of the year. This means we put most strain on the operational areas of the business at one point in time, which also in terms of our underlying business cycle happens to be the busiest time of the year anyway.

One way around this is to start projects earlier – in the previous budget year. The problem here is that we often don't have the money in year one for projects that deliver in year two. Whatever money there is, is focussed on year one's projects.

2. **The tactical planning horizon is longer than the strategic:** It's probably true with all businesses, and it is certainly true with ours, that the market moves so fast nowadays that we can strategically really see only nine months ahead with any degree of certainty. A typical project takes about 15 months to go from start to closure. You can see the problem!

There is a lot of variation: a project could take from three months; it may take two years – but on average it is longer than we can strategically plan. We can't increase our nine-month horizon – that's down to the market and is out of our control. So, we must find ways of shortening our 15-month delivery windows. Classic project management approaches, with emphasis on detailed requirements collection and planning, don't work well in this environment. We continually have to find ways of delivering change and benefits in shorter time windows.

A lot of focus is often given to speeding up the development phase of projects, but this is not really where our time problems come from. The length of a project is often determined by the length of initial planning and the time it takes to do testing and handover. Shortening these phases would be very helpful.

3. **Spotting when to stop projects:** Given the previous challenge sometimes projects become irrelevant, or at least the business case and benefits decline, prior to completion. The competitive environment changes, and what seemed like a great idea when it was initiated is no longer so great part way through the project.

We therefore have to be good at stopping projects when the world moves on. The only way to really do this is by tracking benefits and having regular reviews to make sure they still stack up. Just the fact that a project had a great business case at the start does not mean it still does a few months later. There is a tendency to fall into the sunk-cost trap – "all this money has already been spent, and it will only cost a little more to complete". If the world moves on and the benefits are no longer there, the project should be stopped. We have a limited amount of resource and this must be focussed on the most beneficial projects.

4. **What to do with portfolio delivery staff when there is a lull:** The natural business cycle means there are always peaks and troughs in the workload. One challenge is therefore optimal resourcing. Should I resource up to the peak workload and risk staff being underutilized, or should I staff to the trough and rely on contract staff when I need more. (I'm not just talking about project managers – but all staff working on projects.) Basically we have to find ways to flex up and down.

If you resource to the peak demand then you will find in practice that the lull does not come because people instinctively make new projects to keep busy. They may be sensible projects, but often they are not really priorities, and we waste time doing things just to keep people busy. At the other extreme if you just outsource it all you need to keep an eye on is making sure you have enough of your core skills. If you take a role like business analyst what's the value in outsourcing this? I often think if you bring in contract business analysts all you are doing is paying someone to learn about your business who then leaves.

I think off-shoring offers some interesting possibilities. For example, it is possible to speed up things like testing by doing 24 × 7 testing at reasonable prices.

5. **Keeping the bottleneck at the front end:** *I always like to throttle the amount of work we can do by limiting the number of project managers we have. There is a tendency to staff up with project managers and business analysts, so every project that is wanted can be started. What this means is that projects initiate quickly – but overall delivery is slowed down because you don't deliver projects just with project managers and business analysts! The more project managers employed, the more multi-tasking you tend to get amongst everyone else who works on projects. This just leads to more and more delays.*

It's easy for a senior person to think there must be enough resource for one more project. You see 1000 people in IT or other project-related departments and think you must have enough resource. In reality though there are not 1000 homogeneous skills, but maybe 90 different skill set groups – some of which have very small numbers of staff. Each of these groups can become overloaded and a bottleneck if you start too many projects. Understanding and then managing this is too complex to be practical. There always will be a bottleneck, and it's easiest to manage if it's visible and at the front end.

Of course there's great pressure to put a project manager on every project and start it then and there. But it must be resisted, as although it might give the impression of being helpful, it's really hiding the true resource issues that will occur later in the project. The important thing is speed to deliver, not speed to start! Can I summarize what other executives want from someone in my position? First, they want predictability. If we take on a project and we say we are going to deliver it in a certain timeframe, then they want us to keep to this promise. The second thing they want is balance and fairness. They need an honest broker on the project portfolio. Each has his or her own priorities and needs. They know not everything is going to be done. I can provide a way to get our overall priorities without being biased to one part of the business or another.

MAIN LEARNING POINTS FROM CHAPTER 8

- Execution is the core stage of work for the project manager. It builds on previous work in planning and resourcing and applies the full range of project management tools to ensure the project is completed.

- The tools a project manager uses in execution include risk management, change and configuration management, issue management, assumption management, resource and budget management, scope and requirements management, planning, stakeholder management and benefits management. At the same time the project manager must utilize a wide range of normal management skills such as team management, group dynamics, leadership, communications, relationship building, negotiation and persuasion skills, and responding to organizational politics.

- The project manager must not lose sight of the fact that a project will result in change in an organization and must be planning for operational readiness and change implementation during execution.

- To manage a project effectively the project manager must implement a reliable control system, which typically provides information on progress relative to time, cost, quality and benefits. Although the principles of control systems are universal, each project's control system is unique. The control system is used in an ongoing plan—monitor—control process. Control means taking relevant action based on the control systems' information relative to the plan.

- Control systems rely on estimates of progress. These are often subjective and are a source of risk. Project managers must find ways to verify estimates of progress.
- The project sponsor should support, direct and challenge the project manager, but may need help in understanding his or her role.
- Programme managers usually have a broader role in execution phases than do project managers, especially with regard to longer-term planning, organizational change and benefits realization.
- Portfolio control systems consolidate and extend on information from individual projects (e.g. inclusion of information on cumulative risk and benefits, and on potential new projects).
- The delivery of projects should fall within an overall project governance framework. Project governance applies the principles of corporate governance and extends it to the realm of projects.

REVIEW QUESTIONS AND EXERCISES

1. Consider the work that you have to complete on the remainder of your course. How do you know if you are on track or not? What metrics could you use to track and assess your progress? If you were responsible for all the students on the course what reports and information might you collect, and how would you summarize progress across the student group?
2. Describe a control system for a project. What information would you require, where would you collect it from, and how often? How would you use this information in practice? How often would you modify work on a project in response to information from your control system?
3. Write a role definition in bullet point form for a project manager and a project sponsor. How would you change this if the roles were for a programme manager and a programme sponsor? Complete the set with a role definition for a portfolio manager.
4. What are the attributes of a great project sponsor? How would you expect the project sponsor to interact with a project manager in practice?
5. How do you think culture and management style impacts projects? If you were on the board of a company what styles and culture would you encourage as most conducive to project delivery and why? How would you achieve this?
6. Review Case Study 8.2. How would you approach each of the five challenges Howard outlines? Would you add anything else to these five challenges?

Suggested reading

Managing the execution of projects is a core part of most project management books, although some are more thorough than others.

A good example from a project perspective is

- *Project Management. Planning, Scheduling and Controlling Projects.* Stanley E Portny, Samuel J Mantel, Jack R Meredith, Scott M Schafer, Margaret M Sutton and Brian E Kramer. John Wiley, 2008, pp 247–401

In terms of the roles of sponsors, try

o *Project Sponsorship: Achieving Management Commitment for Project Success.* Randall L Englund and Alfonso Bucero. Jossey-Bass Business & Management, 2006

For a better understanding of project governance, reference

o *Directing Change: A Guide to Governance of Project Management.* APM (Association for Project Management), 2004

Bibliography

APM (Association for Project Management). *Directing Change: A Guide to Governance of Project Management*, 2004.

APM (Association for Project Management). *APM Body of Knowledge,* 5th Edition, 2006.

Committee on the Financial Aspects of Corporate Governance. *Report of the Committee on the Financial Aspects of Corporate Governance.* Chaired by A. Cadbury, Gee & Co, December 1992.

Cooke-Davies, T. "Consistently doing the right projects and doing them right – What metrics do you need". *The Measured.* Volume 4, Issue 2, Summer 2004, pp 44–52.

Cooper, R., Edgett, S. and Kleinschmidt, E. "Portfolio management for new product development: Results of an Industry Practices Study". *R&D Management.* Volume 31, Issue 4, 2001, pp. 361–80.

Gray, CF. and Larson, EW. *Project Management: The Managerial Process.* McGraw-Hill International Edition. 2006.

Knutson, J. "An executive project progress checklist". *PM Network.* January 2001.

Levine, H. *Project Portfolio Management. A Practical Guide to Selecting Projects, Managing Portfolios and Maximizing Benefits.* Jossey-Bass, 2005.

Martinelli, R. and Waddell, J. "Managing programs to success: Key program metrics". *PM World Today.* Volume IX, Issue VII, July 2007.

Maylor, H. *Project Management.* 3rd edition. FT Prentice Hall, 2005.

Phillips, J., Bothell, T. and Lynne Snead, G. *The Project Management Scorecard: Measuring the Success of Project Management Solutions.* Butterworth-Heinemann, June 2002.

Portny, S., Mantel, S., Meredith, J., Schafer, S., Sutton, M. and Kramer, B. *Project Management. Planning, Scheduling and Controlling Projects.* John Wiley, 2008, pp. 247–401.

Rozenes, S., Vitner, G. and Spraggett, S. "MPCS: Multidimensional Project Control System". *International Journal of Project Management.* Volume 22, Issue 2, February 2004, pp. 109–18.

Straw, B. and Ross J. "Knowing when to pull the plug". *Harvard Business Review.* March 1987.

Suda, L. "Linking strategy, leadership and organization culture for project success". *PM World Today.* Volume IX, Issue IX, September 2007.

Van De Velde, R. "Time is up: Assessing schedule performance with earned value". *PM World Today.* Volume IX, Issue X, October 2007.

9

implementation:
delivering and sustaining
change

Organizations invest significant amounts of time and money in project planning and execution. Well-defined and well-executed projects, selected as part of a portfolio aligned with business objectives, result in valuable deliverables. The deliverables provide the opportunity for substantial business benefits. But this presents only a potential for benefits until the deliverables are implemented. Implementation results in business changes. It is through change that benefits are realized and projects can be justified. If nothing changes in a business, there can be no benefits.

Implementation is often the riskiest part of a project. Until implementation starts, the biggest risk a project usually exposes a business to is the loss of the investment in the project and the opportunity costs associated with this investment. There may be a significant financial loss from a poorly planned and executed project. Yet, this can be trivial compared to the risk from implementation. Poorly implemented change can disrupt the existing operations of a business, and in extreme situations can threaten the survival of the business. For this reason understanding implementation is critical for all managers involved with, sponsoring or impacted by projects.

This chapter provides a description of the stages in project implementation. This is based on a standard project management lifecycle and covers the period from completion of the creation of deliverables to project closure. However, there is more to successful change in business than following a series of project steps. Project management can sometimes be viewed purely from the methodological aspects and sequence of steps in a project. This is a risky perspective to take when it comes to implementation. Implementation is fraught with the unpredictability of human nature and the interaction of the relatively simple world of a project with the full complexity of the organization. Stakeholder management is an important aspect of all stages of projects, but it is in implementation that human factors become central. Successful change requires balancing the reinforcing and counteracting pressures arising from different stakeholders.

Project implementation is inherently concerned with business change, and there is another discipline beyond project management that deals with change called, logically, *change management*. This chapter introduces change management and looks at how it overlaps with and differs from project management. It will show how achieving change is more than the technical application of project management.

Although there is increasing use of change management language amongst the project management community, project managers and project management approaches often gloss over change and change management. If it is mentioned at all, it is as something that occurs in the final stages of projects. Change management may be mentioned as dealing with the *soft side* or the *human dimensions* of projects. For some projects this is a fair representation, but by positioning change management like this, project managers can be guilty of underestimating and poorly understanding change. This chapter will show that change management, if anything, is more complex than project management and occurs in a wider range of situations. Whereas project management may be considered as an essential but specialist discipline that the general manager needs a limited understanding of, change management is increasingly seen as a component of every manager's role.

Whilst there is some debate and difference of opinion about the optimal way to manage a project, the variation in viewpoints is minor compared with the limited consensus over what change management is. There are many theories on change and change management, and they are very varied. This variation in views starts with different perspectives on the nature of change in organizations, includes various views on the best way to manage change, and encompasses debates on whether there can be such a thing as a way to manage change. This chapter introduces this debate and compares and contrasts project and change management.

By looking at change the chapter also starts to question the limits of project management, introducing a debate that is revisited in Chapter 13 (Context, culture and the limits to project management). Change is a complex phenomenon, and change management is a large and growing discipline. This chapter can only provide an introduction to these subjects and position their relevance next to projects and project management.

Project implementation

Implementation can be summed up in the instruction a sponsor can give to a project manager to proceed – *make it happen*. Implementation moves a project from the relatively closed and organized world within a project manager's control into the wider arena of the organization. The level of control a project manager has during implementation is inherently limited, because a project manager has little influence over daily operations of a business. Through implementation the project will impinge on the daily operations, and daily operations will impinge on the project. Project managers are often guilty of focussing primarily on deliverable creation and completing a project, rather than on the complex activities involved in achieving sustained change following a project.

Implementation can be anything from a very short phase of a project through to a significant proportion of the overall timeline. Complicated programmes, resulting in major business change, may spend 50% or more of their total duration in implementation. For projects with an objective of delivering enhanced skills or improved capabilities, implementation can be the most significant phase of the project.

During implementation the project manger is concerned with ensuring that the outcome expected occurs, and the necessary quality of this outcome is achieved. It is during implementation that business benefits start to arise, so it is of critical importance to the project sponsor. At the end of implementation all the loose ends of the project should be tied up and the stakeholder community should be satisfied. Following implementation there is an opportunity to reflect on the project and learn from the experience.

Successful implementation builds on the previous stages in a project. It requires quality deliverables that meet the end needs of the customer, based on a true understanding of requirements. Successful implementation also links back to the point of project conception. It is unfortunate that it is often during implementation that there is a realization that the project is not the right thing to be doing. Too often questions like *does this change make sense, is it the right thing to do*, or *is it happening at the right time* are asked during implementation (Bruch et al., 2005). All a project manager can do in implementation is to execute the change in the best way possible. The challenge of performing the right change needs to have been decided up front during the conception, acceptance and prioritization of a project.

The activities within implementation vary considerably depending on the nature of the project. The rest of this section describes four generic steps within implementation:

- *Implementation planning*: which is concerned with ensuring that the organization is ready to change in the way required by the project
- *Testing and acceptance*: which is performed to ensure the deliverables created by the project meet the needs as defined in the requirements
- *Implementation and handover*: when the deliverables are put to live use in the business and handed over to operational departments
- *Project closure and review*: when all remaining activities in the project are completed and a formal review of the project is performed

Depending on viewpoint or project lifecycle, implementation can be considered as the final part of project execution, or it can be defined as the stage after execution.

Implementation planning

The first phase of implementation is *implementation planning*. It is the detailed preparation for implementing changes into live business operations. Implementation planning is concerned with what needs to be done to go from a set of deliverables, to an implemented change and the situation in which the project can be closed. There are two main components to implementation planning:

1. Ensuring the project's deliverables are in a fit state to be implemented
2. Ensuring that the organization is ready to change in the way proposed

One way to consider implementation is as the point of two worlds colliding: the worlds of the project and of business operations. Until implementation the main impact a project has on operations is as a resource drain. A project may take people from operational departments to work on the project. This may be a problem for operations, but it is usually manageable. Otherwise the project and operations are largely independent.

During implementation existing operations will be forced to change as the deliverables are implemented, and this change will cause disruption. Whether the project is implementing improved processes, new IT systems, better performance management approaches or organizational changes, disruption cannot be avoided. Even in construction projects, the building of new infrastructure often affects existing users of current infrastructure. Until implementation the primary objective of the project manager is to progress with delivery; during implementation the desire to push forward and complete the project has to be balanced against the need to minimize disruption to existing operations.

The baseline project plan created at the start of the project should include the implementation phase. However, it is not normally possible to do full implementation planning until the latter stages of a project when detailed information is available. Implementation planning needs to deal with all the details that the project plan may not have considered. Thus, for example, a project plan may indicate that some people will need training, and time in the plan must be assigned for this. The implementation plan will worry about factors like who those people are, how they can be released from their day jobs to undertake the training, where the training will take place, who will develop the training materials and who will do the training.

There often is no black and white boundary between implementation and deliverable creation. In a phased programme, implementation will start and carry on in parallel with continuing development work.

There can be no standard implementation plan, because there is no such thing as a standard project in a standard business with standard operations. However, there are some common steps a plan can be built from, which are described in the rest of this section. There are also many lessons learnt over time that can be applied to avoid some of the pitfalls in implementation.

Operational readiness can be considered as a part of implementation planning, although it can also be considered as a separate activity. As implementation results in a change to operations, this will be easier if the operations are prepared for the change and are operationally ready to accept the change. Operational readiness deals with the assessment of what activities are required to ensure that operations can deal with the change.

Acceptance and testing

Before implementation can begin, the deliverables from a project should be accepted by the parts of the business that will use them and be impacted by them. *Acceptance* is an important milestone in projects, when the deliverables are recognized and explicitly acknowledged as being ready for implementation. *Testing* is performed to support acceptance and to prove the deliverables created meet the end need and are in a fit state to be implemented.

There are several different reasons for testing. Testing is undertaken to ensure the completeness and the quality of deliverables. Testing helps to check whether the project will meet user expectations. Testing supports preparation for change by verifying the usability of deliverables. Testing can ascertain the operational impact of deliverables, and what service levels they will be capable of supporting. Testing may also be linked to contractual issues. For example, a project supplier may not be paid until certain tests have been completed satisfactorily.

Testing is a complicated activity, and there may be several stages of testing. The different stages of testing enable gradually more complex tests to be performed, and more and more of the testing objectives to be met. The nature of testing varies depending on the type of deliverables, and the following example is built up from an IT project. Testing for IT seeks to verify that a product has been well-built, and to validate that it is the right product in that it meets the original needs. In a typical IT project the stages of testing are

- *Unit test*: testing small subroutines and ensuring they do what is expected. By testing small components errors are easier to locate and fix. As errors are almost inevitable in software, a good test is not one that identifies no errors, but one that identifies the most errors.
- *Integration test*: combining the units and ensuring that as a complete software application it continues to operate correctly and meet requirements. Unit test cannot reliably predict the interactions between deliverable components, and therefore integration test is required.
- *Validation or user acceptance test (UAT)*: ensuring that the software meets user expectations as defined in the original requirements specification. Unit and integration tests are usually performed by specialist software testers, whereas UAT should be performed by representatives of the end-users of the systems. (This should not be an opportunity to change requirements, though changes may be requested if it is really the first time users have seen the deliverables. Where compromises have been made against original requirements the users should have been informed and their expectations managed, and UAT should not be the point when they are made aware of these compromises.)
- *Systems test*: the integration of the system with the other existing computer systems in a business. The primary objective at this stage is to ensure that the new software has no adverse effect on other elements of technology.
- *Operational test*: finally trying the system in a live environment to ensure service levels and other non-functional requirements are met, and the system does not generally disrupt business operations. Often the only way to perform reliably an operational test is to implement the system live. This is less of a test, and more of a measurement of what happens in reality. In case there are negative results *roll-back* plans are put in place to reverse the changes out and go back to the previous state. This is not always possible for some changes are irreversible, and hence a source of significant operational risk.

Project managers hope deliverables pass tests. But this, of course, does not always happen. Where tests fail, a decision must be taken as to whether to accept the failure and implement sub-optimal deliverables, or perform some re-work to improve the deliverables. Re-working deliverables can be time-consuming and expensive, and one of the drivers for a quality approach throughout projects is to avoid problems at the testing phase. Having a quality approach to requirements capture, solutions design and solutions development should minimize test problems. Typically, the earlier problems are identified in a development process the easier they are to fix. However, no development is foolproof and some contingency for re-work resulting from testing should be held.

In some situations it may be necessary not only to test deliverables within a business, but to expose them to customers prior to full implementation. This is common with new products where *customer trials* may have to be performed. As well as testing the functioning of new products in real customer environments, trials also provide an opportunity to explore customer attitudes to new products, and attributes of products such as the pricing, branding or packaging.

Testing can be an expensive and time-consuming phase of any project with complex deliverables. There are ways to speed up and perform better-quality testing through parallel and automated testing. Testing can also be outsourced and off-shored. However, assuming the tests are well-designed, the longer the testing, and the more the resources assigned to it, the more thorough it will be. The higher the risk associated with implementation, the more the effort that should be expended on testing.

The length of testing is always a compromise between a business's need to proceed and the risk associated with deliverables being incomplete or liable to failure. Testing is about risk reduction, but it is not foolproof. It is questionable for a complex deliverable such as an IT system or a new product whether fully exhaustive testing is possible. For an IT system exhaustive testing would require every function and combination of functions to be tested against every possible type of data. For a new product, no matter how robust the testing is, it is likely that a customer somewhere will use it in a completely unforeseen manner with unpredictable results.

Successful testing is to some extent a matter of perception. Depending on viewpoint a bug in software can be seen as a failure of testing, or as an acceptable result of the compromise between progressing with launch and test durations. That is not to say that testing cannot be improved. It is estimated that at least one-third of the cost of software failures could be avoided with improved testing (The Economist, 2004).

Having passed testing, the deliverables are accepted and signed off as ready for implementation.

Implementation and handover

Implementation is the point at which a change is made to some aspect of the business. Following implementation the deliverables are handed over to the operational departments of the business, and the project is ready for closure. Implementation is a process of transition from one state, prior-to-the-change, to a new state, following-the-change. *Handover* is the point of responsibility leaving the project team and going to business operations.

The approaches to managing the transition of business operations from one state to another vary considerably. In summary, there are essentially two ways to perform implementation:

1. As a once-off single activity
2. Phased implementation

A single phase of implementation is sometimes known as a *big bang* implementation. The transition to a new state occurs at once with a single implementation, with the deliverables becoming universally used. If the deliverables only impact a limited area of the business, or if the degree of change is restricted, then this is often the most sensible approach as it can be done quickly.

A *phased implementation* is performing change in a limited area of the business at one time, and then progressively expanding the area of the business included within the change. Phasing may be based on a geographic area or functional groups, or within one process in a business. Phased implementation reduces risk, though it does extend the timeline of implementation. A compromise between big-bang and a phased implementation is a *pilot implementation*. Here changes are piloted in one area of the business before being rolled out to the rest.

The factors which should be used to determine whether implementation should be big-bang or phased are

o *The speed with which a project must complete*: The faster a project must be completed, the more appropriate a big-bang style of implementation is.
o *The scale of change and degree of risk associated with it*: The higher the risk the more appropriate a phased implementation.
o *Whether roll back is possible or not*: If roll back is not possible then risk increases, and again a phased implementation is more appropriate.
o *Whether the change can be broken into chunks or not*: Irrespective of the risk some changes cannot be phased, and the only approach is the big-bang one. If a company has one customer database that all systems interface into, then upgrading the database software may have to be done as a big bang.

The level of risk associated with implementation should be taken into account in the testing stage. The more the risk associated with implementation, the more thorough and exhaustive the testing should be.

Assuming that implementation is complete the project is now ready for *handover*. Handover means that future responsibility for the deliverables from the project is taken on by the operational departments. As a project is a temporary management structure, handover must occur at some stage. There are two main audiences for handover: *end-users* and *operational support*. End-users are the users of the deliverables in the live operations of the business. At point of handover they should be fully comfortable with the use of the deliverables.

Operational support are the teams who will provide any support necessary to end-users following implementation. Many deliverables require some form of ongoing support; for example, an IT system needs support in case of software problems in future.

Handover can often be a contentious stage of projects. The project team is normally under pressure from their line managers to complete their project work so they can either be available for the next project or return to operations. Operational departments are often reluctant to take changes or new developments into their responsibilities without sufficient time and resource to manage them adequately. Almost all projects have to make some compromises, and this may give reason for operational departments to delay handover. If handover is delayed, a project team may not be able to be released for other work. Smooth handover is one indication of a well-run project.

Often an important component in preparation for implementation is training. If the deliverables from a project are an improved capability or enhanced skills, training may be the main activity in implementation. Training depends on the need and the impact of the change on different groups of people in a business. Training encompasses everything from simple awareness raising to in-depth explanation and education on how to use and how to support the deliverables being implemented.

An important element of implementation is ensuring that all documentation relating to project deliverables is complete. Until implementation the people most familiar with the deliverables are the project team, but following implementation the deliverables will be used and maintained by the operational departments of the business. There will usually be a requirement for various documents to be available to the end-users and operational support, in an accessible format. The documentation will include requirements specifications, design and configuration documents, procedures and instructions, training materials etc.

Project closure and review

Once the deliverables are handed over the project is ready to close. Project closure is not simply a matter of stopping the project team's work one day, but should ensure that all loose ends of the project are tied up. Typical components of project closure include

- Completing any outstanding activities, or ensuring they are included in the handover to end-users or operational support.
- Releasing human resources at the appropriate time. Project managers are often under pressure to release resources as soon as implementation starts. Problems can occur in implementation and this pressure should be resisted until the change is complete in all respects.
- Thanking and celebrating. Project team members should be thanked appropriately for their contribution to the project.
- Reviewing stakeholder satisfaction and agreeing any actions required to satisfy dissatisfied stakeholders. This includes agreeing what to do with any unfulfilled requirements.
- Project staff appraisals, and for non-project staff feedback to their line managers on performance on the project.
- Finalizing budgets and releasing any money not spent. This requires ensuring all final payments to suppliers have been made. It can take several months after project closure before all costs are realized on a project budget. Some contractual payments may be dependent on performance post-implementation.
- Completing any project documentation, such as handover reports and project closure approvals.

Project closure is an opportunity to agree what happens to any requirements, which, for practical reasons such as time or cost constraints, were eliminated from the scope of the project.

For a project, the end of implementation means the closure of the project. For a multi-phase programme the end of any one implementation may be a time for celebration, but otherwise the programme continues on (see Diagrams 9.1 and 9.2 for a comparison). At the end of implementation decisions have to be made about how to fulfil unmet requirements. They can be rejected, or put forward for inclusion in a future project. In a multi-phase implementation, unmet requirements can be considered for inclusion in latter phases of the programme.

The final activity is to review the project and capture any lessons to be learnt. There will always be components of a project that went well and which should be repeated on future projects, and there will be mistakes and lessons learnt. It is often noted that a major factor in successful organizations is their ability to learn, and review is an important part of learning. A formal review with the project team and project stakeholders should be carried out to capture and document these

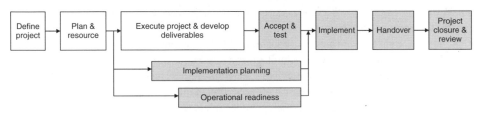

Diagram 9.1 *Project implementation stages*

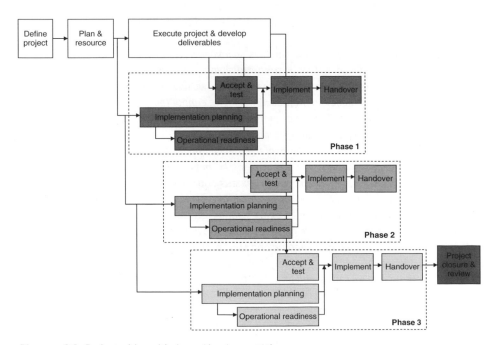

Diagram 9.2 *Project with multi-phased implementation*

lessons to enable them to be disseminated through the organization. Most project management methodologies insist on post-implementation reviews.

The timing of reviews is critical. It should not be performed too late or else many details of the project will be forgotten. On the other hand, if it is held too early the final outcome of the project may not be clear in terms of benefits and impact on the operations. One way to balance this is to perform a project team review within a few weeks of project closure, and then to have a sponsor and stakeholder review of overall success some months later. The second review should also be used to identify any problems with the implementation that need fixing. The second part of the review is important, but unfortunately is often omitted, and true long-term success of projects is often not assessed and lessons are not learnt.

Case Study 9.1   IMPLEMENTATION PLANNING IN EMEDYS

eMedys is a pioneering company providing services to hospitals and their patients. eMedys installs and operates bedside terminals. These terminals provide patient entertainment (TV, telephony and internet), as well as easy access to hospital services, such as meal ordering. The same terminal can be used by hospital staff to access medical applications, for example patient records, when they are providing bedside care to the patient.

eMedys makes use of innovative technology and has a unique business model, which makes its service highly attractive to hospitals. eMedys is a new business, and at the time of writing this case study is winning its first orders. In this case study, the Director of Programmes talks about implementation planning in eMedys.

We are involved in implementing infrastructure and services within hospitals. The implementation consists of installation work as well as a business change. The trigger for an implementation project is winning a contract with a particular hospital (or chain of hospitals). We have started to win our first contracts, and so implementation is becoming core to our business.

Winning a contract within the hospital sector is an involved process. A typical timeframe from initial discussions through to contract closure in this sector is 18 months. Because of the appeal of our product and business model, we have been successful in significantly shortening on these timeframes. Even so, we cannot reliably expect to close a deal in less than nine months. Given this extended timescale it might be thought that we have plenty of time to prepare for an implementation. Difficulties arise because until we have signed the contract we are not sure of the precise range of services the hospital wants – and the order in which contracts will be signed is not certain.

Although we are a start-up, we are a global business and are working with hospitals across Asia and Europe. This means we have to run implementation projects in many parts of the world at once. Selling is not an exact science, and sometimes a specific hospital moves faster than expected in closing a deal, on other occasions it is slower. We track all the sales activity that is running and start preparing for implementation as soon as a particular client reaches a certain point in our defined sales process. Even so, we might think that hospital A may sign first, and that hospital B will some weeks later. In practice, the order can easily reverse. This means we have to be able to shift the focus of our implementation effort very quickly.

To give us the maximum flexibility we outsource the majority of the installation work. Even so, there are core skills which only we possess and which are part of our competitive differentiation. So, we have to continually prioritize where we make those skills available depending on which hospital is at which stage in the sales and implementation process. In addition, every implementation requires a significant capital investment in the equipment we install. Like any business we want to manage our cash flows and do not want to build up a large inventory of equipment until we know it is required. A lot of the equipment we buy is specialized and has long lead times, so we cannot just order it at the last moment. We predict a volume of installation and line up our suppliers to provide the appropriate amount of equipment, but where in the world we want the equipment delivered to can change until the very last moment. We are constantly juggling resources depending on the ever-changing situation.

Although the implementation is not overly complex, in terms of the steps required to install and connect a terminal within a hospital, the environment of a hospital makes things complicated. Simple activities, like drilling a hole in the wall, are more difficult under the need to keep a hospital environment clean and free of infection, and not to disturb patients. Hospitals can't close down to let us do our work – we have to work around them. Access to beds may be for very short periods of time – and we have to know the environment is free from infection so our staff can do their work. Afterwards, the hospital has to be confident the area is again clean, hygienic and suitable for a patient to inhabit.

The physical installation and switch on of our service is not the end point of implementation. The next step is getting people to use the service. In many cases this is automatic, as it is attractive and intuitive to use. However, there is an ongoing change management activity to maximize the use of device both from viewpoint of patients for entertainment services and from the perspective of hospital for medical applications. The medical profession can be a conundrum at times. On one hand, it is at the forefront of technology, on the other, it can be very resistant to change. We have sold a service to our customers, and we want them to maximize the benefits – helping them to engage, get used to it, and make full use of the service is important to us.

What I have talked about so far are the implementation projects we undertake. As we are a start-up, the implementations are just one part of a larger programme to build and develop our business. This start-up programme is not a simple and predictable endeavour, but a highly dynamic and ever-changing situation. A project management approach is a significant help, but we cannot work to a rigid plan. New opportunities arise all the time. We need to be ready for them and flexible enough to take advantage of them.

More information on eMedys can be found at www.emedys.com

Portfolio management and implementation

Implementation of a set of deliverables is the responsibility of the relevant project or programme manager. The portfolio management function has a limited involvement in individual implementations directly. However, successful portfolio management needs to have good information on implementation and should have an influence on the timing of implementation.

Reporting on progress in implementation is critical for portfolio planning. As implementation completes project resources will start to be released and become available for allocation to other projects. Implementation is also the start of benefits realization.

Portfolio management should influence the timing of implementation. The timing of implementation is initially determined by the length of the project. But implementation dates should also take account of the cumulative level of change across a business and any events which impact the ability or desire to change.

A project manager is aware of implementation from the viewpoint of the project he is responsible for. Being able to change successfully is a factor of the *capacity for change* and *willingness to change* in a business, or in any one area of a business. The capacity for change is dependent on a number of factors such as skills for change and readiness for change, but it is also dependent on

- o *The cumulative amount of change occurring at any one time*: Change requires adaptation and learning, and people have a finite capacity for this at any one time. Exposing groups to excessive amount of change at any one time leads to higher risk of change failure, greater disruption and longer implementation times. Although senior operational roles, such as a director of customer services or the chief operating officer, are interested in gaining the benefits from project implementation, one of their main concerns is usually the risk of disruption to the functions they are responsible for.
- o *The amount of disruption that is acceptable*: Change causes disruption as people learn new ways of working and also because of emotional responses to change. Some business functions can accept high levels of disruption with minimal risk to the business. Other business-critical functions, such as customer services, can only manage minimal disruption at any one time without exposing the business to risk.
- o *The impact of other events*: Factors such as volumes of work associated with business cycles or non-availability of staff because of public holidays may impact the capacity for change or the willingness to change. For example, busy periods in sales cycles, such as Christmas for retailers, are times when there is a reduced willingness to change.

The portfolio management function should therefore be looking at the schedule of implementations across projects and programmes, and if necessary re-phasing project implementations to take account of change capacity. Change capacity can be thought of as a scarce resource that the portfolio manager must prioritize access to if there is a potential bottleneck.

To develop an assessment of cumulative change a portfolio manager should look from a functional or process viewpoint, as this is where change impacts. It should also factor in any other events in the business calendar that reduce the capacity or willingness to change. A simple example is shown in Diagram 9.3.

Diagram 9.3 shows five areas of a business: sales, customer service, manufacturing, procurement and corporate. The chart displays the timing of project implementations and other business events over time. This business has a portfolio of 14 projects, numbered p1 to p14 on the chart, which will be implemented in the next few months. Project implementations may be indicated several times on the chart if they impact more than one function. For example, p2 is shown against sales and corporate, as this is a project to implement a new sales-tracking and commission system which will be used by both sales and corporate functions.

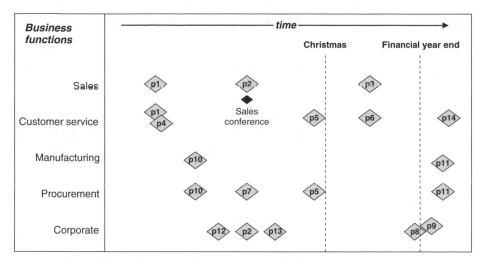

Diagram 9.3 *Assessing cumulative change*

By looking across from each function of the business it is possible to see which implementations will occur at what point in time within which functions. From this chart a number of issues may be raised:

o Projects p1 and p4 may need to be re-phased if they clash in customer services. But note that p1 is also being implemented in sales, and any re-phasing needs to take account of the impact on sales as well.

o Project p2 is being implemented in sales at the same time as the sales conference. The conference may offer the opportunity to communicate on the change, but it also means staff are out of the office. Phasing of the project and sales conference needs to be reviewed. However, p2 is also being implemented in the corporate function, and any schedule change needs to avoid a clash with p12 or p13.

o Project p5 is being implemented in customer services and procurement close to Christmas. This is a poor time to implement changes in some businesses, such as a retailer, as it can risk disruption at a time when there are peak workloads and more staff on holiday. On the other hand, Christmas can be a good time to implement changes in other businesses, such as the introduction of new machinery in a factory, as it may be a relatively quiet period with fewer staff working.

o Projects p8 and p9 may create a change overload for corporate, especially as the implementation is currently planned for the financial year end, which is usually a busy time for the corporate functions.

o The manufacturing function can probably absorb more change than is currently planned for it as nothing is being implemented between the completion of p10 and the implementation of p11.

Of course, a real assessment would be more complex than this and may contain hundreds of projects across scores of functions. A function may well be able to absorb several projects at once, and there will be more business events that have to be considered.

Implementation, business change and change management

The earlier section in this chapter titled "Project Implementation" described a traditional approach to completing projects that will be familiar to many project managers. Some of the language or terminology related to implementation may alter depending on project types. An IT project manager may use slightly different language from a new product developer, but the basic principles of implementation and nature of the steps involved would be consistent. This type of approach has proven itself in large numbers of projects and is the result of years of learning by project managers. However, it is not without problems.

Implementation is often one of the most difficult and contentious phases of projects. Many projects have developed a series of deliverables without major problem only to stumble when it comes to implementation. A key factor in this is insufficient understanding of change and an inadequate application of change management. This issue becomes more critical with projects that have less to do with the development of tangible deliverables such as an IT development, and more to do with the achieving change in its own right, such as cultural change.

The symptoms of failed implementation become apparent with a lack of acceptance of deliverables from a project. Operational departments do not involve themselves in the project or its implementation. When the root causes of implementation failure are assessed it may be found that the operational departments never agreed on the goals of the project in the first place, and even if they did, they may not have agreed to the route taken to achieve those goals. Because of limited operational involvement, staff are not properly trained and the deliverables end up being unused and unusable. Failure is often less overt, when the deliverables start to be used during project implementation, but over a few months following the end of the project the change is not sustained, and people revert to old ways of working. A project has been completed, but change has not been achieved. The project investment has been wasted.

Before getting to implementation it is useful to ask a project manager what he thinks his role is: to create a set of deliverables or to achieve business change. Neither possible answer is wrong, but if the answer is to "create deliverables" then someone else has to be responsible for ensuring that business change occurs. This is a challenge of varying degrees depending on the scale of business change a project results in.

In some projects the resultant business change is trivial. If the project is to produce a new management report, then the action of stopping using one report and starting to use the new one is straightforward and will not require much in the way of change management. On the other hand if the project is to alter the way a business is managed, which requires a new suite of management reports measuring a different set of KPIs from those traditionally used – which is being done to drive different behaviour in the business – then a significant change challenge arises.

Change management is more than the stakeholder management of operational departments. Project managers are adept at managing stakeholders. Projects borrow resources from operational departments, which can irritate and cause problems for operational departments. Good project managers learn the skills of dealing with and smoothing the ruffled feathers of operational managers. But in implementation the impact of the project on stakeholders increases. Change disrupts operations and may make it hard for people to maintain their performance and service levels. Change forces people to work in new ways they may not be comfortable with. In addition, during implementation the response of operational departments to change creates a feedback loop which is unpredictable in nature. Change always creates a response. The response may reinforce the change, or it may counteract change. Most often the response to change is perceived as a *resistance* to change.

Resistance to change is a phenomenon that anyone implementing any kind of change becomes familiar with. Resistance can come about for a whole host of reasons. Sometimes people are resistant simply because something is new, and it conflicts with their experiences and models of the world. Often resistance is due to a real or perceived loss from a change. If something changes in an organization there may be a group of people who are in some way worse off – they may really be worse off, or simply imagine they are. Such people are likely to actively resist the change. On some other occasions resistance is due to completely rational reasons and from a belief that the change is not in the interests of the organization – and this will sometimes be true. Resistance is not simply a force to overcome; it indicates a different viewpoint that should be listened to and explored.

Change management means much more than just implementing deliverables. Change management is about achieving and sustaining a transition from one way of working to a new way. Change management is also about optimizing the experience of the change to minimize the disruption on the organization during change, and to speed up the process of transition. Whereas implementation happens at the end of a project, or at the end of each phase of a programme, change management occurs throughout the life of a project in terms of preparing the ground for change.

From an organization's perspective and particularly from a project manager's view it is important to understand the difference between the creation of deliverables and business change. Deliverables are the final output created by a project, but a deliverable is not a change in itself. Putting the deliverable to use is a change.

Making a change happen at the point of implementation is often not sufficient to realize the full benefits from a project investment. The required result is a *sustained* change. People, groups and organizations often accept change only to revert to previous ways of working. Sustaining a change requires ongoing management after the point of project closure.

The difference between completing a project and achieving change is often one of emphasis. Some project managers are familiar with and well-versed in change management, but the perspectives of project managers and change managers can be different. This difference in perspective between project and change managers is typified by the following definitions (the first was also used in Chapter 1):

> *Project management is the process by which projects are defined, planned, monitored, controlled and delivered such that the agreed benefits are realized.* (APM, 2006)
> *Change management is about modifying or transforming organizations in order to maintain or improve their efficiencies.* (Hayes, 2007)

The remaining sections of this chapter look at the nature of change, what change management is, and the relationship between project and change management.

The nature of change

We all intuitively know what change is, and in business the word is used with great frequency. However, there is rarely though a discussion on what change means, and the danger is that assumptions are made about common understandings when different models are used.

Let us start, therefore, with some thought of what the word change means. Change is used both as a verb and a noun. *Change* means to make something different, ideally in the context of organization change, to make something better. *Change* also refers to the process of making something different. As well, *change* is the name of the outcome of making something different.

There are many views on change. In making something different, what becomes different and how does it become different? Researchers and writers on change look at change from several different aspects. There is change as a phenomenon experienced by the individual. There is change as an experience of groups and of teams. There is change as in organizational change. Finally, there is change as in society and the environment.

From a business perspective the focus is usually on *organizational change*. But organizations are made up of individuals, and those individuals are structured into teams and groups. Therefore, arguably organizational change cannot be fully understood without some appreciation of both how individuals change as well as how teams and groups change. In addition, organizations are part of society, and so changes in society will be reflected in organizational change.

Change may be perceived by a project sponsor as simply an alteration in a way of working. But change is understood and interpreted through the lens of individual and group perceptions and psychology. Change is understood by people not only at a conscious rational and logical level – balancing the pros and cons in their favour – but also at an emotional and behavioural level. Change is not something that simply happens to or is done to people, it is something they experience and interact with changing the end result often in unpredicted ways.

Organizations experience change in different ways. There are incremental changes which may accumulate over time to drive some significant enhancement. This is change that would be understood by people and organizations experienced in approaches like *total quality management* or *TQM*. At the other extreme are transformational changes when the culture, strategy or operations of a business are modified as would be experienced in a major *business process re-engineering* (*BPR*) programme. Change may be considered as an episodic event that occurs occasionally in the life of an organization. In between the episodes of change an organization reaches a state of equilibrium.

Given that change is about transition from one state to another it is often implied in change literature that the change comes about from a state of stability. The father of modern thinking on change is Kurt Lewin. His model of a successful change project is one that goes through three steps: *unfreezing* when an individual or group recognizes change, *moving* when the change occurs, and *re-freezing* when a new stable state is reached (Lewin actually terms it a quasi-stationary equilibrium) (Lewin, 1947). However, some commentators express the opinion that stability is largely an illusion and change is a continuous state for individuals and organizations.

Change is usually thought of in business as arising from a deliberate and planned decision. A new business strategy arises. This results in a certain number of projects. The projects result in change. This is a model that many project managers would use. There is much debate about the reality of this model. If organizations are completely in control of their destiny, then this view of planned change is correct. However, there is plenty of opinion that most organizations do not shape their future, but respond to external pressures and influences, and as such change is largely a response to external events. Successful firms according to this view are not those that have the best planned future, but the ones that respond most quickly to events by avoiding problems and seizing opportunities as they arise.

Rune Todnem By suggests three ways in which change can be categorized (By, 2005):

1. *The rate of change occurrence*: whether it is discontinuous, incremental, bumpy incremental, continuous or bumpy continuous
2. *How change arises*: whether it is planned, emergent, contingency or a choice
3. *The scale of the change*: from fine tuning to incremental change through modular transformation, and finally corporate transformation

These categories reflect the varied nature of change.

One consistent message that comes through change literature is that change is not simply related to implementation. Implementation may be manifestation of change, but change and change management covers the spectrum from strategy and the initial selection of ideas through to sustaining change long after implementation has taken place.

Change management

As well as there being significant differences between views on change, there are also wide variations in the meaning of change management and perspectives on what is a good approach to managing change. Change management is almost universally thought of as important and a key part of management, but there is little consensus as to what exactly makes up change management. Some commentators question the possibility of change management, arguing that change is an outcome that has to be responded to, and is not something that can be planned or managed.

Practitioners, working in business, tend to be less interested in the theoretical views on the right and wrong of change, and want tools they can apply to solve everyday business problems. Even at the practitioner level there is a variety of interpretations of the best way to undertake and manage change. This variation in views can be seen from three articles chosen from respected magazines, which are targeted at senior executives and practitioners. Each of these articles proposes the four factors important in successful change management. Even the titles represent different models of change.

Table 9.1 Key factors in achieving successful change

Lawson and Price, *McKinsey Quarterly*, 2003	Sirkin, Keenan and Jackson *Harvard Business Review*, 2003	Roberto and Levesque *MIT Sloan Management Review*, 2005
The psychology of change management	The hard side of change management	The art of making change initiatives stick
Successful change requires • A purpose to believe in • Reinforcement systems that keep people interested and believing • Availability of the skills required for change. People cannot just change, they have to know how to • Consistent role models	The factors in successful change are • The frequency of formal reviews of change projects • The ability of the team to complete change initiatives on time • The commitment of the most senior leaders in the business to the change and the understanding and belief in the change amongst affected employees • The amount of effort required by employees to make the change initiative work beyond normal workloads. The higher it is, the less likely the change will be successful.	Successful change comes about through: • Chartering, having a clear specification of scope and a well-designed team member roles • Learning and discovering what works and then experimenting • Mobilizing, garnering resources and building emotional commitment • Realigning processes, changing the jobs and the performance metrics

The titles of the articles and the main points they make are summarized in Table 9.1.

Change management theories

There are numerous and ever-expanding theories of change and change management. To give a flavour of the different views four influential change management writers are briefly reviewed below: Kurt Lewin, Andrew Pettigrew, Peter Senge and John Kotter. These are four of the most well-known, dominant and influential commentators on business change.

Many of the foundations of change management derive from the work of Kurt Lewin. Lewin was an academic and practitioner in interpersonal, group and community relationships. Although his work is applicable to business, that was not his primary concern. His work, though often criticized now, underpins a lot of change management theory. His research included work in field theory, group dynamics, action research and the three-step model of change (Burnes, 2004). The three-step model of change through the stages of *unfreezing, moving* and *re-freezing* is often now seen as overly simplistic, though many change management approaches stem from it. He regarded status quo and change as relative concepts, and the result of the balance of conditions and forces.

> *Change and constancy are relative concepts; group life is never without change, merely differences in the amount and type of change exist.* (Lewin, 1947)

In 1990 Peter Senge's book *The Fifth Discipline* was published, which was to have a significant influence over many management thinkers. Senge argues that the companies that succeed are those that continually adapt and evolve through a process of learning. The *learning organization* is one that grows through experimentation and continual advancement. He identifies five components to the learning organization: *systems thinking, personal mastery, mental models, building shared vision* and *team learning*. Systems thinking is the *fifth* discipline of the title, because he claims it integrates the other disciplines into a coherent body of theory and practice (Senge, 1990).

> *The tools and ideas that are presented in this book are for destroying the illusion that the world is created of separate, unrelated forces. When we give up this illusions – we can then build "learning organizations," organizations where people continually expand their capacities to create results they truly desire.* (Senge, 1990)

Andrew Pettigrew is an academic who has written a number of books, which primarily look at the human, political and social aspects of organizations and their strategies. His work has influenced the development of the *processual approach* to change. This approach criticizes simplistic and planned approaches to change, and rejects any prescriptive how-to style of change management approaches. Processualists present change as complex mixture of individual decision-making and perceptions, political struggles and coalition building.

Another highly influential writer on change is John Kotter. Kotter focuses on leadership as the main component of successful change. As may be expected for someone who focuses on strategy and leadership, Kotter promotes the need for a clear goal for change and a logic for how to achieve it as the fundamental parts of successful change. He has identified eight steps titled *The eight stage process of creating major change*. These steps are the responsibility of the leaders of the business. One of the main roles of leadership is to take organizations through the eight steps. In presenting these eight steps Kotter promotes change as something that can be planned and controlled. The eight steps are (Kotter, 1996)

1. Establishing a sense of urgency
2. Creating the guiding coalition
3. Developing a vision and a strategy
4. Communicating the change vision
5. Empowering broad-based action
6. Generating short-term wins
7. Consolidating gains and producing more change
8. Anchoring new approaches in the culture

Change management methodologies

There is a range of methodologies which have developed for achieving change within organizations. These have primarily developed within the manufacturing sector, possibly as a result of the highly competitive nature of that environment, but have gradually spread across a range of industries. Methods such as *total quality management* (TQM), *business process re-engineering* (BPR), *lean* and *Six-Sigma* may not label themselves as change management methodologies, but they are about achieving beneficial improvement – in other words, change.

Each one takes a different perspective on what is important and how to achieve it, but all focus on driving beneficial change in organizations. TQM, lean and Six-Sigma though are more than approaches to individual change; they actually set out to change the way a business is managed, and through this achieve continuous change.

TQM drives to raise the awareness of quality in all members of an organization. From this ongoing, largely incremental, change businesses continually improve. Although TQM is used less explicitly nowadays, the general thinking and approach to TQM have influenced many aspects of business change and performance improvement.

BPR derives from the work of Michael Hammer. BPR focuses the business around its core processes and tasks which add value to customers. Any non-value adding work should be removed, and removal of non-value adding work is one of the key challenges for managers. Hammer is particularly critical of many IT projects which he claimed were simply automating non-value adding tasks rather than improving the way businesses operate (Hammer, 1990). BPR has it advocates and its critics, but irrespective of viewpoint it has brought the view of the organization through processes rather than functions into everyday business thinking.

Lean is an approach derived from the Toyota management system aimed at the identification and steady elimination of waste, the improvement of quality and production time and cost reduction.

Six-Sigma is often linked with lean, but it is a separate methodology that has its roots in statistical process control. Six-Sigma is a methodology originally developed by Motorola aimed at removing defects in processes. A defect is any non-conformity to expected outcome from a process. Although defect is often interpreted simplistically as a fault, it can be variance from any characteristic of a process. Six-Sigma can be implemented through its methods DMAIC (define, measure, analyse, improve, control) to improve an existing process or DMADV (define, measure, analyze, design, verify) for new processes.

So what is change management?

The material included in this section is a summary of a fraction of the most influential authors on change and change management. The main conclusion that can be drawn from the presented perspectives is that change and change management are important. In addition, there is, unfortunately, limited consensus on what drives change and what are the main components of a worthwhile approach to change management. A third conclusion that may be drawn is that change management is whatever it needs to be to result in the change required.

However, if there is no single approach to change management it is possible at least to start to identify some common threads and ideas that are generally presented as being important for change. This should not be considered as a lifecycle in the project management sense, but as a set of building blocks of change management. It is these building blocks of change management that project managers often learn and adopt into their approach to implementation throughout their careers.

Common factors identified as central to successful change management are:

o The role of leadership in setting the direction for change and acting as a role model for the change.
o The importance of objective setting and clarifying what change outcome is desired. Given the volatility of business many commentators stress the need for flexibility in objective setting.

o The need to understand the current state that will be transitioned from in a change. What is the current state and how far is it from the desired state? This is important to determine what actions are needed to go from the current to the desired state.

o The level of preparation and readiness for change within an organization. Readiness is a function of both change skills and the mental state with which a change is received. Preparation requires anticipating responses to change. The response is determined by a complex mesh of factors from rational views and individual psychology through to group dynamics. Change is interpreted, and the interpretation will often be different from that intended.

o The importance of communications in supporting change. Communication is critical in terms of preparing and informing staff for change. Adept communication skills can positively influence responses to change. Communication is a two-way process and it is also critical as a mechanism to develop understanding and to monitor responses to change.

o The need to create acceptance for change. Complete acceptance for change is not always fully possible, but at least negative responses need to be mitigated.

o The need to monitor and manage the responses to change. There will be reinforcing and counteracting pressures, and change will only be successful if the reinforcing pressures are greater than the counteracting. A change is not simply done to a target audience, the audience participate in the outcome of the change.

o The critical importance of aligning performance measurement systems with the objectives of the change. If performance measurement is not aligned with the change it is likely that the change will unravel and will not be sustained.

o The need for ongoing measurement and review post-implementation to maintain momentum and sustaining change efforts. Change needs vigilance after implementation to ensure it is sustained.

o An understanding that change is constantly occurring. The environment that was assessed at the start of a change project will be different by the time implementation completes. By the time implementation completes, needs will have moved on, and as soon as one implementation is complete preparation for the next change should begin.

The relationship between project and change management

There are two disciplines this chapter has discussed – *project management* and *change management*. Each has a role to play in driving change in business, but what is the relationship between project and change management? Project managers often present change as an outcome from projects and act as if change management does not exist or is merely a sub-set of project management. In contrast many change managers do not even refer to project management. A practitioner may ask, *is the initiative I am working on a project or a change? Or should I be using project or change management?* This section helps in answering these questions.

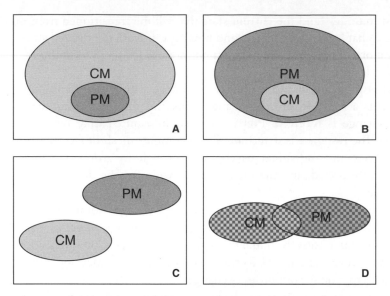

Diagram 9.4 The relationship between project and change management

Diagram 9.4 presents four possible relationships between project and change management. These are represented by the Venn diagrams in the four boxes marked A, B, C and D. In each diagram PM represents project management, and CM represents change management.

- o Box A shows project management as a sub-set of change management
- o Box B shows change management as a sub-set of project management
- o Box C shows project and change management as completely distinct disciplines
- o Box D shows project and change management as overlapping disciplines

Each of these states is correct in different situations.

Organizations often implement major change initiatives under the direction of a change leader, who may be supported by a project manager. A cultural change programme may have a change leader overall. A project manager will support developing and managing the key events in the change programme – such as education or communication events. But cultural change cannot be completely controlled via a plan. Cultural change is about change in behaviour of everyone in an organization, and this is inherently an unplannable series of occurrences. An endeavour of this type is illustrated by the Venn diagram in box A.

Many project management writers present change as an outcome from projects. Change management is shown as a useful aid to implementation as if change management is a sub-set of project management, as shown in box B. An example of this is a major IT systems implementation. A project approach is used to define requirements and develop the system. In implementation people's roles and responsibilities will adapt to the new systems functionality. To achieve this adaptation in roles the implementation is supported by change management.

In contrast, many change management writers do not even discuss project management, implying there is no relationship between the two disciplines, as represented by box C. An example of this could be the daily application of TQM. In a TQM situation there can be hundreds of minor changes underway all the time. These are not controlled or project managed, as they are too small. Each change is defined and implemented under the delegated authority of anyone in the organization who has the right to make appropriate change to his or her working processes. Six-Sigma can similarly result in thousands of small changes across an organization.

Finally, practitioners of change and project management often work hand in hand, and there are increasingly dual-skilled practitioners who use both project and change management as required. In project implementation the skills come together: when working with individuals and groups on small or sustained change then change management is used; when creating tangible deliverables project management is applied. This view is as presented in Box D.

None of these models is necessarily right or wrong, but Box D is the most representative and helpful way to consider project and change management.

Comparing project and change management

This sub-section provides a brief comparison of project and change management. The following areas are considered:

- o Origins and theoretical basis
- o The roles of participants
- o The use of improvisation
- o Scope of the disciplines
- o Outcomes and success criteria

The formalization of project and change management is a twentieth-century phenomenon. Some commentators on project management position it as an age-old skill that must have existed in some form or other for ancient developments, such as building of the pyramids. There is, however, little real evidence for this other than supposition (other of course than the existence of the pyramids!). Change can be proven as an ancient topic of discussion. For example, it is a core part of Buddhist literature, which has existed for thousands of years.

A good starting point for a comparison of project and change management is their theoretical basis. The basis of change management and project management appears different. Project management has developed as a practitioner-led approach. Although it is subject to and improved by academic research and critique, the research tends to look at the validity of project management and comparisons between different project management approaches. Academia has been less involved in the direct creation of project management methodology. In contrast, although many change management approaches are based on practitioner experience, much of the essence of change management has derived from academic theory. For example, Lewin's work, whether still accepted or not, was instrumental in the development of change management. It is difficult to think of an equivalent for project management. (That is not underestimating the impact of thinkers like Goldratt who have influenced the progression of project management.) The understanding of change and development of change management appear to have derived from a more significant basis in research in areas such as individual and group psychology than project management.

There is a difference in roles of participants between project and change management. Change management approaches often emphasize that they are something everyone in a business is involved in. Change management methodologies like TQM, Lean or Six-Sigma stress the involvement and training of large numbers of staff in the organization in the method itself. Ideally, everyone understands and can apply the techniques in their everyday work. Part of implementing a change with Six-Sigma is explicitly expanding the base of people in an organization with those skills. Implementing Six-Sigma is presented as a change in its own right, not merely as a mechanism to deliver change.

Everyone in an organization may also be involved in a project at some time, but project management remains a specialist discipline, and it is not normally argued that everyone in a business should be trained in project management. As part of a project, project managers do not habitually train the project team in project management, and project management lifecycles do not include a step for project management training.

Another view on participation is that change management is the domain of the leadership of the organization, whilst project management is the domain of a professional coterie (similar to other professions such as accountancy or engineering). Whereas project management is largely positioned as a specialist technical skill, change management is often portrayed as a component of general management or leadership skills (e.g. Kotter, 1996).

Project managers try to influence senior managers and leaders, often through the project sponsor. Project management presents such support as a critical success factor. Similarly, change management often stresses the need for leadership involvement. There is a difference in emphasis in change management, where this leadership is *involved* in the change as opposed to *supporting* a project.

It is widely accepted that project management needs to be tailored to suit a specific circumstance. However, in most situations there will be some form of lifecycles with stages that are broadly recognizable to all project managers. Different commentators have varying views on change management. Some describe change management in terms of process-based approaches, whilst others are inherently suspicious of the idea that change can be encapsulated within a simple process. Hope Hailey and Balogun (2002) have the concept of a *change kaleidoscope* which pulls together different contextual aspects and design options for change.

Traditional project management stresses the importance of lifecycle. Project management involves reaching a defined end goal via a lifecycle. Therefore, whilst there may be room for improvisation in terms of activities like solving a specific issue, the overall approach is not improvised. Change management often is less methodological and relies more on intuition and improvised approaches. Many descriptions of change management are tips and tactics, with some tools, yet without a specific description of the order in which they should be used.

Projects may have unexpected occurrences, but they are often undesired. These unanticipated outcomes are not simply a result of poor planning or insufficient project management; they are the result of the different ways individuals interpret change (Balogun, 2006). Many project management tools (e.g. planning and risk management) are available to remove or reduce the unpredicted. Change management, on the other hand, is often specifically about dealing with unexpected outcomes. People who have change thrust upon them are not passive recipients of change, but actively involved (either positively or negatively), and interpret the change in a way that makes sense to them. It is an emergent process and largely unpredictable. Change management is about dealing with the emergent.

It would be far too simplistic though to assume project management is a rigid methodology and change management is pure improvisation and intuition. Some change management approaches, such as Six-Sigma, provide very structured life-cycles and are concerned with delivering planned, tangible, measured change. On the other hand, the use of improvisation and intuition is increasingly accepted and recognized as a valid in project management, especially when dealing with novel or complex situations.

Improvisation is acknowledged as a means by which strategic change is implemented and embedded in organizations, and is required because of the uniqueness of each change. Experienced project managers dealing with complicated people-related situations such as organizational change report that they regularly resort to improvisation and intuition, and are generally comfortable with it (Leybourne and Sadler-Smith, 2006).

There is a difference between completing a project and achieving change, even if it is one of emphasis. Programme managers might respond with agreement, but add that it is the role of programme management to achieve business change. Whereas project management is focussed on the creation of some output or deliverables, programme management is more focussed on business change. This is often true. However, even the most complicated and long-lasting programme has an end point, and arguably change can always reverse or come undone after this end point. Responsibility for sustaining change, therefore, continues after a project has completed.

Change management has a broader scope than project management. Change management starts before any specific endeavour or initiatives, to develop organizational readiness for change. Readiness for change may not be related to an individual change, but is based on a view that as change is inevitable the organization needs to be ready for it and have the skills needed.

Moreover, there is the scenario of continuous change. If change is continuous, it cannot be a project (Lawrence et al., 2006). Projects have end points, a continuous change does not.

For project managers change is the outcome of implementing project deliverables, which results in change. For change managers projects may be required to create the conditions or enablers for the change desired, but it is change management that makes it happen.

Project management is typically concerned with the outcome achieved at the end of the project. Change does not have an end point as such. Even if the state reached at the end of a change process was ideal, change management cannot rest until the change is shown to have been sustained. Sustainability is dependent on the interplay of multiple factors, and also the judgement of sustainability is dependent on the analysis and timing of that judgement (Buchanan et al., 2005).

There are many factors which contribute to change implementation success. These vary from the factors that are traditionally considered as hard and tangible (e.g. the implementation of a new computer system or the design of a modified business process) to those considered as less tangible and soft (e.g. dealing with stakeholders and communications). Soft factors are associated with many areas that project managers are used to dealing with. Projects will often have communications plans, stakeholder management activities and so on. However, there are limits to what a project can achieve. There is a broad continuum of other factors which help or contribute to change success such as psychology (Lawson and Price, 2003) and change readiness derived from the culture of the organization (Jones et al., 2005). These items take time to develop. Issues such as culture, policies and styles of human resource management cannot simply be achieved in projects and delivered like any other deliverable. It is questionable therefore how much projects can contribute to cultural change, as these are not pre-plannable events of a fixed duration.

Combining project and change management

Project managers often imply that project management is change management, as all projects are about making change happen. Strategy specialists emphasize repeatedly that the best strategy in the world is not worth anything unless it can be implemented – often without mentioning either project or change management. Change management practitioners talk a different, but overlapping language, about the need for executive sponsorship, communications and management of resistance. New methodologies arise all the time, like Six-Sigma, bringing new ideas and enhanced capabilities to deliver change. Each of the advocates use related terminology, or worse, the same terminology in slightly different ways.

The project management community is gradually adopting much of the language and approach of change management. The traditional paradigm of projects, where efficiency and control are of paramount importance, and goals are predetermined, uncontested and not expected to change, is moving. Pollack identifies this as the soft paradigm of project management. In the soft paradigm the role of the project manager is more of a facilitator and more focussed on human relationships. Goals are not clear at the start of the work and are not stable. There is an acceptance of uncertainty and a willingness to be flexible with planning. There is also a degree of continuous definition (Pollack, 2007). Pollack then indicates that the tools and techniques of project management may need adaptation and enhancement for this new world. Some of these new techniques are, in reality, the existing techniques of change management.

What is relevant is being able to drive and deliver projects and change, and the application of the most appropriate tools for the right situation. The balance between change and project management is dependent on the specific context. One way to look at this is where the project is on a spectrum from "hard" or "soft". Crawford and Pollack (2004) propose seven dimensions to ascertain the relative hardness/softness of a specific project. (Even these are framed in language that is derived from the world of projects.)

1. *Goal/objective clarity*: are the goals clear or are they ambiguous?
2. *Goal/objective tangibility*: is the output a physical artefact or is it an abstract concept?

3. *The kinds of success measures*: is success to be quantitatively measured or qualitatively?
4. *Project permeability*: how vulnerable is the project to risk outside of the project's control?
5. *Number of solution options*: is there a single solution or are there many alternatives?
6. *Roles*: are the project team experts with no stakeholder participation or are they facilitative practitioners with high stakeholder involvement?
7. *Stakeholder expectations and values*: do the stakeholders value technical performance and efficiency managed by monitoring and control, or do they value relationships, culture and meaning to be managed by negotiation and discussion?

The nascent field of *complex project management* specifically, although somewhat controversially, attempts to bring together some new and some existing ideas from change management into a methodology for dealing with complex projects.

Some situations, such as dealing with small continuous change or understanding how an individual or group will respond to change, are completely suited to the domain of change management. Some other situations, such as the delivery of a tangible product such as the refitting of an office complex, are completely suited to the domain of projects. The truth is that in some situations project management is primary and change management may be secondary or even trivial enough to not exist as a formal discipline. In some other situations the reverse is true. However, many endeavours benefit from the application of both project and change management. The choice of what tools, methods or techniques to apply to deliver a project is something project managers should decide early on in a project's lifecycle, although it can be adapted throughout a project. (This is known as the *project management strategy*.)

Both project management and change management are about delivering value in organizations, and both have a role to play. In the end, the boundaries and relationship between project and change management is an issue of definition. Where the definitions are not universally agreed, and where both subjects are evolving and modifying with time, it is not possible to identify an absolute boundary – and it may not be productive to try to do so.

Case Study 9.2   DELIVERING EFFECTIVE OUTCOMES

In this case study Peter Evans discusses change management. Peter is an experienced change and operational manager. He has in-depth expertise of change management and of a range of methods including Six-Sigma and Lean. Peter has a successful track record in delivering business performance improvements. He has trained, and acts as a coach and advisor to, many Six-Sigma Black Belts and Master Black Belts.

Peter has worked for a variety of organizations including GE, Vodafone, Energis and Virgin Media.

Peter Evans

There is a significant difference between implementing something that sustains versus just completing a project. I have seen companies implement very expensive and complex IT systems that were simply turned off just after being built because they were developed in an IT and project management bubble without the involvement of the end-users of the systems. On the other hand, I have seen process changes that were completely successful, even though they were counter-cultural and challenged the norms and unspoken rules of a business.

The big lesson for me is that there are two aspects of delivering an effective outcome. The first is the quality of the end product from the project. The second is the level of acceptance for this product. When I worked at GE we had an equation that summarized this: effectiveness = quality × acceptance.

Assuming a well-run project can deliver a quality product, the challenge, from a change management perspective, is in ensuring acceptance for that product and the change it will entail. There are two fundamental aspects of achieving acceptance. First, acceptance requires spending time and effort in working with the stakeholder community. Second, acceptance of change needs a high level of leadership from a senior executive. The level of the leadership should be determined by the scale, scope, impact and enormity of the change. Titular sponsorship is no help and in fact can hinder if the organization doesn't feel the heat of the support given.

There needs to be an understanding of stakeholder needs and views, the levels of operational readiness for change, and what the existing rules of work are. Often, assumptions about the current ways of work and unspoken rules of operation have to be exposed, and broken – I call this assumption busting. Assumptions limit change; freeing an organization from assumptions is very powerful.

Assumption busting is best done in a workshop with a group of people. The workshop sets out to identify what the base assumptions in a business are. Once assumptions are identified they need to be analysed and explored to understand why they exist. Typically, I then ask a series of questions. These can start with simple questions like "is that assumption true?" If the answer is "no" then it is already broken, if the answer is "yes" I go onto more detailed questions, such as "can it be made untrue?" or "can we change the basis on which it is made?" By going through a series of questions you will find that many assumptions can be removed.

I have seen assumption busting make radical changes possible. When I worked in the aircraft leasing business one of the key performance indicators was AOG – Aircraft on Ground. Whenever aircrafts are on the ground they are not making money and it is essential to minimize AOG to maximize profitability. One of the key periods of AOG was when an aircraft leased to one airline was moved to be leased to a different airline. Various works are required on an airplane in going from one airline to another. This resulted in an AOG of over 30 days in some instances. Many of the reasons it took this long were inbuilt rules in the business. A classic example was the assumption that preparation for handover to another airline could not be done when the airplane was still being leased by another. Actually some work could start for preparing the airplane for the new airline even when it was in active service with the previous airline. By challenging assumptions like this we were able to find a way to reduce AOG to one or two days.

The essential part of understanding the level of support for the project and maintaining sponsorship is stakeholder management. All project managers know about stakeholder management. Unfortunately a lot of people on projects do stakeholder management at the beginning of the project, and then they forget about it for the rest of the project. Successful project and programme managers keep stakeholder assessments and stakeholder management actions alive throughout the project. They talk about stakeholders at every project meeting. They have a communications plan that is constantly evolving and delivering the right communications to support stakeholder management.

Really good project and programme managers are politically astute, and actively manage stakeholders. I have seen many project managers lose control of projects, or get into difficulty, because they have not managed stakeholders well. Project managers may think they have got agreement from stakeholders, but once they have it they assume it is there for the whole project. Agreement can easily evaporate if it is not constantly tested and renewed. This can be more of a problem in some industries and businesses than others – some industries are very political and project managers need to be aware of this.

Anyone running a major programme either needs to have a professional change manager working in the programme team or has to take responsibility for change management personally. When programme managers take responsibility for change management they need to be willing to spend a significant proportion of their time on change management. There are several great change models available, and programme managers should make sure they have an awareness of them and deep understanding of how to drive change. When I train Six-Sigma black belts or master black belts I spend at least one-third of the time training them on the human aspects of change. When I coach master black belts and project leaders I spend as much time focussed on what they are doing about human change, as on the technical and methodological aspects of their projects.

MAIN LEARNING POINTS FROM CHAPTER 9

- Implementation is the time at which a project moves from the relatively controlled and bounded environment of the project team to the dynamic environment of an operational organization. Implementation is often the highest-risk phase of a project. Many projects have failed due to poor implementation and project managers' over-focus on deliverable creation rather than on the sustained change successful implementation requires.

- Effective implementation starts with good planning. Although implementation should be planned in the core project plan, as implementation approaches it is usually necessary to plan in more detail. However, human nature and response to change is such that no implementation plan will precisely represent what happens in reality.

- A key component of implementation planning is operational readiness, ensuring that the operational departments are prepared for the change that implementing a project entails.

- Deliverables should be tested prior to implementation to ensure they are of sufficient quality to be accepted by operations. Testing is a non-trivial activity that requires sufficient time to complete adequately.
- Following testing deliverables can be implemented and then handed over to operations. Implementation requires flexible and responsive project management as many unforeseen events may occur due to the huge variety of human responses to change and the complexity of a business's infrastructure which will be altered by the project.
- Implementation may occur in one or several phases. The phasing should be determined by considering the risks in implementation.
- Once implemented deliverables are handed over to operations and the project's responsibility for the deliverables is finished. A project closure should be undertaken following handover to tie up any loose ends, and to formalize the learning from the experience of the project.
- At a portfolio level implementation should be analysed in terms of cumulative change as a result of an organization's projects relative to its ability to handle change.
- Successful implementation makes use of change management as well as project management. There are many perspectives on the meaning of change and the best tools to handle it. The most productive approach for project managers is to accept change management as a broader discipline than project management and to apply appropriate change tools.
- Whereas project management is primarily involved with the creation and quality of deliverables and finishing a project successfully, change management is concerned with delivering sustained change.
- Common success factors in change include explicit sponsorship and leadership for the change, regular communications, building acceptance for the change, and consistency of senior management behaviour and performance management systems with the goals of the change.

REVIEW QUESTIONS AND EXERCISES

1. Imagine that you are responsible for a project to manage a major event. Write a description of the event. Create the work breakdown structure for the project's implementation plan.
2. Develop a checklist to give to project managers to prepare for project implementation. What are the advantages and disadvantages of having such a checklist?
3. Why do projects fail in implementation? Create a list of the top ten reasons you think organizations fail in implementation. Write a description of each reason and what can be done to overcome it.
4. How important is context in determining an approach to implementation?
5. Consider an organization you are familiar with. What is its capacity for change? What events in a normal business year impact either its capacity for change or willingness to change? Is the willingness to change consistent across the organization? Where does it vary and why?
6. Which is a more useful discipline – project management or change management? Justify your viewpoint.
7. Do you think it is more helpful to train project managers in change management, or those responsible for change in project management? Why?

Suggested reading

There are many books on change management, and they vary from serious academic studies through to simple "how-to" type manuals. Their scope includes everything from personal and individual change through to organizational change. The first book listed here is a university-level textbook; the second is a widely recognized and accessible volume suggesting one specific approach to change based on research:

- *The Theory and Practice of Change Management.* John Hayes, 2nd Edition, Palgrave MacMillan, 2007
- *Leading Change.* John P Kotter. Harvard Business School Press, 1996

Bibliography

APM (Association for Project Management). *APM Body of Knowledge*, 5th Edition, 2006.

Balogun, J. "Managing change: Steering a course between intended strategies and unintended outcomes". *Long Range Planning.* Volume 39, Issue 1, February 2006, pp. 29–49.

Brown, T. and Gill, M. "Charting new horizons with initiative review". *Harvard Business School Balanced Scorecard Report.* September–October 2006.

Bruch, H., Gerber, P. and Maier, V. "Strategic change decisions: Doing the right change right". *Journal of Change Management.* Volume 5, Issue 1, March 2005, pp. 97–107.

Buchanan, D., Fitzgerald, L., Ketley, D., Gollop, R., Jones, J., Lamont, S., Neath, A. and Whitby, E. "No going back: A review of the literature on sustaining organizational change". *International Journal of Management Reviews.* Volume 7, Issue 3, September 2005, pp. 189–205.

Burnes, B. "Kurt Lewin and the planned approach to change: A re-appraisal". *Journal of Management Studies.* Volume 41, Issue 4, September 2004, pp. 977–1002.

By, R. "Organisational change management: A critical review". *Journal of Change Management.* Volume 5, Issue 4, December 2005, pp. 369–80.

Cardinal, J. and Marle, F. "Project: The just necessary structure to reach your goals". *International Journal of Project Management.* Volume 24, Issue 3, April 2006, pp. 226–33.

Crawford, L. and Pollack, J. "Hard and soft projects: A framework for analysis". *International Journal of Project Management.* Volume 22, Issue 8, November 2004, pp. 645–53.

Hammer, M. "Reengineering work: Don't automate, obliterate". *Harvard Business Review*, July–August 1990, pp. 104–12.

Hayes, J. *The Theory and Practice of Change Management.* 2nd Edition. Palgrave Macmillan, 2007.

Hope Hailey, V. and Balogun, J. "Devising context sensitive approaches to change: The example of Glaxo Wellcome". *Long Range Planning.* Volume 35, Issue 2, April 2002, pp. 153–78.

Jones, R., Jimmieson, N. and Griffiths, A. "The impact of organizational culture and reshaping capabilities on change implementation success: The mediating role of readiness for change". *Journal of Management Studies.* Volume 42, Issue 2, March 2005, pp. 361–86.

Kotter, KP. *Leading Change.* Harvard Business School Press, 1996.

Lawrence, T., Dyck, B., Maitlis, S. and Mauws, M. "The underlying structure of continuous change". *MIT Sloan Management Review.* Volume 47, Issue 4, Summer 2006, pp. 59–66.

Lawson, E. and Price, C. "The psychology of change management". *McKinsey Quarterly, 2003 Special Edition: the Value in organization*, pp. 31–41.

Lewin, K. "Frontiers in group dynamics". *Field Theory in Social Science*, Edited by Cartwright D, Social Science Paperbacks, 1947.

Leybourne, S. and Sadler-Smith, E. "The role of intuition and improvisation in project management". *International Journal of Project Management.* Volume 24, Issue 6, August 2006, pp. 483–92.

Pollack, J. "The changing paradigms of project management". *International Journal of Project Management.* Volume 25, Issue 3, April 2007, pp. 266–74.

Roberto, M. and Levesque, L. "The art of making change initiatives stick". *MIT Sloan Management Review.* Volume 46, Issue 4, Summer 2005, pp. 53–60.

Senge, P. *The Fifth Discipline: The Art & Practice of the Learning Organization*, Transworld, 1990.

Sirkin, H., Keenan, P. and Jackson, A. "The hard side of change management". *Harvard Business Review*, October 2005.

The Economist. "Special report: Software testing". *The Economist*, November 27, 2004.

10
achieving
benefits
from projects

Often there is a wide range of views on whether a project or programme has been successful. These views reflect the perspectives of different stakeholders. Usually their judgements are based on one or more of three factors: the success in creating the specified deliverables within the constraints of the project; the experience of implementation; and what the deliverables are like to use once the project has completed. These are all valid considerations, but arguably the most important measure of success for a business overall is the value it obtained from the project. This value is normally known as *benefits*.

Benefits are the gains made from an investment in a project or programme. The gains may be specified in financial terms, can be defined in terms of other quantifiable factors like increase in customer satisfaction ratings, or may be described as less tangible factors such as achievement of a strategic goal or an improvement in a relationship. Often the benefits of a project are a combination of all of these. Hence, a project could provide a business with increased revenues, decreased customer complaints and better relationship with a business partner.

Project managers use the terms *benefits realization* and *benefits management*, which are essentially synonymous, when talking about the processes for achieving and measuring benefits. Both terms refer to the process that runs from the initial identification of benefits through to the achievement of value. The terms are used interchangeably in this chapter.

At the start of a project a business case is developed which describes the benefits that will arise from the project. Once the project has implemented a change, benefits should start to be realized. For some projects benefits only start to be realized when the whole project is complete; in other situations changes are made

275

to business throughout the life of the project and benefits are realized whilst the project progresses. Large programmes with several phases of implementation will deliver waves of benefits.

Projects have a bad reputation of regularly not delivering benefits, or at least not delivering the benefits as expected or promised. Unfortunately, this reputation is often deserved. At a portfolio level the problem is exacerbated. Many businesses find themselves in the situation where the total theoretical benefits, from the business cases of all approved projects, massively exceed the actual benefits achieved. The simple questions "what did we get from our investment in projects" or "was it worthwhile" remain unanswered and often unanswerable. This is unacceptable for most businesses.

It might be thought that, given this poor reputation, project managers are keen to focus on benefits management. Some practitioners are, but there is often an absence of understanding and application of benefits management. Go into a bookshop with a wide section of books on projects and project management. When you scan the contents and index pages you will find that many books have no information on benefits, or only a cursory paragraph or two. This may be because benefits management is seen as something broader than project management, and therefore not the concern of project managers.

Programme managers on the other hand are often responsible for benefits, and more aware of them. It is also true that programme management approaches such as MSP (Managing successful programmes) place considerably more focus on benefits (OGC, 2007). However, whilst the methodology may exist, even programmes have a questionable reputation for regularly delivering value. In truth, the lack of focus on benefits often extends wider than the project and programme management community. Business leaders regularly start and complete projects without any real understanding of the benefits.

Regrettably, benefits management is not just a great idea that has not been properly applied. Even in organizations which are keen advocates of benefits management, success is not always achieved. The great idea of tracking benefits is harder in practice than might be realized on initial reflection. But with vigilance and perseverance it is possible. There are organizations which have successfully implemented a benefits management process, and regularly deliver value-adding projects.

Benefits realization is a core issue for all managers involved in projects: sponsors or the customers. This chapter introduces the theory of benefits management and describes many of the problems and pitfalls in its implementation. The role of benefits management is typically different within a project from what it is within a programme, so in this chapter both programmes and projects are discussed.

Benefits management in projects

Benefits arise in projects following the implementation of a change. The change is enabled by the creation of projects' deliverables. This is summarized in Diagram 10.1. The deliverables created by a project have many formats. They may be tangible deliverables such as an IT system or a new office block. They can be less tangible, such as delivering an improved capability to a business through training or cultural change. Whatever the benefits are, the fundamental rationale for the project investment is not the creation of deliverables, nor is it achieving a business change; it is

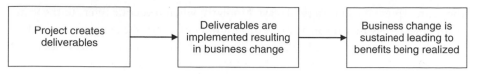

| Project creates deliverables | → | Deliverables are implemented resulting in business change | → | Business change is sustained leading to benefits being realized |

Diagram 10.1 Achieving business benefits in projects

the increase in the value of the business. Benefits management is an approach to achieving benefits as well as measuring them.

Some may argue that measuring benefits is unnecessary as it is measuring what would happen anyway. It is important for three reasons:

1. If benefits are not measured after project completion they have a tendency to evaporate. Measurement encourages the desired behaviours. Many organizations have implemented projects with strong business cases, but not measured the benefits. They find that some time after project completion no metrics in the business actually improve: the expected cost reductions have not resulted in anyone's budgets reducing; the planned gains in efficiencies are not seen in performance metrics; and the identified headcount reductions are not reflected in the actual headcount. The probable reason is that managers are under continuous budget pressure; if benefits are not tracked they are not likely to voluntarily cut their budgets or increase performance targets as a result of projects.

2. It enables rewards in recognition of achievements. Rewarding project achievement is an important part of motivating staff to perform well on projects.

3. It supports learning and improvement. If benefits are not tracked then it is impossible to be certain whether a project achieved what it set out to achieve. The ability to improve project performance needs a way of assessing if projects accomplished what they set out to accomplish. Measuring benefits contributes to this.

Benefits measurement is often required because business rules require the measurement of the returns from any investments.

This section describes the method for benefits management. First, there is a brief discussion on the use of the word *benefits* and *value* in project management. Second, this section describes the traditional approach to benefits management, which is used commonly in business. It then describes the problems with this approach and proposes an enhanced approach.

Terminology – benefits and value

The most common way to describe the outcome from a business investment is in terms of the *value* it achieves. When using the term *value* or *benefit* it is worth being precise as to the meaning in the specific context. The project management community, as well as the general business community, tends to use the term *value* in a vague way, although it has a precise and specific meaning. Value is often used in a similar way to the word *quality*. *Quality* has a formal definition, but is used in different and indistinct ways. When someone talks about the quality of an object they can express it in a variety of ways. Similarly, when someone refers to the value of an object, they may mean any one of a number of interpretations of the word.

The word *value* is used as both a noun and a verb. The deliverables from a project can be valued (verb), and they can have a value (noun). Value is used in a specific sense as in "the project will deliver a value of £100K", or in a more general sense as in "the project will create value".

In terms of benefits management, the word value is normally replaced by *benefits*, where benefits are the gains from a project. Although *value* and *benefit* can be used as synonyms they tend to be used in slightly different ways. Value tends to be associated with a general concept of gains from a project, whilst benefits are seen as explicitly identified and defined gains. The term value can be confusing as it is used in several different ways in project management.

Other phrases which often enter discussion when talking about benefits and the value from a project are *Value Management*, and *Value Engineering*. Value Management is a way of managing aimed at maximizing the overall performance of an organization in terms of the value it achieves. The ideas of value management have influenced the development of approaches to benefits management. Value management starts by defining what value means in a specific context to an organization and a project. It then seeks to ensure measures are in place and to have alignment between the project objectives and the value desired. It also seeks to maximize the outcomes from a project.

Value Engineering is a method used to improve the value of deliverables by examining the function of them and the cost to produce them. Value in Value Engineering has a specific meaning and is defined as the ratio of function to cost. Value can be increased by either improving the function or reducing the cost. Value Engineering may be used on projects in terms of improving the design of deliverables. It is related to some projects, but in itself is not a part of project management anymore than a software development approach is a part of project management.

A useful project management technique is *Earned Value Analysis* or *EVA*. In EVA, the word *value* refers to something different from the same term used in Benefits Management, Value Management or Value Engineering. In EVA, value is a measure of how complete a project is. If a project has completed 50% of the work required, it has earned 50% of the expected value. It is easy to argue that the project has actually earned 0% of the expected value until implementation has resulted in business change and the realization of benefits. This is an argument of semantics and the application of a word in a context. Earned value is a useful tool in measuring project progress, but it has little to do with assessing the benefits from a project (earned value is described in Chapter 8). It is perfectly acceptable to use the term value in the way it is used in EVA, but it should not be confused with the real *value* or *benefits* delivered from a project.

For all of these reasons, this chapter refers to benefits rather than value.

A helpful piece of terminology is *benefits stream*. Benefits can occur from a project at one point in time when the project completes or can be achieved over time. For instance, the benefits from a new piece of machinery in a factory are realized over the life of the machine. The benefits over time are called a *benefits stream*. A benefits stream could be an amount that varies across time such as £50K in the first quarter, £100K in the second quarter, £250K in the third quarter and

£500K in the fourth quarter. The cumulative benefit from these four quarters is £900K (i.e. £50K + £100K + £250K + £500K). Usually in business, it is important to understand the rate of benefits as well as the cumulative amount achieved. The term benefits stream is used to indicate the rate of benefits achieved over time.

The traditional approach to benefits management

Many projects have been executed without any consideration of benefits, but this is increasingly unusual. Most businesses have approval processes for investments like projects, which require some consideration of the benefits that will be achieved from a project. In addition, accountabilities are usually allocated for achieving or realizing benefits once the project is complete.

A common approach to benefits management can be understood by describing the life of a project in five steps, as shown in Diagram 10.2.

The process starts when an idea is generated, which one or more people sponsor as something the business should do. Doing the project requires investment. Investment needs approval. Hence, moving forward with the project is subject to the investment approval processes.

The investment approval process requires someone to formally answer the questions why the project should be undertaken and what benefits will be gained from investing in the project. These benefits are specified in a *business case*. A business case is usually a standard format document used for investment appraisals.

The business case contains the costs and benefits from the project. The costs are a function of the resources required to deliver the project, and where appropriate, to operate the deliverables following implementation. Costs should account for the *opportunity costs* of a project investment, that is, what else could be done with the same money. Financial calculations such as NPV take account of opportunity costs by applying a suitable discount rate.

Costs should consider the relative cost as well as any absolute project costs. For example, a project may cost £20m and provide a benefit of £20m. Without any other reason for the investment, such a project would normally be rejected. However, if there are existing costs for not performing the project, for instance, the costs associated with current methods of operation or maintaining current capabilities, these must also be accounted for. If a project costs £20m, delivers a benefit of £20m and removes existing maintenance costs of £15m, then it has a strong business case.

The benefits can be a variety of gains expected to be made by the project. They may be tangible and quantifiable, or they may be intangible but describable (e.g. strategic alignment or better management information). There is a tendency to favour financial benefits as they ease comparisons between different business cases.

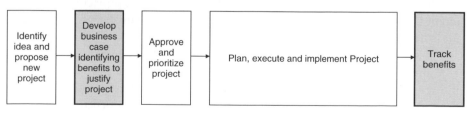

Diagram 10.2 A traditional approach to benefits management

If a positive business case can be constructed then the proposed project is put forward for approval and prioritization as part of the portfolio management process. A successful project is prioritized, and when the appropriate time comes it is initiated. The fourth step is the stage of project management, when the project is planned, executed, implemented and finished. Following project completion the final and fifth step occurs, when the benefits are realized and tracked. *Benefits tracking* is not simply a matter of benefits happening, but of tracking and measuring them over time explicitly. Typically, benefits tracking takes place after project completion.

Of the five steps in Diagram 10.2 there are two steps directly related to benefits management, shown with bold lines and shaded in grey. There is an initial phase, which is about identifying benefits to justify an investment, and a final phase which is about measuring achievement. In between these two phases, from the point of project acceptance to the finalization of delivery benefits, management is largely in abeyance and is not an active endeavour.

This simple and straightforward approach is easy to understand and is applied in many businesses. It is a significant improvement on having no benefits management. However, it suffers from a number of problems which are discussed next.

The problems of benefits management

Benefits management faces a number of problems which must be overcome if it is to provide a reliable mechanism for achieving business benefits. By understanding these problems managers can be aware of them and are more likely to overcome them.

There are four sources of problems with benefits management:

o The nature of benefits themselves
o The origins of projects
o Issues inherent in projects and project management
o Issues arising from the behaviour of sponsors or other managers

Let us look at all of these.

It is easy to understand the theory of benefits management. Identifying and measuring benefits is a simple concept, but in practice benefits can be elusive to identify, difficult to describe and even harder to measure. Having a common-sense feeling that undertaking a project, such as improving office facilities, will result in greater staff satisfaction is simple. Defining what the increase in staff satisfaction will be and how this will result in lower levels of staff turnover or greater productivity is significantly harder. Where benefits are identified and where assumptions are made to estimate them, the benefits are subject to risk of error. Estimating how much a metric such as staff satisfaction will improve from a project is quite a different challenge from actually being able to measure it. Many benefits are hard to measure.

For some types of benefits no way of measuring its attainment exists within a business. Although measures can be put in place as part of a project's delivery, if there is no history of data then it is not possible to understand what marginal improvement a project has brought about. Showing a level of customer satisfaction following a project to improve customer services is meaningless, unless this can be compared to the level of customer satisfaction prior to the project being implemented. Methods like Six-Sigma perform measurement as one of the first tasks in any change activity.

Other problems associated with measuring benefits relate to issues such as the risk of double counting and the inability to track which actions in a business actually resulted in what improvement. An individual project may credibly claim that it will decrease a metric such as level of customer churn by 10%, but this becomes non-credible when several projects claim the same. When the results from multiple projects are accumulated it can indicate that they will result in unbelievable or impossible results such as positive customer churn.

Projects are not the only source of improvements, as operational managers are constantly tinkering with and improving processes, procedures and management approaches. Ever since the spread of the total quality management approach, there has been a trend for managers to try to continuously improve performance as part of their usual work. A project may start out with a target to improve efficiency by 10%. At the end of the project efficiency may have increased by 10%, but it is very difficult to prove whether this was the result of the project or the result of the activities of business-as-usual operational change.

In the desire to justify a project a group of stakeholders can bundle any variety of benefits to ensure the project gains approval. If the type of benefits associated with a project are not relevant or important to business then this is not helpful. Claiming cost reduction benefits in a business in a rapid expansion phase and which has no cost pressure is generally not worthwhile. Similarly, claiming benefits associated with staff or customer satisfaction in a business that is under severe cost pressures and fighting for its survival is not always useful.

Even if benefits are relevant and tangible, it does not mean that their realization is easy. For instance, consider a project which results in a budget reduction owing to efficiencies gained from the implementation of a new IT system. It is quite easy for the finance director to check whether, when the project completes, the budget has been reduced in line with the business case. From an operational manager's viewpoint it is also easy to determine whether the IT system has been implemented, but to be sure that it has delivered the efficiency gains, and therefore be willing to reduce the budget, is much harder.

Problems with benefits can also develop depending on who originates projects. Often project concepts arise not from some need in a business, but from the existence of a solution. The "solution in search of a problem" is common in areas like IT where promises of wonderful new technology can excite the IT specialists. There is no reason why a department, like IT, should not invest time in innovative thinking and suggest ideas to the business for improvements. However, if the idea is taken forward into a project there needs to be a real business commitment to the project and to achieving the associated benefits. Without it projects can commence, which no operational manager has any intention of delivering benefits from. The focus may be primarily on the technology, less on the associated change, and not at all on the benefits.

An associated problem is the allocation of benefits to line managers' budgets without their involvement and understanding. A project may be justified based on some savings, and when the project is complete the savings are realized from

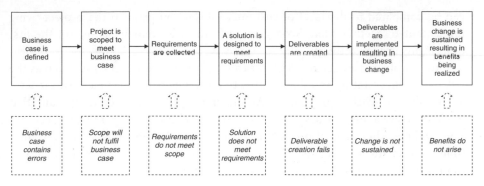

Diagram 10.3 *Risks to benefits across project lifecycle*

various budgets. Unless the budget holders have agreed to this up-front when the project started, this can cause many problems. Insufficient involvement of accountable managers in the design of projects and allocation of responsibility for achieving benefits results in greater resistance to change and reluctance to deliver expected benefits. If managers are insufficiently involved in the project business case development they will tend to resist delivery of benefits.

Some features of projects can also impact benefits. The most obvious one is the inherent risk in projects. When projects are planned, they are usually based on some assumptions and unknowns. This, means that just because a project is planned to deliver benefits, it will not necessarily do so. The impact of project risks occurring often results in underachievement of benefits. There is a huge variety of possible risks in any one project, and they affect every stage of a project. Diagram 10.3 maps some high-level risks onto the steps in a project which, if realized, will reduce or remove benefits.

Projects take time to complete and are subject to change. Every time a change is implemented on a project it not only has a potential to alter the cost or timescale, but it may also modify the level of benefits achievable by the project or the timing of the benefits. If benefits management is only done as part of business case development and once the project is complete, it is quite likely, given the rate of change on projects, that the benefits afterwards will not match the business case.

The change in expected benefits as a project or the needs of a business change should result in projects being reviewed and if necessary stopped. For a number of reasons many managers are frequently unwilling to stop or kill live projects which no longer have strong business cases.

Even if benefits actually stay the same, expectations of benefits can change. Projects that are perceived to be successful can be subject to *benefits inflation*, when stakeholders' expectations are not maintained in line with reality, and they expect more benefits even if there is no real reason to. Although on completion such a project may deliver exactly what was originally expected, it can be perceived as a failure – and may cause problems if business commitments have been made based on the inflated benefits expectations.

The behaviour of the project team whilst working on a project can also impact benefits. The project team may become involved in the development of a business case to justify a project. But once the business case is approved there is a tendency to focus on the details of the project – such as the time and cost and completing deliverables – and to forget the benefits. Once the project team have completed their work, tracking of benefits is usually not their responsibility, as they will be off onto their next project.

It is not only the behaviour of the project manager and team that affects benefits, but also the behaviour of the project sponsor and other managers with an interest in the project can affect the project. One of the issues is that a manager with a strong desire to implement a project can be biased in terms of development of a business case. Benefits are searched for as an excuse for the project rather than as a basis for sensible business decisions, with the attitude of *I want this project – now find the benefits.* Because there may be no single compelling reason for a project, a vast range of small incremental benefits are identified – which will make the benefits tracking process unnecessarily cumbersome. A 0.1% change in some metrics may be impossible to measure, though it is possible to assign a theoretical value in order to gain approval. By assigning theoretical values to a large number of small changes the cumulative benefits from a project may be sufficient to overcome any investment hurdles, yet in practice many benefits will never be realized.

The business case should be an objective comparison for different investments, but it is often biased or abused. Managers may overpromise benefits to ensure a project is started. Overpromising is a particular problem with long-term investments which may outlive a specific manager's time in a role. This is compounded if new managers are appointed during the life of the project, as they may well be less committed to achieving the goals of a project and may not accept ownership of the business case. Also managers may be less fastidious about the accuracy of benefits in businesses where there is no culture of benefits tracking.

Projects may be spuriously labelled with all sorts of intangible benefits. The most notorious of these are *strategic projects.* Having a strategic label sometimes means that the projects do not have to overcome the same financial hurdles as other projects. Surprisingly, it sometimes works, and projects with very poor business cases are approved because of their alignment with some vague aspect of business strategy. This is unfortunate, as on other occasions projects which are truly strategic will achieve greater alignment between a business and its intended strategy, even without significant quantifiable benefits. The overapplication of the term "strategic" results in poorly performing projects and staff cynicism. Any project seeking approval based on the achievement of strategic goals but limited measurable benefits should be subject to scrutiny before approval.

A final fact is that many managers actually do not like the whole process of business cases and committing to benefits and will try to avoid it. Some managers dislike total or detailed transparency, as it removes their freedom to act and ties them down (Carroll, 2006). The willingness to track benefits can be limited both because it can be difficult and time-consuming and because it can make managers' lives hard at a future date.

An enhanced approach for benefits management in projects

With an understanding of all the possible problems of benefits management it is easy to despair and place benefits management in the category of "too hard to make work". Benefits management can be made to work, and many organizations have practical and robust benefits tracking processes. The likelihood of successful benefits management can be increased by four factors.

First, it is possible to design and implement an enhanced approach to benefits management that will overcome many of the issues noted above. Second, awareness of the problems and applying greater management vigilance to activities such as business case development will overcome some problems. Third, a management culture which values benefits and treats benefits realization as an important part of all projects can be developed. All too often benefits management and business cases are considered merely as painful administrative activities that have to be beaten or manipulated to needs. Benefits management is assisted in companies in which personal commitments are treated seriously, and which have a culture of accountability and measurement. Fourth, projects should be designed with achievement of benefits in mind rather than as an afterthought.

This section deals with the first point – an enhanced process for benefits management. The other three are discussed in more detail later in this chapter. The enhanced process is summarized in Diagram 10.4.

The starting point for successful benefits management is to understand business objectives. Where a formalized strategy exists this should be the source of objectives. Benefits should not be pursued as a justification for a project, but because those benefits are related to a business's objectives. With an understanding of objectives it is normally possible to identify ideas or concepts which contribute towards meeting these objectives. The benefits to be delivered by a project should fit in with the business's strategy, for example, there is limited point in investing scarce resources in cost reduction in a business pushing for growth. It is not just about starting the projects with the maximum benefits; a business should select the projects which are most aligned to what the business wants to achieve.

Of course, there are some activities that have to be done irrespective of the business case. Investments such as fulfilling legal and regulatory commitments are an obligation that a business has little choice over (other than the option of choosing the timing and quality of implementation). Such activities should still be subject to benefits management even if it is not for approval and prioritization. A benefits management mindset will seek to maximize benefits from any project investment, even those that are mandatory.

Having identified a suitable project concept a business case must be developed. Business cases are built around the costs and benefits, and ideally are in a common format. A common format allows comparison with other projects, but also with other investments a business may make.

The business case should identify both the benefits and the ownership for them. Who will be accountable for achieving benefits once the project is complete,

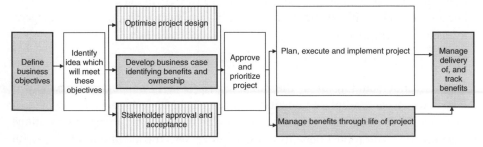

Diagram 10.4 Improved benefits management process

and in what form will these be achieved? For example, if a benefit is a headcount reduction, will this be achieved by a reduced headcount budget, or by a reduction in planned recruitment, or in an increase in output achieved by allocating the free heads to another task? What budget will these benefits be shown in? Each of these is a valid way to achieve a benefit, but it is important to know in what way a benefit will be specifically achieved – not only to ensure it happens, but also because there are implications of achieving a benefit in different ways. As an example, if a project enables costs to be cut by 10%, there is a difference between taking the money away by reducing budgets by 10%, or keeping the money in budgets, but expecting 10% more output to be achieved by those budget holders.

Benefits must be defined in terms of the timeframe for their delivery. The timeframe is critical and it underpins the ability to make business commitments. Managing expectations as to when benefits will be delivered as well as how much they will be is an important part of project management. For instance, in a company of 2500 staff there could be a project to increase efficiency by 2%. To perform the same amount of work will require 50 people less, or the company will be able to do extra work equivalent to recruiting an extra 50 people. At a predefined time after the end of the project either headcount should reduce to 2450, or output should increase to what would have been possible from 2550 staff. If neither of these occurs in the planned time, then the expected benefit has not been realized.

Like other parts of a project, benefits are subject to risk. At the start of a project there will be many unknowns which may result in increased or decreased benefits in reality. Benefits should be shown as a range taking account of risk. If a greater level of certainty is required before approving a project business case, a feasibility study can be used to explore and confirm potential benefit levels.

A business case cannot be created without regard to the nature of the project. During business case development the project concept should be optimized. Optimization is partially about benefits, but also more broadly about project strategy and project design. Project optimization aims to design the project most likely to achieve the objectives with a manageable level of risk. For example, should a project be split into separate components because it is too complex to manage, or because it delivers different types of benefits over quite different timescales? The project should be designed for whichever maximizes benefits.

In parallel with the development of a business case and the optimization of the project stakeholders should be engaged. Their approval for the project should be gained, and where appropriate, acceptance of the benefits ensured. The root of all benefits is someone somewhere in the business will be doing an activity in a different way from now. If nothing is done differently then there will be no benefits. It may be a new activity, or it may be an existing activity performed faster, cheaper or better. It is this change in activity that will generate benefits. A project can deliver the capability for this changed way of working – but it cannot make the change happen. The change can only happen if the people involved, and their line managers, make it happen. The time to gain manager and stakeholder acceptance of this responsibility to deliver benefits is as the project concept is forming, and not at some later date or when a project is complete. Having acceptance is a critical success factor in smooth change management once the project is complete. In addition, as many benefits will not be achieved until long after the project is complete the operational departments of a business have to accept this responsibility.

Involving stakeholders at this early stage creates the linkage between the project and the team or manager who is "benefiting" from it. It is possible to run a project, and at the end to force managers to deliver benefits such as reductions in headcounts or increases in performance. It is far better though to involve the benefits owner up-front and let them support the project optimization and business case development so that they fully support the benefits that have to be achieved. Where there is commitment to benefits there will be a significant reduction in resistance to change and increased commitment to the project. The project becomes a common aim. The reverse is also true! If there is no commitment it is questionable whether the project should be pursued.

Ideally the business case is actually developed by the stakeholders who will be responsible for achieving the benefits once the project is completed. The benefits owners, not the project team, should identify the benefits. Although the project team can support the administration and creation of the business case, it should not be seen as a document that they own or are responsible for achieving.

Once the business case is approved the project can be initiated following a normal project lifecycle.

As part of the project it may be necessary to put responsibilities, processes and systems in place for measuring the identified benefits. This can mean significant amounts of work, but it is often worthwhile. It is not always possible to measure a benefit the ideal way, either because a measure is not possible or it is too hard or expensive to collect. Measures have to be practical.

If measures did not exist prior to the project it may be necessary to collect data for a period prior to making a change, otherwise there is no baseline for the incremental improvement brought about by the project.

Benefits must be managed through the project's life. As project changes occur, or as the reality of project delivery affects either the scale or timing of benefits, the business case should be updated under change control. Business cases should be updated as project progresses the way the project plan is updated, and are subject to progressive elaboration.

Any changes to business case are key information for project reviews, and the resulting decisions to continue, amend or kill projects. Projects are often stopped because upon review they are found to be too late or too overspent to be worth continuing. It could be argued, however, that reviews should focus on whether adequate benefits will still be achieved. If not, the project should be stopped or re-designed. It should never be forgotten during project delivery that the project exists to deliver benefits.

Following project completion benefits should start to be realized. There must be human resources assigned with a responsibility for measuring the benefits. To ensure this does not become a major overhead, the tracking of benefits should ideally be combined into the normal management information systems, and performance management tracking.

The critical success factors for benefits management include

○ A realistic business case, with known and managed assumptions, and an understanding of the level of risk associated with it
○ Ownership for benefits realization, and a culture which holds people accountable for targets
○ Building benefits into budgets. This should not be a stick, but done with the agreement of project sponsors and customers, and must take account of risk levels associated with a project. If they are not willing to build targets into budgets the project should not be performed.
○ Managed expectations as the project progresses
○ A business case subject to review and change control as the project proceeds
○ Tracked benefits and risks

Designing projects for benefits

Benefits management is often presented as something that can be bolted on top of or wrapped around a project. It is usually defined as a more central part of programme management, but even so it could be removed from most methodologies without fundamentally changing the approach to delivering a programme. What is often missing from presentations of benefits management is the impact it has on the way a project is undertaken. Benefits management is not merely a method for justifying and measuring benefits; it is an approach and a mindset to maximizing benefits. The delivery of benefits should be considered not only as an outcome of projects, but as a fundamental aspect of project design and planning.

This section considers the implications of benefits management upon project strategy and the approach to a project. There is no universal checklist of factors to consider in optimizing project design, so the points listed here should be considered as indicative rather than exhaustive.

At the start of a project, the project manager has a range of choices to make. Typical questions include what is the project strategy, what project lifecycle should be used, how should the project be phased, and what is the appropriate balance between time, cost and quality? The selection of project approach and the choice of project strategy usually consider how best to create the expected deliverables. Different project lifecycles and the application of diverse methods and tools can be tailored to suit various types of deliverables.

However, the project's strategy should also take account of the needs to achieve benefits, and the characteristics of those benefits. Projects can deliberately be designed and planned to ease benefits realization. Conversely, if benefits management is only considered as an afterthought it is likely that benefits will not be optimized. Optimization of benefits has to take account of the timing of benefits, the levels of benefits possible, and the balance between different categories of benefits. Examples of such choices are

○ A choice between delivering some benefit quickly or delivering more benefit but at a slower pace
○ To spend more on a project to speed up delivery of benefits versus minimizing cost of a project but consequently slowing down achievement of benefits

o To focus a project on a limited set of deliverables, or to expand scope to deliver associated deliverables that can be developed by the same project team (e.g. whether to use a project to deliver a new IT system to a business, or to also use the project as an environment to improve IT skills by teaching staff a new development methodology).

The first issue to consider in developing a project plan is the timing of benefits. Early realization of benefits is often disproportionately valuable to a business. Partially this is because of the time value of money and the impact of discounting. One hundred pounds in two years time is less valuable than one hundred pounds today. The increased value of early benefits also relates to the relatively short time in any one role for a modern manager. A project which extends beyond a sponsor's tenure in a role is generally of less interest to him or her than one that delivers sooner. More fundamentally, in projects such as new product development, if the project is not completed in a rapid timescale the market opportunity is reduced or may even disappear. A potential benefits stream of £10m in incremental revenues may decrease to £5m or even zero depending on competitive response and the time of launch of a new product or service. The benefits of speed to market and first mover advantage for a new product are well-documented. In these types of situation, a faster project can deliver significantly greater benefits than a slower one.

The need to accelerate the creation of value from a project is often hampered by an unwillingness to increase the total cost or the rate of spending of money, or to manage cash-flow. However, when a full analysis of a project is undertaken it can sometimes be sensible to increase radically the pace of project spending to speed up completion and realization of benefits.

Another effect of the timing of projects upon benefits is where benefits must occur within a specific period, such as the current financial year. If benefits must be delivered in-year then late delivery of a project can have a disproportionate impact on the benefits achieved. For example, consider a project which will deliver £100K per month in savings owing to improved procurement facilitated by a review of all contracts. If the savings are delivered half way through the year, then the benefits will be gained for the remaining six months of the year. This gives a total in-year benefit of £600K (6 months × £100K per month). Now, assume the £600K benefit is the target set for the project sponsor, and the saving has been committed to shareholders. If the project is 2 months late and is completed at the end of month 8, only 4 months of the year remain to accrue benefits. A total in-year benefit of £400K will be achieved (4 months × £100K per month). In this situation the business has a choice: accept the £400K of benefits or try to deliver savings of £150K per month to try to reach the £600K target. Either way presents the project sponsor with a problem: either finishing the year £200K undertarget, or having to find another way to deliver that £200K of savings.

In general terms, the later the project delivery, the more difficult the achieving of in-year savings. Conversely, the earlier the project delivery, the easier the achieving of in-year benefits. Halving the amount of time left in a financial year to reap benefits means doubling the benefits run rate to achieve the same total benefits in-year. Whilst a delay of only a few weeks may have no impact on the total benefits achieved over time, it can make achieving an in-year target hard or even impossible. In some situations, such as where investors have set financial targets for a business, hitting in-year targets is critical.

As businesses grow in complexity, their project needs become more involved and implementation is increasingly complicated. This leads to increasing times-cales to deliver projects. Unfortunately, in many industries the strategic horizon is actually decreasing. Therefore whilst projects take longer, the ability to predict the projects required is becoming weaker. Many projects start with positive business cases, but deliver when they are no longer relevant. For instance, a business develops a new product, but during development the business strategy is revised to exit the market the product is to be sold in. This results in reduced benefits. Shortening strategic horizons encourages rapid delivery of benefits whilst they are still applicable to the business. Shortening strategic horizons disfavours the selection of complex and ambitious long-term programmes in favour of short-term rapid delivery of incremental benefits.

Planning for benefits realization should influence decisions about the phasing of projects. The need for benefits throughout the life of a project increases the attractiveness of phased implementation of deliverables, rather than a single "big-bang" delivery at the completion of a project. A project, or a programme of work, can be designed to deliver an entire set of fully functioning deliverables at the endeavour's completion. Alternatively, the same piece of work may be designed to deliver partial deliverables, which may not fulfil the entire requirements, but will at least fulfil some of them. In this way benefits can start to be accrued earlier. Let us take a simple example of a project which will take one year to complete. If it is phased as a single piece of work, no benefits are delivered until after one year. Alternatively if it can be phased to give partial deliverables every three months then benefits accrue much earlier – this is good for the business, and also enhances the attractiveness of the project's business case.

The phenomenon of scope creep can be particularly harmful for delivery of benefits, and approval of any change controls should consider the impact on the timing of benefits realization. Although by expanding the scope of a project it is possible that in the long term it will deliver a wider set of benefits to a business, in the short term scope expansion increases risk and tends to delay achievement of any benefit. Increased risk is unwelcome as it increases the chances that the project will fail. There is a tendency in live projects to focus on the functionality and form of deliverables over benefits. This tendency should be resisted.

A very different way of looking at a project is to consider the types of benefits it delivers. Different benefits types have different characteristics, which require different management approaches. It is good practice to try and avoid merging different benefits streams into single projects. A benefits stream such as cost reduction will often require a different approach in terms of managing the balance of time, cost and quality (the iron triangle) from a benefits stream related to profit maximization or increasing customer satisfaction. Of course, some endeavours naturally deliver multiple types of benefits, but before combining different parts of projects into a single endeavour it is worth reflecting whether they need a consistent style of management or not. Merging different project components into a single project can seem attractive as one vehicle then serves multiple goals. Before making such a choice the implications of the project for the management and any compromises between factors should be considered. A project manager will struggle with delivery of a project which on one hand requires minimization of cost as it is related to cost reduction, and yet on the other hand requires shortest time to market or highest levels of quality.

The potential to deliver benefits can be used to improve the likelihood of project success, by linking project team performance assessment and rewards to the achievement of benefits. By using project success measures to reward and increase the project team's motivation, the levels of project success can be significantly improved. Similarly, where third-party suppliers, sub-contractors or systems integrators are involved in a project, their payments can be linked to benefits delivery. However, this is dependent on reliable and mutually agreed measurement systems. Tying payments to performance, when there are not reliable and mutually agreed measurement systems, will lead to disputes.

Benefits realization is not only a result of project-led change, but has an impact on the likelihood of successfully sustained change. A project which will deliver benefits that are seen as favourable by the groups undergoing change is more likely to be positively supported. Conversely, benefits that are seen as negative or difficult to attain amongst some project stakeholder communities will create resistance to the project. Projects should be designed and managed to ease change.

To illustrate the above point, let us consider a situation in which a manager has been tasked with a 10% cost reduction. He or she is likely to be supportive of a project which will help to achieve this target. However, if the manager has no tasking, but a project's business case requires the manager to achieve a 10% cost reduction once the project is complete, he or she is likely to resist the project. The resistance comes about both because the 10% cost reduction may be hard for the manager to achieve and also because many managers lack confidence in a project's ability to deliver them the capability to make the cost reduction. Many managers have experienced the situation of having to deliver committed benefits even though a project has not fully delivered the enabling capability to them. Overcoming such resistance requires both alignment of project and operational manager's objectives, and providing the line manager with confidence that the project will actually provide the capability to reduce a budget by 10%.

Case Study 10.1 BENEFITS REALIZATION IN A POST-MERGER INTEGRATION

Two large listed organizations operating in the same sector were seen as obvious merger candidates for years. Due to a number of regulatory and financial issues a merger was not permitted for a long time. However, with some changes in the market it became possible, and one organization made a successful bid for the other. Following the purchase there was a major post-merger integration programme. In this case study, the Director of Integration discusses how benefits were managed in this post-merger integration programme.

We ran a very complex post-merger integration programme that touched every part of the business. Post-merger integration for us meant bringing the businesses together to work effectively as one organization, and to deliver significant synergy savings. The whole justification for the merger was based on the synergies we could achieve by combining the companies.

To gain commitment to the merger, the synergies were committed in advance to shareholders and to the banks that financed the deal. The synergy commitment was defined in terms of financial savings to be made in each of the next eight quarters following the merger. Both the scale and phasing of the synergies were critical. Tracking of benefits delivery was essential, not only for good management, but because they were important numbers that were externally reported and were subject to independent audit. Tracking benefits to the level that you are confident that they are robust enough to be audited by an external auditor is tough.

We started the programme by designing a target organizational structure, and putting in place the people who would run each department. They then had to review the current organizational structures and agree which parts of the two organizations would come into their new department. Departmental level plans which identified the steps needed to merge and the benefits that would be realized were developed. The departmental heads then had to commit to deliver them.

The departmental plans were consolidated by a central programme office into a single programme-level plan. All dependencies between the merger work in different departments were agreed. For example, one department might want to bring two teams to one location to merge them. This could mean that facilities management would have to gain office space big enough for the new merged team, but also would have some smaller offices to dispose of. There could also be a dependency on IT. The new combined team would require the appropriate IT systems, which could mean merging existing systems or choosing the systems from one firm over those used in the other. The dependencies were very complicated, and a delay in one part of the plan could easily spill over into other areas.

The plans were put into action. We tracked progress of the tasks in the plan and delivery of benefits. Benefits did not come all at the end, but were delivered through the project. We might release up some office space, or make some people redundant, and then the benefits had to be claimed.

Where changes or slippage occurred these had to be reported to the central programme office. Each area reporting a slippage would be tasked with finding other benefits to make up for the late delivery. If this was not possible then other departments or functions would be asked to make up the shortfall. Of course, this was never popular, and the social pressure between managers meant that everyone was reluctant to fail on their targets and thus force other managers to increase theirs. There was a level of contingency in the plans, so if we failed to deliver 100% of benefits, it did not mean we would necessarily fail in our external targets.

Total savings were important, but the actual commitments were to in-year savings. Hence, problems had to be resolved not only if benefits turned out to be smaller than expected, but also if they came later. Let me give you an example. Making a commitment to reduce costs at the start of the first quarter of the year would give four quarters of in-year benefits. If this was delayed to the end of the second quarter only two quarters of benefits would be delivered in the year. This would result in achieving only 50% of the

10

expected benefits in-year, even if the absolute value of benefits was the same. Late delivery always led to a shortfall in benefits. Generally, the later a benefit was delivered the larger it had to be to reach in-year targets. However, if anything was delivered earlier it increased overall benefits and made up for shortfalls elsewhere.

Delivery was linked totally to actual benefits and, where, appropriate to budget changes. If people were made redundant they had to be named. Names were checked against HR records, and the internal finance department had to show a commensurate reduction in budgets. Any benefits claim had to be signed off by the project manager delivering it, the operational owner of the budget affected, the internal finance manager, and, where relevant, HR. An external team would then confirm they had been delivered.

We did not have the knowledge to create such a robust benefits tracking system, and we made use of specialist consultants who were experts in both post-merger integration and benefits tracking.

We had many difficulties in the programme, but overall it was a success and we exceeded the externally committed synergy savings. We overdelivered against a set of very ambitious targets. The discipline the external consultants brought at first seemed like a nightmare, far too bureaucratic and completely over the top. In time it became the accepted practice and just seemed the natural thing to do. Although the programme finished over a year ago, we still use the same benefits tracking approaches as the discipline forces people to adhere to plans and makes everyone focus on benefits in every project.

Benefits management in relation to programmes and portfolios

This section overviews the impact of benefits on the design and management of multiple and larger endeavours, as performed in programme and portfolio management.

Programme management

Programme management is richer in approaches to benefits delivery than project management. Methods such as MSP (OGC, 2007) build benefits management in as a central pillar of delivery. Specific areas where programme management extends on project management and offers the ability for enhanced benefits management include

- The common management of projects which contribute to the same benefit or set of benefits
- The phasing of projects within a programme to optimize benefits
- The explicit allocation of responsibilities for benefits management

One of the common issues facing benefits management for projects is the situation in which multiple separate projects affect the same benefits stream. Different projects may each contribute to achieving some larger project or goal. The benefits from several projects may be greater than what any one can individually deliver. In terms of the creation of the deliverables the projects may be separate endeavours, and it may make no sense to merge them into a single project. However, they need a level of coordination and control to ensure they come together to deliver the overall benefits. This coordination and control is provided by structuring the projects into a programme with a single programme manager.

A good example is the merger of two companies. Mergers are often justified based on achieving synergies. Delivery of the synergies will require a number of different components of the business to be brought together and rationalized. For instance, the merger may require teams to be merged, IT systems to be integrated, business processes to be standardized and buildings to be combined and may offer the opportunity for a rationalization of supplier base. Although these are quite separate types of endeavours they can be inter-related – so bringing two teams together may require common IT systems and business processes, and may facilitate rationalization of office space. Removing some IT systems allows a supplier to be removed, and possibly renegotiation for better rates with other suppliers. Each activity is a separate project requiring different skills, but they should be coordinated as a programme of work to deal with the dependencies between projects and to manage the overall delivery of benefits.

Programme management offers the opportunity to bring the projects into a common management structure, where each of the projects is delivered under the umbrella of an overall programme. The benefits are associated with the programme and not the individual projects. This is particularly helpful where a programme requires diverse deliverables combined with a significant element of business change. Each project delivers a part of the overall capability for change; the programme delivers the change.

Where programmes are made up of multiple phases or projects the sequencing of activities should take account of benefits delivery and not simply creating deliverables. Such sequencing is shown in Diagram 10.5. The diagram represents

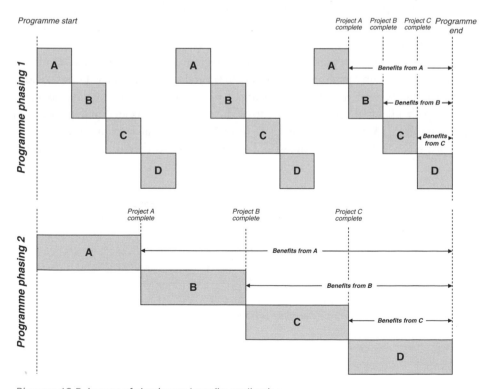

Diagram 10.5 *Impact of phasing on benefits realization*

a programme made up of four projects A, B, C and D. Let us assume there are resource constraints and only one project can be worked on at one time. The programme manager may decide that it is best to try and progress all of the projects at once. Due to resource constraints this results in swapping between projects as shown in the upper half of the diagram, labelled programme phasing 1.

Assuming that the speed of the programme is determined by the available resources the programme manager can phase the projects differently. The component projects can be delivered in sequence as shown in the lower half of the diagram, labelled programme phasing 2. This has no effect on the end point of the programme, when project D is completed, as equal amount of work is done in both phases. However, the speed to deliver benefits from project A, B and C is considerably higher, and from a benefits realization viewpoint this is a better way to phase the projects.

Of course, with no resource constraint there is an even faster way to deliver benefits, and that is to deliver all of the projects in parallel. This uses the maximum amount of resource at any time and hence results in the highest rate of spending, but total spending is the same. Even if there is a human resource constraint which makes programme phasing 3 difficult, it may be possible to overcome it by spending more money and utilizing contract resources. Although the total benefits from the programme are unlikely to change, the speed with which they are achieved will be increased. This is attractive to many businesses.

Theoretically, the total resources consumed and total time spent in programme phasing 1, 2 and 3 is the same. But the time to achieve the stream of benefits, and the total benefits delivered by the time of the original programme end are significantly different. Although this is a very simplified example, it is this type of planning that programme managers should undertake when considering how to maximize benefits from a programme.

In reality, life is often more complex than Diagram 10.5 or 10.6 indicate. Evidence indicates that when the same people perform several tasks in parallel, it can take longer than the cumulative time for focussing on each one and doing them in sequence. On the other hand, projects may have to be done in parallel because of dependencies between them. A programme manager has to be able to answer questions like do the projects use different resources, and so can they be worked on in parallel? What

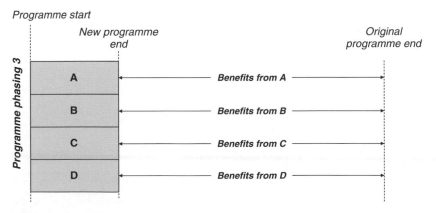

Diagram 10.6 Optimal phasing for benefits delivery assuming no resource constraint

types of resources are required and what is the maximum rate of spending on the project possible? Is there any change constraint in terms of operational department's ability to absorb the change from the programme, which affects the phasing of implementation?

All of these are important considerations, and a programme cannot be planned only on the basis of the fastest time to deliver benefits. But the principle remains that when resource constraints are considered, it is often better to deliver fewer streams of work faster in sequence than to undertake multiple works in parallel.

Portfolio management

Consideration of benefits is also important in portfolio management. The business case developed for any project or programmes is normally the key information in determining its priority within a portfolio. Although there are other factors to be considered, a project with a better business case will tend to be prioritized higher than one with a poorer business case. A well-implemented benefits management process, based on good business cases should result in a better selection of projects.

As projects progress the prediction of benefits to be delivered may change. Periodic portfolio reviews must not only consider which projects are complete and which new projects should be introduced to the portfolio, but also determine which projects should be stopped and which ones should be re-prioritized. There has to be a pragmatic approach to changing prioritizations. There is no point continuing a project whose benefits have decreased below the remaining costs to complete. On the other hand, constantly re-prioritizing based on incremental changes in benefit predictions can lead to chaos and continual swapping between projects without ever completing any.

In making decisions to change priorities, or in extremis to kill off projects with declining benefits stream, decision-makers should avoid two traps. The first is to worry excessively about *sunk costs*. This is when a project is continued, simply because the amount spent to date is so great that no one can face stopping it. The opposite can also happen where a project is stopped because the benefits stream will no longer justify the amount spent to date. What actually matters is the amount left to spend on a project and the benefits relative to this. Consider a project that has already spent £1m, has £250K left to complete, and will deliver benefits worth £500K. This project overall will be a poor investment, as it will cost £1.25m and only deliver £550K. However, it should be completed as the business will be better off achieving £500K of benefits for £250K of spending. The £1m is already spent and stopping the project will not bring it back. Alternatively, if the project has spent £1m, needs £100K to complete, but will only deliver £50K worth of benefits, it should be stopped. A manager may be reticent to do this as it explicitly requires accepting the write-off of £1m, but if the project continues the situation will be worse as £1.05m will be lost (£1m + £100K – £50K).

Of course, any such decisions do need to account for the level of risk in a project. Some projects lose credibility in an organization due to repeatedly changing the prediction of level and timing of benefits.

Portfolios should provide a balanced set of projects which cover the range of a business's needs. Business decision-making tends to favour financial benefits. Financial benefits are easy to understand and easy to compare. This is unfortunate as there can be many worthwhile projects with good benefits streams that are difficult to quantify in financial terms but worth pursuing. An overly strong emphasis on financial benefits can lead to an unbalanced project portfolio. Projects with strong and easily identifiable financial benefits (e.g. those relating to sales, or new product development) will tend to be favoured over those with a less direct financial linkage (e.g. staff capability development). Portfolio managers should be alert to this risk and try to ensure a range of projects providing a balanced set of benefits in line with portfolio objectives are undertaken.

Portfolio management can also be used to review the proposed set of projects and programmes with duplicate or overlapping benefits streams. There is no reason why two separate projects should not independently provide improvements in the same business metric, whether it is something like revenue increases, customer satisfaction improvements, or raising staff skill levels. However, with all metrics there tends to be a maximum level and it becomes increasingly difficult to make improvements as an organization approaches this level. As an example, with a customer satisfaction rating of 50%, it should not be a significant challenge to improve this to 55%. However, changing from a customer satisfaction rating of 94% to 99% is significantly harder. Therefore, where multiple projects in a portfolio are attempting to provide benefits in terms of improving the same business metric, consideration has to be given to the achievable cumulative benefit. It is often found that when three projects independently claim to deliver a benefit level of x, they do not or cannot combinedly deliver $3x$.

In view of this portfolio managers have to consider whether multiple projects attempting to provide similar benefits are really cumulative. It may be that a subset of the proposed projects is a better investment, or that the separate projects are better off combined into a single programme of work. A key factor in making this decision should be which way optimizes the delivery of benefits.

Conversely, portfolio managers should identify projects which are at cross purposes, and which will reduce the ability to achieve benefits. For instance, an initiative aimed at reducing headcount in one area of the business may be non-compatible with one aimed at increasing staff satisfaction. Similarly, an initiative to implement a new financial system in one area of the business may be incompatible with an objective to minimize investment in that area.

Portfolio management should consider the risk and phasing of benefits across the portfolio. Businesses prefer benefits earlier rather than later. Also it is often helpful to have ongoing streams of benefits from a number of projects, rather than occasional peaks, as it can ease financial and general business management. A portfolio can be structured to optimize the rate and delivery of benefits by choosing the best selection of projects to achieve this.

The advantage of optimizing the degree of parallel working across a portfolio has been identified several times in this book. Portfolios should be designed for delivery and completion of work, thus optimizing the delivery of benefits. They should not be designed simply to allow working on the maximum number of projects possible in parallel. Unfortunately, under the pressures of multiple stakeholders portfolios often consist of the maximum number of projects possible, rather than the set of projects that will deliver the optimal level of benefits.

There are many reasons why running multiple projects in parallel is essential. Businesses are complex and do not have the luxury of working on only one activity at a time. A large business has the capacity to do many projects at once, which leads to parallel working. However, in general, too high a level of parallel working will delay benefits delivery. Resource contention between projects should be minimized to maximize delivery throughput.

By bringing together all projects at a single point the portfolio management function can also provide the linkage between project delivery and budget and annual financial planning processes. Financial planning must take account of committed benefits from projects in terms of future projections of budget needs.

Implementing benefits management

This chapter has described an enhanced benefits management process and discussed the approach to benefits management considering its effect at a project, programme and portfolio level. Implementing benefits management is facilitated by having the right, comprehensive process in place. For a process to work, it must be supported by defined roles and responsibilities. It is also enhanced by having the right culture and mindset which appreciates the need to work towards optimizing benefits. This section discusses

- o The roles and responsibilities required for benefits management
- o The leadership needed to develop the right culture and implement benefits management successfully

Roles and responsibilities for benefits management

There are various possible ways to structure the responsibilities for benefits management and there will be variations between every project. In some situations project managers are very much focussed on deliverables, and the project sponsor takes full responsibility for worrying about benefits. In some other situations a project manager will take a more active role in achieving benefits. The variations depend on the nature of the organization and the personalities of the project manager and sponsor.

However, in general terms the following positions are involved in benefits management:

- o Project manager
- o Programme manager
- o Portfolio manager
- o Project/programme sponsors
- o Budget holders and business unit managers
- o Benefits manager
- o Leadership team

The *project manager's* role is to deliver the project, which in turn facilitates the achievement of benefits. The project manager is responsible for the structure and approach to the project. Project managers should take account of optimizing benefits in designing and delivering projects. The *programme manager's* role extends on the project manager's by bringing together a family of initiatives which contribute towards a common area of value. Both projects and programmes are supported and directed by a *sponsor*. The sponsor is accountable for delivery of the expected benefits from a project.

The split in responsibilities between the project manager and project sponsor can be confusing. At the heart of the separation of roles lies the concept of a project manager being *responsible* for delivery and the project sponsor being *accountable* for benefits. A responsibility is an activity which is someone's job to perform. An accountability is an activity or outcome someone must ensure will happen or be achieved, whether or not they actually do the task themselves. Having accountability implies that someone will be held to account or judged on the achievement of the outcome required. As the responsible party the project manager spends most of the time on a project managing the process of creation and implementation of deliverables to a defined specification. The project sponsor must ensure that once implementation is completed the benefits are realized.

In programme management, the split in responsibilities can be less clear as programme managers often take some level of accountability for business change and benefits realization. However, if benefits will be realized after the programme has completed then the accountability has to remain with the programme sponsor. What is most critical is not the general split in responsibilities between project or programme manager on one hand and project or programme sponsor on the other, but that in any one situation specific responsibilities and accountabilities are clear and unambiguous.

The role of the *portfolio manager* with regard to benefits is twofold. First, portfolio managers should track cumulative benefits being delivered across a portfolio to ensure that benefits required are being delivered. Second, the portfolio manager must seek to adjust the portfolio depending on the reality of delivery. Prioritizations should rise or fall depending on the actual capability of a project to deliver benefits as it is implemented. Projects may be added or removed depending on progress towards portfolio objectives.

At the end of the day if a project delivers benefits then somewhere in the organization there must be an alteration in performance. This alteration may be shown in terms of an increase or decrease in a budget; it may be achieved through changes in a business performance metric such as numbers of customer complaints or production volumes; or it may be an intangible change such as improved supplier relationships. Whatever the deliverable, a *budget holder* or a *business unit manager* not only gains from the project, but also has the challenge of realizing the benefit. It is a common occurrence that following a project a business unit manager has to decrease his budget and deliver against higher performance targets.

In some cases the business unit manager may be the project sponsor, but not every business unit manager affected by a project can be the project sponsor. A large programme will impact the performance of multiple departments. In this situation, a variety of business unit managers must each realize part of the benefits. There is a separation of creating the capability for benefits (in a project) from those who actually have to deliver them (a business unit manager).

Some organizations have an additional role of a *benefits manager*. This is an optional role, but it can be very useful. The benefits manager is not project-specific, but works across the portfolio. He should act as an evangelist for achieving benefits. The benefits manager is responsible for ensuring that projects (and possibly other investments) are compliant with the benefits realization process and are being delivered to optimize benefits. Following completion the benefits manager can track whether the benefits are actually being realized. The benefits manager should work closely with the portfolio manager.

Finally, there is a role for the *leadership team* of an organization in terms of implementing and performing benefits management. The leadership team should exhibit behaviours which value benefits management, develop a culture supportive of benefits management, and provide the right balance of enforcement without punishment. The leadership team should also provide direction according to project progress; for instance, what should happen if a project has underdelivered benefits? Is an additional project started? Will benefits simply be tasked onto business unit managers?

Leadership for benefits management

Implementing benefits management in an organization can be a significant change. Moving from a culture in which benefits are not measured, or are assumed and taken on trust, to one in which they are tracked, and managers are held accountable, is not trivial. Fully implementing benefits management requires changes in attitudes and behaviours, and needs the sponsorship of the leadership team. The leadership team must reinforce the importance of benefits management, and continually exhibit behaviour supportive of benefits management. The leadership must be prepared for a prolonged period of focus on benefits management. It can take some time to be embedded – possibly some months, probably a few years – to become standard practice.

The full needs of benefits management should not be underestimated. Many business leaders require the use of business cases for all investments, and assume this alone will lead to better benefits management. Simply mandating that all projects require business cases may be a good start, but will not achieve the full potential of benefits management and the optimization of benefits.

The behaviour of the leadership team is essential to developing the right balance of pressure and support for benefits realization. Realizing benefits needs openness and honesty, along with a balanced approach to forcing realization. If no one is ever held accountable for benefits delivery then it is unlikely that they will be realized. On the other hand too aggressive pursuit of benefits following project completion can be counter-productive. Business unit managers are often forced to provide benefits irrespective of the actual outcome of a project. If a project does not achieve its goals, forcing benefits by actions such as cutting budgets can damage a business.

There is a common mindset in business that if a manager knows he will be accountable for benefits, he will deliver them irrespective of project outcome. There is some truth in this, but it has its limits. Forcing managers to achieve benefits can make them take suitable action to achieve the benefit irrespective of the project outcome. However, if it is possible to deliver benefits irrespective of project outcome, it is questionable whether the project was ever required. One of the costs of forcing unrealistic benefits to be achieved is reduced operational performance. Examples are common where managers have been forced to reduce headcount or budgets because a project was meant to enable this. If the project failed, but the headcount or budget cuts are forced, a lower operational service level will follow. This is rarely desirable.

Leaders need to make balanced judgements in applying benefits management. If the process is applied leniently it will not achieve value for the business. However, if the penalties for project failure are high, then honesty is less likely, and the business will end up suffering.

A lax attitude to realizing benefits almost always leads to reduced benefits delivery. Managers must be held accountable for benefits appropriate to the level of risk and degree of change a project is subject to. A culture must be developed in which success and the rewards associated with success come about because of benefits being realized, not just for completing projects.

Leaders should ensure projects are designed for the achievement of benefits. They should constantly reinforce the message that the only goal of projects is increased business value, whether this value is achieved in terms of financial, performance or intangible benefits.

Case Study 10.2 AVOIDING PITFALLS IN BENEFITS REALIZATION

In this case study Paul Gilhooley provides some ideas and tips on benefits realization. Paul is an experienced programme manager and operational manager, who has in-depth expertise in benefits management. He has worked for a variety of organizations including British Airways, Telewest Broadband and BT.

Paul Gilhooley

The first thing to say about benefits realization is that it is not just about financial benefits. Most people think it is about financial returns, but it should be about any type of benefit. For example, improvements in staff behaviours and greater cultural alignment are important types of benefits. It is a very common misunderstanding in industry that for a benefit to be real it has to be financial. Focussing only on the financial side can underestimate benefits and distort priorities.

The starting point for benefits management is to decide what your baseline is, and to measure it. Without identifying and measuring baseline performance, you can't measure the improvement a project brings about. When you know what your baseline is then you have a way of assessing benefits – as long as you can ensure there is no double counting, and you can ring-fence the part of the business you are measuring improvements in from any other influences. One of the key challenges is being able to measure benefits where there are multiple activities being undertaken; this emphasizes the key rule that the group who measure the benefits must have a holistic view of all activities.

The next important decision is who will actually do the measurement. Responsibility for measurement must be allocated, else it will not happen. Measurement is best done by an independent central function that has visibility across all initiatives. This helps avoiding double counting and makes understanding how different initiatives have fed into one set of benefits easier. It could be the finance function, or it could be a Project Management Office (PMO).

One of the biggest problems in benefits management is when it comes to 'cashing the cheque' and ensuring the benefits are actually delivered. A project might be delivered that reduces some operational task time by four minutes per job. If thousands of these jobs are done a day, that adds up to potentially a big headcount saving; but actually getting operational areas to reduce staff levels can be very difficult. To cash the cheque you must understand what acceptable types of return are. If the business model has changed during the project there could be an argument that you are still cashing the cheque through cost avoidance rather than headcount reduction. Whether this is acceptable or not depends on the situation.

The main mistake that project managers make in achieving benefits is not getting buy-in at the front end of the project. If operational managers are not aware or have not agreed to the goals of a project, it is too late when the project finishes to make anyone cut budgets or increase performance. The solution to this problem is to have a strong governance process which ensures that stakeholders and budget owners are involved up-front, buy-in to the project, and commit to delivery of the benefits if the project delivers. The reasons why a large percentage of projects fail in delivering benefits are a lack of stakeholder engagement and sustainability strategies at board level.

Project and programme managers are very poor at linking escalations and change controls to benefits realization. For instance, consider when a project manager escalates a project to a sponsor because the project is going red, and it is not within the project manager's power to resolve the problems. Project managers cannot solve every problem unaided, and in this situation for the project to come off red needs some action by the sponsor. The project manager may give some options and implications, but rarely does he or she really link through to the impact on benefits. The sponsor then chooses an option, without understanding the implications on benefits. Projects that are subject to many escalations and change controls often end up delivering significantly lower benefits, without anyone being prepared for this.

To make benefits realization work requires, in my opinion, a strong project management office or something similar. A PMO can have the visibility of what is happening across all projects and can act as the guardians of change control and escalations. Whenever change controls or escalations are raised they can help to ensure that all pertinent information on the impact on benefits is considered.

The overall goal across all projects in an organization is to maximize benefits. Maximization requires benefits to be understood in the broadest sense and may include things other than financial improvements, such as regulatory alignment or an improvement in skills or capabilities.

One of the key issues in achieving benefits is the volume of change. To achieve benefits requires change. But operational areas can only absorb so much change, and therefore the rate of benefits realization is constrained by the amount of change operations can handle. There is a need to prioritize which change is done to maximize total benefits achieved. However, as the state of projects alters, or as business needs change, then what should be prioritized highest also changes. Ideally, there is an intelligent PMO that can support dynamic re-prioritization under the governance of all key stakeholders.

Another consideration in optimizing benefits is understanding how benefits link to the project management methodology. Different stages of projects add different levels of benefits. Scoping, planning, business case development and prioritizing may all be essential to delivering the right projects, but in themselves they deliver no benefits. On the other hand, execution and implementation delivers benefits. There should be a step when a high-level business case is created allowing the organization to determine *whether this meets its business criteria and whether further spending should be authorized (in terms of resource allocation, opex and capex). To provide an efficient process it is key that the high-level business case is a sub-set of the main business case. I like to time box all the up-front activity on work like developing a high-level business case, and let the resources spend as much time on execution and implementation.*

A final point about understanding benefits is to challenge organizations to really understand their costs for doing a project. If you do not understand costs, you don't understand the incremental benefits a project results in. How many organizations really cost the time of their staff on projects and understand the costs of project over-runs? If a project is four weeks late what is the cost of the delay to the project, but equally what is the cost to the other project that would be otherwise using the resources and starting on its way to deliver benefits? Having a real understanding on benefits needs this information.

There are many different benefits methodologies and approaches, some of which are very powerful. In general, use of benefits maps to link between benefits drivers that a project will influence, such as time to complete a task, through to the actual benefits, is helpful. Whichever approach is used the fundamentals of measuring from a baseline and ensuring buy-in to realize them are universally critical.

Once delivered there is the challenge of ensuring your improvements have been sustained. This should be through the improved performance being continually measured. It becomes the new baseline. Any future improvement is taken from this new baseline position.

In summary, benefits realization is a continuous management process running throughout the programme life cycle. It should be the core process of any change initiative, the backbone of any programme, involving far more than a few benefits events early in the process. The only valid reason for investing in change is to generate benefits, and without generation of benefits for at least one group of stake holders, there is no justification for investing in change. Benefits are the ultimate deliverable, and should lay the foundations for project or programme management, rather than being, as so often, the afterthought. This approach to benefits realization demands increased quality and rigour in business cases, and meaningful benefit tracking and reporting. Driving benefits out of a project involves working closely with the customer to ensure the "change" gets firmly adopted and embedded in the organization.

MAIN LEARNING POINTS FROM CHAPTER 10

- Benefits are the value a project returns to the organization. Benefits may be financial or non-financial, and tangible or non-tangible. An overfocus on financial benefits can lead to other useful benefits being lost.
- Measurement is an essential part of realizing benefits. When benefits are measured they are significantly more likely to be achieved.
- In assessing benefits, it is important to consider the total value of a benefit, the timing and the risk associated with achieving it. In some cases it is important to understand which budget year benefits will occur in.

- Benefits are only realized if something changes in the business – for example, a budget is reduced or output increases. A project cannot make this occur, but can only create the environment in which it occurs. Delivery of benefits lies with the operational departments of an organization. Buy-in from benefits owners is essential for successful benefits delivery.
- There are many pitfalls to avoid in measuring benefits – from the actual capability to measure, to avoiding double counting and appropriately assigning benefit creation to the right source.
- Benefits should not be seen simply as an outcome from a project or as a means to justify a project. Projects should be derived from the need for benefits in an organization. Projects and programmes can be designed and actively managed to maximize benefits. Considerations for maximizing benefits include prioritization, phasing and timing of project delivery. Also care should be given when mixing non-complementary benefits within a single endeavour.
- As projects evolve and change, the benefits and business case associated with the project should also evolve and change.
- At a portfolio level benefits should be tracked to ensure portfolio objectives are met. The portfolio manager must be aware of the level of risk associated with benefits delivery. The portfolio must be actively managed as benefit streams change or new benefit delivering project proposals arise.
- Implementation of benefits management requires clear roles and responsibilities. The management of an organization must show leadership, actively promote the delivery of benefits and hold people accountable for benefit delivery.

REVIEW QUESTIONS AND EXERCISES

1. What is your experience of benefits management on projects? What was successful and what worked less well?
2. What do you think the difficulties of putting in place a set of measures and targets for tracking benefits in a project might be? How would you overcome each of these problems?
3. Consider a programme to prepare a country for hosting the Olympic Games. What are the main categories of benefits from such a programme? What are the relative priorities and timescales for achieving each type of benefit? How would achieving benefits affect the programme strategy and the design of the programme? How would you ensure that benefits have been achieved? If you were the programme manager which benefits would you be most concerned with achieving and why?
4. If you were a senior executive in a large corporation tasked with implementing benefits management in the business for the first time how would you approach this challenge? What would your concerns be?
5. How can you use benefits management to support implementation and change management? What are the risks associated with benefits management upon successful change?
6. Considering the iron triangle of cost, quality and time, and any other factors you think are relevant, how would your approach to projects delivering the following types of benefit vary?
   - Revenue increase
   - Cost savings
   - Improvement in customer satisfaction

10

- Compliance with new compulsory legislation
- Providing enhanced capabilities and skills for staff

What would your concerns be for a project which delivered benefits of each of these types?

7. Imagine that you are responsible for a major investment programme in a business. This programme consists of projects to increase headcount, expand into new improved office spaces, an enhancement in customer services, implementation of a new performance and financial management systems, launching several new products, and corporate re-branding. Which activities would you do in parallel and which in sequence? Note any assumptions you make. What factors would you consider in making this decision? How will this impact the realization of benefits? Would you change the order of activities if the programme had to be at least 50% self-financing?

Suggested Reading

Benefits management is achieving a gradually higher profile in the project management community. However, the availability of good books on the subject is still limited. One book that does cover the topic reasonably comprehensively is

o *Benefit Realisation Management: A Practical Guide to Achieving Benefits Through Change*. Gerald Bradley. Gower Publishing Ltd, May 2006

Bibliography

Benko, C. and Warren McFarlan, F. *Connecting the Dots: Aligning Your Project Portfolio with Corporate Objectives*. Harvard Business School Press, 2003.

Bradley, G. *Benefit Realisation Management: A Practical Guide to Achieving Benefits Through Change*. Gower Publishing Ltd, May 2006.

Carroll, T. *Project Delivery in Business-As-Usual Organizations*. Gower Publications Ltd, 2006.

Office of Government Commerce. *Managing Successful Programmes*. Stationery Office Books, September 2007.

Reiss, G. *Programme Management Demystified. Managing Multiple Projects Successfully*. Routledge, 3rd Edition, 2006.

Williams D. and Parr T. *Enterprise Programme Management*. Palgrave Macmillan, 2004.

11

understanding and managing risk on projects

Anyone sponsoring, supporting or having an interest in the outcome of a project is likely to have a set of concerns when a project starts and as it progresses. These concerns can be encapsulated in four questions. *Will the project be delivered? When it is delivered, will I get what I want? When I get it, will I still want it? Will it do what I expect it to do?*

Even if stakeholders do not have these concerns, they often should do. Just because a project starts, there is no guarantee that it will end with the expected or desired outcome. Projects do not always succeed, and regularly fail to meet the needs of every stakeholder. Business history is littered with stories of failed and underachieved projects. Projects are inherently risky ventures.

There are many sources of risk on projects, which can be categorized into three generic root causes: uncertainty, ambiguity and instability. First, projects are typified by various degrees of *uncertainty*. A project manager is rarely certain that the work breakdown structure or estimates of task lengths are correct. The information required to be sure that the project can be completed within the expected time and cost is uncertain. Second, projects are subject to *ambiguity*, with many hazy, multiple and sometimes incompatible sources of information. Project managers cannot be sure that their understanding of objectives and scope really matches that of all stakeholders. Stakeholders themselves are often not able to express what they want. Finally, projects exist in an environment of *instability*. Stakeholders' needs alter and evolve.

If uncertainty, ambiguity and instability are the primary sources of risk, they are exhibited in many varied ways on any one project and the degree of risk varies from project to project. In some situations, the level of risk is trivial and the effort expended on risk management is minimal. In other situations, the risk is high and risk management is one of the main activities on the project. Experience helps in risk management, as projects which are alike tend to be subject to similar types of risk. But all projects have a degree of uniqueness, whether it is in the nature of the project itself or in the context in which it is being run. Hence, each project exhibits some individual risks. Therefore, dealing with risk is, to some degree, a different challenge on every project.

For all these reasons, project stakeholders should be concerned about risk. But the impact of risk is not only an issue to those directly involved in projects. Project risk can have a wider effect on business management and operations, as well as on the ability of businesses to make and keep commitments.

A failed project, which, due to risks arising, does not achieve the expected returns, normally becomes one more of a number of management issues to be resolved in the day-to-day running of a business. If, however, it is not just any project than has failed, but the major investment programme for a business, the lack of returns can cause significant problems. More than one construction business has gone bankrupt as a result of a poorly executed major programme. Even if the project succeeds in creating the expected deliverables, a poor implementation can disrupt a business. Talk to any senior executive, and she normally has several stories about painful IT systems' implementations or business changes that caused more trouble than was expected.

There is a significant value to certainty or predictability in business. Managers have to make commitments regularly to shareholders, customers, staff and suppliers. Often these commitments are dependent on projects. Shareholders may be given assurances about an increase in revenues and a decrease in costs. Customers can be promised new products, better services or lower prices. Staff loyalty may be secured with assurances of enhanced facilities, new performance management approaches or improvements in contractual terms. Suppliers may be pledged improved relationships or payments processes, facilitated by new processes and systems. All of these depend on the successful completion of projects, but the commitment usually has to be made before the project is complete. As a project is inherently risky, any such commitment, no matter how confidently stated, is also inherently risky.

For all of these reasons, the existence of risk should be a concern, but it should not cause unconstrained anxiety. Risk is not something that just has to be accepted on a project – risk can be measured; choices can be made based on an understanding of risk; and projects can be managed to cope with risk. Risk is handled in project management through a process called, logically, *risk management.*

Project risk management increases the likelihood of successful completion of a project. Often project risk management is performed to ensure a project is delivered to time, cost and quality criteria, but it can also be used to ensure a project meets any of its success criteria. Risk management links to all other parts of project management. Activities such as project selection, scoping, requirements analysis, resourcing, planning, execution and implementation all contribute towards creating project risk and offer ways to help reduce project risk.

Risk management is an important issue for all managers with an interest in or impacted by projects. Risk management is a central part of project management. This chapter combines standard thinking on project risk management with a broader perspective of the volatility of projects.

Risk and projects

This section provides an introduction to risk and risk management on projects. It describes the sources of risk. It then discusses the importance of risk management, by looking at the impact of risk on projects. Finally, there is an overview of the risk management process. The remainder of the chapter describes each stage of the risk management process in more detail.

The sources of risk

There are many pitfalls that projects face on the journey from initial concept through to complete implementation and the realization of benefits. The root source of all risk derives from an inability to be certain about the future. This uncertainty is compounded by three facts. First, projects exhibit a degree of novelty and innovation, so experience alone cannot fully predict the outcome. Second, the environment projects operate in is unstable and modifying all the time. Even if a project appears to be very similar to a previous one the context in which in occurs will be different. Third, there is usually a degree of ambiguity about many aspects of a project. For instance, questions such as what will a project deliver, what do stakeholders want, whether a deliverable will be acceptable may not have a single definite answer when a project commences.

In thinking about all the sources of risk, it is easy to become despondent about the chance of ever delivering a project. But high-risk projects are delivered successfully all the time. With the right approach risk can be managed. Understanding risk is not a reason to be pessimistic, but should be seen as a way to increase the likelihood of success.

Project management approaches consider risk as the possible occurrence of an uncertain event that will lead to particular consequences. For instance, there is a risk that a supplier may be late in delivering a component of a project, with the consequence that the whole project will be late. That a source of risk exists in a project does not mean that the uncertain event or the consequences will occur, but it means there may be situations in which they do. If a source of risk exists and is ignored, the likelihood of the uncertain event and its resultant consequences occurring are higher than if the risk is managed.

The general sources of risk play out in every stage of a project creating the opportunity for hazards being realized resulting in detrimental impact. It is not possible to write, at least certainly not in a condense form, a list of all the possible sources of risk on a project. This sub-section aims to give a flavour of the typical range of risks.

Common sources of risk are uncertainty, ambiguity or instability which are associated with

- Scoping, objective setting and requirements analysis, and the associated definition of project constraints
- Planning, estimating and scheduling
- Resourcing projects
- Suppliers and sub-contractors
- Executing or delivering the project
- Implementing change
- Benefits realization

- Characteristics of the project
- Characteristics of the environment in which it operates

Let us look at each of these in turn.

The risks that arise from issues with the scope, objective setting or requirements are some of the most fundamental in a project. There is the risk of omissions or errors in scope. If these are not identified the project may not deliver a result that is useful, or may deliver one that is not as useful as it could be. Requirements can suffer from poor specifications or an inability to define what is wanted. There are hazards associated when stakeholders request unreasonable requirements which may be impossible to achieve. There is the risk of incompatibilities in needs between stakeholders. Also, although stakeholders have a general idea of their requirements they may not know precisely what they want from or project, or even if they do, may not be able to express it in a meaningful way.

Risk increases when constraints are forced upon a project without understanding the consequences. Such constraints can come about through aggressive demands upon time or cost, or unreasonable constraints from sponsors such as forcing completion by a certain date. Overly lean staffing on a project to minimize cost, or allowing project completion with available resource also threatens successful project completion. No matter how often a senior manager makes a statement like "this must happen", if it is not possible, it will not. Setting high targets can motivate people to achieve many incredible feats, but it also is risky.

There are dangers in the ambiguous definition of constraints and assumptions related to constraints. Project managers may assume that time is the most important constraint on a project, whereas in reality it may be cost or vice versa. The constraints applied to a project may not really line up with real business needs. Engineers may develop very high-quality systems and technology, whilst in reality the business needed something quick and cheap.

Planning is a major source of project risk. Work breakdown structures can have gaps or contain tasks unnecessary to achieving the goal of the project. Estimates may be wrong – not only in terms of deciding the scale of a task in a plan, but also in assessing progress to the plan. Dependencies may be missed. Even if they are included they often rely on action of people outside of the project manager's control, such as on other projects or on management decision-making. There can be sequencing problems in plans, with missing or the wrong linkages. When a plan is completed it may show zero or very little slack, meaning that the chance of over running on the project is high.

Planning large programmes has specific additional risks. There is the issue of a human's mental capacity to cope with the scale and complexity of the work. Documenting plans helps remove the need to remember details, as does having a hierarchy of plans which breaks details into chunks under separate project managers. Even so, the programme manager has to be able to cope with significant and ever-changing complexity. In addition, large programmes tend to run for long time periods, and there are limits to the real planning horizon in many contexts. Planning a few days to a few months ahead may be reasonably accurate. Planning more than six months ahead in many business contexts is of limited true validity because of the degree of continuous change.

There are risks that arise because of the order in which work is performed. There is a general human tendency to leave difficult and poorly understood work until late, performing easy and well-understood tasks first. On a project this is a high-risk option, and it is always better to initiate high-risk and unclear tasks first as it gives the most time to manage the risk and overcome unforeseen problems.

Risks often arise from the people on the project team. A project team may have insufficient staff or people with the wrong skills or negative attitudes. Project team members may have inadequate experience of the type of project. A project may have a set of individually well-skilled team members with the right experiences, who, unfortunately, cannot work constructively together as a team. The size of the project team may be determined by assuming a certain level of productivity that may not be achieved in practice. Productivity levels vary greatly, and the best team members will typically be several times as productive as the worst. Also, even if they are capable of doing the work in the time required, project team members may be not sufficiently motivated.

Another type of human resource risk is that people leave the project. Organizations are always juggling their resources, and people can be pulled-off projects for short or long terms to work on higher-priority projects. Although this may be the right thing to do for the business overall, it is a risk for the individual project. Staff may be removed from project work altogether. This is common when operational issues arise which need rapid resolution. Project team members are often the most competent and best placed to resolve operational problems. There is a constant tension in many businesses between the need to fix operational issues and the desire to continue with project progress. In addition, people may resign and leave the company. In all these cases it may be possible to replace people on projects, but it will at least cause some disruption and is likely to cause delays.

Not only a project team needs people in it, but the team members need to have clear roles and responsibilities. It is very difficult to create exhaustive role definitions which unambiguously ensure that every aspect of a project is covered. Project teams need to be flexible in how they work and in completing all the tasks in the project plan. The willingness and ability of project team members to pick up unallocated tasks is another source of risk. A classic example of this risk arises with the separation of roles between the project manager and project sponsor. The sponsor is usually responsible for benefits realization, the project manager is not. An inexperienced sponsor may place insufficient emphasis on benefits, and a project manager who sticks precisely to his role definition may not worry about benefits at all. There is a resultant risk that benefits will therefore not materialize.

Human resource risk increases when one considers the impact across projects. Any late delivery in one project means the project team have to work for longer on the project, and this in turn risks delay in subsequent projects requiring the same resources. More complex is the effect on scarce resources of working on multiple projects in parallel. The higher the number of projects a single person works on in parallel, the less productive she is. By enforcing high degrees of cross-project parallel working the risk of project delay is increased.

Many projects rely not only on internal resources, but also on external suppliers. Supplier risk has different characteristics from internal resource risk. With a business's own staff it is possible to develop an understanding of how suitable staff are for a specific project role. With an external supplier, there will often be unknowns about how good team members are. In addition, no matter what promises are derived from suppliers when they win a contract to support a project, it is normally impossible to have certainty about their true levels of commitment. Suppliers will usually be working for several organizations at once, and if another customer is regarded as more important there is always a risk that resources will be pulled off one business's project and allocated to another. Irrespective of any guarantee, an experienced supplier will view all projects with a risk–reward viewpoint. If the rewards are greater on another piece of work, they may be willing to suffer contractual penalties on one project to work on another, to the detriment of one customer.

Suppliers usually work within some form of a statement of work, which defines their role and outputs. The statement of work is subject to a contract between the customer and supplier. There are various risks associated with statement of works and contracts. The most common risk is when customers change requirements. Changes may occur because of misunderstandings, omissions or evolving needs. Often this means a modification to the statement of work. The supplier may be unwilling to agree to the modification, or willing only to perform it with additional charges. This is compounded by the fact that some experienced suppliers will deliberately seek a low fixed price and tightly defined contract to win work. The suppliers are confident that customers will require alterations to the contract and will charge a high price for them. Some suppliers make a significant proportion of profits from work associated with modifications to contracts.

In modern business the relationship between a large customer and a large supplier is often complex and bidirectional. A firm may simultaneously be a supplier to and customer of another. This creates *relationship risk* on a project. For example, an IT company may supply IT services to a telecoms operator, who in turn supplies telecoms services to the IT company. If a linkage is made between these two types of contracts, then a project to install new IT services may be affected by the need to buy telecoms services. This can result in the choice of sub-optimal suppliers and poor contractual arrangements.

Parts of a project, or whole projects, may be outsourced or off-shored to suppliers. Once a project is outsourced much of the work may be done at different locations or countries, and it is difficult or even impossible to monitor progress and quality. Although outsourcing work is often essential to gain the right skills and the best price, it has risks. Outsourced suppliers often deliver excellent work, but there are numerous examples of unexpected delays, poor quality and cost overruns from outsourced suppliers.

In terms of project execution there are several hazards that must be overcome. Many of these threats are specific to the type of project. The fundamental risk is simply whether it is possible to deliver the solution expected and whether it will work or not. For complex projects, especially those of a technical nature, there are also risks associated with the integration of multiple components.

Given the unpredictability and variability of responses to change, implementation is a significant area of project risks. People may reject changes. Changes may not work when taken out of the controlled domain of a project and put into the full complexity of a business. *Transition risk* is the risk associated with going from current ways of working to the new ways following implementation of a change through a project. It is often the risk that experienced managers worry about most. One reason for this is that should an implementation go wrong, it may not only mean the failure of a project, but can also mean major operational disruption for a business.

The primary reason for starting projects and making the investment required is to increase the value of a business in one way or another. This value may be a tangible financial improvement, may be an improvement in some other quantified metric, such as customer service, or may be intangible and unquantifiable. Whatever the benefits, if they are not realized then there is no point in the project. There are many risks associated with benefits realization. The absence of benefits may simply be a reflection of other project risks. But there are risks that benefits may be absorbed or unprovable following project completion.

There are probably an infinite variety of project-specific risks depending on the content of a project and the context in which it operates. Innovative or novel projects are particularly high-risk. This includes everything from new IT systems to untried products. As there is no experience of such projects they are subject to all sorts of possible problems at every phase of a project.

There is a risk from the poor use of project management or the application of a sub-optimal methodology. Choices of projects and project management strategy are subject to error. Practitioners often choose the approach they are most familiar with instead of the one best suited to a specific situation. An IT developer familiar with traditional project approaches will choose a waterfall style development even though an approach like Agile may better suit a specific situation. A project manager familiar with tangible deliverables may not manage a business change project in the right way.

There is risk deriving from changes in scope or requirements and scope creep. Scope creep is a potential risk on all projects, but it needs to be closely watched when evolutionary development approaches are used, which are common with software development. In an evolutionary approach each project iteration may be small, but there can be a tendency for a never-ending sequence of iterations to go on. Features can always be added to software, and, unless managed well, evolutionary approaches can become an open door to ongoing enhancements and continuing cost.

Risk does arise not only from within a project but can also result from the environment in which the project operates. This can be the nature of the business, a national culture or working internationally. Specific work environments can be unstable and not conducive to productive project work. Some businesses have poor decision-making processes and a general lack of willingness to make and keep commitments. Both of these are fundamental to project success. Some other businesses do not have an optimal balance between ambition and caution. Great projects avoid constrained thinking that focuses too much on problems, and steer clear of overly ambitious concepts that do not take reasonable concerns into account. Conservative projects lead to limited returns, but overambition leads to failed projects. Successful projects balance ambition with practical realities.

Projects can also be subject to market risk and changes in the environment in which a business operates. Changes in regulations and legislation can affect a project. Similarly, changes in competitive situations will affect projects. A brilliant project to rapidly develop an innovative product may have an outstanding business case. The business case can be destroyed overnight, if a competitor unexpectedly delivers an equivalent product in advance.

With external risks there will come a point at which the risk becomes an accepted part of normal business operations and is not something a project manager on an individual project has to concern himself with. Taking an extreme example, there is always a risk that a meteor will hit the earth and this will stop a project! However, no sensible project manager will worry about such a thing, not just because it is of very low probability, but also because there is nothing within the constraints of a project that can be done about it. A more realistic example is the impact of a possible economic recession on the success of a new product to be launched by a business. Although the threat of recession may be a real problem for the business and for the project's business case, a project manager or project team has no ability to influence such an occurrence. Whilst it is a risk for the project, it may be decided that it is outside the scope of a project manager's role to do anything about this.

The impact and probability of a risk occurring

Awareness of the many sources of risk may be interesting, but is of limited concern in itself. The reason for identifying the sources of risk is to be able to mitigate the negative impact of the risk on a project or a business.

Understanding the sources of risk enables potential threats to be avoided. But, whilst trying to understand the possible hazards a project is exposed to, it quickly becomes apparent that any one project is open to a huge number of potential threats. A project manager can only manage a limited number of activities to avoid risk. The question for the project manager, therefore, is which risks are worth taking action to avoid? The answer lies in understanding what the impact of a risk will be if it occurs and what the probability of it occurring is. The focus of management attention is then given to the highest-impact and highest-probability risks. This sub-section introduces these two: risk impact and risk probability.

The occurrence of a risk on a project can have an impact at four levels:

o On a project
o Across a portfolio of projects
o Upon a business or organization
o External to a business

If risk occurs, it may stop a project achieving what it set out to do. Risk may stop one or more of deliverables being created, changes being implemented or benefits being realized. In some situations, a project may still finish with the planned outcome though a risk occurs, but it means the project does not conform to the expected constraints. The project may be late, it may spend more money or use more resources than expected, or the quality may be lower than required.

Risk may impact any project success criteria. In the end, risk is about the likelihood that a project will not be a success. But not being a success means different things to different stakeholders (see Chapter 7). It may mean not meeting time and budget, or not achieving the business case. It can be other success criteria, such as not meeting stakeholder satisfaction or not achieving a goal such as increased skills in an organization.

Risk within a project can spill across into other projects. Organizations have limited resources. Any financial overspend or additional time worked on a project by scarce resources resulting from unpredicted risk has to have an effect somewhere else in a business. Usually this is on other projects. If a project overspends there is less money for other projects. If a project is late, then other projects using the same resources will start later. If a project does not deliver its full scope and some requirements are missed, then another project may have to have its scope expanded to fulfil the missing requirements.

Moreover, some projects are inter-dependent. Where there is a dependency between projects, one project can only progress or end upon completion of some actions by another project. This is particularly common with projects in a programme. If a project is subject to a risk which is realized, and so does not complete, this will have a knock-on impact on any dependent projects. A significant factor in successful programme management is the risk management of project inter-dependencies.

Risk on a project can also impact operations. If a project is late or overspent on, the additional resources required to complete it may be allocated from resources assigned to other projects. Alternatively, the project may take resources from business operations. Operational budgets or headcount may be reduced temporarily to fulfil the needs of the project.

There is a risk that is often more significant upon a business from projects. This is *implementation* or *transition risk*. As a project completes, the deliverables are implemented within an organization. The deliverables may be anything from something tangible like a new building, something intangible but measurable such as new IT software, or unquantifiable change such as enhanced training and skills. Transition risk has many root causes. Key amongst these are the facts that human beings take time to adapt to change and in the process of making a modification things are more likely to go wrong. During implementation a business is exposed most often to risk. This risk can sometimes have a significant detrimental impact. Many businesses have reported reduced annual performance as a result of poorly implemented projects. Some businesses have gone bankrupt due to the disruption from a very badly implemented project.

Project risk does not always stop at the boundaries of a business. If pitfalls are not avoided, projects may impact wider stakeholder groups such as customers who wanted new products that are not delivered, shareholders who wanted increased revenues that do not occur, suppliers who do not receive orders for components they expected projects to require, and local communities if a project may cause environmental damage. Some of these groups are not normally considered as a project's stakeholders. It is relatively unusual in a business project to consider the local community as stakeholder and to take their needs and the risks upon them into account. But in some situations it is essential. This is especially true if a project risks a significant detrimental impact upon that community; or else it will create negative publicity and bad feelings towards an organization.

Assessing the impact of a risk if it occurs can be done in different ways. It is common in small projects to use the subjective judgement of the project manager to determine the impact. This usually involves a simple scale of high, medium or low. For many project situations such judgement is adequate.

In assessing impact in more critical situations it is important to be more specific about impact. If the risk will impact schedule – by how much, a few days, a month or an unlimited time? If the risk will impact cost – by how much will it increase costs? Will it result in a 5% overrun, 10% or more? If a risk may result in a project's scope having to be reduced, precisely what requirements will not be achieved? If a risk could lead to a reduction in a business case, how much will the business case deteriorate by? Being specific about impact is crucial when risk avoidance strategies will require additional resources on a project. Increasing a project budget by 5% may not be welcome, but if that additional 5% is to be used to reduce the impact or likelihood of a risk that will delay a project by a year, it would often be a good investment.

Project management practitioners tend to assume a direct relationship between the occurrence of a risk event and the result. In reality, the consequences may be a result of multiple risks occurring and the interplay between them. This can make assessing the impact of risk more complicated.

Another related issue is the vulnerability of a project or a business to risk. Vulnerability is the inability of the project to cope with a risk event. A project in a business with very tight finances will typically be more vulnerable to a cost overrun than one which is cash rich. In situations in which specific types of impact are of greater importance than others, the focus of risk identification should be on risks that could result in that impact. For example, in a cost-constrained environment a risk resulting in higher costs is more important to avoid than one which will result in project delays. In contrast, in very fast-moving consumer markets a delay in completing a project is generally more important to avoid than a cost overrun. In safety-critical situations, risks which impact the quality of delivery are often of more importance than risks which affect the time or cost of the project.

If the impact of a risk is one factor that has to be considered in prioritizing action to manage risks, the other is the probability that the risk will occur. A very high-impact risk may, at first glance, be more important to deal with than a risk which if realized has half of the impact. On the other hand if the very high-impact risk has only a 1% probability of occurring and the lower-impact risk has 50%, then the lower-impact risk would usually be considered of greater importance to a project manager.

Having determined the impact of risk, next it is necessary to determine the *likelihood*. Determining the likelihood of a risk is normally a subjective judgement made by a project manager. Often the same simple scale of high, medium or low is used as for probability. This can be sufficient in smaller and non-complex projects. The purpose of understanding the likelihood is not to do any form of statistical analysis, but only to prioritize action against the risks. Understanding whether a risk is highly likely versus being of low likelihood can be sufficient for prioritization purposes.

By combining impact and likelihood focus on risks can be prioritized, as shown in Diagram 11.1.

However, in more complex projects it will be necessary to be more specific in assessing risk probabilities and to combine this with more accurate assessment of impact from risks. It can be seen in the example of a project to change the systems that calculate and collect a country's tax. The implications of error are huge, and therefore there is a need for highly sophisticated risk management. The difference

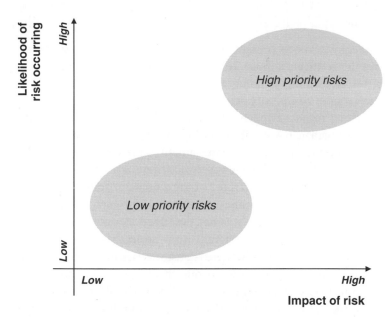

Diagram 11.1 Prioritising risk

between a risk with a 1% probability and one with a 4% probability can be very significant. In a less critical project both a 1% and a 4% probability risk would be considered of low probability and handled in a similar way.

The traditional way to consider the likelihood of risk is as a single probability, as in "this risk has a 50% chance of occurring". Whilst this can work for many situations, it can be too simplistic for others. Most risks are not binary events that either do or do not happen. The risk can occur to different degrees with different levels of impact. For instance, there may be a 25% chance that one project team member will be ill in the next month causing a minor delay. There may be a 10% chance that 2 team members will be ill at the same time, causing greater delay, which is more difficult to resolve. Finally, there could be a 3% chance that 3 or more team members will be ill at the same time, causing a critical delay. Understanding the spread of probabilities and impacts is considerably more involved than considering a simple chance that a risk will or will not arise, but is essential in some situations.

For some risks the impact is so significant that the probability of it occurring is less relevant, and the risk will be managed largely irrespective of probability. Consider the situation in which a project puts a human life at risk. The probability of death may be very small, but in spite of that expensive and time-consuming safety measures will be taken. A similar level of risk management may not be applied for a risk of equivalent likelihood and economic impact, but which does not risk human life.

When assessing risk it is helpful to understand that the perception of risk varies between different businesses. The perception of risk and the attitude to risk is also culturally variable. This is important not only because project management is relevant to all cultures, but because with globalization and the increasing tendency for projects to be international, a project manager may have to understand and deal with the differences. (Culture and its impact on project management are discussed in Chapter 13.)

The risk management process

There are many different ways to present the risk management process. Some are involved; others are relatively simple. This book has selected a comparatively simple model, as this eases understanding and is more practical to apply. Each stage of this process varies in complexity depending on the situation.

Risk management in a project happens at three levels, as shown in Diagram 11.2. First, there is risk management within an individual project, which is the responsibility of the project manager. Risk management approaches are a normal part of project management methodologies. Second, there is risk management across projects. This can be across a programme or the whole portfolio of projects. Programme risk management is often more complex than project risk management, but the principles are the same, so it is not described in any more detail in this book. Portfolio risk management is different from project risk management and is discussed separately later on. Finally, there is business risk management. The wider topic of business risk management is outside the scope of this book, and is shown here for context only. Business risk management should not only take project and portfolio risks into account, but also has to deal with the wider range of risks, such as risk to demand for products, hazards associated with competitors and threats from changing legislation.

The steps in project risk management do not directly align with stages in a project's lifecycle. The potential for risk starts as soon as the project concept is being developed and continues for as long as the project is ongoing. The opportunity to manage risk also starts as soon as the project concept is being envisaged and continues until the project is complete. Although some stages are more risky than others, risk management must occur through the life of the project. Formal risk reviews may occur at project initiation and at different decision points or gates in a project's lifecycle, but this should not lead to an assumption that risk management does not occur between these reviews. Risk management is an ongoing activity throughout the project's life.

Although the level of risk varies, all projects have some degree of risk. Project management is concerned not only with doing tasks with no risk; it enables

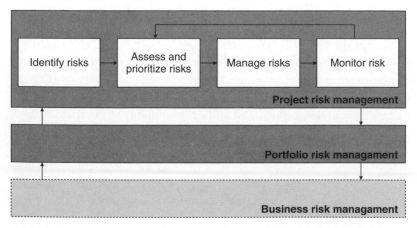

Diagram 11.2 Risk management process

complex and risky things to be done in a controlled and predictable way. In many ways project management is a mechanism for reducing the risk of failure by applying a structured methodology.

Putting a risk management process in place is essential for projects of any complexity. There is a strong linkage between risk management and project success (Voetsch et al., 2005).

Project risk management – identifying risk

The starting point to manage risk is to identify the hazards facing a project. Risk identification applies a general understanding of risk to locate the precise threats that a specific project is exposed to. Identification of risks requires applying experience of previous situations, and determining whether there are lessons for the current project, and projecting forward to identify new potential problems. Reducing risk on projects is done with a mindset of finding the right way to do things and avoiding the wrong ways.

When hazards are identified there is an opportunity to take action to counteract the risk. To allow action to be taken it is important to understand that risk identification is about detecting the sources of risk, not the outcome or impact, if the threat happens. As an example, late delivery is not a source of risk, it is an outcome. A source of risk could be poor planning or poor estimating which may lead to late delivery. It is easier to solve a potential cause of problems prior to a risk occurring, than dealing with a broader non-specific problem like late delivery.

Risk identification involves detecting potential problems, but does not deal with current issues. If a project has an existing live problem, such as it is behind on schedule or overrun on cost, then it is too late for risk management. The problem has to be dealt with and overcome now. To differentiate from risks, current problems on projects are known as *issues* and managed via *issue management*. Issue management is described in Chapter 8. Risk management seeks to take action to avoid issues before they occur.

Identification of risks is helped by having an understanding of a number of factors. It is essential to have an appreciation of the sources of project risk. It is very helpful to have knowledge of previous projects, to understand where risks arose, and to know how to avoid common mistakes. However, experience of previous projects can only go so far, as every project is different. Therefore, it is useful to be able to identify innovative or novel aspects of a project. Typically the more innovative the project, the higher the associated level of risk.

There is no single way to identify risks, and it is best to apply a combination of approaches. Common ways to identify risks include

- Reviewing similar previous projects
- Analysing project documentation, such as the scope and plan, the project strategy, and the solutions design – especially to identify novel or unusual approaches
- Interviewing and discussing the project with project participants
- Group meetings including brainstorming sessions
- Applying risk checklists
- Identifying and reviewing assumptions

- Consulting and reviewing with experts or other experienced practitioners
- Ongoing monitoring of projects

Let us look at each of these in turn.

Although every project has a degree of uniqueness, most share many features with previous projects. One project to deliver a new telecoms service has many features in common with another. A project to implement a new accounting system is likely to be comparable with a previous project to implement an accounting system. By reviewing similar previous projects it is often possible to identify the problems which arose and determine actions which could have avoided those problems. In addition, it is useful to identify what else might have gone wrong had it not been for the deliberate action of the project team. Such a review can be performed informally by having project team members from previous project apply their knowledge to the current situation. However, it is often better to perform a formal review session and identify the lessons for the current project.

An experienced project manager can identify many risks by reviewing project documentation. Helpful documents to review are the scope, objectives and the project plan. In reviewing the documents the project manager should be asking questions like

- What was unknown when developing these?
- Are there any gaps or omissions that could cause problems later in the project?
- Which parts are most likely to change, and will this cause any difficulty?
- Is there anything here that may not be specified in the way the originator meant or could be interpreted wrongly?
- What might go wrong?

A review of the project plan can assess each individual element of the plan to identify risks. Gaps or omissions in plan may be identified. A review also allows clarification of areas of the plan that are risky because they are poorly understood or contain new approaches.

Another very helpful way to identify project risks is to use the knowledge of the project team. Simply discussing concerns with project participants, whether in informal chats or formal interviews, can throw up many hazards that were not identified. Such a dialogue should continue throughout the life of the project. As well as with the project team members, discussions can be held with stakeholder representatives. Asking stakeholders to review and sign off key documents such as the scope and requirements often leads to the identification of areas of ambiguity.

People are often more creative in group sessions rather than in one-to-one conversations. One of the most productive ways of identifying project risks is to run a risk identification session with a selection of project participants. If the project team is large, it can be helpful to run several separate sessions. The team is brought together specifically to identify risks. Everyone should be encouraged to raise all their concerns. Techniques such as brainstorming are particularly good in identifying possible risks. Whilst not everything generated in a brainstorming session will turn out to be relevant, it will often pinpoint a wide range of threats.

Many organizations, and some risk management books, provide generic check lists to review to identify risks on a project. These risk checklists are based on previous experience and are developed over time. Best practice is to maintain and update such checklists after the completion of every project. Reading such a checklist can appear daunting, as some have hundreds of potential risks, but in reality reviewing them should not be an overly demanding task. A single sentence or phrase describing the sources of risk on previous projects can prompt the real-ization of the existence of a hazard on the current project. To be most useful, it is important to make sure that the risk checklists contain references to sources of risk and not outcomes. Listing down that a project may be late, may be overspent on or may not deliver sufficient value is of limited help. Pointing out specific problems, for instance, in an IT project a problem such as the risk from integration of sub-systems, can be very helpful.

One of the main sources of risk on projects is assumptions. Everyone makes assumptions all the time, and often it is essential to make them. If assumptions were not made it would be difficult to progress with any complex task, as it would have to keep stopping to verify every aspect of information on a project. Assumptions are very helpful, but it is inherent in an assumption that it may be wrong. It is critical, therefore, to identify all assumptions being made on a project. Every assumption has an associated risk profile – what is the chance it is wrong, and what will the effect on the project be if it is? All assumptions should be documented and visible to the project team. By documenting and sharing assumptions any ambiguity and difference in opinion on assumptions can be clarified. As the project progresses new assumptions should be added to this documentation.

Assumptions should not only be documented; they should be managed. Management of assumptions requires each assumption to have an owner tasked with keeping the assumption up-to-date. If the assumption changes or when it becomes a fact, the documentation should be updated. When an assumption is modified it may need adaptations to the project to be made. The assumption owner should seek to reduce the risk from assumptions by verification and con-verting them to facts. Where there is a major risk to a project from an assump-tion, it is worth expending significant effort to verify the assumption. At the end of a project there should be no assumptions left, all should be converted to facts. (If the assumption is still an assumption it was probably not relevant to the delivery of the project, although it could still be relevant to the project's busi-ness case.)

Most organizations have a wide range of expertise available, either in the staff in the business or through relationships with consultants. For important projects, it is good practice to talk to anyone with relevant experience to gain their insights into potential risks. For critical projects bringing in an expert to perform a review of the project and to advise the project manager of areas of risk can be a productive way of identifying risks the project manager or project team have not thought of.

The final way to identify risks is by the ongoing monitoring of a project. Part of the role of the project manager is to perform a continuous review of project status throughout the life of the project. The earlier a risk is identified the better, as it enables the most time to take action. But remember that hazards will arise or be detected throughout the life of the project. A project manager must be constantly alert for new risks, and should encourage all of the project team to keep her informed of any risks they identify. In high-pressure situations, there can be a reluctance to acknowledge risks and the flagging of risks can be covertly discouraged. This tendency should be discouraged. Identifying risks is not negative, but positive, as it increases the likelihood of success by being able to take action to mitigate risks.

One specific way to identify risks is through the monitoring of trends in progress on a project. Trends such as budget declining faster than progress, contingency disappearing, and gradual slowing in progress, all indicate underlying problems that may need action to resolve or to avoid getting worse.

In a standard business project a typical way to identify risk is to run a risk identification brainstorming session at the start of the project, and possibly at periodic intervals through the project. A risk checklist may be referred to early on in the project's life to trigger thinking about potential risks. As the project progresses additional risks are identified by the project manager and project team members as part of their normal work. The responsibility for risk identification and management will be with the project manager.

For a large business-critical programme a more thorough approach may be used. In addition to the techniques used on a small project, the programme manager could initiate risk management with expert reviews of project scope and plans. Assessments of novel parts of the project or innovative techniques which are to be used can throw up further risks. Assumptions will be formally logged, tracked and assessed for risk. Risk interviews will be performed regularly with programme team members and stakeholders. Although the responsibility for risk management is the programme manager's, he may be supported by a dedicated risk manager as part of the programme team.

Whether risk management is a small activity on a simple and well-understood project, or a major piece of work on a complicated innovative programme, as every risk is identified it must be documented. The risks can be documented in a standard template. All of the risks can be collected into a single database or spreadsheet, normally known as a *risk log*.

Project risk management – assessing and prioritizing risks

Knowing that risk generally has an impact is a good start, but a project manager needs to decide whether he needs to do anything about a risk or a group of risks. In the complicated and resource-constrained world of a busy project it is not possible to take action against every risk and it is essential to prioritize efforts against the most significant risks.

There are two ways to assess risk: *qualitative* and *quantitative* risk assessment. Qualitative is simple, but subjective. Quantitative is more involved, but can provide both a more objective understanding of risk and more information on risk. Qualitative risk assessment provides a way to prioritize risks and understand their relative criticality. Quantitative assessment enables a more absolute assessment of risk criticality, but it also can provide information to enable the sizing of project contingency and management reserves.

Qualitative Assessment

The classic approach to assess a risk is to make a subjective judgement of the risk impact, which is an estimation of the magnitude of consequences upon the project, and the likelihood or probability that it will occur. Qualitative risk assessment is useful because it is easy to perform, and can be done quickly. It suffers from two problems: First, it is subjective and therefore open to error and variability. Second, it only provides a relative assessment of risk. Project managers often think of qualitative assessment as best practice, whereas it is in reality only a common practice.

A typical approach to qualitative assessment is to make estimates along a three-point scale for impact (high, medium or low) and a three-point scale for likelihood (high, medium or low). Sometimes qualitative approach can appear as quantitative if instead of using an adjectival score a numeric score is used, such as 1, 2 or 3. This is still qualitative as, in this context, 2 is not twice 1, anymore than *medium* is twice *low*. An example of using such an approach is shown in Table 11.1.

Qualitative risk assessment can be improved by having clear definitions of what should be considered as high, medium or low probability or impact. Although determining the actual magnitude of probability or impact is still subjective, scoring against the scale becomes objective. Such definitions are situation-specific and depend on the organization's and project sponsor's vulnerability to and appetite for risk. An example is shown in Table 11.1.

Where a more detailed hierarchy of risks is required the probability and impact can be split into more categories. For example, they could be scored on a scale of 1 to 5, or 1 to 10. This provides greater granularity in decision-making, but it is important to avoid the trap of assuming that because there is increased granularity the associated decision-making is any more objective.

Another way to improve qualitative risk assessment is by using multiple opinions and not basing assessment on the sole judgement of the project manager. Risks can be assessed after discussion with a group of experienced professionals. Decisions based on subjectivity viewpoints are not necessarily a bad thing, if the judgement is based on experience. Using multiple experiences tends to improve the assessment.

Qualitative risk assessment is adequate for many, typically smaller or less complex, projects. Although it does not provide a true numerical understanding of risk, it is sufficient to prioritize action against risk. With enough experience in the type of project being managed, qualitative risk assessment is often sufficient.

Table 11.1 Qualitative risk assessment categories

	Probability	Impact
High or 3	>40% probability of occurring	Project objectives or business case are at risk
Medium or 2	10–40% probability of occurring	Project constraints are at risk by >10% (cost or time)
Low or 1	<10% probability of occurring	Significant inconvenience to the project

Quantitative Assessment

Where qualitative risk assessment does not provide sufficient information to manage risks it is necessary to do some form of quantitative assessment. The main situations in which qualitative assessment will not provide sufficient information are

- o *There is a need to understand absolute risk levels*: for example, to support financial investments. Saying a risk is high is often not enough for a business case. Usually a more precise measure of probability and a costed impact is required.
- o *Removing risk has a significant cost associated with it*: Therefore it is only done when the cost of removing the risk can also be assessed and shown to be lower than the cost of incurring the risk.
- o *It is important to be able to accumulate risks across the project to understand total risk a project is exposed to*: Adding up several qualitative risks is largely meaningless. Assessment that there are three quantified risks related to cost – one with 10% chance of a £10m overrun, a second with 20% chance of a £5m overrun, and another with a 40% chance of a £2m – can be used to provide an overall expected cost overrun. In this case it is £2.4m ($£10m \times 0.1 + £5m \times 0.2 + £2m \times 0.2 = £2.4m$). This type of information is also useful in making portfolio decisions.

If quantitative assessment is to be undertaken, it is not actually necessary to do qualitative assessment for risk prioritization. The information provided by quantitative assessment can be used equally well for prioritizing action against the risk. However, it is normal to do both, as qualitative assessment is quick and easy to do and can provide rapid prioritization before quantitative is complete. Quantitative assessments can be done against the most significant risks only.

There is a variety of quantitative techniques and describing them in detail is outside the scope of this book, as many are complex and can require a reasonable understanding of statistics and probability distributions. This section introduces only the most common forms of quantitative assessment.

One of the easiest ways to quantify risk is by the use of assessment tables. RAMP proposes the use of risk assessment tables to help with assessing risks (Faculty of Actuaries, 2005).

The simplest form of quantitative assessment is *sensitivity analysis,* which determines the sensitivity of a project to risk. Sensitivity analysis is based on the realization that all risks will not be equally damaging to projects. For instance, when there is slack in a plan, even if a task is made late by a risk, unless the slack goes to zero it will not impact overall delivery dates. On the other hand, any delay in a task on the critical path (or critical chain), will cause a delay in the project. Sensitivity analysis calculates the effect, on the whole project, of changing one of the risk variables. The impact on schedule delays, cost overruns and business case can be assessed by sensitivity analysis. By performing this analysis for multiple risks it is possible to both see the sensitivity to each risk and determine where the greatest sensitivity lies.

For simple plans sensitivity analysis, at least to schedule delays, can be performed by visually inspecting the plan. For complex networks a computer can be used to calculate and identify the most sensitive parts of a plan.

Where the overall effect of risk is required for a project, *probabilistic analysis* can be undertaken. Probabilistic analysis specifies a probability distribution for each risk, and then considers the effect of all risks together. There are many possible probability distributions to use (e.g. normal distribution, uniform, triangular), but usually more important than the distribution is the choice of maximum and minimum levels, or the range the distribution is over.

The most common form of probabilistic analysis is *Monte Carlo Simulation*. To perform a Monte Carlo Simulation three estimates of values for each element of a project plan are taken – the most likely, the highest and the lowest. A random calculation of a value that falls within the probability distribution is performed. The likely project outcome is determined by combining values selected for each risk. The calculation is performed many times, each time choosing a different starting value. It is not unusual to repeat the calculation 1000 times. The result is a probability distribution for the project. The more the number of calculations that are performed the more accurate the project probability distribution, although the benefit of each repeated calculation declines above a certain level.

Monte Carlo Simulations are almost always done with computer software. Given the volume of calculations per iteration and the need to repeat the calculations hundreds of times it is impractical to do them manually. Simulation software can be used to calculate distributions for costs and durations.

Project risk management – managing risk

As a result of understanding and prioritizing the hazards a project faces, it is possible to take action to manage the prioritized threats. A project can be managed to generally reduce its exposure to risk or to resolve specific risks that cannot be removed by general actions. The management action to resolve specific risks must be tailored to the risk. Sometimes, a well-chosen action can remove a risk altogether, but on other occasions it only mitigates the threat: either by reducing the risk's probability of occurrence or by lowering the impact if it does occur.

Managing risk can be understood by looking at three different topics, which this section covers. First, there are general risk reduction activities. These are the strategies and approaches which will lower a project's overall risk exposure, although may not resolve specific risks. Remaining risks following general risk reduction must be handled on a case-by-case basis. The second topic, therefore, provides an understanding of the options employed to overcome individual risks. Finally, there is a section concerned with the process of selecting and implementing the most appropriate option.

General risk reduction

The most helpful way to remove risk from a project is to avoid it in the first place, or at least to reduce the level of threat. There are a number of risk reduction strategies a project manager can undertake. The most effective way to reduce risk is usually by applying general good management practice. In the situation of a project, this means using the right project management approach, choosing the right team for the project, and having the right experience available to the project team.

Most standard project management activities are essentially concerned with removing uncertainties and ambiguities, and generally reducing risk. For example, clarifying objectives and scope, planning and estimating, and change control all help to lower risk by reducing uncertainty and ambiguity. Activities which ensure what was planned is what gets done, including the use of control systems and progress monitoring, decrease the risk of project problems. Specific techniques which apply only in certain situations (such as the use of Earned Value), prototypes, testing, implementation planning and change management also help to lower the likelihood of failure.

Where there is insufficient information to plan a project with an acceptable level of risk, ways should be sought to improve understanding before progressing and risking a wasted investment. Feasibility studies provide information to enable better, less risky, decisions to be made about whether to proceed with a project or not, and upon proceeding, how to proceed.

Project management methods emphasize the creation of many documents. From requirement specifications to plans, from issues and risk logs to change control forms, from scoping documents to project closure forms, project managers spend a significant proportion of time creating and reviewing documents. The reason documentation is so important is that it enables information to be shared in a consistent way, understanding to be common and information to be challenged. The simple technique of documentation may create a significant project overhead, and the level of documentation should be designed to be appropriate to the scale and complexity of a project. However, in general terms appropriate levels of documentation reduce risk.

Good project management makes assumptions and decisions explicit rather than implicit, and subject to review and challenge. Again this reduces risk and lowers the likelihood of misunderstanding and mistakes.

Of course the most obvious risk reduction strategy is to put a risk management process in place. The risk management process should ensure the ongoing identification, assessment, action taking and monitoring of project risks. It is not uncommon to find projects with no risk management or a cursory once-off risk review at the start of the work. A more thorough risk management approach, which is a component of active management throughout the life of the project, will be considerably more effective. But effective risk management is not just implementing a process and ensuring that the steps are followed. Good risk management is dependent on the project manager and the project team having a risk mindset. This means an awareness of the possibility of risk; alertness for the existence of sources of risk on a project; and a willingness to take proactive action to remove, reduce or resolve risks.

Risk management needs to be appropriate to the situation. Good risk management can save lots of problems, but it has a cost. The project manager needs to consider the appropriate level of risk for an organization and a specific project. She needs to think in terms of what risks are worth overcoming at what cost. How important is a project, and what happens if it goes wrong? If a project is not important and has limited impact if it goes wrong, then risk management can be less intense.

The project strategy and the way projects are designed can be tailored to reduce levels of risk. Very large innovative programmes tend to be associated with high levels of risk. Where there is a high level of complexity, unknowns and novel ways of working or use of new technology, projects can be broken into smaller, more manageable chunks to reduce risk. Similarly, the order of tasks on a project can help increase or decrease risk. Simply performing the most risky and unfamiliar tasks as early as practical in a project will reduce risk. There can be a tendency to leave unfamiliar or difficult tasks to the end. This is bad strategy as it leaves the least time to overcome unknowns and deal with problems. By facing difficult tasks early on there is a greater opportunity to overcome issues and problems, and if necessary to appropriately manage expectations.

Another key factor in risk reduction is the right size of a project team. Insufficient resource is a risk factor on many projects. But more important than the quantity of resource is the quality of people in the project team. The best quality people on a project will be several times as productive as the not so good ones and can often make up for significant shortfalls in resource. The most productive team will provide capacity to deal with the unexpected. In addition, the best people tend to work together more constructively. Most importantly, they will not be daunted by problems and challenges but will find creative solutions to overcome them.

Good project management makes sense out of incoherency, removing ambiguity, and limits the need for changes in scope or requirements. Risk is reduced when project-related information is as specific as possible. For instance, a plan should not just indicate that one person is required to do a task, but show the named individual responsible. Accountabilities and role definitions should be clear. Specifications should be complete and subject to sufficient review. Objectives must be precise and commonly understood. Any ambiguities or uncertainties in the trade-off between time, cost and quality should be removed. It is essential to understand which of the time, cost and quality constraints are most important and what are the boundaries that cannot be exceeded. However, making information specific does not mean making information concrete when it is not possible to do so. There is a risk in forcing the creation of precision and detail when insufficient work has been done to make it happen or there are too many underlying unknowns. In such a situation any specifics will be assumptions, which in turn introduce risk.

A common source of risk on many projects is when unusual approaches and solutions are chosen. These approaches may be completely innovative, or may simply be new to a specific organization. Being innovative provides organizations with a way to improve their competitive situation. However, innovation is generally risky. Therefore another broad risk reduction strategy is to decrease the level of innovation.

Reducing innovation does not necessarily mean not doing anything new. Innovation can sometimes be achieved by using existing knowledge and capabilities in novel combinations. Deliverables like new products and new IT systems can be developed from existing and well-understood components. Total avoidance of innovation is not a good strategy, but neither is unnecessary adoption of new ideas simply because they exist. Some functions of businesses may be attracted to novel solutions because they are interesting, rather than because they add value. Wherever new technology or techniques are introduced they should be challenged: Is there an existing and well-understood way to achieve the same?

One way to decide whether innovation in a project is required is to focus on the benefits and value achieved by a project and not on the implementation of a specific solution. If the only way to accomplish the benefits desired is with a novel solution, then it should be chosen. If the same can be achieved with well-known methods, then these should be considered as preferable.

Where innovation is essential, the risk can be lowered by running small pilot projects and feasibility studies to explore new techniques and technology. Where innovation cannot be avoided or where the opportunity from new technology and techniques is great, it must be well-managed. The most innovative components of a project should be identified and progress closely monitored. The sponsors and customers of any project with novel components must understand the threat of the unexpected occurring, and build appropriate levels of contingency into the project plan. Basing significant business commitments on innovative projects is always risky.

If a project is really uncertain, ambiguous and subject to ongoing change, then a project manager can put in place a structure to reduce uncertainty and ambiguity, but there are limits to how much clarity is possible. In these situations, even expectations management links to risk management. In a highly volatile situation stakeholders' expectations need to be managed to help them understand that there are limits to predictability. A plan is a prediction of the future, but it is a prediction built on current understanding and assumptions about the future. If the future is different in an unpredictable way, even the best and most experienced project manager may fail. A project's success criteria should be aligned with level of risk. Meeting expectations is normally a measure of success, even if it is implicit. Therefore, in highly risky situations it is essential to manage expectations as risk occurs, so the project may still meet stakeholders' expectations.

Different types of projects are variably susceptible to general risk reduction activities. Hard projects are typically more amenable to uncertainty reduction than soft projects (Atkinson et al., 2007). Soft projects are associated with ambiguity, and some predictions almost certainly will be wrong. Delivering a project successfully in such a situation comes down to whether the sponsor and stakeholders trust the project manager and the process she is using as the best way to get to an as yet undefined end point. Some managers have a much greater tolerance of vagueness than others. In some circumstances a willingness to accept ambiguity is required to enable exploration of the topic. The project manager's role is to bring different views together into a coherent structure as the project progresses. The willingness to let the project manager do this requires trust. If there is no trust in the project manager, then failure may be inevitable.

General risk reduction strategies will not remove all risk from a project, and there will still be a need to identify, assess and manage individual risks. However, by approaching a project with an awareness of risk, and applying good project management discipline, it is possible to reduce risk significantly. By ignoring hazards and designing projects without any consideration of threats, the challenge of risk management will increase dramatically.

Although it will not in itself reduce risk, it is important for the project manager to have some level of guidance of what is an acceptable level of risk, both at project and portfolio level. Without this project managers may ignore certain risks, or regard a level of risk as personally acceptable, which may not be acceptable at a corporate level.

Options for managing individual risks

If a risk is not removed by the application of general risk reduction strategies and good project management, then it is necessary to consider taking specific action to resolve it. Different actions are possible, and they can be considered through a decision tree as shown in Diagram 11.3.

The first consideration is whether a risk is *known* or *unknown*. This may sound like a nonsensical statement. Surely if a risk is unknown can it not be dealt with? Unknown risks, by their very definition, cannot be specifically resolved. However, it is in the nature of any future event that some risks are unknowable. The future is not fully predictable, and we cannot even predict the full range the alternative outcomes. Known risks can be dealt with by actions targeted at each specific risk. It may, on first consideration, seem impossible to deal with unknown risks.

However, by understanding characteristics of a project such as the scale and complexity of the programme, the degree of novelty and innovation, and the experience of the project team, it is at least possible to develop a general perspective on the level of risk associated with the project. Although no action is possible to resolve unknown risks, there can be an acceptance that there is likely to be a level of unknown risks occurring related to the characteristics of the project. Depending on the relative level of unknown risk possible more or less contingency can be built into the project plans. Contingency can exist in the form of time, resource and financial buffers to account for unpredicted problems. This type of contingency is sometimes called *management reserve.*

Management reserve is usually a percentage increment on the values in the baseline plan. A 4% financial reserve may be held and a 5% time reserve. Typically, management reserve provides a low percentage of contingency. Determining the level of management reserve is experience-based and situation-specific. There

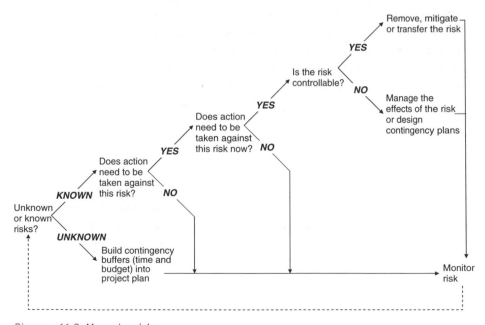

Diagram 11.3 Managing risks

are heuristics that can be applied to calculate the level of management reserve depending on the characteristics of the project. The reserve gives the opportunity for the project manager to handle unexpected risks and still achieve the project objectives within the project constraints. There are some pitfalls associated with management reserve. The most basic one is that the knowledge that there is some slack available can reduce project manager and project team motivation. To avoid this, management reserve should only be available on approval by the project sponsor and with clear identification of the specific, unpredicted risk that has caused it. Management reserve is a contingency for risk, and not a buffer for poor management or low motivation.

When the risks are known the options for managing them are much clearer. The first consideration with a known risk is whether it is worthwhile taking any action to resolve it. Action needs to be taken against the risk only if the probability and likelihood of the risk are sufficiently high. In identifying risks many small threats come to light, which are either very unlikely or will have a very minor impact that the project has limited vulnerability to. In many cases it is not worth the time or effort to resolve them. The cost or time to remove the risk may be too great, and a decision to accept the risk is taken. It is perfectly legitimate for a project manager to make a conscious decision to accept a risk. However, having identified a risk it is worth keeping track of it in case the status of the project changes to such an extent that the risk increases in probability or impact.

Although the outcome may appear to be no different, it is important to differentiate between a decision not to take action against a risk and ignoring a risk. Managers can be overoptimistic or unwilling to consider risk. This is common if they have made personal commitments based on delivery of a project. Deciding not to take action against a risk is not saying there will never be action, as the situation may change. It is merely saying that at that time it is not necessary to take action, and from the current viewpoint it will not be. Being aware of the risk, it is still possible to monitor it. Consideration also has to be given to the cumulative impact of small risks. A large number of low-probability risks may, cumulatively, indicate a risky project, and therefore may need action taken to mitigate them.

Even if it is necessary to take action to resolve a risk, it may not be essential to take action immediately. Although early action against risk is generally preferable as it increases the likelihood of effective results, in some cases it is better to leave dealing with a risk until later. If a risk is not imminent and is poorly understood, it can be better to continue to progress the project and monitor the risk until it is better-understood. In addition, projects do not usually have excess resource, and any action against a risk will use some resource – so delaying action may be essential.

In the situation where a risk is not an immediate threat it can make sense to prioritize action for later. If possible, a *trigger* for action should be determined. A trigger is the definition of a state when action is required. It may simply be a date, or the risk level rising above a certain level, or a minimum period before a stage of the project. For instance, a risk may be identified that must be resolved at least 20 days before the second phase of the project is started.

It is important to differentiate between a need to respond urgently to a risk and a high-priority risk. An urgent risk is one which is highly imminent. A high-priority risk is one with relatively higher impact and higher probability. It may be quite sensible to leave resolving a high-priority risk that may only occur in four months time, whereas a lower-priority risk that may occur tomorrow should be dealt with. However, in dealing with urgent risks rather than high-priority risks, the urgent risks must not crowd out any action against the high-priority ones. Overall, it is more important to deal with the high-priority risks than the urgent ones.

When a decision is taken to deal with the risk now, the next question arising is whether it is actually possible, from the perspective of a project, to *control* the risk. Some risks are *controllable* by a project. If they are controllable it means that it is possible to attack the origin of the risk and take action to stop it occurring or at least to minimize the level of threat.

Where a risk is controllable, it can often be dealt with early in the project's life.

The actions that can be taken to stop a controllable risk occurring or impacting a project are varied, and risk-specific, but generally fall into four categories:

- o *Removal of the threat*: for example, the situation in which a project is threatened with losing team members to fix high-priority operational problems. By escalating this risk to a senior level the project manager receives commitment that the resources will not be pulled off the project, and hence the risk is removed.
- o *Mitigation by reducing the likelihood of the risk occurring*: for example, dealing with possible estimation errors in a plan. If there is concern over the estimations a more experienced colleague can review the plan. Although this will not remove all estimation errors for certain, it will decrease the likelihood of them.
- o *Mitigating by lowering the impact of the risk should it occur*: for example, the situation where there is only one member of the project team having a critical skill set. If there is a risk that this team member will leave the company, it can be mitigated by training another team member. By training another team member, the risk of the first team member leaving has not changed, but the impact on the project is reduced.
- o *Transferring the risk to a third party*: in contracts with a third party for the third party to accept the risk. For example, a business running a construction project may use sub-contractors. A sub-contractor may bear the risk of cost overruns on parts of the project they are sub-contracted to complete. Although the likelihood or probability of cost overruns has not changed, it is no longer a problem for the business. Another common example is the use of insurance.

Not all risks are controllable by a project. Risks may arise because of conditions in the business or in the market in which it operates. If a risk is *uncontrollable*, it is not possible for the project manager to stop the risk occurring. In this case, rather than dealing with the source of risk the project manager has to be prepared to deal with the effects of the risk. Again the precise action taken is dependent on the specific risk, but generally falls into two categories:

- o Preparation to deal with effects as they occur. This may be associated with action to decrease the vulnerability of a project to a particular category risk, or with increases in contingency.
- o Contingency plans

A classic example of an uncontrollable risk is where there is a threat of a strike in a business due to failure in negotiations between a union and managers over a pay deal. A project team has no ability to influence whether the strike does or does not happen, but they can plan to handle the resultant problems on the project if some staff are unavailable to the project.

Contingency plans are additional plans in a project which are contingent on some event happening. Contingency plans should not be confused with *contingency* that exists as a buffer in the main project plan. Contingency plans are a series of actions to be taken to deal with the effects of risk and are designed to deal with the occurrence of an uncontrollable risk. They are initiated in response to a predefined trigger. Often the trigger is the occurrence of risk, but it can be more complex than this. If a contingency plan is designed that will take six weeks to implement, it has to be triggered up to six weeks before the results from it are required. If the risk can occur at any time resulting in immediate delay to the project, it may be necessary to implement the contingency plan straightaway.

Contingency plans which are implemented prior to a risk occurring are a form of insurance. Although the results from the contingency plan may not be required, as the risk may not occur, the investment is made to reduce the risk to the project. Let us illustrate this by the example of a project to run a major company-wide event that needs staff to travel from several locations to the business's headquarters. The business wants staff to travel together by train and everyone is booked a train ticket. Some weeks before the event a series of strikes on the railways starts, and the rail service is disrupted. The alternative way to get staff to the event is by coach. Ideally, the project team could wait until the day before the event and book coaches if the strike is ongoing, but the coach company needs two weeks notice for a booking. A decision is made therefore to put a contingency plan in place to book coaches two weeks before the event, if the rail strike is still going on, and there are no signs of imminent completion of the strike. Even if the strike is still going two weeks before the event, it may still stop in time, but the event is of such importance that the business does not want to take the chance. Hence, it invests in booking coaches that may not be required.

An example of a contingency planning decision is shown in Diagram 11.4. A project starts at time t0. At time t1 a key activity on the critical path starts.

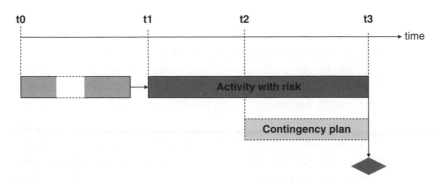

Diagram 11.4 The timing of implementing a contingency plan

The activity must be completed by time t3 to ensure a milestone is reached. This activity is risky, so a contingency plan is identified to ensure it can be achieved. Irrespective of whether any risk is realized the contingency plan must be started on or before time t2 to be effective. If it is started any time before t2 it will still be effective. If the risk occurs before time t2 the contingency plan can be triggered effectively. However, assuming by time t2 no risk has arisen a decision must be made. Either implement the contingency plan, at cost, to remove a risk which may not occur or do not trigger it, but leave a chance the project will be delayed if the risk does occur. This is a typical trade-off decision a project manager must make regularly.

Selecting actions to resolve and remove risks should not be seen as purely the mechanistic application of a series of steps. Resolving risk situations relies often on great creativity. The design, for example, of an effective and efficient contingency plan can require ingenuity and inspiration.

The process for managing individual risks

Managing risks starts with an acceptance that risk exists. Denying or ignoring risk happens, but is a dangerous approach to project management. Once a risk is accepted as existing, and is assessed as worth taking action to resolve, it can be managed.

The process for managing an individual risk has a straightforward set of steps:

- o Identify and log risk in a risk register
- o Assess, prioritize and assign ownership
- o Generate ideas for action
- o Select optimal action
- o Determine trigger event to implement action (if appropriate)
- o Document risk plan (if required)
- o Update project plan (if required)
- o Monitor for trigger event and, when appropriate, take action

Logging risks is usually done with standard templates that most businesses have available. The details of all risks should be maintained in a risk database containing the information from all the risks, with visibility to all the project team.

Generating ideas to overcome a risk and identifying creative ways around risks can be some of the most valuable actions a project manager or the project team take. For some risks the action to overcome them can be absorbed into the normal work of the project team. For others, it is necessary to review options in terms of what is the most effective approach and the cost of the action. The relative cost and benefit of any risk reduction action includes impact of risk. Some activities remove risk; with others the risk remains, but the probability or likelihood is reduced. A cheap action that reduces a risks probability by 75% may be preferable to a very expensive option that removes the risk altogether.

In selecting an action to overcome a risk, especially in more complicated situations where the action is a significant piece of work in its own right, it is necessary to be aware of *secondary risks*. A secondary risk is a new risk introduced by an action taken to overcome risks. There is a secondary risk associated with every risk mitigation action – the action may not work and it may create additional risk upon the project unrelated to the initial risk.

If the risk action is not to be taken straightaway, a trigger event must be determined. This may be when certain criteria occur, such as a risk increasing in probability, or may be as simple as a date or a known event in the future. Choosing the right trigger event is critical.

Complicated risk reduction activities may need their own plan, but this is not always necessary. Where individual risk management strategies are to be implemented in future they should be built into the project plan. The cumulative impact of all risk management activities also has to be accounted for in the plan. Although risk management is essential, it can be a significant drain on project resources, and, if a project was poorly scoped to begin with, may result in the need for re-planning.

Project risk management – monitoring risk

The whole project risk management process is built upon a general awareness of risk and vigilance in tackling the threats facing a project. Risk management is not an activity that can happen only once, or even at occasional periodic intervals, on the project. Risk management must be a live and ongoing process throughout the project.

If risk management is to remain an active part of project management it is necessary for the project manager, supported by the project team, to keep monitoring risk. The project manager should

- Continuously be alert and identify any new risk arising
- Frequently monitor status of existing risks; be attentive to changes in probability or impact
- Regularly check results from implementation of risk actions, and if they do not work, take subsequent action
- Periodically monitor trends in risk and overall level of risk
- Often check that stakeholder expectations are in line with the current level of risk

Monitoring risk does not just involve the identification and monitoring of known risks. Risk monitoring links to the other domains of project management. Events may occur on projects which change the risk profile. The project manager should be aware of trends across the project. Is there any progressive delay, overspend or increase in issues? Each of these may have a well-understood cause that can be resolved, but they tend to indicate a project in trouble and with increasing risk of failure. The earlier such trends are identified, the easier it is to take effective action.

Particular attention should be paid to the trend in the reduction in contingency reserves. A perfect project will not use any contingency, but typically the amount of contingency declines as the project progresses. The contingency should not be declining faster than the project is progressing. Unless the level of contingency is explicitly monitored it can be a source of problems. An apparently well-performing project can in fact have significant problems, if the appearance of being on track is being achieved by covertly using up the contingency. The danger is that, as the project appears to be under control, no action is taken to bring the project back on track. All of a sudden, when the contingency is exhausted, the project switches from being understood as on track and without problems to being in a difficult situation. Once the contingency is exhausted the project will often become progressively late. When contingency is exhausted the project manager has lost a powerful tool to manage a project successfully.

The level of contingency should have been based on an understanding of the level of risk associated with the project, and has to account for both the known and the unknown risks a project is subject to. Obviously, quantifying the latter is by its very definition imprecise, and there is always a risk that it is wrong.

Good management relies on open communications, and the way risk monitoring is performed supports this. Communication is required to understand, to take action and to be heard by managers and sponsors of projects. Ongoing risk management requires ongoing dialogue to identify, assess and take action on risks. Successful risk management needs openness and honesty, and this will only happen in an environment in which it is encouraged to explore and overcome problems, and not in one in which it is better or easier to hide bad news. Regular communication should exist between the project team and the project manager, and between the project manager and project stakeholders.

At the completion of a project the information on risks and the experience of managing risks should form part of an organization's learning for the future. It should result in updates to a business's risk checklist.

Portfolio risk management

Whereas project risk management is concerned with specific events on individual projects, portfolio risk management is more concerned with the average level of risk and spread of risk across the portfolio. Project portfolio risk management can be considered as analogous to an investment fund's risk management. An investment manager responsible for a financial portfolio is often willing to take high levels of risk on a proportion of funds under investment, as long as this is balanced with some lower-level risks or investments in assets with contrary trends. Similarly a portfolio manager is concerned primarily with the balance of risk across projects. Whilst in the case of one project it may be good practice to minimize risk, in the situation of many projects it is quite acceptable to have some high-risk projects as long as they are balanced with more certain project investments.

The portfolio manager must consider whether to accept an individual project into the portfolio both in terms of its own risk and in terms of what its potential impact on the overall portfolio is. Portfolio objectives should help in determining maximum acceptable levels of risk on any one project investment, as well as across the portfolio as a whole. The aim of portfolio risk management should be to reduce vulnerability of the business to any one project risk, and to increase the likelihood of meeting portfolio objectives.

Risk must be considered during the initial review and acceptance of a project into a portfolio, and at regular review points during the life of a project. At the initial acceptance of a project into a portfolio, the portfolio manager should seek to select the best projects, request modifications to projects if the risk is too high, and ensure projects' business cases reflect the appropriate level of risk. During the delivery of projects, the portfolio manager should be both monitoring for any changes in project risk levels and responding to risks occurring on projects and making the necessary adaptations to the portfolio.

The starting point for portfolio risk management is to choose the right projects in the first place. To achieve this, the portfolio manager should have a view of what is an acceptable level of risk for an individual project, and for the portfolio as a whole. This is organization- and sector-specific. Some industries, such as oil exploration or certain financial services companies, are used to taking up and managing very high-risk projects and having a high level of overall portfolio risk. Some other sectors, for example local government or pension funds, may be constrained by regulation or by their culture to a maximum level of risk. In very low-risk environments, it may not even be possible to balance a high-risk project with several low-risk projects, and all projects must exhibit low risk.

If a project does have too high a level of risk then the portfolio manager has a range of choices. The first is to simply reject the project. The second is to try and change either the scope of the project or the approach to its delivery to reduce risk to an acceptable level. The third is to review the project in the context of what else is happening in the project portfolio. If there are many low-risk projects then it may be acceptable to have some higher-risk initiatives.

It is important in accepting and prioritizing a project to ensure that the business case has taken account of risk. A £1.5m return from a project sounds better than a project with a £1m return. The former project may be prioritized higher. However, if the former has only a 50% level of certainty, and the latter has 95%, then the latter would usually be considered as a better investment.

Acceptance of project, its prioritization and the level of monitoring required – all are impacted by the level of risk. High-risk projects usually require more monitoring and more robust control systems.

During project delivery the portfolio manager should be monitoring project risk levels to be aware of changes. Ideally project risk will decline as a project progresses. This is often true, as there should be fewer uncertainties and ambiguities to be resolved as a project progresses. Projects which exhibit increasing risk as they progress should be of concern, and must be monitored. If the risk reaches too high a level then the project should be stopped or changed. There is a tendency not to review overall project risk as projects progress. This is a mistake, and robust portfolio management is as much interested in the shifting risk on in-life projects as in the risk assessed at the time of project approval.

Portfolio managers should also be monitoring resource risks across the portfolio, and planning actions to take, should a project be delayed in terms of impact on subsequent projects. The portfolio manager should resolve any conflicts in priorities, which occur as risks occur. Part of minimizing risks associated with human resource should be to optimize the levels of parallel working.

The portfolio manager and project governance should continually encourage the reduction of risk through the use of the most appropriate project and programme management approaches. Most project management disciplines such as scoping, planning and having a control system are fundamental to good risk management.

Positive risk and opportunities

This chapter has reviewed project risk management and presented risk as potentially having a detrimental impact upon a project or business. Modern risk management approaches realize that risk can take the form of an opportunity as well as a threat, and have a potentially positive impact on a project. There is a probability that a project will perform less well than expected, but also that it may perform better.

Positive risk management is sometimes called *opportunity management*. The aim of opportunity management is to maximize the return on investment and benefits from projects, and to generally improve any measure of success of a project. Opportunity management can use the same general approach as risk management. As risk management seeks to avoid or reduce the impact of risks, opportunity management seeks to maximize the scale of any opportunities, and to increase the likelihood of them being achieved.

The same approaches used to identify negative risks can also be used to expose opportunities. Brainstorming sessions, expert input and continual monitoring can be used to identify opportunities. Assumptions, as well as being a source of risk, can be a source of opportunity, if they are overly conservative. When opportunities are identified they can be assessed and prioritized. Following prioritization they can be managed and monitored.

Often simply challenging a project team with a series of questions can prompt the identification of many opportunities. Examples of typical questions that can be asked to identify opportunities are

- Can the project be done better, cheaper or quicker? Can more value be added to the business in any way?
- Is there any way the project can achieve more with the same resources?
- Can scope be trimmed to deliver same business value overall?
- Can the team learn more or gain more experience?
- Can components be delivered that can be re-used in other situations? For example, technology, business or project processes, learnings or deliverables?
- Can anything be added (be wary of scope creep) for no additional cost?
- Can suppliers to the project be leveraged to deliver more in response for getting project work?

Having identified an opportunity the project manager and project sponsor can decide whether it is worth pursuing. In a similar fashion to risks, opportunities can be assessed in terms of the potential benefit if they are realized and the probability of achieving this benefit. Following assessment opportunities can be rejected or prioritized and pursued.

Opportunities exist at a portfolio level as well as at a project level. A portfolio manager can seek opportunities to improve a portfolio or to improve the returns from a portfolio. An example of a portfolio opportunity is combining two projects with similar deliverables into one, and thus reducing the resource requirement whilst achieving the same level of benefits.

Earth Tech is a provider of design, engineering and construction services, targeted at the water and waste sector. Earth Tech is a global corporation and is part of the Tyco International family of companies. In this article Tom Connolly talks about the radical change programme the UK subsidiary of Earth Tech undertook to improve its project management performance.

Tom is the Project Services Director and he along with the Board of Directors drove the change process.

Tom Connolly

We started a major change process about two years ago to improve our project performance. As our core business is in delivering projects, it is an area we have a great deal of expertise in. The size of the projects we undertake varies, but a typical project budget is about £20m.

The success of our business is dependent on the margins we make from projects. However, our margins were too low, and there was too much variability in margins. Because of a number of factors our relationships with our customers were not as strong as they could be, and in some areas we were seeing a decline in sales. To overcome these problems we needed to radically change the way we were doing projects.

Our business revolves around delivering infrastructure projects associated with the water, wastewater and waste industries, and our customers are mainly the water utility and waste management companies. Such companies have an ongoing need for infrastructure developments, and they regularly tender for work. We bid in response to their tenders. When we win a bid, a project is setup to fulfil the customer requirements. The project is the responsibility of the project manager.

Historically, a project manager was almost like a mini-MD running a small independent business of her own. The goal of the project managers was to deliver our customers' contracts and to ensure they were delivered to expected margins. The project managers were supported by a matrix-based organization which provided the various skills to the different projects as required. Often, some people would be working on several projects at once.

There was a great deal of freedom for the project managers. But this meant that they each worked in his or her own ways. Although they had freedom, project managers did not always feel supported by the business. We had a culture which was inclined to penalize failure, so there was a tendency not to share information on projects which was not positive. The lack of transparency was visible to our customers and led to some mistrust which strained relationships. Risks and plans were handled differently on different projects. Projects operated as independent silos, and this caused problems as what was good for one project was not necessarily good for the business as a whole.

Let me give you a practical example of a problem we had. We had one supplier who provided a variety of components we required on many projects. Deliveries from this supplier were often on the critical path for our projects. We decided to talk to this supplier to find out why they were always in this situation. On review we found out that each project approached the supplier in a different way, provided different sorts of information and asked for delivery in varied timescales. As a result it was virtually impossible for the supplier to consistently meet all our needs.

Of course, we performed monthly reviews of projects. The problem was that we did not get a clear-enough picture of progress, and got a limited visibility of use of contingency. It was not uncommon for projects to report being on target for several months in a row and then suddenly for problems to appear. What was happening on some projects was that any problems the project manager had he was overcoming by use of informal contingency he had built into the plan. On these projects there were effectively two types of contingency. There was the official contingency that could only be used on approval and as a result of risk events. But project managers also hid "jam jars", where they might build small amounts of fat into the plan here and there. This meant there was some room for them to deal with some problems, but it also meant it was invisible to the rest of the management of the business, until all of this fat was used up.

There was a tendency for the project managers not to consider the long-term implications of any decline in contingency. As long as they could solve today's problems they tended to report the project as on track. The only time we would know there was a problem was when their hidden fat ran out and there was nothing left to deal with the unexpected. The leadership of the business, rather than getting an awareness of risks up-front, would suddenly be confronted with problems that could be difficult to resolve.

So we embarked on our change process. There are a number of elements to the change. Our projects start as a response to winning a customer bid, and we had to improve the handover from winning the bid to starting the project. Historically, the project manager was involved when the bid was won. Now we involve the project manager earlier. He or she has to sign off acceptance of the bid timescale, price and the designs of our solution. This means that we start in a realistic situation that the project manager believes is achievable. Any changes that occur during the project also have to be signed off by the project manager. There can be three types of changes: tender mistakes, client-led changes, which we will negotiate with our customers, and design developments. Design developments are generally improvements which are advantageous in one way or another for us to do, and so are accepted as being overall beneficial.

We have re-arranged our project staffing matrix. Rather than a project manager managing across a matrix, the team with the most relevant experience works full-time on the project. Our business is effectively organized around projects. As well as easing the challenge of delivering a project, this helps to develop and retain skills most relevant to particular project types. So someone who develops expertise in an aspect of "waste" projects, on completion of one project will move to another "waste" project of a similar type. This best utilizes our resources. The only time this does not happen is if someone prefers to do a different type of project for career development purposes.

To avoid the risk of projects working as a silo we have a number of checks and balances working across projects. For example, as a project starts up it will need the support of supply chain. Procurement is a significant part of all of our projects. The procurement strategy is developed against the project's work breakdown structure. The project manager is expected to apply our standard procurement policies, but can move away from them if he or she justifies it and gets the supply chain management function to agree with this. The procurement strategy for a project is signed off both by the project manager and by the supply chain manager, who works independently of the project. This process of dual sign-off by the project manager and an independent expert helps to ensure best practice and consistency across projects.

Another example of a check and balance is that every month project managers produce a cost report on project progress. This report is checked and signed off by our independent cost engineering function. Thus we know that the cost report is not only the project manager's opinion, but that it has been checked by an independent expert. We have other independent checks and balances working across projects, related to key aspects of our business, such as resource management, training, design engineering and process excellence.

Each month the project managers produce a detailed project report which is reviewed by our project board made up of the executives of our business. As part of our improvement to processes we have moved all our projects to be run according to the Theory of Constraints, and utilizing the ideas of Critical Chain. One of the key reports reviewed by the board is a comparatively simple, but very powerful, one-page diagram. The diagram shows the progress in completing the longest chain in the project versus the usage of buffers. In simple terms, as long as the project is progressing no more quickly than the rate of buffer usage, we know both that it is on track and that there will be no hidden surprises in contingency being used up.

It has taken us about two years to complete this change, and the results are very positive. The margin on our projects has increased, and the variability in margin has declined significantly. Finally, openness and communication has generally increased, and our relationships with our customers are improving. Executing the change had to do a limited degree of staff change, but in the main we have driven the improvements with the existing project staff. The success of the change programme is evident in the fact that whilst making the changes we have had our two most successful years.

More information on Earth Tech can be found at www.earthtech.co.uk or www.earthtech.com.

MAIN LEARNING POINTS FROM CHAPTER 11

- Risk is inherent in projects. It has many sources, including assumptions. In general terms it comes about because of uncertainty, ambiguity and instability in projects. The existence of risk on projects conflicts with a business's desire for predictability.
- Risk can not only affect the success of a project, but risk in one project can also impact other projects, have a detrimental impact on business performance and can even have a negative impact outside of an organization.
- Each project is unique and the risk it faces will be unique. Innovative and novel projects tend to be more risky.
- Risk can be identified and can occur at any stage on a project, from initial concept to project closure. The earlier the risks are identified the greater the opportunity to resolve them. Risk should be monitored for the entire life of the project.
- The first way to reduce risk is by only selecting projects with a manageable level of risk. Second, good management and the application of appropriate project management processes and tools will reduce risk.
- Risk can be managed. The steps in managing risks are identification, documentation, assessment, management action and review.
- Risks can be assessed by qualitative and quantitative approaches. Qualitative approaches are simple to use, but only provide relative and subjective assessments.

Quantitative approaches provide more objective and absolute measures of risk, but are complex, and many project managers are not skilled in them.

- There will always be an element of unknown risk on projects. This can be mitigated by the use of contingency or management reserve.
- Known risks can be directly managed. Some risks are controllable and can be removed, transferred or mitigated. Uncontrollable risks can be dealt with by contingency plans.
- Portfolio management provides the opportunity to manage risk by choosing the right projects and balancing risks across projects.
- Risk does not have to be detrimental. Positive risks, or opportunities, may also occur on a project.

REVIEW QUESTIONS AND EXERCISES

1. Find three examples of major failed projects that have been discussed in the press. What do you think were the main risks on each project? When would you have identified these risks, and what would you have done about it? Do you think that with better risk management these projects could have been more successful? Would you have rejected any of the three as an investment from the outset, given your perspective on the projects' level of risk?
2. Choose a project you will have to complete as part of your academic studies. Identify the risks associated with this work by considering what is uncertain, which requirements for the project are ambiguous, whether the work is likely to be subject to change, what could go wrong, and what assumptions you are making about the work. Prioritize the top five risks and decide what you will do to stop them occurring or to minimize their impact if they do occur.
3. Design a template form for capturing information about risks. What information do you need on the template? Who would you expect to complete this template on a project? What would you do with the information on the form?
4. What can project portfolio management learn from the way risk is managed in an investment portfolio? Provide examples.
5. Is innovation a good thing in business? Why? What are the risks and how can these be overcome? Find an example each where innovation has been well-managed and where it has failed. What differentiates the approaches?
6. In your experience how well have opportunities on projects been identified and acted upon? What are the benefits of putting a formal opportunity management process in place?
7. How would you decide whether a business was overly ambitious or overly cautious? How would you find the right balance, and what is the role of risk management in doing this?

Suggested reading

Risk management is a central component of all project and programme management approaches. Most project management and programme management books have a section on risk management, for example,

- *Project Management, The Managerial Process.* Clifford Gray and Erik Larson. McGraw-Hill, 3rd Edition, 2006. Chapter 7, pp. 205–40.

There are many more specialized books on risk management for projects. An accessible book, which covers the topic well and is strong on explaining the linkages between risk management and other areas of project management, is

- *Identifying and Managing Project Risk.* Tom Kendrick. Amacom. 2003

(Although this is written from the perspective of technical projects, most of the book will be of interest to any project manager.)

Supporting the books on project management, there are several formal and detailed risk management approaches. In some situations the domain of project risk management overlaps with more general risk management approaches. The PMBoK and APM BoK both contain risk management approaches. The APM have an additional text on risk management beyond the contents of the APM BoK. This is the *PRAM*, or Project Risk Assessment and Management. The Institution of Civil Engineers working with the faculty of actuaries have produced *RAMP*, or Risk Analysis and Management for Projects. Although this was developed for civil engineers it does have wider applicability. Sample references are

- *Project Risk Assessment and Management.* APM, 2004
- *Risk Analysis and Management for Projects (RAMP).* Faculty of actuaries, 2005

Bibliography

APM (Association for Project Management). *Project Risk Analysis and Management.* 2nd Edition, 2004.

Atkinson R., Crawford L. and Ward, S. "Fundamental uncertainties in project and the scope of project management". *International Journal of Project Management.* Volume 24, Issue 8, November 2006, pp. 687–98.

Chapman, C. "Key points of contention in framing assumptions for risk and uncertainty management". *International Journal of Project Management.* Volume 24, Issue 4, May 2006, pp. 303–13.

Chapman, C. and Ward, S. *Project Risk Management: Processes, Techniques and Insights, 2nd Edition: Processes, Techniques and Insights.* John Wiley and Sons Ltd, 2nd Revised Edition, September 2003.

Costa, H., Jarros, M. and Travassos, G. "Evaluating software project portfolio risk". *The Journal of Systems and Software.* Volume 80, 2007, pp. 16–31.

de Camprieu, R., Desbiens, J. and Feixue, Y. "'Cultural' differences in project risk perception: An empirical comparison of China and Canada". *International Journal of Project Management.* Volume 25, Issue 7, October 2007, pp. 683–94.

Faculty of Actuaries. *Risk Analysis and Management for Projects (RAMP).* Thomas Telford Ltd, 2nd edition, November 2005.

Kendrick, T. *Identifying and Managing Project Risk: Essential Tools for Failure-proofing Your Project.* Amacom, April 2003.

Olsson, R. "In search of opportunity management: Is the risk management process enough?" *International Journal of Project Management.* Volume 25, Issue 8, November 2007, pp. 745–52.

PMI (Project Management Institute, Inc). *The Guide to the Project Management Body of Knowledge*, version 3, 2000.

Voetsch, R., Cioffi, D. and Anbari, F. "Association of reported project risk management practices and project success". *Project Perspectives, Periodical of the Project Management Association, Finland.* Volume XXVII, 2005, pp. 4–8.

Winston, R. "Rethinking the Risk Management Process: The Reasoning and the Impact 'Assuming communication in risk management – Has it been working for us?'" *PM World Today.* Volume IX, Issue IX, September 2007.

12

building a delivery capability

Most businesses need to implement projects regularly. Whether a project directly provides new products and services to customers, or improves some facet of operations, projects are a key element of almost all commercial activities. The range of projects is enormous, and their potential to add value to organizations is huge. Project and change management approaches are subject to debate and continue to evolve and improve. Questions often arise about the merits of one approach over another, but the underlying requirement for projects is unquestioned. Projects affect almost all staff in an organization, either as active participants or because they have to live with the results. Projects are essential to and impact every aspect of business.

If projects are so fundamental, organizations must have access to a capability to deliver them. This project management capability should be able to fulfil the demands of the range of projects an organization has. The challenge facing the general manager is not to understand all the details of project management and so become an expert project manager. The general manager needs access to skilled professionals who can deliver the projects he requires. An organization needs to understand how to build a project management capability, and to learn sufficient about projects to be able to lead and manage this capability.

This chapter sets out the broad considerations in building a project management capability. It looks at what a project management capability is made up of; what the capacity of this capability needs to be; where project managers can be sourced from; and how they should be managed to deliver successful projects. But a capability simply to manage projects is of limited use on its own. To deliver projects requires more than project managers and, in most situations, simply delivering projects is not enough. The real requirement is to deliver value-adding change. Although project managers are an important component in the delivery of change, they cannot do it on their own. This chapter therefore considers what other skills are required in addition to project managers, and what the other determinants of a successful project and change capability are.

This capability to deliver value-adding change has many labels. It may be referred to as a *project management competency*, an *execution* or *implementation capability*; it can be called a *change capacity*, and various other combinations of these words. From different perspectives these phrases have various meanings. In this book, it is referred to as the *delivery capability*, which is the capability to transition successfully from ideas and concepts to value-added change in an organization.

For the general manager who is not interested in project management but who needs to have projects delivered on a regular basis this may be the most important chapter in this book. The opportunity for performance improvements, better returns and improved competitive positioning is dependent both on having a sound strategy and good concepts for change and on the ability to execute this change. Substantially better results can be immediately achieved by improving execution capabilities.

Developing a competence in project management

A delivery capability is made up from a number of components. The first one, which is most relevant to this book, is to acquire access to a team of project managers. The project managers must have the necessary competence to manage the delivery of the organization's chosen projects. The term project management is applied to a very broad range of endeavours, and project managers perform a highly varied set of roles. There are generic skills required in all project managers, such as the ability to structure work into a logical sequence, but many aspects of the skills and knowledge required are role-specific.

The project management challenge

The starting point for developing a project management capability must be to determine what sort of capability is required. Although all organizations require projects to be delivered at some time, the range and types of projects vary considerably. There is an element of project management that is truly generic, but many aspects of being a successful project manager are context-specific. A great project manager in the construction business may struggle with a complex business change, and similarly a business change expert may not have the correct range of skills to manage a construction project.

To understand the variations in types of projects, projects can be characterized along several dimensions. Key characteristics of projects are

- Application area
- Industrial sector
- Complexity
- Culture
- Responsibility for delivery – in-house or outsourced
- Novelty and uncertainty
- Pace

The application area of a project is the most obvious variable. Is a project an internal IT development, a business change, a new product launch, a construction project or a programme for the defence industry? The application area of projects is closely related to a business's industrial sector. Banking projects have common features, such as a need to be conformant to financial regulations that projects for a supermarket chain do not have. However, even within one business, operating in one sector, there can be requirements for different sorts of project management expertise. In a telecommunications firm, the challenge of managing the building of a new telecoms network is quite different from a call centre improvement programme; yet both are common projects within telecoms businesses.

Different levels of project management capability are able to deal with various levels of complexity of a project. Complexity has to account for a range of factors such as scale of a project, the number of departments involved in a project, the number and type of stakeholders, the variety of locations, and the type of solution being implemented. A project manager, used to working for a single manager in one location, may not succeed managing an international programme with hundreds of different stakeholders. Complexity can also relate to the level of uncertainty and ambiguity associated with a project, and hence to its level of risk.

Culture is usually an implicit criterion in selecting project managers, but often it should be more explicit and deliberate. In some situations an ability to work across cultures is required and understanding detailed cultural variations is essential. Culture includes the obvious such as the languages a project manager must be fluent in. It can include the need for awareness of differences in the legal and regulatory systems. It also encompasses the less-transparent variations in culture such as the degree of autonomy people expect, the distribution of power in an organization, how decisions are made, styles of interaction that are appropriate and effective, and the levels of patience expected, as well as the social hierarchy. Culture is important as project managers move between industries, but it is even more important when working internationally and with a globally distributed multi-cultural project team (Mäkilouko, 2006). A successful approach to managing a Chinese team may be less successful if applied to an American or French team. If the team is combined from all three countries, it poses yet another challenge.

Projects may be delivered by in-house resources, or can be outsourced or sub-contracted. If the work on a project is outsourced, the style of project management must be adapted. A project manager on an in-house project typically has visibility of the detailed working of each project team member and has some authority over the project team. A project manager dealing with an outsourced supplier usually has no visibility of the detailed workings of the project team and has no direct authority over them. With an outsourced project, the project manager can usually only manage by monitoring milestones. Where external suppliers are used, the style of project management is also impacted by the contract type. Managing a fixed-price contract is a very different challenge from working in a shared risk–reward situation.

Projects have various levels of novelty or innovation. Some can utilize existing technology and implement it via current development methods; others make use of new and unknown technology by experimental development methods. The focus on risk management versus the expected pace of delivery will vary significantly. Working on an R&D project is quite different from launching a new product built from well-understood components.

The ability to handle the pace of project work is also a critical factor in selecting project managers. Delivering on a single project every few months or years, is a very different challenge from delivering a constant stream of 20 small projects in parallel. Project managers who manage multiple projects in parallel need additional skills to those used by single-project project managers (Patankul and Milosevic, 2005). Knowledge of inter-dependency management, multi-tasking and simultaneous and inter-project process become more important.

The project manager must have the relevant knowledge to be able to communicate with the project team and stakeholders. The world of financial systems development uses a different set of jargon and concepts from the domain of developing weapons for the defence industry. The range of skills required varies as well. A project manager in the construction industry will almost certainly spend time negotiating with and managing a wide range of sub-contractors. A specialist in business change may have to call on the support of consultants, but will primarily be working with the staff within the organization.

The final question is whether the business sees project management as a core skill of the business or not. Competitive advantage can be achieved through projects. But competitive advantage comes about mainly because of the types of project delivered rather than through project management skills in themselves and how the project was managed. However, where factors such as speed-to-market or low-cost projects are essential to commercial success, an exceptional project management capability can assist in achieving this. The resultant question is whether the organization needs competent project managers, or best-in-class project managers with differentiated skills from those working at competitors.

In summary, whilst there are generic elements to project management that are applicable in every situation, a project manager needs a variety of context-related skills and knowledge to be effective in a specific situation. There is a range of criteria to consider when selecting project managers.

Types of project managers

In developing a project management capability it is important to be aware of the different types of project managers that exist. For a small organization with a series of relatively non-complex projects it may not be necessary to have professional project managers. It is possible to deliver projects utilizing line managers in the organization who have project management training and experience, but who do not work 100% of the time as dedicated project managers. For some projects, such as business change, it can be advantageous for the person leading the work to be a line manager in the area being changed.

Part-time project managers are a useful resource to call on, but they are unlikely to deliver the more involved projects that most businesses regularly have. Most businesses need some level of professional, full-time project management support. New product development is not an occasional activity in many businesses, but is a permanent stream of work, with a constant demand for project managers, and therefore justifies the allocation of dedicated project management professionals.

Anyone involved in selecting project managers will soon come across an assortment of titles. Project managers are given various job titles, and there is typically a hierarchy associated with project managers of increasingly greater skills. A typical hierarchy of titles is

o Junior project manager
o Project manager
o Senior project manager
o Programme manager
o Programme director

As an individual moves up this hierarchy he or she, typically, would be responsible for endeavours of increasing complexity and scale, and will usually be working with and interfacing to people of greater seniority in the organization as a whole. The more senior project managers may often manage initiatives with increased levels of ambiguity and uncertainty, and may, in addition to pure delivery, become accountable for benefits realization. Unfortunately there are no commonly used standards on job titles, and selecting project managers based on job title, without understanding the context in which that job title was given, is not a reliable mechanism to choose staff of the right level of skills. A project manager in one organization may well have significantly more responsibility than a programme director in another, although the job titles would suggest the reverse.

A hierarchy of project managers does not correspond to a hierarchy of line management. Seniority is related to project management capability, and not line management ability. In some situations the boundary between project management and line management skills is blurred. In some organizations project and programme managers all report to a line manager with a different category of job title, such as head of project management. In some other situations the manager of project managers is called the *programme manager*, even though he manages no programmes but is a line manager responsible for normal staff management duties. This means that irrespective of job title it is essential to understand the specific experience a project manager has before determining whether he or she is suitable for a role in an organization.

Whilst job titles do need to be treated with caution, it is important to understand the difference in role between a project and programme manager. Although this book has not emphasized the role of the programme manager, an experienced programme manager can bring a significantly enhanced skill set to a project manager. The basic skill set of a programme manager is similar to that of a project manager, but she is typically competent to manage initiatives of significantly greater complexity and scale. Programme managers are not only experienced with larger endeavours than are project managers, but they are usually more capable of dealing with multi-phase initiatives, benefits realization and business change.

As well as considering the seniority of project managers needed, it is helpful to consider whether specialists with in-depth knowledge of an aspect of project management are required. In some situations it is appropriate to consider developing in-depth expertise in areas such as planning and scheduling or risk management. This can require the recruitment of dedicated planning or risk management experts. These experts have a narrower range of capabilities than a normal project manager, but understand their specialization in much greater depth. Such experts can provide a range of services. They can be used as consultants or advisors for project managers when the latter have particular projects they need additional help on. They can work across projects to ensure the overall quality of an area that is important to a specific business. For instance, in high-risk situations it may be necessary to ensure project managers are managing risks in an optimal way. Specialists can provide central support and look at plans and risks from a portfolio level. They may report to a programme manager on large programmes which have complex plans or difficult risk management challenges.

Finally, an organization should decide whether it requires a *project management office* or *PMO* (for a definition of PMO see Chapter 1). PMOs can provide a variety services and can be set up for different reasons. The PMO may directly support individual project and programme managers or an organization as a whole. PMOs can have a role in developing and encouraging compliance to project management standards. They can act as a centre of knowledge in best practice (and if expert planning and risk managers are recruited they can be part of the PMO team). A PMO can provide administrative support to project managers. The PMO can be the consolidator of information across projects and provide reports on progress, change, issues and risks across a business's project portfolio.

Skills required

Once a decision is made that a project manager(s) is(are) needed the next question is what skills are required. The skills required in a project manager (Diagram 12.1) include

- Technical skills
- Context-specific knowledge – both of project and of the type of organization
- Personal capabilities
- General management and leadership skills

Let us look at each on of these in turn.

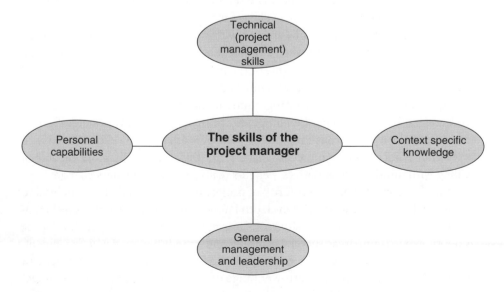

Diagram 12.1 The skills of the project manager

Technical skills refer to the core project management skills of a project manager. Technical skills encompass all the skills needed to manage a project from initial concept through to final delivery. This includes scoping and objective setting, planning, project execution, issue and risk management, change and scope control, and implementation.

Project managers gain their technical skills either through experience or training. There is a range of project management qualifications available. The qualifications have a strong bias towards the technical components of project management. Bodies such as The Project Management Institute, the International Project Managers Association and the Australian Institute of Project Managers offer various types of training and accreditation. There are also accredited training courses in specific project management methodologies such as PRINCE2 and MSP. Groups such as the Association of Project Management stress continuous professional development (CPD). The APM offer schemes to track project managers' involvement in training courses and seminars. Most of these types of accreditation come about following short training courses, with durations of days or a few weeks. Increasingly there are broader and more involved qualifications in the form of undergraduate and postgraduate degrees. The available qualifications are continuously evolving, for example, the emergence of complex project management and associated accreditation (Dombkins and Gray, 2006).

Having a project management qualification or levels of accreditation can provide useful guidance as to the knowledge of a project manager. By recruiting project managers with similar types of accreditation an organization can ensure that a common base level of project management understanding exists, and that there is a consistency in approach. However, care needs to be taken before assuming too much based on qualifications alone. An individual may have project management qualifications but this does not necessarily make her a good project manager. Project management is a practical discipline. Understanding the theory of project management and having a good knowledge of various tools and techniques is very helpful. But unless the practitioner can make them work in real-life situations, when dealing with various people, it is of limited value. Training can improve on purely experiential knowledge, but training should not be seen as a substitute for experience. Even a challenge as fundamental as developing a project plan is very different when done for real than when created in a class room.

It is important to note that whilst competency in the technical aspects of project management, and an ability to use the tools and methods of project management, is critical for project managers, project rarely fail because of technical reasons alone (Hyväri, 2006).

Projects are context-specific, and a project manager must have relevant knowledge of the organization and the application area of a project. But context knowledge should not be overemphasized. The role of the project manager is to manage the tasks on the project, and not to *do* them, and therefore the project manager does not need to be an expert in all the activities on the project. He does need to be able to talk productively to the project team members and to plan and manage their work. This requires an understanding of any language or jargon associated with a business or a project application and a familiarity with the concepts used in the project.

The context of a project can drive the need for specific areas of knowledge that project managers must have, for example,

o *In banking and finance*: an appreciation of financial regulations and risk and their implications upon the project
o *In construction work*: an understanding of health and safety requirements and the ability to select and manage sub-contractors. This will necessitate having negotiation skills and experience of different styles of contracts – from fixed price, time and materials through to shared risk and rewards.
o *In IT development*: knowledge of software development lifecycles, an appreciation of business analysis and software development, and an understanding of systems integration and testing.
o *In business change and performance improvement projects*: there may be a requirement to understand methodologies such as Six-Sigma or Lean.
o *In defence projects*: an understanding of government procurement and development processes.
o *In new product development projects in a fast-moving consumer goods business*: an appreciation of the customer and an understanding of marketing concepts.

Projects can be both a rewarding and a demanding environment to work in. Anyone selected for a career in project management should think the implications through carefully before progressing. There are certain personal skills or attributes which indicate a better likelihood of enjoying and thriving in a project environment. The ability to multi-task is essential. It is rare, even on the smallest project, for a project manager to be working on one task at a time. Even on the most well-planned projects unexpected problems will arise, that may cause feelings of anxiety or an expectation of failure. Project managers should therefore have a positive disposition, tempered by a realistic view of the challenges and risks a project presents. Project managers should have a capability to solve unexpected and often difficult problems. Because of the degree of multi-tasking, often high expectations and the levels of risks, projects can be stressful environments to work in. Project managers should, therefore, have the capability to handle personal stress, without it becoming detrimental either to themselves or to the project.

A project manager must be culturally aware and able to adapt behaviour to different situations, exhibiting behaviour that is consistent with an organization and a situation. Projects work within an organization and impact the organization. The behaviour of the project manager must be aligned with the organization and adaptable to different parts of the organization. Although project managers can successfully deliver projects without exhibiting all expected behaviours, it makes life difficult. Exhibiting aggressive and self-focussed behaviour in an organization that works on consensus is liable to create problems on a project, but so is the inverse, when a project manager seeks consensus in an organization that favours individual assertiveness.

It is not just the organization's culture that a project manager's personality type should be aligned with. Project manager's personality must suit the needs of an individual project. Projects will be more successful when managed by project managers whose personality profile matches the project, and project managers will be more successful managing projects that match their personality types. Factors such as the ability to handle differing degrees of complexity, technology and technological uncertainty, novelty, and pace are all affected by different personality types (Dvir et al., 2006).

Project management methods can be prescriptive in a way that is not always optimal. Real life varies considerably from situation to situation, and one approach may not work in all. Project managers often have to improvise or be able to respond flexibly to different situations (Gallo and Gardiner, 2007). Creativity in projects is normally thought of in terms of overcoming problems or in choosing a project approach or strategy. But creativity may be required in terms of adapting the project management methodology or lifecycle. This can create a conflict with the ideal of standardized approaches in an organization and does conflict with the idea of a project as a common control structure. A balance must be found which enables project managers to adapt approaches when they are not optimal for a particular situation and yet not allow unconstrained adaptation of well-designed methods. The challenge is to give freedom, whilst also questioning whether an individual project manager will really come up with a better approach than one that has evolved from the knowledge of scores of experienced practitioners. Whatever balance is chosen, an ability to assess situations and to respond flexibly is an important skill for project managers.

On top of the specific project management skills, the project manager has to be able to exhibit more general management and leadership skills appropriate to the seniority of the role. For instance, a programme director is usually relatively senior in an organization and is expected to exhibit the behaviours and skills appropriate to that level in a hierarchy. Most organizations have expectations of general skills in their staff depending on seniority. Many organizations want to recruit people who will fit in with their business culture. For project managers to be successful they should meet company expectations on line management skills and cultural alignment.

There is a wide range of possible management and leaderships skills required. Critical amongst these are

- Communication
- Networking
- Team management
- Group dynamics
- Stakeholder management, and organizational politics
- Motivation
- Organizing and planning
- Influencing, conflict management and negotiation skills
- Understanding of the business context

All aspects of communication are particularly important to project management. The need to understand and collect information, to keep people informed, to direct action, and to set expectations are all aspects of good communication. Project managers must communicate frequently with project team members and project sponsors. Successful project managers can communicate both in the terminology of projects and in the general business language of the organization. Successful project managers are good listeners as well as transmitters of information.

Project team management shares some aspects of normal team management, but often has unique aspects. Project team members can often be geographically distributed. They may be used to working in a function made up of people sharing their core skill. A lawyer or accountant may find it odd to be managed by someone without skills in their subject area, but a project manager will sometimes have to do this. Team members often do not line-report to the project management, and have a permanent line manager who can influence their behaviour both for the advantage and detriment of the project. Team members can be senior to the project manager, but have to work under her guidance and control. Managing teams in this context provides specific challenges for the project manager.

Typically the most important characteristics of a successful project manager are that she must be able to communicate and motivate people, and she should be decisive (Hyväri, 2006). Generally, the project manager's leadership style influences the degree of project success, and different leadership styles are best for different situations (Müller and Turner, 2007).

There is a range of models which describe generic levels of competency in project and programme management and which can be used to improve the management of project management (APM, 2007). Such models can be used to develop an organization's skills definitions, to assess existing levels of competency against, and to support the development of skills enhancement plans.

Size of project management capability

The size of the project management community is a function of the volume, scale, complexity and pace of the projects required. This can be determined from a forward projection of the expected project portfolio. In reality, it is very difficult to be precise about the number of project managers required, as there will be a level of change and fluctuation in demand. In addition, projects may turn out to be less or more difficult than expected.

Therefore, irrespective of how detailed planning is possible, the project management team needs to be flexibly resourced. An organization has to choose between

- Scaling the project management team to expected demand
- Controlling the volume of projects to match the project management resource available

In most cases a balance between these two options is found, with a relatively fixed-sized team of employed project managers, and flexibility provided by the use of contract resource.

Whilst sizing the project management team it is important to understand variations in demand. In some organizations there is a relatively constant demand for projects, in others there are fluctuations. These fluctuations can be linked to annual budget cycles, sales or variations in customer demands.

Sizing a project management team needs to factor in the time it takes to recruit project managers. From the point of deciding a project manager is required to the time at which someone is employed in a project management role can take several months. In addition, a newly employed project manager is unlikely to be fully productive for some months until she has had time to gain familiarity with the organization and develop a network within it. Where someone is needed quickly, and when an existing employee with project management skills is not available, it is usually necessary to find a contract project manager. Unfortunately even locating, selecting and negotiating with a good contract project manager can take a few weeks.

Selecting and sourcing project managers

With an understanding of the skills required it is possible to develop a competency definition, against which project managers are selected. This competency definition should be built partially on standard, transferable project management skills, but also enhanced with specific competencies required in a particular business. The next activity then is to source and select project managers or people with the potential to be project managers.

There is a number of ways to source project managers which can be summarized as

- Training and develop the skills of existing staff with an interest in projects
- Recruiting experienced project managers as permanent employees
- Utilizing contract or consultant project managers on a project-by-project basis
- Outsourcing projects

Each of these approaches has different strengths and weaknesses.

By selecting internal staff and providing project management training and development, an organization can choose staff with a known track record and strong context-specific knowledge. In specialized areas, the context-specific knowledge can take a long time to develop, so training existing staff as project managers can be a good approach. However, it does not give immediate access to the resources required to run all projects. Like many other competencies, it can take years to develop a strong and reliable project management capability. Not all staff, even those who have been very successful in their current role, will make good project managers.

Recruiting experienced project managers as permanent employees is a good way to build a new project management team, if no capability exists in the organization. It suffers from all the problems associated with recruitment. Recruitment can be resource-intensive, and it can take considerable time to locate the right people and convince them to join the organization. No matter how thorough screening and interviewing is, it is not a fully reliable way to select ideal candidates. If an organization has no existing project management competence it can be difficult to be sure that the people recruited are as strong in delivery as they may initially appear. Moreover, no matter how good the individuals' project management skills are, if they are used to working in a different environment, it can take some time before they are fully productive in a new organization.

Project managers do not have to be employees of a business. The opportunity to outsource projects of a specialist nature, or to temporarily contract project managers for the life of a project, is useful for many businesses. This is especially true in light of the often variable level of demand for projects and project managers. Contracting project managers for short term to deliver a project can be a good way to enhance a project management team that is not large enough for peaks in demand. There are many contract and consultant project managers available. Some organizations will contract to provide a variable number of project managers on an ongoing basis, providing a flexible resource pool.

Outsourcing a project takes the delivery of the project completely away from an organization. This can be common in areas such as IT development. Outsourcing projects has a mixed track record of success, but if well-managed can reduce risk, and sometimes cost, by using a company expert in the type of project to take responsibility for it end-to-end. However, it is important to understand that outsourcing a project does not mean an organization provides no resources, or is not impacted by the project. An external company that takes full responsibility for a project will still need access to potentially significant amounts of staff time to define requirements and perform acceptance testing. In addition, once a project is complete, it still must result in some change in the organization which cannot be implemented without impact on the organization. Finally, even an outsourced contract has to be managed.

The availability of external resources and outsourcers can provide significant flexibility in how an organization approaches projects. However, there are several downsides. External resources may be more expensive than employees (although with off-shoring staff also may be significantly cheaper). External consultants and contractors are paid to manage a project to the point of delivery, and they may lack commitment to the final outcome once the project is complete and their role is finished. Long-term benefits realization can be compromised. Finally, repeatedly using external resources can build up a dependency on them, and any learning a contractor makes on the project is lost to the business as soon as the project finishes and they leave. This can be a particular problem if a project develops intellectual property, which may be lost or not stay confidential to a firm. Determining the number and source of project managers must include considerations of the learning and intellectual property development needs.

Project management infrastructure

If project managers want to be fully productive they are required to develop of a set of methods, tools, systems and processes called *project management infrastructure*. The infrastructure provides productivity aids such as planning tools; ensures consistent ways of working which are easier to monitor and manage; and avoids re-invention and re-learning at the start of each project. This infrastructure is an important part of a project management capability.

Components of the project management infrastructure include

- o Project management standards, processes and tools
- o Governance and portfolio management processes
- o Knowledge capture and learning support tools
- o Software tools to support areas such as planning, resource management, portfolio management, along with reporting tools with common access
- o Document access and team working tools
- o Training materials
- o Reference guides such as standard risk checklists

The project management infrastructure should be appropriate for scale of organization and the volume and complexity of the projects undertaken. It can be developed over time, and enhanced by the project management teams. The infrastructure not only should be sufficient and robust for the needs of the organization but also should be flexible. Various projects present quite different management challenges, and an overly rigid infrastructure, which enforces one way of working, can inhibit optimal delivery.

Managing project managers

A delivery capability is often best provided by a proportion of project managers being employed directly by a business, where the proportion is context-specific. The project managers may be organized into a team, or distributed throughout the organization. Either way the project managers need management to be fully productive. In some ways managing project managers is like any other staff management task, but it has some unique features.

A business should allocate responsibility for the project management capability in the organization. There must be one or more manager(s) of project managers. The role may be the sole responsibility of a single individual, or may be part of the roles of many people who have one or more project managers in their teams. The way this responsibility is allocated links to the way the project managers are organized. (This is different from the organization of projects which is discussed in the section titled "Other considerations in developing a delivery capability".) At its simplest, project managers can be organized into either a single project team or a project division, or they can be dispersed throughout the organization. There are different pros and cons of each approach.

Typically, there are senior managers who have, as a core part of their role, an ongoing responsibility for the delivery of projects. For example, the CIO may have a significant operational responsibility, but also has an important ongoing project role for IT applications development. Similarly a role like Head of Product Development, who runs a series of new product developments and product enhancements, is a senior delivery manager or delivery executive. Project managers can be centralized into a single team under a Head of Project Management, or a similar title.

Centralizing project managers creates a single team that can be consistently managed. Allocation of project managers from a single team to projects can be easily controlled via prioritization processes. The role of a project manager is different from other roles in an organization. A team of project managers provides a way for the management and development of project managers to be tailored to the needs of project management roles. A single project team can facilitate the development of and conformity to project standards.

A distributed team of project managers tends to result in less consistent management of the project managers. It can be more difficult to ensure project managers are working to the priorities as defined by portfolio management. The approach to project management may vary from department to department. However, dispersed project managers can be faster-reacting and greater experts in local departmental context and needs.

The choice of centralized versus decentralized approach is a business-specific decision and depends on whether standardization and control are more important, or rapid response and an understanding of local departmental context is required. A balance can be found using a combination of organization structures, with some project managers embedded into the line and others remaining in a central

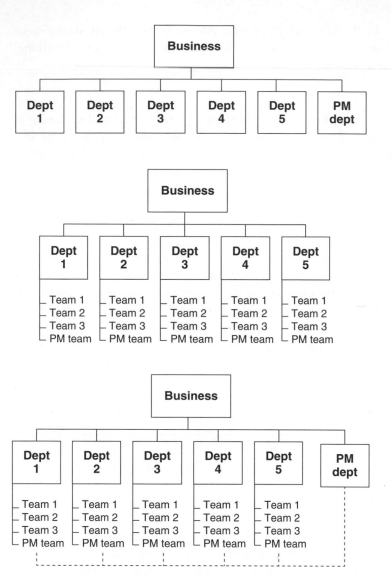

Diagram 12.2 *Different ways to organize project functions-centralized, distributed and combined*

dedicated project management team (see Diagram 12.2). For instance, the central project managers can deliver the larger programmes, any central infrastructure developments, and any projects drawing on common resource pools such as IT. The distributed project managers can support operations with smaller initiatives using departmental resources, and implementing local business change which may require detailed understanding of local staffing, processes and procedures.

Often project managers are located in departments which naturally are involved in large numbers of projects, such as the IT department. There is nothing inherently wrong with this. But in placing project managers in the IT department, there needs to be clarity as to whether these are IT project managers who only manage IT projects or the IT components of programmes or whether they are business project managers who happen to be managed by the IT department but who may be responsible for a variety of business change initiatives.

The management of project managers has to ensure that there are sufficient project managers within the organization to fulfil the business's needs. The project managers should be selected to fit with the requirements of the business. The level of resource may vary over time and needs to contain the right balance of internal and external resource.

Once a project management organization has been defined, it can be enhanced by a set of methods, processes, tools and reference materials. Common components of this are

o Competency descriptions to select and performance manage project mangers against. These can reference the various generic models designed to improve the management of projects. A summary of these models is available in *Models to Improve the Management of Projects* (APM, 2007).
o A defined career structure, with role definitions for the hierarchy of project management roles that exist.
o Development and training materials. These should be aligned to competencies and career structure and include technical, role-specific and general management skills.
o An appropriate project management infrastructure, which builds upon the knowledge and best practice commonly available, but is made practical and relevant to the situation.
o Portfolio management processes.
o A performance evaluation approach.

A structured performance evaluation process is a central block for managing, motivating and developing all staff in a business. For performance evaluation to be effective it should align rewards and encouragement to the behaviours wanted and the outcomes desired. Clarity should exist as to what behaviours and outcomes are required from project managers.

It may seem best to align performance evaluation to the value delivered from projects. The greater the value delivered, the higher the reward and encouragement a project manager should receive. The problem is that most project managers do not choose, or even have any real influence on, the projects they are allocated to. Even the best project manager will struggle to deliver a project which is poorly resourced or supported. For example, even if a project is managed very well, if it was designed to deliver £100K worth of benefit it is unlikely to deliver more than a less well run project but with a potential for £1m worth of benefit. Therefore, one approach to performance management is to measure performance in terms of delivery to plan and expectations, compliance with expected behaviours, as well as conformance to and enhancement of company standards.

Managing a project management capability should also ensure that the skills and capabilities of the project team are enhanced over time. Some project managers hold a conservative attitude towards expanding their knowledge and rely on existing skills, especially if they have been successful in the past. There is always an opportunity to improve, not only from widening exposure to a fuller range of project management techniques, but also from looking at related disciplines.

Projects offer a great opportunity to learn, and learning will occur opportunistically on most projects. But the quality and quantity of learning will be limited if it is not deliberate and structured in the right way (Sense, 2007). Learning may be an implicit or explicit goal of a project, and people may be encouraged or enticed to work on projects because of the opportunity to learn. But learning may take time and resources, so it needs to be built into the plan, and project managers need to have the remit to scale resources accordingly. Ironically, the optimal learning experience may come about by the use of sub-optimal resources. The most experienced and highly skilled resources may perform best on a project they are familiar with, but simply because they have most experience they will learn least. However, whilst using the least experienced staff may provide the best learning opportunity, it may present too high a level of risk. One compromise, to allow inexperienced staff to learn whilst reducing the risk associated, is to combine inexperienced and experienced team members or to use the most experienced staff as mentors and advisors to the less experienced.

Successful project management is concerned with real-life situations. Management of project managers should look at the behaviour and culture of the project management team and ensure it matches the range of needs of the real business. This may require different project managers for different types of businesses. The style of working in an engineering project can be very different from that required when working with a sales team. For greatest flexibility individual project managers should be selected to be able to work in the widest range of situations, but even so there will be limits.

Managing a project management capability involves line management of the project management staff and building an environment in which projects and project managers can thrive. The business culture must be supportive of project management. The wider management community must be willing to perform roles such as project sponsor. An environment in which commitments are made and held to, in which decisions can be efficiently made, and in which staff are aware of how their actions impact projects will increase the likelihood of project success.

To ensure that the whole management community of an organization can work in a way that helps rather than hinders project delivery, there may be a need for training and education outside of the project management team. Everything from explaining project management processes through to education on the role of the project sponsor will help. The delivery executive should support the development of a suitable project governance process.

The delivery executive has to direct and control the project management community and provide support to them. An environment which is appreciative of good project management will help to encourage the right performance. As with all project management, expectations management is fundamental to success. In the end no organization provides a perfect environment for projects, and many organizations, especially those that are not project-based, cannot structure themselves simply to optimize project delivery. Project managers have to be able to deliver in sub-optimal situations, such as imperfect sponsorship or unclear remit. The manager of project managers has an ongoing role supporting project expectations management in imperfect situations.

It should be understood that developing a project and change capability is a change in itself, and all the guidance of good project and change management applies. The objective of the team should be understood. Building the team should be approached in a structured way. Successfully building a project capability needs sponsorship, communications and buy-in. It is helped by rapidly showing success and building a reputation for good delivery.

Case Study **12.1**   **HOW DO YOU BUILD PROJECT MANAGEMENT CAPABILITY?**

Kevin Muraski is an experienced programme director. He has worked for several organizations involved in high technology, telecommunications and media. He is currently a programme director at BT.

Kevin Muraski

There is no single universal answer to your question. Whenever I am required to improve a business's project management capability I start by asking myself "what capability are we trying to achieve – what is the real business need?" Whatever is built has to fulfil the business's real needs. In truth, many elements of this need will be the same in any situation, so I have a general model in my head of what is required, but it has to be tailored to the context.

Let me give you a typical example.

The normal starting point when I am asked to build a project management capability is that the organization has a whole load of projects going on, but does not really know what they are and what their status is. In terms of resources, there are usually a few project managers, of varying levels of competency, dotted around the organization.

I bring the existing project managers into my team to begin with; normally I would immediately try to add a couple of good people I know, and then start some recruitment to complete the team I need.

In parallel with the recruitment I begin to address the needs of the business. To do this I focus initially only on the few top managers who run the business. If they've had no project function before (or a poor one), the starting problem usually is that they have no visibility of what is going on. So, my first challenge is to give them that. I seek to be able to tell them quickly what projects are underway, and what their real status is.

Once the senior managers have this view, and once they see that the information is reliable, their confidence increases. I then start to put some control around the existing projects. This can be as simple as binary information and binary decisions – is a project in a good state, or is it in trouble? Should we continue the project or should we kill it?

When this debate happens the senior management team starts to feel engaged in the live projects, and also with the whole process of project management. The interesting thing is that once you give them this level of engagement they give you support, but they also give you distance to manage your job because they start to trust you.

At this point I go down a level, not only in terms of project management, but also in terms of whom I am working with. The project reports start to become more specific and detailed, and I start engaging with the next level of managers.

In parallel I would have started to build the team I need. This means a review of existing staff and recruitment. I put the team structure in place to take over existing projects, which must also be able to start any new work the business requires. The team might be a pool of project managers with a set of account managers, or it might be a series of project management teams aligned to business units – it depends on the situation.

In terms of my recruitment I try to avoid the trap of thinking all project managers are the same. They aren't. I don't just mean that some are good and some are incompetent – I mean there are different skills for different situations. In my world the project manager needs good commercial skills, client relationship management and ability to work truly from end to end (from initial idea through to complete implementation and operational handover), but at the same time has to be able to go in detail in specific specialist areas. Other businesses have different needs.

I find skills by looking at experience more than qualifications. Qualifications and accreditation can help, but it's not my primary interest. I'm not against accreditation. Specific qualifications tend to help weaker project managers by giving them a reliable approach. They also help by giving a degree of common language. Beyond that I'm not convinced. I think if you are an external supplier selling project management services qualifications probably help in giving you the right badge – but as an internal support organization, it's less important.

The question I am trying to answer when I select someone is, do they have a real track record of delivery, and can they demonstrate it? I'm not interested in theoretical skills or an obsession with process. As much as anything I am looking for an attitude of getting things done and a desire to meet real business needs.

Beyond this there is the whole debate as to whether you create a central project management function or you distribute it across the business. Again, that depends on the situation and can probably be answered a bit later on when you are consistently delivering projects.

The capability to deliver

Many businesses have a project management capability, in some form or shape, which has developed over time. Unless the organization is a specialist project management consultancy, few firms need a project management capability for its own sake. What they really require is a capability to deliver projects and change. This requires a broader set of competencies than those associated with project management alone.

Other skills to deliver projects

A project manager can be compared to the conductor of an orchestra. Although a great conductor can help to create a brilliant symphony, the conductor alone creates no music. The conductor needs the support of musicians. The more complex the music, the more musicians are needed. So is it with projects, project managers and project teams.

This may seem self-evident. But it is not unusual to find that the solution to the problem of needing a project delivered in a business is the recruitment of a permanent or temporary project manager. A resourceful project manager will find a way to get the work done, even if he is not formally allocated a project team. But the only way he can achieve this is by carving time out from other work people are already doing. Increasing the number of project managers without simultaneously increasing the project team members will result in increased multi-tasking and delayed delivery of a number of projects using the same people.

The additional skills required in a project, beyond the project manager, are obviously project-specific. Construction projects require civil engineers and people to do physical labour. Financial services projects require banking experts. IT projects require business analysts, solutions designers, software developers, systems integrators and testing specialists. Each of these types of projects may have its own methods and approaches. A construction project may use a defined approach to managing a shared-risk-and-reward contract. An IT project may need to use a development methodology such as SSADM or Agile.

A successful portfolio requires sufficient resource to undertake the prioritized projects. This resource ideally has a balance of all the necessary skills to do projects, with each skill area proportionately resourced. In practice, this is very hard to achieve, and given the constantly fluctuating demand for skills on projects, there will always be relative shortages in one area and relative excess supply in another. The aim of resource management should be to minimize the levels of oversupply and undersupply of skills.

There are many skills which managers in organizations are well aware that project managers cannot have. Unfortunately there can be a tendency for project managers to become responsible for a variety of tasks on a project simply because no one with the right skills is available. If the project manager has the necessary skills, and if he has the time available on top of doing his project management task, then it may be appropriate for him to pick up these tasks. However, managing a project of any significant complexity is a full-time task. In the same way that a conductor may be a brilliant pianist, but no one would seriously expect him to conduct an orchestra and play the piano at the same time, no one should assume that a project manager should be doing anything but project management.

Examples of areas of work that project managers can be swept into, and which are often better done by professionals in the associated field, include business analysis, change management, systems integration and testing, supplier negotiations, contract and legal work, project office and business communications (Newton, 2005). An experienced project manager, with sufficient time available, may be able to take full responsibility for any of these tasks. Where the tasks are minor, and the risk associated with mistake is small, then it is probably appropriate for a project manger to undertake the task. But is should not be assumed without some evaluation. It is also context-specific. For example, a construction project manager would almost certainly be expected to deal with sub-contractor negotiations, whilst a project manager used to managing internal software developments may not have the appropriate skills and may need specialist support in dealing with external suppliers.

In addition to various specialized resources, projects require business-as-usual resource. This is not just because projects have tasks that need people to do. Projects need access to people with a current understanding of how an organization works and what the organization requires in order to implement business change. If there is a continuous stream of projects there always must be excess resource or "fat" in the operational departments of the organization to provide this.

There is a danger that overzealous financial management may demand that this fat is cut out once projects are complete. The logic is that if the operational departments were able to cope with this resource allocated to a project, then they do not really need it. Occasionally, this can be the right thing to do, but more often it is short-termist and should be avoided. Making staff redundant when projects finish reduces the desirability of working on projects; often removes the people with the best skills; loses the knowledge that has been developed on the project; and the same people may be needed again soon.

The capability to change

Projects are undertaken to achieve beneficial change. Depending on the type of change, realizing it may require more than project management. The change may directly result from a project, or a project may be just one part of making a change occur. Given that change is critical for the long-term success of many businesses, it is important that organizations have a capacity for change. This may require capabilities to be developed which are broader than those typically associated with project management. The capacity to perform change has three components:

1. Capability to change
2. Capability to maintain daily operations in situation of changes
3. Capability to implement subsequent changes (Meyer and Stensaker, 2006)

For those changes that are best delivered as a project, of the three components of a change capacity, only the first, *capability to change*, is related to project management. It is worth noting that projects are not always the best vehicle to achieve certain types of outcomes (the limits to project management are explored in Chapter 13).

There are change methods which can work in conjunction with project and programme management, and which can enhance and extend them. However, the lifecycle of change and project management are different. Change management starts before project management in terms of setting the environment for and gathering enthusiasm for change. Change management also continues after the implementation of deliverables and the completion of a project. Change management should ensure that operations are optimized following the change and also that the change is sustained.

The capability to maintain some level of daily operations is critical for many businesses, even during project implementation. Irrespective of the importance of an individual project, unless a business is a project business such as a construction company, the organization's survival is dependent on daily operations and not projects. Projects threaten the operations because they take resources from operations to work on the project. Moreover, the activity of implementing change disrupts operations.

The ability to maintain daily operations in the situation of change is an important capability, essential to any business that undergoes regular modifications. This ability to work, without compromising daily operations, is a key consideration in change planning and change execution. It relies on the skills and capabilities of operational managers and their team as well as the project team.

Planning a change project cannot ignore the requirements of business operations. Some activities undertaken to support a change, or even seen as essential to a change can be detrimental to operations. For example, John Kotter, the authority on business change, stresses the need to create a sense of urgency and even a crisis to generate support for a change (Kotter, 1996). This generation of a crisis may energize the change team, but it can be detrimental to existing operations. Similarly ensuring there is participation in a change from operational staff can be detrimental for current operations although it is essential to the change.

The change in a business is never finished in one single initiative. There is a continuous and ongoing need to modify and adapt businesses to their environment, to respond to competitive threats and to seize opportunities. Project management and much of change management regard changes as individual initiatives. There is an underlying and often unspoken assumption that if one initiative can be delivered successfully, the next one can as well. But changes are not independent entities. Actions and responses to actions in one change influence the level of success in the next. An organization can only absorb so much change at any one time, and the pacing of a series of changes is a key decision in overall success, as well as in the maintenance of daily operations. Staff experience of one change influences their attitude to the next one. Employees need a positive view of change to support the future changes. A poorly executed change can make the next change much more difficult.

Developing a delivery capability requires the building of a change management capability as well. It may be a component of the project management capability or separate. A business needs the development of the skills to maintain daily operations during change and has to plan and design projects with consideration of the need to implement subsequent changes. Success cannot be viewed purely in terms of return on a project investment, but also must consider the impact on operations and the impact on the ability to make subsequent changes.

Other considerations in developing a delivery capability

Whatever components a delivery capability is built up from, and whatever the precise needs of a specific business, the delivery capability has to work within the environment of the organization. The successful application of delivery methods and tools, and the productive use of the skills of experienced project managers, is affected by characteristics of the organization. Characteristics as varied as the way decisions are made or the way the organization is structured, whilst not directly related to project and change, have a strong influence on the ability to deliver successfully.

In some situations it is appropriate to adapt the characteristics of an organization to facilitate better delivery of projects. In other circumstances it is not, especially in organizations whose primary role is to provide customer products and services via its business-as-usual operations. For instance, construction companies are often organized to support the delivery of civil engineering projects that are their core business. In contrast, a bank is more likely to be organized for daily operational efficiency and to support the provision of banking services to customers than to optimize project delivery. Whether an organization can be adapted to meet project needs or not, it is at least worthwhile understanding what characteristics of an organization may impact the ability to deliver projects.

Examples of characteristics of organizations that can affect delivery effectiveness and efficiency include

- The level of participation, involvement and support for projects
- Decision-making processes
- Responsibility for the development of a delivery capability
- Organizational structures
- The flexibility of the organization

Successful project management requires the active participation of and general support from senior management team. Governance processes are the responsibility of a company's executive. Portfolio management needs the ongoing involvement of senior stakeholders. Successful change needs the active and visible sponsorship of the leaders of the affected areas of a business.

If the general management community is to be effective in supporting projects they need to have a good awareness and understanding of project management concepts, such as risk. It is the responsibility of project managers to communicate to the business community in business language and not in project management jargon. However, some project management concepts are powerful, and it is helpful for all managers to understand some project terminology. Without this there is a danger of regular conversations between project managers and business leaders not achieving effective communication.

Projects often need decisions to be made by senior managers. Whether it is budgetary approval to start a project, a decision to continue with a project following the results of a feasibility study, or agreement to one option for a solution amongst many, decisions are a key task in project plans. Where decision-making processes are responsive to project needs, it is easier to keep projects to timelines. Where decision making is involved and slow, projects will regularly find that the needs for decisions are on their critical path, and the project may fall behind schedule.

Responsibility for the development of a delivery capability needs to be clear. There are different strengths and weaknesses of centralized and decentralized approaches to developing project capabilities, but whichever approach is chosen it should be explicit. Significant amounts of time and resource can be repeatedly wasted on projects trying to decide which set of delivery resources are responsible for which set of activities on which projects.

In project-based industries ownership for project management may be allocated naturally. If what the business does is projects, then building and enhancing a project management capability is core to most senior roles. However, in non-project-based businesses, responsibility can fall onto those departments most closely associated with projects, such as IT.

There are different ways to organize the team working on a project. Theoretically, this is independent of a business's organizational structure. But in practice, the organizational structure will influence and constrain the types of project organization that are possible. The most effective structure for the delivery of projects is a project team with dedicated project resources only working for a project manager. This is not always possible. The next most effective is the matrix team, where people report in a line fashion to a line manager who may be a functional or process owner. The same staff report for the period of a project to a project manager. The least effective is the pure functional project team structure (Hyväri, 2006). An extension of a project organization with fully dedicated resources can be to move the project team intact from project to project. Of course, what is ideal for the project may not be what is best for the organization overall.

Finally, project and change success is related to levels of organizational flexibility. Projects result in change. Repeated changes are easier in organizations that can adapt to required modifications in a flexible way. Flexibility can exist in all components of an organization, whether it is in processes, IT systems, or organizational structures. For example, a project may result in modifications to job roles for some staff. In some organizations this will be a major problem that will require negotiations with staff over job content, rewards and training; in some others, job roles are defined flexibly and staff expect them to change regularly and adopt changes readily.

Flexibility does not arise accidentally – it can be deliberately planned and designed. Building flexibility into an organization accepts that the future is unpredictable in terms of specific changes that will be required, but also accepts the need to respond to change on a continuous basis. Flexibility can be designed into IT systems, office layouts, factory designs, organizational structures and so on.

Flexibility has a cost associated with it. Few organizations need completely unbounded flexibility, and it is questionable whether it is achievable. But flexibility in areas such as an ability to introduce rapidly new products, change the pricing of products and the way products are bundled together for sales greatly assist in efficient delivery of change.

Case Study 12.2   FINDING SOMEONE TO GROW A BUSINESS

David is an entrepreneur who has been involved in the startup of several businesses. In this short article he talks about his experience with Rated People, a company he co-founded with Andrew Skipwith and Dafydd Hopkin in autumn 2005. Rated People provide a service to link consumers with local trades people, to fulfil work they require done on their homes. It provides facilities for consumers to place adverts for projects, as well as providing ratings and feedback on trades people. Rated People is the United Kingdom's leading recommendation site for trades. It is growing rapidly. At the time of writing this article the service has had over 100,000 home improver customers, and over 12,000 trade suppliers are registered with them. These numbers are increasing quickly.

David Caswell

Q: How do you go about building the capabilities you need to grow your business?
We have been in business for about two years now, although a fair proportion of that time was spent getting ready for trading. We started actively trading about nine

months ago. We have been very successful and are growing faster than we originally expected, which is obviously great, but it gives us a management problem in making the jump from a small to a sizable business earlier than we expected.

Making the change from the scale of business we are, to the scale of business we will be requires a major enhancement of our infrastructure as well as the recruitment of a new expanded leadership team. The development of our infrastructure and increase in headcount has to be balanced by our growth as a business – so development is not purely a technical issue, but is intimately tied to our commercial success.

Right now, we are still a relatively small business. We have 10 people directly employed in the United Kingdom, plus a number of suppliers we use for some of our operations. This includes an outsourced offshore call centre. The challenge for us in expanding our headcount is to find the right people who can work in the environment of what is still a relatively small business. We are probably never going to employ thousands of people and our culture and environment is very different from a big business.

To make the changes, we need someone who can lead and manage the delivery of our enhanced infrastructure and expansion. But as a small company we cannot recruit a specialist purely with delivery skills. We need someone with a combination of marketing, operational and business change abilities. As well as doing the role we are recruiting for, the person has to free up time in our existing leadership to focus more on strategy.

Of course, it is a lot to expect to find someone with all of these skills, and in reality any candidate is likely to be a compromise in one area or another. In any area that the candidate is weaker we will consider what team he needs around him to complement his skills.

Given our success to date and our growth plans, we need to recruit someone with significant experience. That means someone with an established track record from an established business. However, anyone joining us has to understand that we are different from a big business. Probably as important as the candidate's specific skills in any area is his ability to fit in with the culture and scale of the organization. Although we are ambitious, when you are a small company you do not have the luxury of all the support and services that a large company has. So we need someone who is both able to work at a senior level and lead and direct people, as well as someone who is not afraid to get his or her hands dirty and muck in with the day-to-day work.

In a big business everyone at a senior level tends to have the same bag of basic competencies. Whether it's man management or negotiation skills, they will have them. This is not true in a small business, where people are employed because they can add energy, work with its pace of change, and create value in the business. Relationships tend to be closer and can be more intense. Anyone moving from a big business to a small business has to understand this cultural difference and be able to work in it.

Delivering our enhanced infrastructure is key to our success, and finding the right person who fits with our business is essential to that. That person has to bring a hybrid skill set including both business change and development, as well as the ability to drive the daily growth and expansion of a business.

More information on Rated People can be found at www.**ratedpeople.com**.

MAIN LEARNING POINTS FROM CHAPTER 12

- With regular streams of projects, organizations need to develop a project management capability.
- Considerations in building such a capability include the seniority of project managers, the size of the team, the balance of part-time and full-time staff and in-house versus contract resource, and the organization of the team.
- A centralized project management team can more easily provide controlled and standardized project management, but it may be remote from business operations. Decentralized teams can be close to business operations, but may be more difficult to control, standardize and fit with HR policies in individual departments. A useful compromise is to have a small central team and decentralized project managers.
- Project managers should be able to manage in the environment of the organization, for example, sector, application area and culture, and the complexity, pace and novelty of projects.
- Project managers need appropriate technical skills, context-specific knowledge, personal capabilities and general management and leadership skills.
- Project managers' skills can be improved with training, but training and qualifications should enhance rather than be a substitute for experience. A culture in which learning is ongoing and projects are regularly reviewed should be encouraged.
- Project managers need an infrastructure to support their work, for example, systems, standards, processes and tools, and document management and sharing facilities.
- Developing a project management capability is assisted by HR polices which support the recruitment and development of project managers, and appropriate performance evaluation linked to project work.
- Delivering projects requires more than project managers, for example, access to other specialist resources and operational staff for projects.
- The most effective way to manage staff on projects is by direct line control; the least effective way is a pure functional structure. Matrix management provides a practical compromise.
- The nature of the organization and its ability to change whilst maintaining daily operations are key determinants of project success. Flexibility can be designed into an organization.

REVIEW QUESTIONS AND EXERCISES

1. Write an interview questionnaire for selecting project managers. What are the most important questions? How would you test the answers given to give yourself confidence in the candidates you select?
2. When selecting a project manager which is more important, qualifications or experience? Justify your answer.
3. Imagine that you are presented with the challenge of building a new project management team in an organization. How would you approach this challenge? Note any assumptions you make.
4. Review a project you are familiar with from your work experience. What range of capabilities and skills were required to complete this project? How important were project management skills?

5. What are the relative advantages and disadvantages of outsourcing a project to a third party? When would you consider outsourcing? When would you insist a project has to be completed in house?
6. Choose three companies which you have some familiarity with and which have different styles of organizational structure. How do you think the different ways of organizing impact the ability to deliver projects? Which is the best? What actions can project managers take to mitigate any problems which arise from organizational design?
7. Describe, at a high level, the alternative ways to organize a team of project managers, the team working on a project and the departments in a business. What is the relationship between the way the organization, the project managers and a project team are organized? For each, give an example of a business in which it is the primary consideration in organizational design.
8. Identify several examples of flexibility in organizations. How do you think this will assist in delivering change? Do you think the cost of flexibility in these situations is less than the potential benefits?

Suggested reading

Carroll's 2005 book contains a helpful chapter on building a project management capability:

> o *Project Delivery in Business-As-Usual Organizations.* Tim Carroll. Gower, 2006, Chapter 3, pp. 25–86

One way organizations can gain an understanding of their level of capability, their strengths and weaknesses in project management, and develop a plan to improve their capabilities is by the use of maturity models. The Association of Project Management has produced a guide which introduces various models for understanding and improving project management competencies:

> o *Models to Improve the Management of Projects.* Association of Project Management, 2007

Examples of specific maturity models described in detail are

> o *Organizational Project Management Maturity Model (Opm3) Overview.* Project Management Institute, 2004
> o *Project Portfolio Management Maturity Model.* James S Pennypacker (ed.). Center for Business Practices, 2005

References

APM (Association for Project Management). *Models to Improve the Management of Projects,* 2007.

Carroll, Tim. *Project Delivery in Business-As-Usual Organizations.* Gower, 2006.

Crawford, L., Morris, P., Thomas, J. and Winter, M. "Practitioner development: From trained technicians to reflective practitioners". *International Journal of Project Management.* Volume 24, Issue 8, November 2006, pp. 722–33.

Dombkins, D. and Gray, N. *Project Management and Organisational Change (Delivering Tangible Change Outcomes Using Innovative Complex Project Management),* 2006.

Dvir, D., Sadeh, A. and Malach-Pines, A. "Projects and project managers: The relationship between project managers' personality, project types, and project success". *Project Management Journal.* Volume 37, Issue 5, December 2006, pp. 36–48.

Gallo, M. and Gardiner, P. "Triggers for a flexible approach to project management within UK financial services". *International Journal of Project Management*. Volume 25, Issue 5, July 2007, pp. 446–57.

Hyväri, I. "Project management effectiveness in project-orientated business organizations". *International Journal of Project Management*. Volume 24, Issue 3, April 2006, pp. 216–25.

Jugdev, K., Mathur, G. and Fung, T. "Project management assets and their relationship with the project management capability of the firm". *International Journal of Project Management*. Volume 25, Issue 6, August 2007, pp. 560–68.

Kotter, J. *Leading Change*. Harvard Business School Press, 1996.

Longman, A. and Mullis, J. "Project management: Key tool for implementing strategy". *Journal of Business Strategy*. Volume 25, Issue 5, 2004, pp. 54–60.

Lyneham-Brown, D. "Business analysis and project management – Roles and inter-relationship". *Project Manager Today*, Volume XIII, Issue 3, March 2001.

Mäkilouko, M. "Multicultural project leadership". *Project Perspectives, Periodical of the Project Management Association, Finland*. Volume XXVII, 2006, pp. 16–19.

Meyer, C. and Stensaker, I. "Developing capacity for change". *Journal of Change Management*. Volume 6, Issue 2, June 2006, pp. 217–31.

Müller, R. and Turner, J. "Matching the project manager's leadership style to project type". *International Journal of Project Management*. Volume 25, Issue 1, January 2007, pp. 21–32.

Newton, R. *The Project Manager, Mastering the Art of Delivery*. FT Prentice Hall, 2005.

Nieman, R. *Execution Plain and Simple – Twelve Steps to Achieving Any Goal on Time and on Budget*. McGraw Hill, 2004.

Patankul, P. and Milosevic, D. "Multiple-Project managers what competencies do you need?" *Project Perspectives, Periodical of the Project Management Association, Finland*. Volume XXVII, 2005, pp. 28–33.

Sense, A. "Structuring the project environment for learning". *International Journal of Project Management*. Volume 25, Issue 4. May 2007, pp. 405–12.

Suda, L. *Linking Strategy, Leadership and Organization Culture for Project Success*. 1st UTD Project Management Symposium. August 2007.

13

context, culture
and the limits
to project management

The basis for many descriptions of project management is an attempt to capture an understanding of *best practice*. The thinking is that by documenting project management best practice the optimal repeatable and standardized method for delivering projects is created. There are a number of advantages to a repeatable and standardized method. In theory it should be effective and efficient. In addition, the consistency that a standardized approach brings means it is relatively easy to measure, manage and control when compared with a unique approach for every initiative.

Unfortunately there are a number of difficulties with the best practice approach. What purports to be best practice rarely is confirmed by validated research to be so. It is usually just the general experience of practitioners of what has worked in the past. Over time such experience translates into *accepted practice*, but there can be a significant difference between accepted practice and what is truly best practice. Theoretically, it may be possible to define best practice, and in some situations accepted practice might be best practice, but without evidence it is equally likely that accepted practice is not best practice. On the other hand, even if what is called *best practice* is really only *accepted practice*, if it achieves results, why should anyone worry whether it is best practice or not?

The debate on whether a particular approach is effective and whether it is the best possible will continue as experience grows and research develops. However, there is a fundamental issue with accepted practice and best practice in relation to project management. The issue is whether the concept of a generic approach with regards to managing a project is meaningful. Can the experiences from one situation be used as an adequate model for a different set of circumstances? Part of the definition

13

of a project is that it is a unique endeavour. Surely unique endeavours need some degree of individuality in how they are tackled. Moreover, even if many projects are in practice quite similar, the context in which they are being executed can be significantly different. Is it really possible to ignore the situation in which a project is being delivered when defining how to manage it?

This chapter shows that whilst there may be many common components to most projects that are best handled by a universal approach, many aspects of the approach to project management have to vary depending on the context in which the project is being delivered. Context can encompass a broad range of factors, and in this chapter the focus is on three aspects: the application area of a project, the sector of business the project is being run in, and the culture of the environment the project exists in.

If project management must be adapted depending on the context then there may be boundaries to project management. At some point the context may be so different from what was assumed in the creation of project management that it might no longer work. This chapter also explores the limits to project management.

This is a wide-ranging debate, and this chapter raises awareness of the issues concerned with the limitations of project management and the need to tailor project management approaches to the situation. It is probably not possible to write an exhaustive description of different aspects of context, and therefore this chapter aims to trigger thinking rather than provide an answer to every possible question or situation.

The material in this chapter relates to all the other chapters in the book. To differing degrees each component of project management needs to be considered in view of the context in which a project is being undertaken. It is particularly relevant to the development of a project management capability described in Chapter 12.

Context and its impact upon project management

There are significant advantages to standardized approaches to management. Standardized approaches can be efficient as they avoid re-learning. Time is not wasted in working out how to manage an endeavour as the management activities are already defined. Standardized approaches can be effective and help to reduce risk. A known and proven way to solve a problem will usually be less risky than an untried approach. From a governance perspective it is far easier to monitor projects that go through similar stages, using the same language, concepts and tools. A standardized approach can be subject to quality audits and continuous improvement, with modifications being applied as it is used and learning occurs. It is reasonable to assume that through continual optimization a widely used standard approach will become ever closer to best practice. Standardization also increases the opportunity for skills transfer, as there is a level of comfort that a project manager from one area has common knowledge that can be applied in a different situation.

The challenge to standardized practice does not arise from debates over whether one technique really is best practice or not, but from the fact that a completely standardized approach will not always work. Projects are unique endeavours of a huge variety, and any project can throw up unexpected challenges. A standardized management approach defined in one situation may not work in another. The techniques used in managing the development of a new type of weapon in the defence sector in the United Kingdom may not be applicable to managing the creation of a TV series in Japan. The approach to developing a small piece of software for a finance application that is needed within a few days is different in many aspects from that used to develop a major part of the national infrastructure that takes years to come to fruition, such as planning and building a new motorway.

On the other hand, we do need some degree of standardization or else project management as a discipline becomes irrelevant. If every single project has to be handled in a totally unique way then the concept of project management is meaningless. The questions are, therefore, which parts of a standard project management approach can be applied to a situation and which parts of the project need individually tailored approaches.

Project management disciplines should be defined in a way that eases common application. As project management becomes more detailed it typically becomes more specific and less universal. The basic steps in risk management – for example, identify risks, assess risk and take action – are probably universally applicable. However, a risk checklist is more likely to be context-specific, as is the knowledge to judge the impact and probability of a risk, say, in a software project compared to a risk in a civil engineering programme. In some situations risk management will be trivial, whereas in some others risk management will be one of the main workstreams. Similarly the concept of developing a project's scope and objectives is probably universally useful. For some projects understanding scope and objectives is the result of an hour's conversation with the sponsor and is done at the start of a project. But in some other projects one of the main outcomes from a project, after months of work involving large numbers of people, is an understanding of scope and objectives. Scope and objectives will have evolved as the project progressed, and may still be evolving as the project enters its implementation phase.

The solution, therefore, is to try to understand the characteristics of projects that indicate sufficient similarity for them to be managed in a common way. There are many possible dimensions to characterize projects. Given the wide applicability of the concept of project management – to manage the process from the realization of an idea or concept through to the creation of a deliverable, where the idea and the deliverable could be anything – it is probably not possible to provide a completely exhaustive description of all characteristics.

Often writers on project management propose an approach to the discipline based on their experience or background, without consideration of the need for variation depending on situations. These approaches often have many features which are biased to the needs of one situation over others. It is often comparatively easy, for example, to differentiate project management texts that have been written by experts in software development from those written by professional civil engineers, even if the books' titles do not make this explicit.

In contrast, there are some commentators who have explored the characteristics of project management to highlight the need for differences in approach. Characteristics include the scale of projects, the complexity, the degree of novelty, the pace of the project, whether the project is intra- or inter-organizational, the cultures involved in the project and so on.

In this chapter projects are characterized in terms of

- o *Application area*: a definition of the content of the project, for example, is it an IT development or a new product development?
- o *Industrial sector*: for example, is the project being undertaken in financial services or in a hospital?
- o *Culture of the environment the project is being undertaken in*: for example, is it happening in China or the United Kingdom?

This section discusses the application area and industrial sector; culture is explored in the following section.

The impact of application area and sector upon project management

Different contexts require varying ranges of skills to successfully deliver projects. It may be argued that some of the differences are not in project management, but in an understanding of the industry. If the industry-specific jargon and concepts are removed then perhaps the underlying project management is the same. This view is problematic for two reasons. First, it is incorrect. There are some unique aspects of project management in different situations. For example, earned value analysis (EVA) is a technique that is commonly used in construction engineering and is part of many definitions of project management. However, EVA is rarely applied in software development. Understanding EVA is considered as a central part of project management for some project managers. Project managers working in other environments may not even have heard of it. Second, if it is only with knowledge of an industry that project management skills can be applied, then separating project management from context knowledge is artificial. Having knowledge of project management that cannot be applied is not useful!

Let us review some examples of industries and situations that place specific requirements upon project managers.

In IT projects, all of the following are essential: a knowledge of software development lifecycles, an appreciation of business analysis and software build processes, and an understanding of systems integration and the various stages of testing. A project manager structuring an IT project, who does not understand issues such as testing and systems integration, is unlikely to develop a reliable or useful plan. IT project lifecycles tend to be based on a software development methodology.

In organizational change and performance improvement projects human behaviour and the response and reaction to proposed and actual change have to be understood and factored in into the plan. Business change plans often have to be more fluid than other project plans. The results from change are not fully predictable, and the timescales and all the activities associated with change cannot be planned in detail. Business change projects may also require an understanding of performance improvement methodologies such as Six-Sigma or Lean. Project managers used to working in environments in which a complete documentation of requirements is the norm, and in which delivery, subject to change control, is aligned to those requirements, may find it challenging to work in the often ambiguous and dynamic world of organizational change.

In new product development (NPD) projects, especially in sectors like fast-moving consumer goods (FMCG), an appreciation of customers and an understanding of marketing concepts are often required. An NPD project lifecycle, which contains stages for creating and testing a concept for a new product, developing products, undertaking market trials, deciding on pricing and packaging, preparing for product launches and so on, is different from any other types of projects. The culture and language of the marketing department is often different from those of functions such as operations or production.

The creative industries pose specific project management challenges. Although it is not recognized by all project managers, a creative enterprise such as a theatre is a project-based organization focussed on the delivery of an event. Many parts of the cultural sector, such as museums, are involved in events. An event is a project. Simon's study of the activities involved in creative projects (video games industry, multimedia, advertising, and a circus) presents a very different view of the role of a project manager than might be gathered from reviewing a traditional project management text (Simon, 2006). In the management of a creative team working on a creative endeavour the project manager is less involved in the classic plan and control than in helping people in the team and around it to work towards an unclear goal by fostering creativity. The role focuses on providing the team members with meaning and collective understanding, knowledge sharing and a balance of challenge and support.

Many creative industries such as film and TV production are examples of businesses which are increasingly inter-organizational. Few TV distributors produce all their own content nowadays. Film companies often develop movies involving a web of companies. Outsourcing of projects and the need to manage external suppliers as a core part of project management is not unique to creative industries, but it is particularly important therein.

In banking and finance, an appreciation of financial regulations and risk has implications upon projects and the way they are run. Over time a whole host of different regulations have come in place many of which are unique to financial services, and to some extent are unique to the jurisdiction the financial institution is operating in. Understanding financial regulations is a core skill. A project manager without an appreciation of this will struggle to deliver projects. That is not saying a project manager has to be a regulatory expert, but he has to at least be aware of the issues that regulation places upon projects.

In defence projects an understanding of government procurement and development processes is necessary. A project's lifecycle may be structured according to the phases in procurement processes. Many project managers from other industries will be completely unfamiliar with the scale, range of involved parties and duration of a defence procurement contract. Defence projects can often last for many years. The combination of a public sector or government customer and private sector firms brings specific challenges. Combining public and private sector is not unique to defence, but is also relevant to health sector and many construction projects.

Construction projects need an understanding of health and safety requirements, and the ability to select and manage sub-contractors is considered as a normal requirement of many projects. Health and safety rules and regulations place a variety of requirements on a project, for instance, the need to undertake health- and safety-related risk assessments. Managing sub-contractors necessitates having negotiation skills and experience of different styles of contracts, from fixed price, time and materials through to shared risk and rewards. These different contract types result in varied project structures and styles of management.

Construction businesses usually rely on a complex network of contractors and sub-contractors. Managing a project made up of groups of customer and supplier organizations is very different from managing an internal workforce to deliver a project. A supplier often has a different perspective on risk, importance and the specific priority of a piece of work than the project owner they are sub-contracted to. Managing staff whose performance can be influenced by the controls and performance management levers of an organization is different from managing a supplier within the boundaries of a contract and relying on inter-organizational relationships.

Construction and defence companies are often completely *projectized* – the business of these companies is projects. This tends to result in a good understanding of and support for projects across the organization. Relevant project management skills are ingrained in many aspects of these businesses. In some cases the whole organizational structure is subordinated to the needs of projects. The organization is a project organization, and staff are managed in project teams without another line management structure. Managing sub-contractors is an essential element of project management in such situations.

A project manager moving from a defence or construction business to a company with non-project-based core operations may find some aspects of the way projects are managed surprising. For example, project managers in non-project-based industries often spend a significant proportion of time throughout the project maintaining access to staff for the project team. Project team members can drift off projects or be allocated to other work at any time. Staff often work on many projects in parallel, as well as having operational tasks to perform. In addition, compared to projectized industries, non-project based companies often expend relatively little effort on project budget management and cost control, especially in relation to the cost of staff time on projects.

Another area of difference between organizations can be the degree of parallel working a project manager is expected to undertake, that is, the number of separate projects the project manager is meant to take on at any one time. In some situations project managers ever manage only one project at a time; in some others, they will be expected to manage two or three projects in parallel; and in still other businesses project managers can be working on tens of projects at the same time. When working time is split across many projects, only a limited amount of time can be spent managing any one project. This means that the style of project management has to change. Project managers working on many parallel projects apply a cutdown project management approach. The skill is in multitasking and using appropriately light-touch project management, as opposed to using the full range of project management disciplines as may be required when one is dedicated to a single large project.

So far the differences in project management approaches between organizations have been compared, but even within a single business the style and needs of project management can vary hugely. The concepts and styles of working favoured by departments such as marketing, sales, engineering, productions, supply chain and operations can be very different from one another. Whilst project managers may try to work in a consistent way across such functions, they have to adapt to the style of those departments, to be fully successful. Also, projects being undertaken for different customer groups require various adaptations in approach. Some customers, such as the government, may insist on using an approach like PRINCE2. Some others, such as large enterprises, may be very familiar with the language and concepts of project management, and thus be easy for a project manager to interact with. Such familiarity with project management techniques may be absent when dealing with small businesses or retail customers.

Why does this matter? It matters because there are implications for using the wrong approach to manage a project. Using the wrong approach will make. the project manager's life harder. Not understanding concepts, not being aware of situational requirements or not being able to use the language of project customers means that a project manager can struggle to scope, plan and deliver the project. Using the wrong and inappropriate approach adds risk to projects and increases the likelihood of project failure. On the other hand, using the best approach for a given situation will significantly increase the likelihood of project success.

Effective context-specific project management

To make project management appropriate and effective to different situations, a project manager needs

- An ability to use the language, terminology and concepts relevant to the situation
- An understanding of implicit rules, expectations and assumptions of a business
- Skills and knowledge specific to an industry or area of application
- An awareness of how project management should be applied in an industry or type of project
- A good knowledge of the fundamentals of project management

Appropriate language, terminology and concepts are essential to communication. Each business, and sometimes each area within a business, has a set of terminology which expresses concepts which are regularly used in that business. This may be referred to as *jargon*. The word *jargon* often has negative connotations, but whether or not jargon is liked, it is important. The language of a business includes concepts that are core to that business. Areas like health services or IT contain a huge amount of unique terminology, or terminology used in unique ways. If the jargon of a business is not understood then communication will be inefficient as concepts have to be explained every time a word is used, and there is a risk of continual miscommunication. A project manager who misinterprets what is told to her is unlikely to be able to manage a project successfully.

Every business has a set of rules, expectations and assumptions that are ingrained into the way decisions are made, and the way people work and interact in the business. Some of these rules may be explicit, for example, regulations applying to industries such as telecommunications and banking. Some of the ways of working are implicit, as in a principle that no one ever misses budgets or time targets. In some businesses a verbal commitment is a binding agreement; in others only written commitments are valuable. Most organizations place customers as central to their way of working, and in some businesses this influences the way everything is done. However, in some others the bias is towards cost efficiency. The rules, expectations and assumptions will shape the way people work on projects, the approach to project delivery and the daily decisions made on projects. For instance, compare a business in which staff satisfaction is of paramount importance to one in which meeting business commitments is most important. If there is a project which is running behind schedule, and is due for delivery by the end of the year, a project manager in the former is less likely to ask staff to work over the Christmas holiday than one in the latter. Moreover, staff are much less likely to expect to be asked to work in holiday times in the former compared to the latter. A project manager who does not understand the rules, expectations and assumptions of a business will find it difficult to manage projects.

Many industries have skills and knowledge that are specific to that industry. Whether the sector is civil engineering, banking or retail services, there is specific expertise that is fundamental to the ongoing ability of the organization to survive in that industry. These skills and knowledge may often be used on projects, and so the project manager has to be aware of them. The project manager does not have to be an expert in every area, but he has to acquire sufficient familiarity to be able to plan projects, to communicate with team members, to direct them and to extract useful information from them.

The existence of varying project needs has lead to the growth of a range of project management tools that are not universally applicable. There are components of project management which would be regarded as essential in some situations, but which project managers working in other situations may not use and even may not be aware of. There are numerous examples earlier in the chapter. Some instances are

- **Project control systems such as earned value analysis (EVA)**: EVA is core in many civil engineering projects, but not used in business change projects.
- **Risk management techniques**: most project managers apply qualitative risk management techniques. Many project managers are less familiar with quantitative risk assessment techniques such as sensitivity analysis and simulation and modelling techniques such as Monte-Carlo. In some situations a lack of knowledge is a reflection of poor skills, but often it is simply a matter of not needing those techniques for specific projects.
- **Benefits realization**: benefits realization techniques are central to some types of projects such as new product developments, and not to others such as cultural change.
- **Resource management**: resource management techniques will vary according to the organization of a business. A pure project-based structure will pose different resource management challenges from a functionally designed organization.

The very scope of project management can vary between organizations. For instance, some project managers would not regard negotiation skills as part of project management, whereas in other industries it would be considered as core. Project managers delivering process change or performance improvements in organizations must understand change management, whereas a project manager on a defence project may not consider change management as a part of project management. Moreover, the meaning and use of the terms like *project manager* and especially *programme manager* vary significantly from organization to organization.

Of course there is a common core set of fundamental project management skills, for example, developing a project plan. Project plans are based universally on the concept of decomposition of a large piece of work into smaller, more manageable and better-understood tasks. Whether or not such a decomposition is called a work breakdown structure or something else is a matter of semantics; the fundamental process will be the same in all situations.

Successful project management has to build on the common core of project management and be enhanced by the specific standards that different situations require. The challenge is to learn and review skills from one area and if appropriate apply them to new situations, with suitable adaptation. If skills were not transferable between sectors then project management might have remained a niche skill within the defence and construction sectors. Proof of its widespread applicability is the fact that over the last few decades it has spread to many industries. A more recent example can be seen in Agile. The Agile development approach has grown up in software development, and some of the concepts are software-specific. However, there are lessons from Agile that can be applied to other areas such as new product development.

Case Study **13.1** IS IT A PROJECT OR NOT?

This case study deals with the provision of services by a major telecommunications service provider. The company sells products to a broad spectrum of customers from large enterprises, through small and medium size businesses, to individual residential consumers. In this case study the Director of Service Delivery talks about the way services are provided to customers and how project management has shaped this approach.

We provide a wide range of telecommunications and related services to customers all over the country. We offer everything from services to individual households to those needed by very large corporations. One of my biggest issues is in continually improving the way we deliver services to different types of customers. This includes optimizing our use of project management.

Let me start by talking about our smallest pieces of work. These are for retail customers to use our consumer products in their homes. I guess you can think of each one of these as a project, and each one does have some unique elements – the house layout, the length of cable and so on. But in reality, thinking of them as projects is not that helpful. We don't even call them projects – they are installations. We have a standard installation process, and we have teams who travel around in vans and do the installs. A good team will do eight to ten installations a day. At the end of their day's work we will have eight to ten new customers we are providing service to and earning money from. In doing this work we obviously want to get it right, make the installation work and satisfy the customer – but alongside this we want to minimize the cost of the install as it makes a big difference to our profitability. If you are only making a few pounds profit every month, having too expensive an install process can easily reduce profitability to zero – or less! Success is achieved through efficiency and standardization – not by project management of every install. We have learnt from the ideas of project management and applied them in designing our installation process, but few of our residential installers know much about it.

At the other end of the scale we have the really big customers. They may buy a service which requires us to do installation work at hundreds of sites, providing service to thousands of their employees. Such work can take months to plan and to complete. These pieces of work are absolutely unique, and although we learn skills from one instance to apply in another, each piece of work is a project without doubt. We make use of a full range of project management disciplines, and even assign dedicated project managers to get them done.

The issue is with the middle-sized pieces of work. They are always projects, but in situations in which we are providing a very cost-effective solution to a small business the margin for us can be very limited. We cannot afford the overhead of professional project managers, and we can't spend time going through all the normal project management stuff like scoping and planning. It's not necessary, and it does not add huge value. A standard process will do. On the other hand, some of the work we do for smaller customers can be quite complex. They're never as complex as the installations we do for large enterprises, but are sufficiently complicated to require some level of project management. The skill is, first, in deciding when it is appropriate to use project management – and that is a function both of the complexity of the work and the amount of money we are charging. Second, if it is appropriate to use project management, determining in what way project management needs to be used. It's no good using an off-the-shelf process for a complex install, but on the other hand, there's no value in using every aspect of project management for small pieces of work.

One thing we have done is to have an intermediate level of management, which is more coordination than project management. We have complex-installation coordinators who are responsible for many small installations at once. I would not call them project managers, but they do use some elements of the project manager's toolkit. It's important to understand that I don't think of them as junior to project managers: they do a different job. Although each job is not very complex they can be coordinating 20 or 30 installations at once, whereas our project managers will ever do only 1 or 2 at a time.

Whether a customer's order is treated as a project, a complex installation, or something managed through a standard process partially depends on the decisions my department makes, but is also influenced by how the service was sold to the customer. Some sales people try to get everything treated as a project to benefit from the personal touch and reliability of a dedicated project manager. It is not always justified. Some other sales people try to get everything treated as a standard product so it is done quickly and without the costs of a project manager being charged to their budget.

We cannot afford not to use the full range of strong project management disciplines for our big customers. We would never achieve what we do if we do not apply project management. Without project management, we could not coordinate our customer work and manage their expectations. At the other extreme, we cannot economically afford the overhead of applying project management to our retail customers. We get an order and we deliver it. The aim is to try and deliver every order in the same high-quality fashion. It's more an operational process than a project. The stuff in the middle – well, that depends on the situation. We have to tailor the approach. Our choice of approach may not be right always, but we are getting better all the time at selecting the right balance of standard process and tailored project management.

Culture and its impact on project management

An awareness of culture is important to project managers for a number of reasons. First, projects may be used as vehicles to influence culture. Projects are a common structure to deliver organizational change. Modifying culture is often an important component of this change. Second, project management needs to be adapted to different cultures to work and to be acceptable in that environment. Project managers need to be aware of and account for different cultural biases. This is particularly important with increase in multi-cultural initiatives, where project managers must aim to minimize problems from multi-cultural working and maximize any advantages it offers. Third, culture has a direct influence on project management approaches. This section focuses on the impact of culture upon projects and project management.

Understanding and adapting to culture is critical to project success. Working in harmony with a culture can ease problems and help project teams to work together, whilst working against a culture will create blockages to project progress. The goals of a project, and the approach to managing a project, need to be aligned with culture. If the project is delivering something which is counter-cultural, then it must be managed to account for this. Delivering counter-cultural outcomes is a significant management challenge, but it can be done.

Culture is built up from a complex range of issues, including ethnic, geographic, economic, legal and historical factors. Culture is a very broad concept. It encompasses manners of communication, the degree of autonomy expected, the levels of individualism versus collectivism, social hierarchy and relationships between people, relative levels of patience expected, how decisions are made, the distribution of power in an organization, work practices, approaches to feedback, rewards and punishments, time and activity orientations, and the styles of interaction that are appropriate and effective. Culture affects how people work, how they expect others to work with them, and the level and type of response if people do not conform.

Culture is a powerful force, operating at many levels. The phrase "*the culture*" is misleading, as there are usually multiple cultures in existence in any one situation. There are ethnic and national cultures, organizational, departmental and group cultures, and as a project progresses there will be a project team culture. The project manager must seek to align the project and the project team with the wider set of cultures.

The culture of an organization or team can affect the acceptance of the discipline of project management. Members of staff may simply not comprehend the need for or advantages of project management. Creative people sometimes find project management too restricting. Sales professionals often complain that project management is too slow and bureaucratic when they just want to get on with the work. Corporate lawyers may ignore project constraints feeling they are working to a higher company agenda and be unwilling to be subject to the direction of an often more junior project manager. Even if a project manager feels that all of these groups are taking unreasonable positions, they have to be handled. In building a project and change capability within an organization, business leaders should seek to adapt the culture, over time, to support projects and change.

The need to fit within a culture affects whether a project manager is suitable to undertake a project or not. For instance, a project manager must be fluent in the language of the project team. Project managers should have an awareness of the formal aspects of an organization's culture, such as the strategy, mission, vision and performance levers, and the informal, such as expected behaviours in different situations.

Occasionally, it is not possible to align a project and project team with an organization's culture because what a project team is trying to do is counter-cultural. If a project is counter-cultural it will struggle to be delivered, unless the project team's work can be insulated from the culture. For instance, some organizations have a faced-paced can-do attitude, some are risk-averse and will only move forward when there is certainty that the right decision is being made. What if a project needs a faced-paced attitude, but is being started in a risk-averse culture? One answer is to separate completely the project team from the rest of the organization. Project teams are physically separated from an organization to do rapid developments of new technology or products in time scales that the core organization cannot achieve. A famous example of this is Lockheed Martin's *skunk works®* approach (see http://www.lockheedmartin.com/aeronautics/skunkworks). It is not uncommon for large organizations to set up completely separate divisions to implement projects which would not be achievable within the culture and environment of the main organization.

Culture is an important consideration when project managers move between industries. In moving between sectors a project manager should check whether his style of working will be appropriate in a different organization. Awareness of culture is also important when working internationally and with a globally distributed multi-cultural project team (Mäkilouko, 2005). A successful approach to managing a Chinese team may be less successful if applied to an American or French team. If the team is combined from all three countries, it poses yet another challenge.

An ability to adapt to culture, or to separate a project from its influence, is essential to working effectively. Culture has a direct impact on how various components of the project management toolkit work. For example, all of the following are affected by cultural factors:

o Measures of success
o Estimation and evaluation
o Risk

- o Change
- o Leadership styles
- o Learning

Project managers have to be able to adapt to culture to be successful, but also the measure of success varies dependent on culture. Some cultures take a relatively long-term view, whilst others are short-termist. A programme like the development of Concorde would be regarded as a disaster financially on a short- to medium-term basis. But on a longer term, and considering its impact on the development of aerospace in Europe, it is possible to consider it as a success. Different cultures factor in very varied aspects into assessments of success. For instance, personal relations (guanxi) between client and contractors are the most important criterion of project success in Chinese construction projects (Wang and Huang, 2006). Whilst many Western projects would favour ending with good client and contractor relationships, it is less likely to be seen as the main measure of success.

The development of a project plan, and the understanding of a wide range of project factors such as risks, depends on the estimation and evaluation of uncertain parameters. Making decisions using estimates and evaluations is iterative and subject to progressive elaboration, and often requires making assumptions. Ideally all estimates would be fully objective, but complete objectivity is not possible. Estimates are inherently subjective, and this subjectivity is influenced by culture.

In a culture that favours "hard science", emphasis can be placed on making estimates as detailed as possible and based on rigorous theory. Cultural pressures in this sort of environment can favour the creation of precise estimates, whereas in reality only approximations are possible. The risk is that the culture of valuing unambiguous accuracy ends up with estimates that are precisely wrong, whereas it would be preferable to use estimates that are approximately right, even if there is some explicit uncertainty associated with them. In some cultures there is a tendency to evade responsibility when it comes to estimates and to worry more about process than the end result. In such a culture plans may be associated with the documentation of a series of assumptions. Estimates are based on the assumptions, without any care for how realistic the assumptions are. At the end, as long as the estimation was correct relative to the assumptions, irrespective of the outcome, the estimator feels safe. In a "can-do" or "macho" culture, estimates can be taken on face value without challenge and be surrounded by a "conspiracy of optimism", and even a reluctance to raise concerns for fear of "getting shot". This results in risk being hidden and sometimes even obviously wrong estimates being unchallenged (Chapman et al., 2006).

Estimates will usually require some assumptions to be made. Assumptions are a source of risk that should be managed. This reinforces the need for project managers to make assumptions explicit, for challenge and debate to be encouraged, and for groupthink to be avoided. Cultures which discourage challenge and encourage unquestioning agreement can struggle with some projects.

The tolerance of risk varies across cultures. When there are low levels of tolerance to risk, project managers have to ensure all risks are well-understood and mitigated. Local government organizations are often relatively risk-averse. Where there are high levels of tolerance to risks project managers may have more freedom to act, but on the other hand they need to ensure that the organization is not blind to risk. Some financial services companies are used to dealing with risky financial investments and are more willing to invest in high-risk projects. Some of the best risk management capabilities exist in sectors which are more open to taking risk because it is part of their normal business to manage risk. Tolerance to risk affects not only the way projects are managed, but also the choice of projects. What might be an acceptable level of risk in one situation, will not be in another. There is little value in proposing high-risk projects in cultures which are risk-averse.

Tolerance to risk is not only an issue of absolute levels of risk acceptable, but also affects the type of risks, and how these risks are assessed. For instance, Chinese and Canadian decision-makers differ in terms of the relative importance they place on various risk factors and the importance they attach to the probability and impact factors of risks (de Camprieu et al., 2007).

Different managers have different levels of acceptance of vagueness depending on the context. This impacts not only the levels of risk, but also the willingness to undertake certain change activities where the objectives and deliverables become apparent only as the project progresses. Projects which can be categorized as *voyages of discovery* or *walking in the fog* (Obeng, 1994), in which the participants start out only with vague concepts and do not precisely know what is wanted or how to do it, are risky as they can result in wasted investment and no valuable output. On the other hand, such endeavours can lead to valuable novel and unexpected outcomes. Only cultures which value learning and are willing to take risks with project investments will permit this style of working.

Organizational change activities are particularly sensitive to culture. Part of the role of organizational change is to adapt culture, but even where this is not an explicit rationale for an initiative, anything that adapts what people do or how they do it will be affected by culture. Some cultures are more open to change, whereas others favour the *status quo.* The latter provide a greater challenge for change initiatives. Those cultures that are open to change, and have a high readiness for change, will tend to be easier to deliver a change initiative into.

The leadership styles of project managers and project sponsors need to be adapted to cultural differences, and take account of any multi-cultural situations. What is an appropriate style of leadership in one culture may be completely inappropriate in another. Very directive leadership, where the leader owns the vision and commands the project team members, may be effective and expected in some situations. A consensual style of leadership, where the leader facilitates the development of ideas and consensus about the ideas, is required in others.

Culture influences the ability to learn from projects. A culture of collaboration and trust is more likely to develop the habit of learning from projects. Organizational culture is one of the key enablers or barriers to learning. A culture which encourages individuals to create and share knowledge and also to define what knowledge is valuable will result in more learning (Adenfelt and Lagerström, 2006).

Projects are not just influenced by culture, they create their own cultures. Depending on the organization this may be a sub-culture, for example, the IT delivery team in a bank, or it may be the predominant culture in projectized industries, such as in the construction, defence and theatre sectors. Culture will develop even if it is not deliberately shaped. Project managers and those with a leadership responsibility towards projects should seek to develop project cultures that are focussed on successful outcomes and are complementary to the environment in which they exist.

The limits to project management

Project management has shown itself to be a highly flexible discipline that is applicable to a wide range of situations. It has successfully been used to deliver endeavours as varied as theatre productions or the building of a nuclear submarine. So far, this chapter has shown that this flexibility is dependent to some extent on tailoring the application of project management to the context. However, there are some contexts which push project management beyond its capabilities – there are limits of project management.

Projects often fail, or are less successful than they could be, because of a poor application of project management. Sometimes they fail because some situations are better dealt with in a non-project way. This section looks at situations in which project management is an ineffective, inappropriate or sub-optimal mechanism to achieve the desired results, however it is applied. The limits are defined in terms of situations that project management is unsuitable for.

Project management is ineffective in dealing with the following types of situations:

- Problems which are inconsistent with the assumptions of project management theory
- Operational management activities (non-unique, repetitive, without a defined end point)
- Small tasks
- Various aspects of organizational and business change

Let us look at each of these briefly.

Traditional project management has developed from a specific approach to problem solving. Project management is reductionist, that is, it is based on an assumption that complex things can be understood by decomposition into simpler things. In reality, some problems cannot be understood by decomposition, and are more than the sum of their parts. For example, complex problems that can be described in terms of systems dynamics, with interactions and feedback loops, cannot always effectively be understood by decomposition.

Project management is aimed at problem solving rather than problem structuring and tends to assume that projects are based on clear and stable goals – hence the assumption, in many project management descriptions, that there is a defined, and implicitly enduring, corporate strategy. Where the basis for a project is not clear, project management aims to reduce uncertainty. But reducing uncertainty may not be the way to optimize all situations. For example, in a creative situation uncertainty may be ideal in enabling unconstrained imagination and inventiveness.

Traditional project management is suited to situations in which efficiency and control are paramount and goals are predetermined, uncontested and expected to stay that way. Project management struggles with highly volatile situations. Although project management has change control to accept modifications to projects, in reality there is often a reluctance to accept change, and change is often portrayed as the enemy of successful project delivery. But if constant variation is in the nature of the environment, continually rejecting change because it will stop a project from being delivered will just end up with valueless deliverables.

Project management is not a suitable way to run an operational department. Some operational tasks could theoretically be structured as projects, but it is an inefficient way to achieve a repetitive task. As shown in Chapter 1 there are three key characteristics of projects: projects exist for a limited period of time; each project is different; and a project is done to reach some predefined goal. Although some projects push the boundaries of these characteristics, they are always broadly true. With a task such as running a production line in a factory, or a customer call centre, none of these characteristics is true. Operational management, and the ongoing improvement of operations against performance goals, is quite different from project management and will not be optimal if run as a project.

Project management adds an overhead to any endeavour. The work of the project manager, and the activities associated with project management, such as maintaining plans or risk management, do not in themselves add to the outcome from the project but do require resources to achieve. Once a project is complete the project management tasks and documents are largely worthless (except as materials for future projects). For many endeavours this overhead is justifiable in terms of risk reduction, and making the other resources on the activity more effective and efficient. The overhead that project management adds is often significantly less than the efficiencies gained from other project team members. The need for project management disappears with small tasks and very simple initiatives. On very small initiatives project management often cannot be justified. This can be seen in Case Study 13.1. In that case study large sales to enterprise clients are managed as projects, but small sales to residential customers are not. It is not that project management could not be applied to deliver the installation of a telecommunications service to a house, but it cannot be done within the other constraints in terms of overhead, resources and time to deliver.

Project management has a valuable role to play in supporting organizational change. But it is far too simplistic to state, as some project management advocates do, that project management or programme management is change management. There are several aspects of organizational change that extend beyond projects, and are not best managed as a project, including

- Types of change that do not fit a project structure
- Change management activities that go on outside the boundaries of a project's lifecycle
- Unanticipated outcomes, derived from an inability to plan and predict all change situations

Project management theory of change tends to assume that there is an explicit management decision to make a change that is planned and deliberate. Projects are often successful in delivering such change. Such changes may be significant or relatively minor. But not all change fits the model of being deliberately planned. Business-as-usual change carries on all the time. Approaches like Total Quality Management (TQM) stress the need for incremental and continuous change that is a natural component of operations. People improve their procedures and work instructions as they perform their normal role. Each change is not explicit, but modification goes on in the detailed operations of a business all the time. Every change may make only a modest difference, but the cumulative impact of changes over time makes a significant difference. Such small changes do not need a project.

Change management has to go on before and after project events. As well as delivering specific modifications, change management is involved in setting the environment for change, and the development of an appropriate change capacity. Such an environment ideally should respond to change flexibly. Developing such an environment is a part of the ongoing management of a business. Change management is also involved in sustaining change once a modification has been made. Although projects portray change as a deliverable, change is not an event; it is a continuous process. Just because a project starts and finishes does not mean a change has started or finished. It just means some components towards change are delivered. Sustaining the change is an ongoing management challenge, not a project-based activity.

Project management controls by definition of deliverables and prediction of how to create them. Change cannot be predictably planned, and the deliverables cannot always be defined in advance. Project management tends to assume that change can be controlled in a top-down fashion. In reality, all senior management can do is set the direction for change (Balogun, 2006). Project managers often assume that comprehensive plans that take best practice into account, including communications, stakeholder management, training, clear responsibilities and so on, will result in successful change. The change process is not fully predictable because of the unpredictable nature of people's responses. Changes result in unexpected responses and unintended outcomes. Unintended outcomes are not simply a result of insufficient planning or poor project management; they happen as individuals make sense of the change and respond to it (Balogun, 2006). Better planning would not remove such outcomes.

Classic project management is based on a *hard paradigm*, rooted in clear goals, with a predictable structured approach to achieve them (Pollack, 2007). In response to the failures of project management to deliver some changes, project management is evolving. There are newer *soft paradigms* of project management in which the role of the project manager becomes more focussed on human relationships. He becomes more of a facilitator and encourager rather than controller. In addition, in the soft paradigm goals are not clear at the start and are not stable. Hence, there has to be an acceptance of uncertainty and a willingness to let go of detailed plans. This is supported by a flexible attitude to planning where the plan and the project needs require constant re-definition. However, there is a risk that with constant re-definition projects get caught in the loop of never-progressing. Newer approaches are attempting to provide ways around this.

The emergence of the concepts of Complex Project Management (Dombkins, 2007), whether or not accepted as valid, does indicate at least some demand for ways to overcome the limits to project management.

In the end the limits to project management may be, at least partially, an issue of definition. There are clear limits to traditional project management. It cannot easily deal with operational situations, or those involving continuous change. On the other hand, with more modern descriptions of project management defining and scoping the discipline is much harder, but the claimed applicability is wider. If project management is defined by what it is meant to achieve, then it is completely flexible, although arguably less helpful to a manager in a specific situation looking for a straightforward set of tools. If project management is defined by a specific approach then it will only work in certain situations, although as the approach evolves and expands the range of situations will increase.

Project management is a broad discipline, with people utilizing a variety of approaches. It has definite limits, but continues to evolve and develop. As it does it increases its ability to take on a wider range of situations.

Case Study **13.2   USING PROJECT MANAGEMENT IN A NON-PROJECT SITUATION**

This case study refers to a business start-up providing products and services to the hospital sector. Each sale will require a complex project to be implemented within a hospital. At the time of writing, this organization is involved in a number of sensitive deals and therefore the case study has been anonymized. The case has been written by the organization's Programme Director.

I was brought into the business after it has been attempting to start up for some months. Lots of great work was done before I got involved. The idea for the business was established, there was some limited financing, and potential clients were starting to get interested in our proposition. My role was to make the proposition real and to develop the capability to deliver on our promises.

We are resource constrained, both in terms of headcount and finances. Currently, to save money, none of us is being paid salary. In compensation we are all getting an equity stake in the business. When our first orders come in we will release more finance, and we should start taking a salary – and we should be able to recruit a few more people and expand our capability to deliver. A lack of funds focuses the mind on delivery, but it also means prioritization is essential as without more funds we can only service a few customers at a time.

The organization has a very strong culture of delivery, based on a small team, with significant opportunities for rewards from success. The team is very focussed on the end goal of making this a successful business. There is no challenge to motivate people, and the team will work pretty much whatever hours are required, seven days a week. But there is a significant challenge in terms of maintaining direction. Everyone has different views of what is most important to get our business up and running. I have to try and keep us going in one direction, or at least as few directions as possible.

As we all are stakeholders in the business, and especially as no one is getting paid, we can't work by top-down direction, but have to use consensus and influence to get things done. It's almost like trying to work with a group of volunteers – though a very motivated group of volunteers. On one hand, this can be frustrating, but on the other, when consensus is achieved, the speed and quality of results is amazing.

Although we are a small team we are very ambitious, and are trying to start a global business. We are a multi-national team, and I have to deal with different styles of interaction. For example, the French members of the team tend to be precise and value significant detail, whereas some other nationalities have a tendency to dive into action. One of my roles is to balance these extremes, making sure we never get stuck in defining more and more detail, but also that we do not start every activity as soon as it arises without at least understanding the objectives and approach to achieving it.

The main thing I am doing is preparing for delivery to first customers. The delivery will take place once we have a contract. Getting a contract in this type of business takes a long time. A typical process from initial conversation to contract being signed with a hospital takes 18 months. We are progressing about a dozen primary contracts at once. They are all progressing at different speeds and every week the progress changes. Sometimes contracts shoot ahead; on other occasions they are unexpectedly delayed. Hospitals are very political organizations with lots of stakeholders. I have to constantly juggle which contract we will sign first, and where we will be delivering our services to first. This could be in very different parts of the world.

On top of this we are constantly coming up with new sales leads, and given our limited resources, we have to find ways to manage expectations. For new leads we actually need to slow down the sales process – as we don't have even the resource to go to all the meetings the customer wants, or we have to drop something else we are doing. This can be really hard: if you say to someone "stop working with a customer who you have been developing for 6 months", they can get quite annoyed – especially, if you then add, "please travel 5000 miles to work with another client"! We all know we are trying to get to the same end point, but we don't always agree about how to get there.

The whole focus of our work changed about two weeks ago. We now have the opportunity to buy an established competitor who have been in business for a few years and have built some great infrastructure. They are in financial trouble. They have been for sale for a while, but now their owners are increasingly keen to sell the business. We think we can buy them very cheaply, as they have a terrible reputation. We know we have the skills to turn the business around. However, it is a complete change in priorities and will mean for some time slowing down the other parts of our business. I see taking over the competitor as a low-risk and fast way to get to our goals, but not everyone does. Some of our other team members don't like the culture of the competitor. Also some of our sales professionals want to sell – because that is what they know how to do and are good at. Buying a business seems like a complete diversion to them. So, again we have to debate priorities and try to get a consensus.

I am called the Programme Director, but very little of what I do fits into the normal way you think of project or programme management. I know my end goal – build a successful business. But every day the way we are going to achieve that changes. I spend a lot of my time getting consensus on priorities, making sure we all understand what we should be doing relative to those priorities, and also ensuring everyone can change what they are doing tomorrow as priorities change again!

I do have various plans for implementation, but they are like contingency plans. I may use none of them if we don't get contracts or if we can't buy the competitor, but they have to be there, being constantly updated in case we pull off one or another deal. The situation is such that we are not ready for detailed project management, but we need to be prepared for the time when we are ready. I use the mindset and approach of a project manager – making sure there is clarity, getting actions and timescales agreed, making sure work is performed and so on – without actually doing very much project management. There's no single end goal at which point the work will be over.

13

MAIN LEARNING POINTS FROM CHAPTER 13

- There is an inherent conflict between the ideals of project management best practice and the reality of each project as a unique endeavour in a unique context.
- Standardized approaches to project management have advantages – they are efficient as re-learning is not required; they can reduce risk by being well-understood; and they can facilitate easier project governance. But they will not work in all situations, and assuming they will increases the risk of project failure.
- Variations in project approaches are required to handle different application areas of projects, respond to the needs of different industrial sectors, and deal with the effects of various national and organizational cultures.
- Irrespective of the project and the approach chosen, a project manager must
    - Use language, terminology and concepts relevant to the situation
    - Have an understanding of implicit rules, expectations and assumptions of a business
    - Apply relevant skills and knowledge specific to an industry or area of application
    - Have an awareness of how project management should be applied in an industry or type of project

This should be supported by a good knowledge of the common fundamentals of project management.

- Project management is not a universal approach that will overcome all management problems. It is unsuitable for many endeavours, for example, situations of continuous change, managing operations, handling very small endeavours, and dealing with complex problems that cannot be understood by decomposition.
- In recognition of the limits of project management there is a constant evolution in the definition, tools and techniques of the discipline, which project managers should strive to understand.

REVIEW QUESTIONS AND EXERCISES

1. What skills would you regard as essential for any project manager working in the business sector you are most familiar with? Which of these skills are specific to your sector, and which are generically useful to all sectors?
2. Which business sectors do you think is most aligned with the needs of project management, and which are most difficult? Why?
3. Which attributes of company culture are helpful to project and project management, and which are not?
4. When building a project management capability in an organization, how much would you consider the organization's culture or any context-specific requirements? How would you tailor your approach to choosing a project team depending on the culture or context of the organization? Give examples.
5. Which components of project management are relatively consistent irrespective of the context? Justify your answer.
6. Describe an objective that can be best reached as a project and one that would not be achievable as a project. What are the main characteristics of these two situations that create this difference?
7. In Case Study 13.2 the author states, "I use the mindset and approach of a project manager. ... without actually doing very much project management". What does this statement mean to you? Use examples to explain your description.

Suggested reading

There are few books which explicitly cover the context and cultural implications for project management, or the limits to project management. For a perspective on some of the theoretical foundations of project management and challenges to them, try

- ○ *Making Projects Critical*. Edited by Damian Hodgson and Svetlana Cicmil. Palgrave Macmillan, 2006

Bibliography

Adenfelt, M. and Lagerström, K. "Enabling knowledge creation and sharing in transnational projects". *International Journal of Project Management*. Volume 24, Issue 3, March 2006, pp. 191–98.

Balogun, J. "Managing change: Steering a course between intended strategies and unintended outcomes". *Long Range Planning*. Volume 39, Issue 1, February 2006, pp. 29–49.

Chapman, C., Ward, S. and Harwood, I. "Minimising the effects of dysfunctional corporate culture in estimation and evaluation: A constructively simple approach". *International Journal of Project Management*. Volume 24, Issue 2, February 2006, pp. 106–15.

de Camprieu, R., Desbiens, J. and Feixue, Y. " 'Cultural' differences in project risk perception: An empirical comparison of China and Canada". *International Journal of Project Management*. Volume 25, Issue 7, October 2007, pp. 683–94.

Dombkins, D. *Complex Project Management: Seminal Essays by Dr David H Dombkins*. BookSurge Publishing, October 2007.

Green, S. "The management of projects in the construction industry: Context, discourse and self-identity". *Making Projects Critical*, Palgrave MacMillan, 2006.

Ivory, C., Alderman, N., McLoughlin, I. and Vaughan, R. "Sense-making as a process within complex projects". *Making Projects Critical*, Palgrave MacMillan, 2006.

Kirsilä, J., Hellström, M. and Wikström, K. "Integration as a project management concept: A study of the commissioning process in industrial deliveries". *International Journal of Project Management*. Volume 25, Issue 7. October 2007, pp. 714–21.

Lawrence, T., Dyck, B., Maitlis, S. and Mauws, M. "The underlying structure of continuous change". *MIT Sloan Management Review*. Volume 47, Issue 4, Summer 2006, pp. 59–66.

Lindgren, M. and Packendorff, J. "Performing arts and the art of performing – On co-construction of project work and professional identities in theatres". *International Journal of Project Management*. Volume 25, Issue 4, May 2007, pp. 354–64.

Mäkilouko, M. "Multicultural project leadership". *Project Perspectives, Periodical of the Project Management Association, Finland*. Volume XXVII, 2005, pp. 16–19.

Newton, R. *The Project Manager, Mastering the Art of Delivery*. FT Prentice Hall, 2005.

Obeng, E. *All change! The Project Leader's Secret Handbook*. FT Prentice Hall, 1994.

Pollack, J. "The changing paradigms of project management". *International Journal of Project Management*. Volume 25, Issue 3, April 2007, pp. 266–74.

Simon, L. "Managing creative projects: An empirical synthesis of activities". *International Journal of Project Management*. Volume 24, Issue 2, February 2006, pp. 116–26.

Suda, L. *Linking Strategy, Leadership and Organization Culture for Project Success*. 1st UTD Project Management Symposium. August 2007.

Vaasaagar, A. and Andersen, E. "On task evolution in renewal projects". *International Journal of Project Management*. Volume 25, Issue 4, May 2007, pp. 346–54.

Wang, X. and Huang, J. "The relationship between key stakeholders' project performance and project success: Perceptions of Chinese construction supervising engineers". *International Journal of Project Management*. Volume 24, Issue 3, April 2006, pp. 253–60.

appendix:
course assignment and
additional questions

This appendix provides additional questions to be used by students and lecturers to help to explore the ideas presented in this book. The questions are presented in two sections:

- ○ *Organizational review of project management*: which contains questions of the form *how well does organization X do project management*?
- ○ *Project/programme review*: which contains questions of the form *how well was project/programme Y managed*?

The first set of questions is targeted at the general manager interested in understanding how well project management is done in an organization. The second set of questions is targeted at project or programme managers interested in understanding how well a specific project was managed.

The questions can be utilized in three ways:

1. As additional review questions, beyond those included within each chapter, to help to reinforce the ideas in the book.
2. To perform a review of a specific aspect of project management in one situation. For example,
   - Using the questions in the first table in the row titled "resource management" to explore how resource management is undertaken in a business
   - Using the questions in the second table in the row titled "risk" to discover how risk management was done on a specific project.
3. As a course assignment to perform a comprehensive review of project management in an organization (using the first set of questions), or a detailed review of a whole project (using the second set of questions). Doing this requires in-depth knowledge of an organization or a project – or access to people from whom relevant information can be gathered.

Table A.1 Organizational review of project management

Topic area	Questions	References	
		Chapter	Chapter title
Project management awareness	• Does project management have a useful role to play in this organization? • What do the terms *project management*, *programme management* and *portfolio management* mean in this organization? • What is the general level of understanding of project management across the organization? • Are there any issues related to the level of knowledge of project management? • How can these problems be overcome? • How does project management relate to and work with other management disciplines in the business?	1	Overview of project management
Strategy	• How meaningful is strategy in the context of this organization? • Is there an organizational strategy or mission? Are there multiple strategies? How does this impact the choice of projects? • How aligned is project and change activity within the organization with strategy? • What level of awareness and understanding of strategy do those responsible for project delivery and implementation have? • How could the implementation of strategy via projects be improved?	2	Strategy, project management and the project portfolio
Portfolio management	• Are there defined (or implicit) portfolio management processes in place in this organization? How are priorities set? • What are the current portfolio objectives? Are they explicit or implicit?	3	Selecting projects and creating the project portfolio

	• What types of projects are included in the portfolio? What projects are done without being assessed via portfolio management? • How effective is the portfolio management approach? Will the set of projects chosen meet the portfolio objectives? Do actual priorities match those set? Is the scale and scope of the portfolio appropriate to the level of resource in the organization? • How could portfolio management be improved? How would you approach making this improvement?		
Resource management	• How does project resource management link to budget planning and finance processes? Is this effective? • How does this organization understand and monitor resource availability? What tools exist to support resource management? • Are there common resource management objectives? What are they (e.g. flexibility, maximum utilization, minimum cost, maximum throughput of work etc)? How do resource management actions match with these objectives? • How are resources managed and allocated to project and change initiatives? Are projects selected with consideration of the resources available? • How well does the level of resources match the scale of projects underway, and the aspirations for project delivery? • What problems are associated with resource management in this organization and how could they be overcome?	4	Project resources and resource management
Requirements	• Do projects generally result in the expected deliverables? Do those deliverables meet real needs?	5	Evolution of requirements and designs

Topic area	Questions	References	
		Chapter	Chapter title
	• How are requirements managed in the organization? What happens to requirements that are not fulfilled in a project? • Are different approaches to requirements analysis and design of solutions understood? • What lifecycle(s) is/are used to convert requirements into designs and then implemented solutions? Could other lifecycles be more appropriate?		
Planning	• Are the types of project undertaken, and the environment in which they are delivered, suitable for accurate planning? • Is predictability important in this organization? Are projects delivered predictably in this organization? • How well are the following performed: determining tasks in the plan, estimating task length and duration, identifying dependencies between tasks and identifying suitable milestones? • How much effort is spent on reviewing and improving project plans presented by project managers? • Are project strategies generally consistent with project objectives?	6	Planning projects
Success	• How successful are projects in this business in general? • Do projects have explicit success criteria? • Do project managers use the success criteria in determining which management actions are required at different stages of the project? • Do the explicit success criteria match the ways people really measure project success?	7	Defining project success

Execution	• How well are projects controlled? Does the organization always have a good understanding of project status? • Are expectations managed in line with real project status? • Is there an available pool of project sponsors who understand the role of a project sponsor and assign adequate time to sponsorship? • Are there defined or implicit governance processes in place? Are they effective? • Is/are there (a) senior manager(s) with regular responsibility for delivery of projects and change? Do(es) he/she/they understand his/her/their role and execute it effectively? • How well is the portfolio actively managed as a response to the changing situation of the business?	8	Managing the execution of projects
Implementation	• How successful is this organization at reliably achieving the desired outcomes from projects? • How well is change management understood? What is understood by the term *change management*? • How is cumulative change assessed? • What are the constraints on the level of change in this organization? • Are there any standard change management approaches in use? • Who is typically responsible for delivering change? • Is a change capability actively developed in the organization?	9	Implementation: Delivering and sustaining change
Benefits	• Is benefits management recognized in this organization?	10	Achieving benefits from projects

Topic area	Questions	References	
		Chapter	Chapter title
	• How often are projects designed and managed with benefits realization in mind? Can you find examples of projects or programmes where the phasing has been designed to optimize benefits delivery? • How is the effect of change on projects factored in into benefits management? • Does the management community generally have confidence that benefits will be delivered? Why? What can be done to improve on this?		
Risk	• How is risk considered when selecting projects? • How well is risk understood and managed on projects? Is there a defined process with supporting checklists? • How are project risks fed through to overall portfolio-level risk? How aware are managers and the executive of project risks? • Are there any common sources of risk in this business? What is done about them? • Are opportunities proactively identified and seized?	11	Understanding and managing risk on projects
Capability	• Is the concept of a delivery capability understood in this organization? • What sort of capability is required? • Is that capability available? How is it sourced? Is this the most appropriate source of the skills needed? • What tools and supporting infrastructure exists? Is it appropriate? • How are project managers managed? How are they organized? Is this the most appropriate organization? • Does project management fulfil the role it is meant to in this organization?	12	Building a delivery capability

	• How has the knowledge and understanding of projects and change been enhanced over time?		
Context	• Are there any specific features of this organization, or the environment in which it operates, which have to be considered when delivering projects? • How does the culture of this organization help or hinder project delivery? • Is project management an appropriate way to deliver all initiatives in this organization? What alternatives to classic project management are used? • Are there initiatives which should be handled as projects that are not? Are there activities managed as projects which should not be?	13	Context, culture and the limits to project management

Table A.2 Project/programme review

Topic area	Questions	References	
		Chapter	Chapter title
Project management awareness	• Would you define this endeavour as a project or a programme? Why? • Was any consideration given to the different ways of managing this project? Could it have been more successful if a different project management approach was chosen? • What components of project management were most relevant to this project? • Are there areas of project management that were not utilized in undertaking this project? Should they have been?	1	Overview of project management

Table A.2 Continued

Topic area	Questions	References	
		Chapter	Chapter title
Strategy	• Why was the project done? Was it the right project to be undertaken when it was, given the resource constraints in the business? • How did the project relate to corporate strategy? • How did the company's strategy affect the day-to-day running of and decision-making on this project? Find some examples of decisions that made reference to strategy.	2	Strategy, project management and the project portfolio
Portfolio management	• Had the project been approved and prioritized? • What was the priority of this project? • What portfolio objectives will the project help in fulfilling? • Were there any problems caused by the project's priority, in terms of the interaction with other projects and programmes?	3	Selecting projects and creating the project portfolio
Resource management	• What resources did the project need? Did the planned resource requirement match what was used? • Were the resources required available? What was done to match needs with availability? Was the project budgeted for? • What problems were there (or could have been there) with resources, and how did the project manager deal with these? Could it have been handled better? • How were the resource needs of this project affected by other projects? How well was this interference managed?	4	Project resources and resource management
Requirements	• How well were the scope and objectives understood? What risks were associated with the scope and objectives or their level of definition? • How were requirements collected on this project?	5	Evolution of requirements and designs

	• How were the requirements converted to a solution? • Could this have been done in a different or better way?		
Planning	• What approach was taken to developing the plan? Did the project have a plan with an appropriate level of detail in it? • Did the project manager make use of all available sources of information and advice in creating the plan? • How well were tasks defined, duration and resources estimated, and dependencies identified? Was the WBS the most appropriate or could a better WBS have been selected? • How much risk did the plan create for the project? • How could the plan have been improved?	6	Planning projects
Success	• How well were the success criteria for this project understood? • What were the success criteria for the project? • Was the project successful? In what way? Were any success criteria not met? Why? What could have been done to make it more successful?	7	Defining project success
Execution	• Did the project have an effective control system? • Did the project manage issues effectively? • Was there an effective change control process in place? • Did the project manager manage the team well? • How were stakeholders and expectations managed? • Was the role of the project sponsor understood and applied? • How did the company's governance processes affect the project? Was this a help or a hindrance?	8	Managing the execution of projects

Table A.2 Continued

Topic area	Questions	References	
		Chapter	Chapter title
Implementation	• How well was the project's implementation planned? • Was the testing and acceptance process effective? • How well was handover managed? Was there sufficient business change preparation? Was the organization ready for the change the project resulted in? • Did the project team predict and manage the response to the project and its deliverables? What unexpected outcomes arose and how were these handled? • Did the project result in both quality deliverables and sustained change?	9	Implementation: Delivering and sustaining change
Benefits	• Were the benefits expected from the project understood in advance? • Was the project planned and managed to optimize delivery of benefits? • Did the project stakeholders accept responsibility for achieving the project's expected benefits? • Did the project deliver the benefits expected?	10	Achieving benefits from projects
Risk	• How well were risks identified? • Were risks appropriately assessed and prioritized? Which risk assessment method was used, qualitative or quantitative? • Were the actions taken to manage risks effective? Were contingency plans used? If so, what benefits did they provide? • Was risk handled as an ongoing part of the management of the project?	11	Understanding and managing risk on projects
Capability	• Did the project manager have the appropriate skills to do this project? Could any additional skills have been useful?	12	Building a delivery capability

	• Was there a range of necessary supporting skills available to deliver the project?		
	• How has the knowledge in the business been improved as a result of what has been learnt on this project?		
Context	• What challenges were specific to the context this project was run in? How were these handled? Was it effective?	13	Context, culture and the limits to project management
	• Was the culture of the organization or department supportive of the project and its objectives?		
	• Did the project team develop its own culture? Did this help or hinder the project? In what ways?		
	• Were there any aspects of the project that project management did not provide tools to deal with?		

index

In this index tables are indicated by (tab.), diagrams by (d.), appendices by (app.)